Growth in a Traditional Society

THE PRINCETON ECONOMIC HISTORY

OF THE WESTERN WORLD

Joel Mokyr, Editor

---

*Growth in a Traditional Society: The French Countryside,
1450–1815* by Philip T. Hoffman (1996)

Growth in a Traditional Society

THE FRENCH COUNTRYSIDE, 1450–1815

Philip T. Hoffman

PRINCETON UNIVERSITY PRESS

PRINCETON, NEW JERSEY

Copyright © 1996 by Princeton University Press
Published by Princeton University Press, 41 William Street,
Princeton, New Jersey 08540
In the United Kingdom: Princeton University Press,
Chichester, West Sussex

Library of Congress Cataloging-in-Publication Data

Hoffman, Philip T., 1947–
Growth in a traditional society : the French countryside,
1450–1815 / Philip T. Hoffman.
    p.   cm. — (The Princeton economic history of the Western world)
  Includes bibliographical references and index.
  ISBN 0-691-02983-0 (cl : alk. paper)
  1. Agriculture—Economic aspects—France—History. 2. France—
Economic conditions. 3. France—Rural conditions. 4. Agricultural
productivity—France—History. I. Title. II. Series.
  HD1943.H64   1996   95-31936
  338.1′0944—dc20

This book has been composed in Times Roman

Printed in the United States of America by
Princeton Academic Press

10 9 8 7 6 5 4 3 2 1

Contents

Illustrations

Tables

Acknowledgments

LIKE ALL AUTHORS, I have piled up debts in writing my book, debts that I can never repay. All that I can do is acknowledge those who have been so generous with their advice and support. My thanks go, first of all, to the institutions that have funded my research: the American Council of Learned Societies, the California Institute of Technology, the George A. and Eliza Gardner Howard Foundation, and the John Randolph Haynes and Dora Haynes Foundation. Thanks go as well to those who have allowed me to use illustrations and to reprint the small part of this book that has previously appeared in journals. The History and Special Collections Division, Louise M. Darling Biomedical Library, at the University of California, Los Angeles, graciously authorized the reproduction of engravings from François Rozier's *Cours complet d'agriculture*. The Economic History Association let me incorporate portions of my article "Land Rents and Agriculture Productivity: The Paris Basin, 1450–1789," *Journal of Economic History* 51 (1991): 771–805. With equal generosity, Philip T. Hoffman, "Institutions and Agriculture in Old Regime France," *Politics and Society*, vol. 16, nos. 2–3, pp. 246–47, copyright (c) 1988 by Sage Publications, Inc., is reprinted by permission of Sage Publications. And obviously I am obliged to the archivists and librarians who assisted my research, and to the editors, secretaries, and assistants who typed in data and helped prepare the manuscript. Here, Rosy Meiron ought to be singled out: her expertise in several languages spared me many a misstep.

Last but not least are the debts to scholars who have offered me their assistance and their advice. I have benefited from the reaction of audiences at the California Institute of Technology; the Ecole des Hautes Etudes en Sciences Sociales; Northwestern University; the University of California, Davis; the University of British Columbia; the University of Illinois; Washington University; the Yale University Law School; the Second World Congress of Cliometrics; and several meetings of the Society for French Historical Studies and the All–University of California Economic History Group. I am particularly grateful to the historians and economists who lavished suggestions and intellectual encouragement upon me: Robert Allen, Jean-Michel Chevet, Lance Davis, Robert Forster, George Grantham, Shawn Kantor, Morgan Kousser, Peter Lindert, Ted Margadant, Joel Mokyr, Larry Neal, John Nye, Douglass C. North, Scott Page, Angela Redish, Ted Scudder, Ken Sokoloff, and David Weir. Several individuals—Robert Bates, Philip Benedict, Greg Clark, Stanley Enger-man, Avner Greif, and Gilles Postel-Vinay—went out of their way to read long portions of the manuscript and offer detailed suggestions. Finally, there are Jean-Laurent Rosenthal and Kathryn Norberg, who took time from their own research to read chapters over and over again. I owe them special thanks.

Abbreviations

AD	Archives départementales
AESC	*Annales: Économies, sociétés, civilisations*
AHEW	*The Agrarian History of England and Wales*. Edited by H.P.R. Finberg and Joan Thirsk. 8 vols. London, 1967–
AN	Archives Nationales
BM	Bibliothèque municipale
CAHEW	*Chapters from the Agrarian History of England and Wales: 1500–1750*. Revised edition of vols. 4 and 5 of *The Agrarian History of England and Wales* (1967). Edited by Joan Thirsk. 5 vols. Cambridge, 1991.
HESF	*Histoire économique et sociale de la France*. Edited by F. Braudel and E. Labrousse. 8 vols. Paris, 1970–82.
HFR	*Histoire de la France rurale*. Edited by G. Duby and A. Wallon. 4 vols. Paris, 1975–76.
JEH	*Journal of Economic History*
Ln or ln	Natural logarithm
SA 1840	*Statistique de la France: Agriculture*. 4 vols. Paris, 1840–41.
SA 1852	*Statistique de la France, 2e série. Statistique agricole recueillie avec le concours des commissions de statistique cantonales instituées par le décret du 1er juillet 1852*. 2 vols. Paris, 1858–60.
SA 1862	*Statistique de la France: Agriculture. Résultats généraux de l'enquête décennale de 1862*. Strasbourg, 1870.
TFP	Total factor productivity

Growth in a Traditional Society

INTRODUCTION

ECONOMIC GROWTH is the great enigma of history and the social sciences. For better and for worse, it remakes society and does more in the long run to improve material welfare than any of the static reshuffling of resources that fills elementary textbooks of economics. Yet growth remains a perplexing mystery. It can accelerate, persist without flagging, and surpass what one would expect given increases in the stock of capital. It can also collapse or stubbornly refuse to budge. It might be thought a simple matter of mobilizing capital, of transferring novel technologies, and of copying successful institutions from developed nations. But the world is more complex than that. Indeed, we still cannot explain why some countries have grown rich, while others remain mired in abject poverty.[1]

Our inability to explain growth is all the more astounding in light of the extraordinary attention devoted to economic growth ever since the time of Adam Smith. Marx aimed to account for growth, in *Das Kapital*; so did Max Weber, in seeking the religious ideas that seemed to launch the West on the path toward riches. Within the discipline of economics, although growth still does not occupy center stage, it has nonetheless attracted luminaries like Simon Kuznets and, more recently, inspired whole new literatures on the institutions of developing countries and theories of endogenous growth. It has intrigued a number of talented economic historians as well.

Economic growth has engaged historians untrained in economics, too. It was long the focus of the social history of the Industrial Revolution in Europe. For earlier periods of European history—particularly the early modern history that stretches from the end of the Middle Ages to roughly the French Revolution—growth (or its absence, stagnation) also excited considerable interest. This was particularly true of the history written in France between the 1930s and the 1970s: the golden years of the French journal *Annales*, when gifted scholars from Marc Bloch to Emmanuel Le Roy Ladurie influenced the writing of history throughout the world. Much of their work concerned early modern France, especially French agriculture. Always lurking in the background was their desire to explain why the French economy—and especially French agriculture—seemed to perform so poorly, at least by comparison with England. They fastened on early modern agriculture because of the widespread belief that growth could only begin with a transformation of the rural economy, a transformation that France seemed to have missed.

Today, it is true, growth and stagnation have by and large been pushed

off to the eaves of European history in general and French history in particular.[2] The reason, at least for early modern France, may well be the very
success of the *Annales* historians. They reached a consensus about the
agrarian economy of early modern France that closed the issue off for further research. In their view, there was little doubt that French agriculture
stagnated during much of the early modern period. The evidence was persuasive: it ranged from the frequent subsistence crises that demographic
historians detected in the seventeenth and early eighteenth centuries to the
anemic records of agricultural output that historians teased out of tithe returns.[3] The causes of the stagnation were equally clear. France—especially
rural France—was a *société immobile*, where rigid mentalities and social
structures made economic growth impossible. Having thus dispatched the
problem of growth and stagnation by classifying France as a société immobile, the *Annales* historians and their intellectual heirs helped push historians off toward other, more fertile areas of research, and growth was
consequently forgotten, at least among historians.

This book aims to revive interest in economic growth and stagnation in
early modern Europe. It addresses itself not only to historians in general, or
to economic historians, who have never lost interest in growth, but to all
social scientists with an interest in the past, be they economists, anthropologists, sociologists, or political scientists. It takes up what European historians might consider one of the premier examples of a stagnant economy,
and in that economy the most backward sector: agriculture in early modern
France. In the eighteenth century Arthur Young faulted French agriculture,
as did agronomists in France. Scores of French historians, from Marc
Bloch onward, have done the same, as have scholars outside of France.
Even revisionist economic historians who believe that the French economy
performed extraordinarily well complain about French agriculture.[4] If
France was a société immobile, then its agriculture dragged the whole
country down.

Given grain riots and the fear of famine, contemporaries were aware of
the failings of French agriculture, at least by the eighteenth century, when
its performance relative to England became something of an obsession. But
concern with agriculture was not just an Enlightenment mania. Even before
the eighteenth century, agriculture was matter of concern to authorities
who wished to provision armies or collect taxes in the countryside. The
subsistence crises saw death rates jump when crops failed, and although
recent research has blurred what was once a simple connection between
mortality and hunger, chronic malnourishment among the poor still seems
to explain a significant proportion of the high mortality rates under the Old
Regime.[5]

What makes French agriculture even more important is that it provides
an example whose importance reaches far beyond the discipline of history.

The French case in fact bears upon a number of issues of current interest to development economists and specialists in economic growth. For far too long, it is true, development economists neglected agriculture, because they knew that it would naturally decline in importance as incomes rose. At best, they thought, it would provide industry with a reservoir of labor, food, and capital. Today, though, they have changed their tune. They realize that by virtue of its very size in an underdeveloped economy agriculture has much to contribute to economic growth, particularly when growth is in its early stages. If agriculture is not nurtured, or—worse yet—if it is exploited, then the whole economy may be dragged down by famine and rural poverty.[6]

Here, early modern France provides a fascinating laboratory, one that lets us weigh what factors throttle rural growth in traditional economies. What accounts for growth and stagnation in the countryside of early modern France? Is it a flaw within French agriculture, as most of the existing research suggests: rural property rights, the peasants' mentality, or the small scale of their farms? Or is it instead a problem outside of agriculture: politics, the tax system, or the meager opportunities for trade? Similar questions can be asked of nearly any country in early modern Europe and of nearly any undeveloped country today, and the answers, even if in a historical setting, have much contemporary relevance.

As far as early modern France is concerned, the time seems particularly ripe for a historical reconsideration. Several of the *Annales* historians (notably Emmanuel Le Roy Ladurie) have begun to revise their own stories, while younger social historians have begun to distance themselves from the metaphor of the société immobile.[7] At the same time, the new economic history (now well into middle age) has been pounding at the door of continental Europe with great insistence in recent years. It finally threatens to renew French history in the way that it has already refashioned the past of England, Ireland, and the Netherlands.[8] My book is part of the process of renewal.

· · ·

This journey into the economic history of the early modern French countryside has taken, I confess, far too long. Beyond the usual excuses—the scattered archival sources of rural history and the time taken to help care for two children—there is yet another cause for the delay. When I started on my way, my road map was traced by two generations of social history. Following Marc Bloch and other historians, I believed that the failings of French agriculture derived from the small size of peasant farms, the lack of English-style enclosures, and the behavior—or better yet, misbehavior—of French landlords. I was particularly interested in the nobles and other privileged landowners who had appropriated increasing amounts of peasant land in the early modern period. How they managed their estates, so I believed, would help explain the performance of French agriculture, and their role in the countryside would address issues that excited social and cultural historians, issues that extended well beyond growth, from rural clientalism to village politics and the tenor of agrarian life.

Accordingly, I planned a book that would mix economics with social and cultural history of a more anthropological flavor. To avoid parochialism, I ruled out a local study, since even the best microhistory can sometimes slight larger issues. But I did wish to capture some of local history's immediacy and detail. My initial decision, therefore, was to follow a handful of separate villages scattered across the country. That seemed the best way to combine generalization with vivid detail. I ended up collecting evidence on eight rural communities: two near Paris, and one each in Normandy, Brittany, Lorraine, Provence, the Lyonnais, and the Pyrenees mountains. Each represented a different type of agriculture or a different economic or social structure. Each was selected for the richness of the relevant sources, from notarial records and land registers (*terriers*, *cadastres*) to local histories, communal deliberations, and criminal court archives. Those were the documents that would shed light on landownership, property management, and the nature of village life. To these eight communities, I later added three others, chosen because they had undergone the sort of enclosures that were common in England but so rare in France: Bretteville-l'Orgueilleuse, in Normandy, and Roville and Neuviller, in Lorraine.

It was while sifting through the copious records of these villages that my conception of the book began to change. In part it was the ever sharper focus on economic growth, which dictated a different organization. But I was also reacting to colleagues and to works of economic history that had begun to appear. I came to realize—much to my dismay—that I would have to seek out other sorts of evidence besides the village records. I now doubted the assertion that French agriculture nearly always performed miserably, and I distrusted the evidence that historians marshaled to demonstrate agrarian stagnation in France. Finding a better measure of agricultural productivity became a paramount concern, launching me on a long and arduous search for leases and prices in both printed and manuscript sources. I had to discover whether French agriculture really did as badly as nearly everyone supposed, and it was not possible to restrict my search to the handful of villages I was originally studying.

Measuring productivity growth with leases and prices also meant learning more about agricultural improvements and about the labor market and the rental market for land. That entailed searching for account books and examining the vast literature on agronomy and estate management. From there I moved on to agricultural capital and the workings of the local economy, adding to what I knew by looking at tax records and probate inventories. My final task was to compare agricultural productivity in France with that in England and Germany, where, fortunately, a host of printed sources lay at my disposal.

The project was now transmogrified. The old book—following a sample of villages—had vanished, leaving behind only vignettes scattered here and there. My initial hypotheses had tumbled by the board as well. The role of the privileged landowners had lost much of its importance, because their behavior—their use of sharecropping, for instance—no longer seemed to block economic growth. As for the social and anthropological topics, they retained a prominent place, but they were now tied to growth and to the workings of the rural economy. Village politics, for instance, were now linked to the political economy of enclosure. Similarly, the village insults and rural clientage that gave agrarian life its tenor fit into the local market for credit, as did the peasants' notions of reputation and honor.

Insults, clientage, and village reputations are not the usual subjects of economic history. I include them, though, not only to explain the workings of the rural economy, but to entice readers who might otherwise spurn a book devoted to economic growth. The lamentable truth is that we academics often hesitate to quit our specialized cloisters. Social and cultural historians tend to overlook economic history, while many economic historians stick to the economy. Similar rifts cut across anthropology and political science, dividing those who use economics from those who shun it. For my part, I want to reach across these divides. I hope to appeal not just to economists, but to anyone intrigued by the workings of traditional societies and the causes of growth, from general historians to political scientists and anthropologists. Such readers, even if they be indifferent to economic growth itself, will therefore find much of interest in what follows. A political historian will learn, for instance, that high politics—the politics of warfare and taxation—had more effect on agricultural growth than demography or enclosure. A social or cultural historian will learn that common rights, which most consider social insurance for the poor, were often the monopoly of the rich. (The common rights were shared rights to use common lands, especially for pasturing; the common lands, or commons, might include waste, fallow, forest, or the stubble on an open field.) Similarly, the language of moral economy (so often invoked to defend the commons in the name of the poor) was often little more than a mask for the interests of wealthy farmers.

Here, it is true, some historians may balk. Traditional societies, they might say, are simply not amenable to economic analysis. Whatever its power, economics does not suit the countryside of early modern France. Its suppositions about behavior are too crude for the age of Luther, Calvin, and Loyola, and it lacks the interpretation and local detail that make history persuasive. Such objections, it should be noted, are not peculiar to history. They have fueled debate over the use of economics in anthropology and political science too.[9] The argument, in a sense, reaches back at least to Max Weber: for him, the sort of rational calculation that economics seemed to presuppose was peculiar to the modern age and impossible without modern markets.[10]

One hesitates to question an argument that stretches back to revered thinkers like Weber, particularly when examples of economic historians' mangling of the past readily come to mind. Yet it is certainly possible to apply economics to traditional societies, without abandoning detail and interpretation. Whether this book does so, I leave to readers to judge, but there are numerous other examples in economic history, and in fields such as political science as well.[11] Furthermore, one can question the whole case against economics, in particular Weber's assertion that the economist's rational calculation is peculiar to the modern age and impossible without markets. Undoubtedly, Weber's views here reflected his own psychological quest for meaning in a modern world that seemed increasingly devoid of significance.[12] But it is hard to reconcile his contention that rational calculation presupposes modern markets with what we know today. Economics is not what it was in Weber's day (1864–1920) and certainly not what it was at the time of Adam Smith (1723–90). Having changed greatly since the 1940s, its metamorphosis continues; it is no longer simply the study of perfect markets under conditions of perfect information. It is certainly compatible with the customs and practices of traditional societies, as can be seen from work in game theory, development economics, economic history, political science, and law and economics. It can be invoked to explain reciprocity, gift giving, and the importance of kinship, honor, and reputation. It need not lead to conservative conclusions, and it is hardly simplistic. Indeed, it might predict a variety of possible outcomes, with the one we observe depending on historical accidents or on the peculiarities of the surrounding culture.[13] Economics is now employed by scores of anthropologists, not just in the economic wing of their discipline but even within cultural anthropology—for instance, by Clifford Geertz.[14] And shunning it does a terrible injustice to the dead, by denying that they were capable of strategic behavior.

The opponents of economics thus seem guilty of two misconceptions.[15] The first is to suppose that economics concerns perfect markets alone and that it therefore has no place before the advent of impersonal transactions and atomized individuals. Again, economics is hardly limited to perfect markets. Rather, it involves trying to make the best of one's situation, be it in a modern market or in arenas that witnessed more personal dealings, from families and peasant villages in the sixteenth century to the internal culture of a twentieth-century corporation. It is not restricted to the realm of modern markets.

The second error is to assume, as Weber in effect did, that economics presupposes conscious rational calculation, the sort of rational calculation that becomes prevalent only with the triumph of capitalism. This too is a misconception. Men and women may make the best of their situation by following custom or rules of thumb. They do so today, just as they did in the past. As a consumer, I may behave just as an economist would predict, yet in filling my grocery cart I have yet to catch myself solving the sort of calculus problem that crops up in a microeconomics text. Similarly, a corporate executive may maximize profits, but he may well do so without explicitly calculating marginal costs. And whether a consumer or a corporate executive calculates and thinks like an economist is usually irrelevant. The point is simply whether his behavior conforms to economic analysis. One can make the same case for early modern Europe. The institutions were obviously different, and so was the intellectual and cultural context. But as we shall see, early modern behavior still seems concordant with what we know about economics, even in the backwaters of rural France. Such a conclusion is in fact borne out in the work of a number of historians, including many who are untainted by any direct association with economics.[16]

. . .

In what follows, I have tried to address readers in a number of fields, an endeavor that entails certain rhetorical problems. Throughout, I have tried to make the manuscript accessible to those who have no quantitative training and no knowledge of economics. Nearly all the mathematics has therefore been consigned to the footnotes and appendixes, and what remains in the text (in Chapter 4) should be intelligible to readers with only a dim memory of high school algebra. If it is not, they should jump ahead to the verbal explanations I provide. Similarly, when I use notions from economics (Chapter 4 is again a good example) I try to make them clear to the utter novice.

Economists and economic historians may have to bear with an occasional explanation of what seems obvious. They may also have to endure my efforts to justify models that they consider perfectly natural. The problem is that noneconomists often find economic reasoning utterly bizarre, and one risks howls of execration if one simply thrusts a model in the average historian's face. Economists may also resent the rich historical detail, but that again is needed to win the confidence of historians and of readers from other fields, such as anthropology, where detailed local research proves a case. By the same token, historians will have to tolerate my discussion of larger issues: generalization is the hallmark of the social sciences.

There are also some problems of vocabulary. Economists often talk of equilibria, a term that sends shudders up the spines of anthropologists and some historians. I will use the word on occasion, but for me equilibrium simply means a likely outcome, once everyone has made the best of his or her lot in life. I speak of equilibria without any implication that rural society was static or self-regulating or that it veered toward a situation in which all people were happy with their fate. Similarly, I shall often speak of traditional society, even though this term also causes anthropologists (and perhaps some historians) to cringe. In doing so, I do not want to suggest that all traditional societies were the same, that they were timeless and unchanging, or that the members of a traditional society were bovine creatures of habit, completely incapable of innovation. In fact, given my attacks on the notion of a société immobile, it will be clear that I am adamantly opposed to such a view of the early modern world.

Given the breadth of my subject, I had to leave out issues dealt with elsewhere: rural industry, the subject of fascinating work by Liana Vardi and others; the seigneury, which has received expert treatment from scholars such as Robert Forster and Jonathan Dewald; and the role of the peasant family in economic growth, illuminated by the excellent recent book of Jean-Marc Moriceau and Gilles Postel-Vinay.[17] Regrettably, I was also forced to bring my story to a halt with the French Revolution. I do hazard some guesses about the Revolution's effects on agriculture, but the changes wrought after 1789 brought most of my documents to an end and, worse yet, made it impossible to pick up the trail using nineteenth-century sources.

Some may lament these omissions, but they are not likely to affect my story. In much of Old Regime France, for example, the seigneury did not bear down heavily. Seigneurial dues were generally low, and obligatory labor—the corvée—unimportant. Seigneurs did claim rights to common grazing land, and their claims certainly had the potential to affect agriculture. But grazing rights is a subject that I do consider. Similarly, while the family did play an important role in managing tenant farms and mobilizing agricultural capital, my story would remain unaffected whether a tenant's capital came from his family or from his landlord. In any event, what I say is likely to mesh well with what other scholars say about the family, the seigneury, and rural industry.

The book begins with the consensus that historians have forged about economic growth in the early modern countryside. I review the historical literature, including the writings of Annales historians, and discuss relevant works outside history, from the classical social thought of Marx and Weber to modern works in the social sciences. Next, in Chapter 2, I take up the role of the peasant community and communal property rights, which both historians and social scientists have long considered a barrier to economic growth. Thereafter I turn to the neglected topic of the rural markets for labor, credit, and land rental (Chapter 3). Studying the markets is a necessary prelude to a new measurement of growth, but it also allows the economics to speak in an exciting new way to sociologists, anthropologists, and social and cultural historians about issues such as village reputations.

Measuring growth is the task of Chapter 4. After exposing the shortcomings of earlier measurements based on grain yields and tithe returns, it appraises productivity growth via a new methodology, which is first applied to the Paris Basin and then to other parts of France. The chapter compares agricultural productivity in France, England, and Germany and concludes with estimates of the growth of the food supply in France. I then turn to explaining the pattern of growth and stagnation (Chapter 5). I consider the sources of productivity growth in early modern France and ask whether small farm size and the lack of enclosure were major obstacles to growth, as many historians and social scientists maintain. I look outside agriculture as well and consider a variety of other causes of stagnation and growth, from warfare and the exactions of the fiscal system, to urbanization, capital improvements, and gains from trade. Finally, the conclusion weighs the effects of the French Revolution and then summarizes the book in terms that should interest historians, economists, and social scientists alike.

CHAPTER ONE

Peasants, Historians, and Economic Growth

THE CLASSIC WORKS of French rural history—Marc Bloch's *Les caractères originaux*, Pierre Goubert's *Beauvais et le Beauvaisis*, or Emmanuel Le Roy Ladurie's *Les paysans de Languedoc* and *Montaillou*—stand practically alone on the tribune of historical honor. Translated, reedited, and reprinted without end, these books have reached an audience far broader than is usual for academic history. Bloch's volume influenced the social sciences, as did *Les paysans de Languedoc*, while Goubert's work helped launch historical demography. As for *Montaillou*, it became a best-seller in several languages. Such success, it goes without saying, is practically unique in rural history. In the comparable English or German literature, nothing has attained such fame, and even the heralded examples of Italian "microhistory" lack the same scholarly impact.[1]

What, though, do these books teach us about the French peasantry? And what do they tell us about the more general problem of growth and stagnation in traditional economies? Obviously, there was more to rural life than economic growth, but growth was an issue that was crucial to Bloch and to Le Roy Ladurie as well. If it seems less imperative to historians today, it is only because scores of social historians have reached something of a consensus about growth, at least as far as rural France is concerned. That consensus holds that the French rural economy stagnated from the end of the Middle Ages until the middle of the Enlightenment, and perhaps well beyond. The reasons for the stagnation appear practically self-evident. The French countryside was rigid and unchanging, a *société immobile*. Its peasants clung tenaciously to their tiny plots and to their outmoded technology, and their village institutions stifled innovation. So persuasive is this consensus that a historian can safely make it the point of departure for exploring more exciting terrain—peasant culture, violence, or religion. Thus Robert Darnton uses it as a foil to investigate village culture under the Old Regime.[2]

Yet despite its persuasiveness, the consensus deserves reconsideration, for what it says about the rural economy seems doubtful at best and misleading at worst. A similar line of argument has echoed throughout European history and the social sciences ever since the time of Marx, and it has seeped into the literature on economic development. There, too, it deserves reexamination.

As fashioned by Bloch, Goubert, Le Roy Ladurie, and other social historians, the consensus about the French countryside is certainly clear. It is layed out quite lucidly in the classic works of French rural history and in two syntheses published in the 1970s, the *Histoire économique et sociale de la France* and the *Histoire de la France rurale*.[3] The consensus begins with a large number of subsistence peasants, who farmed in isolation from markets. For Bloch, these were the peasant smallholders, who emerged from the Middle Ages owing what was generally only an insignificant rent to their seigneurial lords. With hereditary tenure, they in effect became proprietors of their small plots of land. In England, so Bloch maintained, such peasants lost control to the lords, who could demand high rents; in eastern Europe, they were simply pushed off their fields. But in France, their petty holdings still covered much of the countryside.[4]

Cultivating tiny plots, relying on family labor, and producing primarily for their own consumption, the subsistence peasants existed alongside a much smaller sector of market-oriented farmers, typically tenants on large seigneurial holdings. According to the social historians, such large-scale tenant farmers provided the only element of capitalism and innovation in the countryside. For Bloch, they were "in economic terms capitalist[s]."[5] Similarly, Le Roy Ladurie contrasts the large estates that they worked with the peasants' miserable plots: "The plots correspond to the sector of the economy worked by the peasant, which provided . . . his family with subsistence. . . . The large estates, on the other hand, were directed towards the market. . . . They were often leased to well-equipped and relatively rich farmers."[6] Goubert repeats the same refrain. For him, the subsistence peasant pursued a single goal, self-sufficiency for his family: "His deeply rooted ideal was to 'live self-sufficiently,' producing everything that was necessary for material life—food, drink, heat, clothing, tools, even furniture and housing."[7] As Goubert acknowledges, perfect self-sufficiency was impossible, because many subsistence peasants did not possess enough land to feed themselves and their families.[8] But it was still the ideal that governed peasant behavior.

Here, Goubert was undoubtedly influenced, as were many others of his generation, by the work of Ernest Labrousse. An economic historian, Labrousse argued for much the same contrast between the market-oriented tenant farmer and the small-scale subsistence peasant, who employed family labor and lived "essentially from what he himself produced." For Labrousse, the subsistence peasants formed a lethargic "peasantry of stagnation," while the tenants constituted a much more vibrant "peasantry of growth."[9] Quoting Georges Lefebvre, the noted scholar of the French Revolution, Labrousse maintained that the typical subsistence peasant "did not seek to make money by producing for sale. He merely hoped to harvest enough to eat."[10]

One corollary here is that the subsistence peasants lived beyond the reach of markets and of economic analysis. True, they were affected by the rise and fall of population, the variation of wages, and the scarcity of land. And they certainly had to work on the side to make ends meet when their plots shrank, just as they had to sell produce to pay the fisc. Yet the ideal governing their behavior was always self-sufficiency, not profit or gain, which for many historians would seem to rule out economic analysis altogether. Ironically, any role for economics was further marginalized as Labrousse's influence over French history waned. He at least had focused on prices, but once his grip weakened, even prices lost their relevance. As Le Roy Ladurie commented,

> The movement of prices is, of course, an important factor in rural history. But it is true, nevertheless, that most agriculture produce was consumed by its producers, exchanged through barter, or handed over to some Lord and Master in the form of dues in kind. It did not pass through the explicit mediation of market prices, even if such prices were actually used as unofficial measures of produce. So there were other criteria than prices . . . in this 'post-Labroussian' phase of our research.[11]

Since prices and markets seemed irrelevant for the large numbers of subsistence peasants, it was easy for the social historians to downplay some of their own evidence. If peasants specialized in producing wine for market— as in part of Burgundy in the eighteenth century—that still did not constitute an "agricultural revolution," despite what economists might think. An agricultural revolution required something quite different—namely, more large tenant farms growing abundant quantities of grain.[12]

The contrast between the subsistence peasants and the large-scale tenant farmers had other implications as well. It tended to reduce rural history to demography, to the story of population growth and the resultant distribution of property. If a rising population fragmented holdings and increased the number of subsistence peasants, then French agriculture stagnated, for the subsistence peasants dragged down the agrarian economy. What France needed, according to the social historians, were additional large-scale capitalist farmers, for they were the wellspring of economic growth. They abounded in England, where they had brought about a true agricultural revolution of engrossment and enclosures—or so Le Roy Ladurie and others argue. In France, however, they were only a minority. True, their numbers, which varied over time and from place to place, undoubtedly increased during the sixteenth and seventeenth centuries. But their activities met with resistance from the horde of subsistence peasants. To quote Le Roy Ladurie, "in France, . . . the English-style agricultural revolution of enclosures ran into ferocious opposition from the mass of the peasantry."[13]

As a result, French agriculture suffered. For Pierre Goubert, it "hardly progressed," whereas elsewhere, and particularly in England, agriculture "experienced profound and rapid change."[14] With a few exceptions, agricultural productivity in France seemed to stagnate until 1750, when it finally began to improve. Le Roy Ladurie speaks of "a long period of stagnation . . . even . . . from the fourteenth to the seventeenth century" followed by "true growth" in the eighteenth century.[15]

Here, it is true, not all French historians agree with the details. Michel Morineau in particular has argued quite vociferously against any takeoff in the eighteenth century. Yet he too believes in much the same general picture, in a ceiling that limited agricultural productivity. His ceiling, admittedly, is placed quite high, and it therefore allows for considerable variation in output because of wars and famines. Still, it is a ceiling, in his case one that endures not just until 1750 but well past 1800.[16]

Whether the ceiling lifts in 1750 or after 1800, the evidence mustered by the social historians does seem to point to slow agricultural growth. Subsistence crises wracked France into the early eighteenth century, and even after the subsistence crises had subsided, the fear of famine remained very real. The population seemed unable to break through levels reached in the Middle Ages, as if held in check by a lack of food. And the tithe returns—seemingly an excellent index of agricultural output—were stunted. They too failed to surpass what had already been attained in the Middle Ages.[17]

To explain such miserable performance, the social historians have cited a variety of obstacles. They argue, for instance, that the subsistence peasants were simply stubborn: they clung to their outmoded technology and obstinately refused change. Alternatively, their mind-set—their *mentalité*—blinded them to innovations from the outside world. Their conservative Catholicism (so it is claimed) deprived them of entrepreneurial spirit, while the aristocratic ideals of Old Regime society had the same effect on seigneurial landlords. The social historians have invoked a host of other structural weaknesses as well: poor transportation, a paucity of capital, and a political system that drew innovators toward government office.

But the thrust of their argument has always derived from the twin handicaps that the large number of subsistence peasants imposed on the French countryside: small farm size and a village community full of subsistence peasants who were hostile to innovations such as enclosure. Here, as the social historians from Marc Bloch to Emmanuel Le Roy Ladurie have repeated lay the true flaws of French agriculture.[18] Whereas farmers in England worked large, enclosed, and consolidated farms, France was stuck with too many of the minuscule and inefficient subsistence holdings. In some parts of France one could find large farms—Bloch noted some in Normandy, and Le Roy Ladurie saw them on seigneurial farms or outside cities—but they drowned in a sea of tiny parcels. The French countryside simply resisted the English model of large productive farms.

Most of the countryside also escaped enclosure, which would have merged the fragmented parcels, put an end to customs such as communal grazing on the open fields, and facilitated the introduction of new crops. Peasant villages opposed such capitalist improvements, particularly in northern and eastern France, where peasants farmed scattered strips of land and enclosure was in greatest need. There, the village community defended open fields and communal property via suit and collective violence, particularly in the eighteenth century. The battle was all the fiercer because it pitted the subsistence peasants, who depended on the commons, against the seigneurs and their large-scale tenant farmers, who usually favored enclosure. On the eve of the French Revolution, the conflict thus joined hatred of the seigneurial system with opposition to capitalism, defeating enclosures in France. With enclosures rebuffed, French agriculture fell behind.

If the social historians are correct here, then farm size and the lack of enclosures must hold the key to understanding French agricultural stagnation. Bigger farms must have been more productive, but some obstacle must have kept French farms below the efficient size. Similarly, enclosures must have faced hurdles that damaged agriculture as a whole. Existing enclosures must have raised productivity, while resistance prevented similar enclosures from being established on large areas of land. Finally, the most ferocious resistance to enclosure and the reform of communal property rights must have come from the subsistence peasants. Here, to be sure, we should allow for nuance, for as Marc Bloch noted, resistance to enclosure could have come from a variety of different quarters, depending on the interests involved. But as Bloch himself stated, it was among the humbler peasants "that the shock troops of rural resistance were . . . recruited all over the country, declaring war on landlords who attempted improvements and on the enclosure edicts themselves."[19]

French social historians are not alone in holding such opinions. Similar ideas resonate throughout the historical profession. To review one rather illuminating example, let us consider the case of Robert Brenner, a historian of England, who is perhaps best known for his sharp attacks on Le Roy Ladurie's brand of rural history. The gist of Brenner's argument is that Le Roy Ladurie places far too much stress on Malthusian crises and population growth. Yet despite the disagreement over demography, Brenner still shares with Le Roy Ladurie a belief in the evils of strong village communities and small peasant-owned farms. In Brenner's opinion, smallholding peasants were too obsessed with risks to innovate and invest; and because they produced for subsistence, they never specialized as producers. Furthermore, their villages isolated them from the competitive forces of labor and land rental markets, which would have forced innovation and investment upon them. The only way traditional agriculture could improve, therefore, was to eradicate smallholding peasants and replace them with capitalist tenants working large farms. The markets for land and for labor would then propel agriculture ahead. Once again England provided the perfect model.[20]

Such a diagnosis is quite common outside history. In fact it permeates social thought, uniting such disparate figures as Marx and Weber. For Marx, who drew upon his own reading of English history, the subsistence peasants were an obstacle to be swept away in the process of primitive accumulation that initiated economic growth. They had to be stripped of their land and their common rights and reduced to wage labor. Only then, when they had lost their property and their common rights had been suppressed, would growth occur. In England, Marx believed, the peasants had already been replaced by tenant farmers, whose large, capital-intensive farms fostered commercial agriculture. The same transformation would of course be necessary on the Continent. As for Max Weber, despite a nearly antithetical approach, he too contended that the European peasantry raised obstacles to economic growth. In his view, the peasants' communal property rights, their devotion to tradition, and their ingrained habit of producing for subsistence rather than for profit kept them from becoming rational agents of growth. Economic growth required the rise of markets, the spread of individual property rights, and the "disenchantment" of the peasants' traditional mentality.[21]

Deeply entrenched in Marx and Weber, in the ubiquitous notion of a transition from feudalism to capitalism, similar ideas have taken root in more recent works of sociology, anthropology, and political science as well. Perhaps the clearest case is in the work of the political scientist James C. Scott, whose influential *Moral Economy of the Peasant* pays homage to Bloch and Le Roy Ladurie. Although economic growth is not Scott's focus—his major concern is explaining rebellions in Asia—Scott does suggest why peasants generally resist innovation. The reason, he argues, is the risk that innovation involves, because most new techniques cause incomes to vary. Unfortunately, even a slight drop in income can translate into a catastrophe among subsistence peasants, particularly those who are smallholders or landless. Peasants will therefore oppose most innovation. They may even rise up to block new technologies.[22]

In Scott's book, peasants thus resist the onslaught of capitalism. Here, Scott not only draws upon Marx but also upon the historian E. P. Thompson, who linked social protest to the spread of capitalism in England. For Thompson, the cause of such protest might be the commercialization of the grain trade, when it drove prices up beyond what the poor considered just. Or it might erupt when communal property rights fell victim to the ravages of capitalism; for communal property, Thompson suggested, provided a form of social insurance for the poor.[23] Scott shares this interpretation of traditional property rights and social arrangements, and in both his and Thompson's work, the ultimate losers are the poor, the landless, and smallholders.

It is worth noting one additional source for Scott's work: the economic historian Karl Polanyi and his numerous acolytes within anthropology. Polanyi may have exercised relatively little direct influence in France itself, but his view of traditional societies resembles what the French social historians said about the early modern peasant economy.[24] Polanyi in fact drew upon his own reading of early modern history (as well as classical sociology) to paint the rise of the modern market economy in cataclysmic tones. Like Scott and the French historians, he made a sharp distinction between modern commercialized societies and traditional ones. The implication was that one of the major obstacles to economic growth lay in the social arrangements and attitudes prevalent in traditional societies: the insignificance of markets, the absence of profit maximization, the widespread custom of reciprocity, and the concomitant devotion to group subsistence rather than individual gain. What is clear here are the parallels with the historians' arguments about peasant mentalities and village communities. The conclusion, of course, is that until the peasantry was swept away—in what Polanyi believed was almost inevitably a violent transformation— markets and economic growth would be held in check.[25]

To explain slow growth in traditional societies such as France, the same causes are thus invoked by historians and social scientists alike. They reach the same diagnosis despite sharply different methods, which range from the neo-Malthusianism of Le Roy Ladurie and the Marxism of Brenner to the cultural arguments of Weber and Polanyi. Why then question what seems like a solid consensus, one firmly in place for well over a generation? One reason is a problem with the very evidence that the social historians have summoned to demonstrate stagnation in the countryside. The tithe returns, for example, have been subject to attack ever since they first appeared; and as we shall see in Chapter 4, they may well underestimate economic growth.[26] Even if they do not, they differed so much from region to region that an overall verdict of stagnation may do an injustice to areas where the rural economy was thriving. Obviously, what needs explaining are the factors that made these regions stand out.

Much the same holds for the arguments about population. Even if the French population failed to break through a medieval ceiling, there was still enormous room for regional variation.[27] Furthermore, recent research in demographic history casts doubt upon the Malthusian model underlying the arguments about population.[28] Total population may bear only a remote relationship to agricultural productivity; the fraction of the population living in cities is presumably a much better indicator. Finally, as for the subsistence crises, they no longer seem to be clear evidence of agriculture's failings or even of famine. More often than not, the crises resulted from epidemics. If they were linked to a poor harvest, it was because harvest failures sparked migration and migration in turn spread disease. Rather than the failings of agriculture, the true culprits were more likely the social structure, troop movements, and the inadequacies of relief for the poor.[29]

Yet another reason to question the consensus comes from recent work on the French rural economy, work that has begun to illuminate the flaws in the consensus account. The most striking example of this new rural history was actually begun decades ago, but it only appeared in print between 1977 and 1988—Jean Meuvret's posthumous masterpiece, *Le problème des subsistances à l'époque Louis XIV*. Curiously, although Meuvret influenced Goubert and many other French historians, he drew quite a different picture of the French countryside. Downplaying demography, he gave careful consideration instead to agricultural technology, to transportation, and to legal and institutional arrangements in the countryside. In his portrait, peasants were no longer always hostile to innovation. Their technology made efficient use of resources, and if they opposed a particular innovation, it was likely to be for a good reason.

To Meuvret, one must add the insightful work of younger historians. Some is ingenious social history.[30] Some is part of the new economic history that has begun to cover France.[31] Whatever the approach, the authors view the countryside through a different lens. They may well see growth, where before only stagnation was visible.[32] They find change, where before there was only stasis. And when they do encounter stagnation, their explanation for it is different. Their evidence harmonizes with the pathbreaking scholarship about agriculture elsewhere in early modern Europe.[33] It also fits what economists and a number of political scientists now say about the peasantry: that peasant customs are not uneconomic, that even subsistence peasants are engaged in a considerable amount of trade, and that peasants themselves are really not obstacles to economic growth. All of this literature points to a very different argument. Indeed, it suggests that the real obstacles to growth lie elsewhere: with politics, with institutions, and with the rest of the economy—in particular, with the economy's ability to provide human and physical capital and opportunities for trade.

There are thus problems with the consensus. Some we shall take up in subsequent chapters: whether French agriculture really did as poorly as is assumed, whether growth was unknown in France before 1750, whether enclosures and large farms were the elusive keys to growth, or whether it was something else—politics, transportation, mentalities. In short, how much growth was there and what were the causes lurking behind it? We shall also postpone asking whether France's rural economy actually behaved as the social historians believe. Was it really dominated by a subsistence sector in which smallholding peasants farmed in isolation from markets? Did the subsistance peasants behave differently from their counterparts on the large capitalist farms? Did they blunt the forces of competition by escaping the markets for labor and the rental of land? And how did the local economy and local markets actually function? These questions shall be put aside for the moment in order to deal with one issue: the role of subsistence peasants and the village community in blocking enclosures and the reform of communal property rights.

CHAPTER TWO

Common Rights and the Village Community

FOR OVER A CENTURY, the parishioners of Varades battled to save their commons, first from the depredations of their seigneurial lord and then from other usurpers who encroached upon the community's rich pasture. In this parish situated on the edge of Brittany, alongside the Loire upstream from Nantes, the fights over the commons began in 1639 and continued into the 1740s. Such conflict was hardly extraordinary, for many other communities in Brittany witnessed equally ferocious battles over their own commons. Throughout the region, commons happened to be extensive: they served as pasture during the long periods when they were not under cultivation. But increasingly, local seigneurs sought to lay claim to the communal pasture and limit access to it. They did so by granting use rights to individuals who would enclose and cultivate what seemed to be little more than wasteland. Known as *afféagements* in Breton law, such grants grew increasingly widespread in the early modern period, particularly in the eighteenth century. They had the backing of the royal government, which used the afféagements to raise money from the royal domain. They also had the support of the local sovereign law court, the Parlement of Rennes, which buttressed the local seigneur's claims to dispose of all the local commons and waste.[1]

In Varades, the seigneurial lord and the other usurpers tried to enclose portions of the communal pasture, but the parishioners of Varades persisted in grazing their animals there. The parishioners were fined and their animals seized, but the grazing did not stop. The parishioners in fact did everything they could to frustrate their adversaries. They uprooted boundary stones that marked off the seigneur's claims, filled in the ditches that formed the enclosure, and threatened the haywards (*forestiers*) who cited them when their livestock strayed upon the seigneur's portion. In court one of their tactics was noncooperation. When interrogated in criminal proceedings, they played dumb, denying everything. They claimed not to know who had removed the boundary stones—a clever ruse but hardly a plausible one in an early modern parish, where gossip was rife and privacy nonexistent. Similarly, they failed to appear when the court replaced the stones or evaluated the damages that the seigneur had suffered. They also used the courts to defend the commons, pursuing seemingly endless legal battles in Rennes and Paris. And they even resorted to violence. In 1732, some fifty parishioners disguised as women set upon workmen who were delimiting the commons with markers. They beat them up and fired gun-shots, forcing the workmen to jump into the river to escape.[2]

Like similar incidents in Brittany and elsewhere, the events in Varades would seem, at least at first glance, to be a perfect example of what the consensus invites us to believe: the struggle between a valiant peasant community and a capitalist seigneur. On the one side stands the seigneurial lord, who in France is the agent of capitalism: he simply wishes to put wasteland to more profitable use in commercial farming. On the other side stand the poor subsistence peasants, defending their traditional property rights against enclosure and the onslaught of capitalism. Given the sketch of the consensus in Chapter 1, we can readily imagine what to expect: because the subsistence peasants benefit from the commons—a form of social insurance for the poor—they will join together to protect communal property rights from capitalist attack. They will oppose capitalism and commercial farming, and their resistance will block a necessary reform of property rights.

That is what the social historians who fashioned the consensus would anticipate. It also fits what was envisaged by social thinkers from Marx and Weber to the present. Yet the reality was quite different, as we shall see by examining the case of Varades and several other examples in detail. Throughout, our concern will be the generalizations of the consensus: that the poor subsistence peasants opposed capitalism, that they benefited from the commons, that they united to defend communal property, and that their opposition barred enclosure and reform of property rights. Sadly, when scrutinized, these generalizations will fail.

What then was taking place in Varades? Was it poor subsistence peasants who were pasturing animals on the local commons and defending their communal property rights? It certainly appears so. In 1661, for instance, a number of parishioners of Varades were accused of putting animals out to graze on the lord's portion of the commons, of ripping out his boundary markers, and of threatening the haywards. To judge from their occupations, many were probably poor: the day laborer, Jacques Gaultier, or the spinner and washerwoman, Jeanne Dany. Of the twenty-seven who were interrogated in detail in December of 1661, twenty-six were accused of letting animals feed on the seigneur's portion. Of these, fifteen were day laborers, boatmen, weavers, or spinners—not prosperous occupations. Of the eleven charged with ripping out markers or threatening the haywards, nine came from the same modest background.[3]

Yet what is most interesting about the defendants in December of 1661 are the animals they were tending. Of the twenty-six individuals charged with letting animals feed on the lord's holdings, all but one were accused of grazing sheep. The more modest defendants sometimes pastured a few head of cattle too, but what predominated on the commons were sheep.

Gaultier, for instance, admitted to letting forty sheep graze, though he denied that they had strayed into the seigneur's portion. Dany admitted to tending an equal number of sheep. Such herds of sheep, however, were not what we would expect of subsistence farmers, who might pasture a cow or perhaps a horse, but not sheep, and certainly not forty of them. Indeed, if one believes probate inventories from the period, parishioners in Varades typically possessed only a few cattle apiece. Sheep, by contrast, were extraordinarily rare. In fact, of thirty-seven probate inventories drawn up in Varades during the years 1645–57, only one mentions any sheep at all.[4] Sheep were in fact a commercial enterprise, raised for sale because they could be transported long distances. The parishioners watching over the sheep may have been modest, but they were engaged in capitalist agriculture, usually in partnership with merchants who leased them sheep in return for a share of the profits. Jeanne Dany said she had gotten hers from a merchant named François Lohier, who was also one of the accused. He had also let sheep on shares to Jacques Legendre, who permitted them to stray on to the seigneur's portion. The situation in the early eighteenth century was much the same. There, too, sheep predominated on the commons, even though they were rare among Varades' peasants.[5]

Apparently, the poor of Varades were in league with agricultural capitalists, such as merchants and livestock dealers. Together they used the commons to raise livestock for sale. As elsewhere in the west of France, the trade may well have involved shipping animals long distances—perhaps as far as Paris. Although the poorer members of the parish did let their own cattle graze too, the common pasture was not the preserve of subsistence farming. Rather, it was the meeting place for nascent rural capitalism, the locus for a curious alliance between modest peasants and the agents of commercial agriculture. What, though, about the seigneurial lord who was trying to encroach upon the commons? If the evidence from the rest of Brittany is any indication, his afféagements did nothing to improve productivity. Throughout Brittany, seigneurs and the authorities of the royal domain leased out the commons for what was at best a temporary reclamation, but after a few years the land typically reverted to waste. Little of the landscape was affected, and when the afféagements were at their peak, agricultural productivity in Brittany was stagnant or falling. The afféagements, in short, were simply attempts to redefine property rights for the benefit of the seigneurs.[6] They were redistribution pure and simple—or in blunter terms, class robbery—made possible by the law courts and the royal government's thirst for revenue. They were not harbingers of capitalism, and in Varades at least the seigneur was hardly the capitalist vanguard.

Although Varades is only one example, it obviously casts some doubt on the historical consensus. But beyond the doubt that Varades raises lies yet another problem with the consensus—namely, the unity that it presupposes among peasants. It is not just that the subsistence peasants were supposed to oppose capitalism; it is that they would unite to defend their interests and guard their commons. They had to do so consistently, just as they had done in Varades. For if they faltered, if their defense of the commons was only sporadic, then how could they constitute a main obstacle to capitalism and the reform of property rights?

This assumption of unity—the assumption that peasants in traditional villages would act collectively to protect their interests—has a curious intellectual history. It entered the consensus from Marxism, where it was reinforced by evidence about peasant villages derived from nineteenth-century German scholarship. Yet the German scholarship—a curious offspring of both romanticism and efforts of liberal reform—was seriously flawed. In particular, it greatly exaggerated both the solidarity and the continuity of the medieval village. The archetypal image was that of a compact nuclear settlement with cooperative open-field farming, where peasants pastured their animals in a communal herd and tilled scattered strips of land according to a communal crop rotation. The open-field farming unified the community and engendered cooperation. That allegedly was the norm in Europe from time immemorial, until markets and the state wreaked havoc in the countryside.[7] The open-field farming underwrote cooperation in daily life, and from day-to-day cooperation it was only a short step to the assumption of united action to defend the commons.

Such an image, though, is now quite outmoded. Nuclear villages with open fields and communal farming were far from ubiquitous, and in much of Europe they were a fairly recent creation of the late Middle Ages, not a relic of the past. Dispersed habitation—in Varades, for example—was quite common, particularly as one reaches farther back in time. There was in any case no link between settlement type and day-to-day cooperation.[8] If anything, cooperation was the exception, and strife the rule, whatever the shape of the village. The communities that fit the archetypical image—the nuclear villages of the open fields in northeastern France, for instance—hardly engendered the sort of cooperation assumed by scholars, even extraordinarily gifted ones such as Marc Bloch. In one such village, Vionville in Lorraine, hundreds of fines were levied each year for violations of the rules of open-field farming: trespassing, encroaching on a neighbor's parcels, or letting animals wander into his meadows or fields of standing grain.[9] There and elsewhere, fights provoked by trespass, wandering animals, and abuse of the commons were the norm on the open fields. The rules of open-field farming—the bylaws, which regulated planting and harvesting—aimed to minimize such conflict and to keep suspicious neighbors from one another's throats. Nor was strife of this sort unique to the open fields. It was frequent whatever the pattern of settlement, the shape of the fields, or the nature of local agriculture.[10]

Ill will within villages amounted to more than altercations when animals went astray. On occasion villagers could even fail to aid one another in times of need. They might stay inside when a neighbor was assaulted and screamed for help in the middle of the night.[11] True, their uncharitable behavior could be reasonably attributed to fear, or to a belief that the neighbor in distress deserved chastisement. Or it might be argued that such cases were exceptions, lurid incidents culled from criminal records, and thus hardly representative of everyday experience. Even so, it is hard to maintain that cooperation prevailed in most rural communities. Contemporary works of literature, by authors who tended to idealize village life—Noel du Fail in the sixteenth century and Rétif de la Bretonne in the eighteenth—still leave traces of discord in rural communities.[12] Modern studies of villages only amplify the evidence. In book after book, by social and cultural historians and anthropologists alike, it is suspicion and dissension that seem to rule in rural communities. Even a shared faith, which ought to have unified villagers, could just as well divide them, as different factions vied for control of chapels and confraternities.[13]

Admittedly, there were individuals and institutions that attempted to pacify the community: magistrates and village consuls, who sought to arrange an end to feuds, or the Church, which in different ways before and after the Counter-Reformation tried to establish peace. And it was certainly possible to triumph over the squabbles of daily life and mount a united defense of common lands. The case of Varades suggests as much, for there rich and poor parishioners had fought among themselves over the very commons that were under siege. Nonetheless, collective defense of the commons was far from the rule. Elsewhere in Brittany a united campaign against enclosures was possible only because of threats against villagers who were tempted to implicate their neighbors during judicial investigations. A mock gallows was erected to warn those who felt such temptation, but the desire to bear witness against a troublesome neighbor might well have been irresistible. Collective action to protect the commons was therefore difficult, as was any united action in a rural community. That was perhaps one reason—as E. P. Thompson noted—why relatively few protests ever erupted against enclosures in England. Perhaps the lesson for historians is that they should not be too quick to assume solidarity in villages or, for that matter, in other small groups. They should keep in mind the obstacles in the way of unity, the gnawing disagreements and the delicious opportunities to take advantage of one's neighbors—what political scientists would call the free-rider problem. Perhaps historians are too much in the thrall of the sort of anthropology that in effect supposes cultural unity within villages. It keeps their focus on the shared culture within a community, but it blinds them to dissension. It also blinds them to the essential role of forces outside the community, forces of law and politics.

Had it not been for the support of the royal government and sovereign law court, for instance, the seigneurs of Brittany might never have dared to pursue their afféagements.[14]

Whether or not villages could unite to defend their commons, we could still ask about yet another part of the historical consensus: whether the commons benefited the village as a group, or at least the poorer villagers. Did the commons provide social insurance for the poor? In Varades the more modest villagers did graze their own personal animals on the communal pasture in 1661, but ninety years earlier the pasture was apparently overrun by the wealthy. Here, as Jean Meuvret has stressed, we must distinguish between two very different sorts of common rights: first, the rights to feed on the stubble that remained in the open arable after the grain was harvested, and second, the rights to graze on pasture or waste, as in Varades. Rights to the stubble concerned only sheep, which were by and large the monopoly of the wealthier villagers. It follows that the poor usually gained little from the stubble in the open fields.[15] Rights to pasture and waste, on the other hand, were under contention as in Varades, making it difficult to generalize about the share that the poor had. In some communities, the poor clearly benefited from such commons, though as Varades demonstrates, they may have used the commons to profit from commercialized agriculture. In others, sometimes in the very same regions, the poor were largely excluded from the commons. In parts of Provence, in southern France, for instance, communal pasture was leased out and the poor excluded. The money from the leases helped offset the village's tax assessment, to the benefit of rich villagers, who usually owed most of the taxes due.[16]

The same was true in La Grande-Paroisse, southeast of Paris. There in 1782 three prosperous tenant farmers opposed a scheme to divide revenue from the village's commons, which consisted of meadow that the village had been leasing out. The three tenant farmers, all related, were quite explicit about their motives. As one of them explained to a landlord, the revenue from leasing the commons paid a portion of the village's tax assessment. If the commons were divided, the three wealthy farmers would have to pay much more in taxes, and that would limit the rent they could pay. Meanwhile, local smallholders—vinedressers and agricultural day laborers—had no access to the commons in La Grande-Paroisse and derived little benefit from the revenue generated by leasing it. They actually wanted to use the revenue from the commons to pay a schoolmaster and a vicar and then divide the rest among themselves. They had no stubborn attachment to communal property; indeed they argued that the commons actually hurt the village poor: "Although all the inhabitants of a parish supposedly have an equal claim to the commons, the revenues from this meadow nevertheless benefited primarily the rich, to the detriment of the poor."[17]

During the French Revolution, when villagers were actually asked whether they wanted to divide their common pasture land, the poor over-whelmingly voted in favor of division, at least in the villages in the Paris Basin and southeastern France whose records Kathryn Norberg has ana-lyzed. In her communities, it was not the poor or the subsistence peasants who wanted to preserve the commons. Rather, it was the rich. They monop-olized the common pasture and were therefore the ones who wanted to preserve common grazing.[18] As one knowledgeable eighteenth-century ob-server noted, "the commons are called the patrimony of the poor," but in many cases it would be better to say "the patrimony of the rich."[19] It is true that contemporaries did defend the commons as the refuge of the poor, but their language should not always be trusted. Often it cloaked more self-interested motives, as in eighteenth-century Lorraine. There, the judges of the local sovereign law court—the Parlement of Nancy—opposed the divi-sion of common pasture, arguing that tenant farmers and agricultural day laborers depended on the common grazing. But their real motives were more likely the grazing rights that the judges themselves possessed as seigneurial lords and major landowners.[20] The men and women of the Old Regime were not fools. They knew how to use language strategically and could easily clothe self-interest in the vestments of charity for the poor. Although it runs against the grain of much cultural history today, we can-not always take their language at face value. Rather, we must always ask what interests lay behind the words they chose.

In many communities, then, the poor derived scant benefit from the com-mons. If there was conflict over the commons—and there was a great deal in the eighteenth century between seigneurs and villagers—it was not be-cause the commons was the paupers' last defense against the onslaught of capitalism. Rather, it was because the rising value of land made it worth fighting over common rights. It was also that changes in legal practices and state policies made it cheaper for both sides—seigneurs and villagers alike—to wage legal battles over the commons. Aided by experts in feudal law, seigneurs could start to encroach on the commons. Villagers could fight back in the courts with their own legal help.[21] At various times the state also encouraged encroachment, whether it was for fiscal reasons or in the belief that agriculture would improve.

No matter who actually benefited from the commons, one might still ask whether the rural community blocked the reform of communal property rights. Was it the village community that spared France the sort of enclo-sures that swept across early modern England? Marc Bloch believed that it was, and Emmanuel Le Roy Ladurie cited collective violence by villagers to explain the lack of English-style enclosures in France. Both historians maintained that French agriculture suffered as a result, because it never underwent an agricultural revolution like England. The type of enclosure

Bloch and Le Roy Ladurie imagined here would have transformed the open fields of northern and eastern France. It was not the sort of partitioning of the commons that was seen in Varades, for in Brittany and elsewhere in western France enclosures were routine and had little to do with agricultural productivity. What Bloch and Le Roy Ladurie envisaged was a much more drastic affair. It would have consolidated scattered plots into large efficient holdings and put an end to communal grazing rights on stubble and pasture. Farmers would then have been free to plant new crops and explore new crop rotations. That sort of enclosure in the open fields, Bloch and Le Roy Ladurie argued, would have given France what made English agriculture superior; yet it was stopped by the peasant community.[22]

Northeastern France did remain unenclosed. Yet the reasons why remain unclear, as do the ultimate consequences for the rural economy. If we examine the evidence Bloch and Le Roy Ladurie marshall to explain the lack of enclosures, it appears to be rather scanty, particularly when it comes to identifying the precise obstacles. Bloch rested his case on investigations undertaken by the government when it was interested in agricultural reform. The records contain much discussion by lawyers and officials of the pros and cons of enclosure, but they say relatively little about exactly who—in real villages—actually halted enclosures.[23] As for Le Roy Ladurie, he built his case on evidence drawn from Pierre Saint-Jacob's work on Burgundy. Saint-Jacob does cite cases of protests against enclosure of pasture by landless artisans, but his evidence too is surprisingly thin. Although Saint-Jacob speaks of resistance to enclosure, it is not at all clear who is involved.[24] And none of his evidence concerns attempts to undertake an English-style enclosure, the sort that would not just have fenced in a pasture but transformed an entire village—what we might call a general enclosure. That was certainly the sort of enclosure Bloch had in mind.

Yet there is one extraordinary case in which we can determine who made trouble for such an enclosure, and it deserves detailed attention. It concerns two villages in Lorraine, two villages that were among only a handful in France to undergo something close to an English enclosure. During 1768–71, the king's intendant in Lorraine, Antoine de Chaumont de la Galaizière, reshaped the fields in Roville-devant-Bayonne and Neuviller-sur-Moselle, two adjacent communities south of Nancy where he was seigneurial lord and a major landowner.[25] With the consent of the other landowners, he rearranged the parcels in the villages' open fields, consolidating each owner's fragmented holdings, redrawing each village's paths and roads, and reorienting its furrows. Consolidation, he believed, reduced the costs of fertilizing: no longer did an owner have to manure scattered parcels of land. It also gave each owner access to his fields without crossing his neighbor's land. Not only would this reduce the endemic strife over damage caused by trespass, but it made the villages' traditional regulation of planting and harvesting—regulation designed to prevent trespass and theft at sensitive times of the year—completely unnecessary.

Finally, and most important, La Galaizière's reorientation of the furrows promised to resolve serious problems with drainage. In Roville and Neuviller, as in other parts of Lorraine, clay under the topsoil caused water to gather, blighting seeds and rotting crops. If the furrows paralleled the slope of the land and were coordinated, they would carry the water away, but all too often they merely flooded neighboring parcels and roads. Fearing inundation, each farmer adopted a defensive strategy that in the end made everyone worse off: with his plow he piled earth up at the center of each of his narrow strips and cut furrows deep enough around the edges to collect any runoff water. The middle of each strip remained dry, but the deep furrows along the edges were stripped of topsoil and almost permanently flooded. Given the dimensions and number of the strips—there were 2,010 of them in Neuviller's 441 hectares of cultivated land alone—the resulting losses were enormous. Estimates ran to 25 percent of the crop or more. La Galaizière aimed to cut these losses by specifying the direction of the furrows on each piece of property during the consolidation of holdings. The furrows would be coordinated to promote drainage, and their direction could not be changed. Presumably the consolidation of holdings itself would also reduce the losses from deep plowing around parcel boundaries.[26]

The evidence, though far from perfect, suggests that the improvements La Galaizière undertook were extremely successful. The best indication of his success is that land rents rose, a sign (as Chapters 4 and 5 show) that agricultural productivity had increased. Surviving leases from Roville and Neuviller in the late eighteenth century are hard to find, but one of the other large landowners in Roville and Neuviller, a religious order known as the Tiercelins, watched the rent on its farmland in Neuviller jump 55 percent after the rearrangement was completed, even though the number of acres the Tiercelins owned had not changed. Some of the increase, however, may have been due to changes in prices. If we estimate the effect of the price changes by looking at rental rates in neighboring towns where no such rearrangement of fields took place, we are still left with approximately a 32 percent real increase in rent, which we can reasonably attribute to higher productivity.[27] It was no wonder that nineteenth-century agronomists sang La Galaizière's praise.[28]

Rents and agriculture productivity climbed, but La Galaizière's general enclosure aroused considerable resistance within the two villages. In the list of grievances (*cahier de doléances*) drawn up for the meeting of the Estates General on the eve of the French Revolution, the villagers of Neuviller requested the suppression of the royal letters-patent that had authorized La Galaizière's project. Their real concern was that the project had abolished the communal herd's grazing rights on village pasture. They wanted these rights restored to the state they had been in before the enclosure. Roville voiced similar concerns. The villagers there lamented the suppression of grazing rights, and they denounced La Galaizière for appropriating and enclosing over half of the village's pasture. They demanded the return of their pasture; if not, they wanted a restoration of grazing rights on the portion that he had enclosed.[29]

At the time the villagers drew up their cahiers, Roville was in fact battling La Galaizère in the courts over the communal pasture and the grazing rights that the enclosure had suppressed. The suit had apparently begun in 1781, when the shepherd François Gillet led the communal herd across a ditch barring access to part of the pasture that La Galaizière had enclosed. La Galaizière's tenant farmer, Georges Louis, went to the seigneurial court, and not surprisingly he got a judgment against Gillet and against the village of Roville, which employed the shepherd. In its ruling the seigneurial court cited the letters patent authorizing the enclosure. But Roville was not stopped by this decision. It appealed to the Parlement of Nancy, and it did the same in other cases of trespass by the communal herd onto pasture enclosed during La Galaizière's project. Now embroiled in the suit, La Galaizière protested that his enclosure had abolished common grazing in Roville, but the Parlement ruled against him. It ordered La Galaizière and his tenant to return the damages to the village shepherd.[30]

In vain, La Galaizière asked the court to reconsider its decision. He then brought the matter before the king's council. Like many court suits under the Old Regime, the affair dragged on for years: it was still unsettled at the outbreak of the French Revolution. With the suit still under way, in 1788, Roville asked the recently established provincial assembly for help in the affair, for how could a poor community like theirs plead their case before the king? In their petition, the villagers complained that La Galaizière had appropriated the best of their commons, reducing them to distress. How happy they would be if the commons were still in their possession! They had only gone along with La Galaizière's enclosure because of his threats. "Those who balked," they complained, "were threatened with prison." La Galaizière had also slapped them with judgments when the communal herd attempted to exercise its grazing rights. The fines rained down particularly hard on the "poor day laborers," who needed the commons most.[31]

It seems a perfect case of a village's opposition to enclosure, opposition undertaken in the name of the subsistence peasants and the poor. Yet there is still room for doubt. After all, court cases were not usually pressed so far unless substantial interests were involved.[32] Elsewhere in Lorraine, we know, wealthier peasants often monopolized common grazing, leaving little or nothing for the poor. That was the case, for example, in the nearby village of Laneuveville-devant-Bayon, where the seigneur's farmer devastated the common pasture with an enormous herd of sheep. The same monopoly lay at the root of La Galaizière's struggle with the Parlement of Nancy over a 1771 royal edict that limited grazing rights and permitted division of the commons. The judges in the Parlement refused to register the edict (thus depriving it of the force of law) because it infringed on grazing rights that they owned as seigneurs, rights that they leased to prosperous tenant farmers.[33] Roville, of course, may have been different. Although we do not know whose animals made up Roville's communal herd, the documents mentioned both sheep and cattle. The precise numbers are not clear, but conceivably the cattle did belong to the poor.

The real question, though, is whether the village community was the major obstacle to La Galaizière's general enclosure. Whether it was the wealthier villagers or the poorer ones who stood up to La Galaizière, was it the village's opposition alone that blocked his way? Here one must acknowledge a factor that historians have tended to ignore because of their focus on life within the village community: namely, the help that the peasants of Roville received from outside their own village. Their court suit would probably not have received such a favorable hearing on appeal, had the judges of the Parlement not been rankled by previous battles with La Galaizière.[34] Roville had the support of the Parlement, and the village community was not the only obstacle to La Galaizière's project. There were barriers outside the village community as well.

But even inside the village community, La Galaizière confronted other hurdles besides the grazing rights on the communal pasture, hurdles that were ultimately far more difficult to surmount than the village's opposition. His problem was that his general enclosure required the unanimous consent of all the local landowners, for each landowner could threaten to sue and thereby block the project. Given the Parlement of Nancy's hostility to La Galaizière and the legal structure of the Old Regime, this was far from a hollow threat. The Parlement would probably have looked with favor upon appeals from La Galaizière's own seigneurial court, and even without the support of the Parlement, his opponents could take advantage of overlapping jurisdictions and the disconcerting lack of finality in the legal system to file suits against the project even years after it was complete. True, La Galaizière could resort to intimidation to prevent such suits. The villagers of Roville claimed that he had used coercion to get their agreement, and even if the villagers exaggerated in their plea to the provincial assembly, there is little doubt that La Galaizière could easily have cowed smallholders. The same would be true for any powerful seigneur.

But large landowners were a different matter altogether. They could threaten to sue. The village of Roville had gone to court; they could easily do the same. Obviously, as substantial landowners, they all stood to profit from the general enclosure, from its consolidation and improved drainage, and especially from its higher rents. Yet although they all might benefit from the enclosure, the possibility of a suit gave each of them what amounted to a veto over the project. Each one then had an incentive to withhold his consent and threaten to block the enclosure in the hope of appropriating a share of the other landowners' gains. The threat of suit and the need for unanimous consent transformed each of the major landowners into a monopolist and left the project at their mercy.[35]

This was far from a theoretical problem, and contemporaries were well aware of it.[36] It plagued La Galaizière's general enclosure and was in fact the major hurdle he faced. He had to pay off recalcitrant landowners, those who were undoubtedly behaving strategically in an attempt to appropriate a share of the profits. Compensating the recalcitrant greatly reduced the profitability of his enclosure; it may have even made the project more expensive than it was worth. La Galaizière himself paid all the bills. It cost him, he reported, 32,641 livres. Of this only 11,141 livres was spent on surveying and legal costs. The rest, nearly two-thirds of the total expense, went for concessions to win the landowners' consent (all the land for roads came out of La Galaizière's holdings, for example) and for payments to the most stubborn among them. He had to bribe these holdouts by buying their land at above-market prices. The biggest bribes went to the likes of Sieur Mirbeck, a rentier in Neuviller, or to Monsieur Guenin, the second-biggest landowner in Roville.[37] These were hardly paupers.

How much of the increased income from the enclosure did such payments absorb? We can get a rough estimate by assuming that, like the Tiercelins, all the landowners in the two villages experienced a 32 percent real increase in rent (in other words, an increase due to the enclosure and not to higher prices). At contemporary rental rates and land values, the increased rent provided somewhere between an additional 2.4 and 4.8 livres per hectare per year. Over the two villages, it amounted to an increase in land values lying somewhere between 29,000 and 76,000 livres. In the jargon of economics, this is the present value of the increased income that the enclosure generated.[38]

Whatever the precise figure, it is obvious that the costs absorbed a major portion of the increased income that the enclosure produced. Indeed, it may well be the lower estimates of increased income that are most reasonable, since not all landowners may have fared as well as the Tiercelins—say about a 30,000-livre rise in land values, which is slightly less than the project's cost. If so, then the enclosure was apparently a loser, particularly, it would seem, for La Galaizière. Although he was a major landowner, he still reaped only a fraction of the benefits. Had it not been for the 6,000 livres spent on buying off the most stubborn landowners and the 15,500 spent on smaller bribes and on land sacrificed for the roads, the project as a whole would have been in the black, with a rate of return of 12 percent or more, at a time when long-term loans were earning under 5 percent.[39] Even La Galaizière would have emerged a winner. The problem was that the cost of achieving consent absorbed far too much of the benefits.

Fortunately, the government reimbursed La Galaizière for his bills, because his general enclosure was supposed to serve as an example for other villages. In his request for repayment, La Galaizière acknowledged that the cost of achieving unanimity was his greatest expense: "Forced to do everything by the path of agreement, the opposition of every holdout forced me to start all over again numerous times. . . . I had to obtain their votes by enormous sacrifices, which would have ruined me had you not had the good will to reimburse me."[40] La Galaizière claimed that seigneurs in neighboring villages wanted to undertake similar projects, but only if the government helped limit the costs of winning the other landowners' agreement. Their fears were justified, for they undoubtedly would have had to pay dearly to get unanimity. After all, they could not intimidate the recalcitrant as effectively as La Galaizière, who was the king's intendant. To help them, La Galaizière proposed an edict allowing the rearrangement of parcels if the owners of a majority of the land so voted— something analogous to the private enclosure acts in England. By breaking the costly requirement of unanimous consent, such an edict would have facilitated rearrangement for drainage and other improvements, but it was never adopted.[41]

The major obstacle to the sort of general enclosure La Galaizière envisaged was not the peasants' village community. It was strategic behavior by other landowners, who took advantage of the legal system to siphon off the profits of the enclosure. The community was at most a hindrance, since villagers, too, could take advantage of the courts. But the damages involved when they let their animals graze upon enclosed meadows were probably rather small and not enough to put the enclosure into the red.[42] The big expense was the money needed to win the assent of the other landowners, particularly the rich and powerful ones, who could not easily be coerced. If La Galaizière is to be believed—and he had little reason to hide the costs of the difficulties he encountered—it was these landowners who were the real barrier to general enclosures.

Although Roville and Neuviller are only examples, it thus seems that the village community did not stop enclosures. Villages were too divided to defend common property rights consistently. Furthermore, they often had no reason to do so. The villagers were not necessarily opposed to commercial farming, and grazing rights were not the preserve of subsistence peasants and the poor, as many historians and social scientists suppose. The real barriers to enclosure lay elsewhere, with strategic behavior and with the legal system that made strategic behavior possible.

Yet there remains one question: were enclosures themselves the key to growth? Whatever the real obstacles to enclosure, was it a reform of property rights that would set France's traditional agriculture in motion? The answer must await a better measure of productivity growth in early modern agriculture. But before we can measure productivity, we must first come to a better understanding of the rural economy, in particular its labor and rental markets.

CHAPTER THREE

Labor Markets, Rental Markets, and Credit in the Local Economy

THE GIFTED HISTORIANS of the French countryside devoted relatively few pages to rural markets. They acknowledged their existence, and particularly while Ernest Labrousse held sway, they paid attention to market prices. But they tended to ignore a number of critical questions: precisely how the rural markets functioned and how prevalent market transactions were in the countryside. Fortunately, the neglect has begun to give way to attention, at least as far as certain markets are concerned. Jean Meuvret and Steven Kaplan have shed considerable light on the market for grain, while other scholars have illuminated the trade in products such as wine and livestock.[1] Still others have explored land sales, not just in France but in England and Italy.[2] Yet the rental market for land and the labor market have continued to suffer neglect, at least until recently, an omission that clouds our understanding of society and culture in the early modern countryside.[3] These two markets deserve further investigation for a variety of reasons. Not only will examining them yield a fresh perspective on rural society; it will also make possible a new measure of productivity growth.

That rural markets remained in the shadows so long is certainly understandable. Given the consensus that France was overwhelmed by subsistence peasants, markets seemed relatively unimportant. Although large tenant farms produced for the market, according to the consensus the subsistence peasants did not, and they were far more numerous than the tenant farmers.[4] Implicit in the consensus was a picture of subsistence peasants tilling their own plots for their own consumption and relying almost exclusively on family labor. Even if they did occasionally peddle crops to pay taxes or work a bit on the side to make ends meet, their lives were still governed by an ideal of self-sufficiency. Clinging to self-sufficiency and preferring the independence of family labor, they by and large shunned markets.

The problem with this picture is that it is terribly misleading, even as an ideal. In the first place, it is difficult to see why peasants preferred self-sufficiency to market involvement. The usual argument is not the readily understandable one that markets were too distant and the cost of transporting crops for sale too high.[5] Rather, it is that markets were too risky, with the uncertainties of abandoning subsistence production presumably offsetting any gains from trade. Such a claim, it should be stressed, has been advanced by a number of distinguished historians and social scientists, and it is certainly true under some circumstances. But in early modern Europe it does not seem to apply. Indeed, a detailed analysis suggests that early modern markets probably reduced the variation in peasant income.[6]

Still, there is some historical evidence that can be marshaled to support the risks of the early modern market. Perhaps the best derives from the demographic crises that ravaged the parts of northern France that had specialized in grain production. The specialization, it could be argued, resulted from production for the market, and it left the regions vulnerable to famine when the grain harvest failed. Yet as we know, demographic research has clouded what once seemed to be a simple connection between demographic crises and the market price for grain. More often than not, the crises resulted from epidemic disease; the ultimate causes were the social structure, troop movements, and the nature of relief for the poor, none of which derived from production for the market. In fact, the evidence for northern France suggests that the demographic crises subsided when markets expanded. As markets grew more integrated, grain prices had a diminishing effect on mortality.[7]

There is a second and even more severe problem with the belief in self-sufficiency: it simply fails as a description of reality in the countryside, at least in the early modern France. Whatever the appeal of self-sufficiency might have been, it is clear that few peasants had enough land to attain it. Self-sufficiency, early modern historians generally agree, required at least 5 hectares of arable, unless the soil was particularly fertile or the parish blessed with an unusually large amount of commons. Indeed, the most careful examination of the issue, by Jean-Michel Chevet, suggests that it would more likely take 10 hectares (or nearly 25 acres) to support a family, feed livestock, and pay all the necessary taxes, even on the fertile soil of the Paris Basin.[8]

A rudimentary calculation supports Chevet's figure. If we take average yields for France as reported in the agricultural census of 1840 (yields in the Old Regime were no higher) and subtract minimal amounts for seed, taxes, and the tithe, then a family growing wheat and oats might be able to feed itself on a 5-hectare farm. Less optimistic assumptions could easily push the figure up to 10 hectares, as could the demand for animal feed. If, for example, the family hitched two horses to its plow—a typical number—then the plow team would require some 93 hectoliters of oats a year, plus straw and fodder. At 1840 yields (net of seed) and an 8 percent tithe, that would take 7.35 hectares sown with oats, or a 22-hectare farm under a three-field crop rotation.[9] Tax rolls and probate inventories convey the same impression. Horses and plows did not appear until a farm was well over 5 hectares in size.[10]

Few peasants owned that much land. North of Paris, in the village of Goincourt, only three of the ninety-eight peasants owned more than 10 hectares in 1717; ninety-four of them owned less than 2 hectares. Property ownership nearby was much the same. Further west, in the Norman village of Bretteville-l'Orgueilleuse near Caen, there were large farms, but few were in peasant hands. In 1687 the 31 peasant families in the village owned on average only 0.77 hectares each. Only one of them (with 4.7 hectares) even approached 5 hectares. Further south, in Languedoc, peasants in the village of Lespignan did possess farms over 6 hectares in the thinly populated fifteenth century—53 of the 103 village families had more than 6 hectares in 1492. But by the seventeenth century owners of this sort had dwindled to a minority: in 1653 only 34 of the village's 262 families had that much land.[11]

The examples could easily be multiplied: from eighteenth-century Brittany, from sixteenth-century Normandy, and from nearly any century in the Paris Basin; from sunny fields of maize near Toulouse, or from the kingdom's cloudy northern borders. The numbers differ somewhat from place to place and from century to century, but the point is nonetheless clear: few peasants were self-sufficient.[12] True, rights to the commons might make even smallholders self-sufficient. But in arable districts, the commons consisted of little more than grazing rights to the stubble, rights often monopolized, as we saw in Chapter 2, by the wealthy peasants and the local elite. Where the commons were more extensive—in the mountains or in western France, for example—peasants were in any case involved in the market. They specialized in dairy products or in livestock, as in the isolated Pyrenees valley of Barèges.[13] To find peasants with enough land to be self-sufficient, one thus had to look elsewhere: to the yeomen farms worked with family labor in seventeenth-century England, or to eastern Germany in the late fourteenth century, after the Black Death had decimated the population but before the Junkers had constructed their enormous estates.[14] Even then it is doubtful that the English yeomen or the Prussian peasants were isolated from trade.

What could land-poor peasants do? One possibility was to work in cottage industry or cultivate labor-intensive crops such as grapes. Or they could rent land from the country's numerous absentee landlords.[15] Vineyards or cottage industry would in any event draw them into the market, but not all peasants had such alternatives. And even where they were available, they hardly filled everyone's time.[16] Renting land was also out of reach in many instances. As we shall see, landlords hesitated to rent to just anyone, and many peasants lacked the capital—the livestock and equipment—that tenancy often required. In the few instances where we can count how much land peasants both owned and rented, few managed to lease enough to amass 10 or even 5 hectares.[17]

With such small holdings, peasants rarely were fully employed at home. In an arable district, a male adult could farm perhaps 14 hectares. If he owned or rented less than 10 hectares (and if he did not plant labor-intensive crops such as grapes), he would not be fully employed. As for women and children, they were not fully employed (except perhaps at harvest time) until a farm attained nearly 25 hectares. It is hardly surprising then that many peasants not only tilled their own meager holdings but worked on the side.[18] They served as village artisans or hired themselves out for a day's work, perhaps with a horse and cart. They harvested crops—sometimes migrating long distances to do so—and, particularly if they owned property in a village, toiled for large landowners as outdoor servants or day laborers. They might do the same for smaller farms during the long period before the farmer's own children were old enough to be of real assistance.[19] And particularly if they were younger, they might serve as farm domestics until they inherited land or saved enough for marriage.[20] Their very existence thus depended on rural labor markets.

The uneven size of farms thus guaranteed a supply of labor, ranging from servants hired for the year to local day laborers and migratory harvest workers. There was demand for labor as well, particularly on the large farms of absentee owners. There were even tasks to do in the winter months, such as threshing grain. Other opportunities for work arose from the seasonal demands of crops and from differences in climate. Outside Paris, for instance, vintners harvested wheat, because vineyards required little care in the wheat-harvest months of July and August. They were assisted by migrants from the uplands of Berri and the Limousin, where the grain harvest came later and haying did not conflict with harvest work in the Paris Basin.[21] Rural households were thus not isolated from markets, in particular from labor markets.

Here social historians might raise a reasonable objection. A real labor market, they might say, would require much more. Work on a neighbor's farm or at harvest time was simply not enough. It was merely part-time employment, and those who resorted to it retained their own property, which absorbed their allegiance and their time. At bottom, they were still tied to subsistence farming. Their participation in the labor market—or in any market—remained minimal. The rural economy would still be partitioned into two hermetically sealed sectors: the subsistence peasants on the one hand, and the capitalist tenant farmers on the other. Not until the subsistence peasants were stripped of all their property and reduced to pure wage labor would capitalism and market relations permeate their sector of the rural economy.

The argument is one that reaches back to Marx, who believed that capitalism required a "complete separation" of laborers from any property.[22] A rejoinder, unfortunately, is not easy. At the very least, it would require evidence for how much time subsistence peasants devoted to wage labor and how much of their food they purchased from others. If they passed most of their day working to buy food, it would at least suggest that their involvement in the market was extensive. And if many of them were actually propertyless, it might even persuade social historians. The problem, though, is that we do not know how many hours a day subsistence peasants spent working, nor how much food they actually purchased. We can estimate (from documents such as *terriers* and *cadastres*) how much property they owned, and we can guess at how much food this property produced. But they could have rented additional land, although telling how much they rented is nearly impossible. Leases for a given village are typically scattered far and wide. Those that can be located may well lack the information needed to determine how much land subsistence peasants actually farmed. Even the agricultural censuses of the mid nineteenth century shied away from that difficult question.[23]

Perhaps the only sources usable here are eighteenth-century fiscal investigations and tax rolls, which in some cases list how much land everyone owned and rented. The right sort of rolls are not available for all of France; nor are they perfectly reliable. Where they exist, though, they do reveal a substantial group of peasants who had to work to purchase nearly all of their food, even if they consumed every crumb that they themselves produced. In Bretteville-l'Orgueilleuse, for instance, the tax roll of 1735 labeled 48 families (out of the 109 on the roll) as day laborers, servants, or threshers—families clearly dependent on the labor market for their existence. Owning practically no land and renting little more, these families used their labor to buy 97 percent or more of their food.[24]

Admittedly, Bretteville is an extreme case, because agriculture there was heavily commercialized and land ownership was concentrated in the hands of a family of local nobles. But even the most remote and supposedly backward regions of France yield similar results. The sort of tax rolls we need exist, for instance, in the uplands of Auvergne, in regions isolated from commerce by rough terrain. There, in the community of Arches—today in the department of the Cantal—the tax roll of 1769 listed forty-eight families, of whom fully fifteen were day laborers and rural artisans. Only one of the fifteen owned or rented any farmland at all. The others could only cultivate gardens or bits of land that could periodically be reclaimed from the region's extensive commons and then left to lie fallow for years. But as the government's agent responsible for the roll remarked, the reclaimed land would only give the day laborers enough food for a quarter of the year. For the rest they would have to work. Apparently, they could not even support themselves by grazing animals on the commons, for three of the families had only one goat and nine others had no livestock at all.[25]

True, other peasants farmed more land and purchased less food. And the number of those who worked to buy most of their victuals varied over time. Precisely how many did so is impossible to say, for the right sort of fiscal records do not exist before the eighteenth century. In the sixteenth and seventeenth centuries, it is likely that peasant landownership declined.[26] Perhaps more peasants therefore produced their own food back in 1500. Typically, though, the land that peasants lost between 1500 and 1700 was sold to absentee owners, so that rather than being reduced to wage labor by the 1700s, the peasants merely shifted from ownership to tenancy.[27] In any event, the number of peasants heavily dependent on wage labor was large. In 1700, according to contemporary estimates, perhaps three quarters of the rural families in France were headed by an artisan or a day laborer. The percentage may have climbed even higher by the eve of the French Revolution.[28]

Whatever the exact number, in the end it probably does not matter. Neither does the exact amount of land that the average peasant worked. Regardless of what Marx argued, peasants did not have to lose all of their property before they responded to market incentives. They merely had to have some involvement in markets. Whether they spent 20 percent of their time working for wages or 80 percent, they would presumably divide their time at the margin so that the returns to tilling their own plots and working for others would be about the same. They would in all likelihood do the same with crops grown for their own consumption and those produced for the market, even though their own fare of dark bread or porridge might be very different from the wheat that they sold.

In short, it seems wrongheaded to divide the peasants into hermetically sealed classes of subsistence peasants and market-oriented tenant farmers. Empirical studies tend to reject such a simplistic division in developing countries, and in early modern France it clearly does violence to reality. In particular, it does violence to the abundant evidence that peasant families exported labor, while others hired it on the labor market. It does violence to the data from the nineteenth century as well, when the peasantry was undoubtedly stronger than it had been under the Old Regime. Until the 1860s, wages in the countryside tracked urban wages closely, and the earnings of peasant proprietors seemed to match those of semiskilled urban workers. That is hardly what one would expect if a large fraction of the peasantry had been isolated from markets and was clinging to subsistence. Fragmentary records from the Old Regime argue much the same.[29]

The peasants' involvement in markets (especially in the labor market) has at least one important implication: it rules out the popular models of the peasant economy, advanced by A[leksandr]. V. Chaionov and others, which focus on household labor and assume that labor markets simply did not exist.[30] Obviously, all peasants employed some family labor. Nearly all grew some of their own food as well, for to do otherwise would have been foolish given the high costs of transporting crops to market. But they were nearly all involved in markets. They sold crops, bought livestock, rented land, paid for plowing, and hired or sold labor. If their commerce with the outside world was sometimes limited, they at least traded with one another in a local economy.

The functioning of this local economy deserves much more attention—particularly the working of the local land rental and labor markets. Here economists might wish to begin with the labor market. They would be eager to know whether labor was grossly misallocated, with scores of idle paupers haunting the countryside. Yet the evidence discussed above suggests that labor allocation was not a serious problem, for farm laborers and peasant proprietors earned as much in the countryside as they did in the city.

Other scholars might want to ask how extensive was the peasantry's involvement in the labor market. They might pose similar questions about the rental market for land or for agricultural capital and about other rural transactions. Yet as we know, such questions are nearly impossible to answer. We cannot tell how many hours peasants toiled, nor how much land or capital they leased. A precise answer about how much produce they sold is equally elusive.

A more profitable starting point might lie in another direction, with questions that at first glance might seem more appealing to social historians. What were the problems involved in hiring farm labor? What was the relationship between master and servant? What were the practices, the institutions, and the unstated expectations of the rural labor market? And are the transactions between master and servant even amenable to economic analysis? Analogous questions arise quite naturally in the rental market, and they in fact permeate the local economy as a whole. They will obviously intrigue social historians and perhaps even anthropologists. But they should also interest economists. They revolve about important economic issues: "moral hazard," for instance, the label economists apply to undesired behavior that is difficult to detect or control, such as farmhands' loafing when their master was in town. Even more important, the answers to these questions shed light on a major barrier to that economists' obsession, economic growth.

RURAL LABOR MARKETS

Eighteenth-century treatises on agriculture are not the usual hiding place for striking images—far from it. One might consult them for the details of agricultural technology, but not for visual stimulation. Yet in one of the best of the treatises—Abbé Rozier's *Cours complet d'agriculture*—in a lengthy account of a model farm, there lurks a chilling image, one that rivets the historical attention and illuminates the workings of agricultural labor markets under the Old Regime.

Figure 3.1 Abbé Rozier's Model Farm. Reproduced from François Rozier, *Cours complet d'agriculture*, 10 vols. (Paris, 1781–1805), 6: 504, courtesy of the History and Special Collections Division, Louise M. Darling Biomedical Library, UCLA.

Rozier's model farm is ringed by walls and barns; the entire courtyard is enclosed and surrounded. There is only one exit for master, servants, and animals alike (figure 3.1). The reason is simple, according to Rozier; it is so that the farmer can see everything that comes and goes and thereby keep himself from being cheated: "It is one of the most effective ways to avoid being robbed. . . . One might argue that I carry mistrust too far, and that I assume all servants and hired hands are corrupt. I admit it, but even if we suppose that they are honest, we risk nothing in eliminating the temptation to become plunderers. It only takes one to lead the others astray." Rozier's problem is the servants, the farm's hired help. Because they cannot be trusted, they must always be watched. If they do prove honest, pay them well, Rozier advises, but be forever on guard, for once they begin to waste your property, there will be no way to stop them. Indeed, they require such vigilance that the whole farm is designed to ease the master's surveillance. From inside his window, perhaps from behind shutters left slightly ajar, he can see everything the servants do; there is simply no place for them to hide: "There is no nook, no cranny, no hiding place at all that can block his view of the loafer or the ill-willed."[31]

Rozier's model would seem more appropriate for a penitentiary than for the countryside, and although his description of it was published six years before Jeremy Bentham's *Panopticon*, one would commit only a mild anachronism in calling it a panopticon farm. To make sense of it, historians might of course wish to grasp their copies of Michel Foucault and interpret Rozier's image in terms of power, the power of master over servant. But neither Foucault nor power is the answer here. Power, after all, has characterized relations between master and servant since time immemorial. Interpreting Rozier in terms of power simply belabors the obvious. A much more promising avenue of inquiry would be to look at the problems of agricultural labor markets. The problems not only make sense of Rozier's panopticon farm, but they also resolve an annoying paradox: they reconcile Rozier's mistrust and suspicion with the loyalty and reciprocity that, at least ideally, were supposed to characterize master-servant relations under the Old Regime.[32]

Rozier's complaint highlights a major difficulty in the rural labor markets of early modern France. From what he says, it is clear that an early modern farmer could not nonchalantly hire so many hours, say, of a skilled plowman simply by offering the going wage. The reason was that plowmen and other farm domestics were untrustworthy and extraordinarily difficult to supervise. Perhaps in the intimate quarters of an urban lodging it would be easy to keep an eye on servants; but on a farm it was impossible. The domestics were scattered over the courtyard, inside the barns, or out on the fields, while the farmer could be only one place at a time. Worse yet, agricultural servants and laborers were entrusted with crucial tasks. They sowed, plowed, and harvested, and they cared for expensive farm animals. If they did a shoddy job out of ignorance, laziness, or sheer ill will, they could devastate the crops, spoil the harvest, and cost the farmer a fortune in livestock. True, the farmer might be able to detect the damage by inspecting what they had done. But that would take the farmer away from other valuable tasks, and in some cases—injury to livestock, for instance—it might be impossible to distinguish an accident from mischief.

Rozier voices such concerns, but he is not alone. These concerns appear repeatedly, and not just in the physiocratic treatises of the eighteenth century.[33] In the sixteenth century, for example, Charles Estienne recommended vigilance on the farm in similar terms in his *L'agriculture et la maison rustique*. Estienne advised farmers to reside on their farms and to avoid leaving when any agricultural work was to be done. He even counseled farmers to enter and leave their quarters via a secret backdoor. The reason for the vigilance and secrecy was obvious: it was to keep the servants at work, or in Estienne's terms, "to keep them doing their duty all the time." Several decades later, in his influential *Le théâtre de l'agriculture*, Olivier de Serres adopted similar tones, warning that farm workers required constant attention. Only supervision could "make the lazy diligent" and counter the "malign nature of most hired hands, which is the very reason why they merely feign any effort when their master is away."[34]

To judge from the surviving diaries and journals of farmers, such concerns were hardly theoretical musings. In the Norman village of Bretteville-l'Orgueilleuse, for example, a family of minor nobles, the Cairon, farmed their own land and employed half a dozen agricultural servants even in winter—shepherds, *valets de harnois*, and maidservants. The Cairon fired servants who did not work out or who were caught stealing—the *petit valet* Varin "driven out" in 1700, or another, named Charles, "dismissed for having taken trees" in 1698.[35] Farmers elsewhere were beset with similar problems. South of Paris, in the village of Brétigny, a tenant farmer named Pierre Buard returned from selling sheep in Paris in 1753 to discover that one of his servants had broken into his strongbox and absconded with an enormous sum—nearly 900 livres that Buard had amassed to pay his own rent and the village's taxes.[36]

The problems with servants were in fact nearly universal. They preoccupied farmers and landlords in England and Germany, and they were hardly peculiar to the early modern period. They figure in a number of biblical passages, and they remain an issue today. Throughout much of the world, in fact, most farms are still run by families because it is nearly impossible to supervise workers whose tasks cannot all be brought together at the same time under a single roof. As a result, individual farms have rarely employed large numbers of hired laborers, except in unusual cases of monoculture. Nor has agriculture developed specialized managers who supervise farm labor from afar.[37]

In early modern France—as in the modern world—the problems of supervising and motivating servants were compounded by the possibility that servants could leave. There was always the possibility of mobility, always the possibility that a truly bad servant could flee with something of value, like the thief employed by Pierre Buard. Historians tend to ignore such mobility in the early modern countryside, largely because demographers have noted the peasants' tendency to marry in their home villages. But the demographic sources overlook the young and the propertyless, who shuttled about rural districts working as farm servants. They might return home to marry, but in the interim they moved about in search of employment. Others might travel longer distances in search of work or even migrate to cities.[38] Though slight by modern standards, their movements were still enough to provide a dishonest servant with an avenue of escape.

What could an early modern farmer with servants do besides firing those who were idlers and thieves? What strategies could he devise to keep them honest and make them work? A number of solutions were conceivable. Some tasks—some types of harvesting, for instance—could be paid via piece rates, which would encourage workers to exert themselves. But even where piece rates would apply, they could pose problems for harvesting certain crops—hemp, for example, which could easily be damaged by workers hurrying to increase their take. There were a number of different payment schemes for the workers who harvested grain—shares of the crop, a fixed payment per acre, or a daily wage—each with its advantages and disadvantages. Paying a shepherd entailed its own difficulties. He might be paid a wage, but that offered little incentive for diligence. Instead, he was often allowed to keep his animals in the farmer's herd and feed them at the farmer's expense. That sort of compensation, however, gave rise to a number of abuses, which contemporaries knew only too well. Not surprisingly, the shepherd's own animals always turned out bigger than the farmer's, they yielded more wool, and, in the words of a proverb, they never seemed to die. An alternative—one that apparently gained ground in the eighteenth century—involved mixing the shepherd's wage with a bonus. The bonus was proportional to the number of animals and the amount of wool that the farmer's herd produced for sale, with the bonus amounting to perhaps three times the shepherd's wage.[39]

For the servants who toiled year-round on large farms, there were several strategies a farmer could adopt. One was to reward honesty and assiduousness with a raise.[40] Much of the servants' pay took the form of food and perhaps lodging, but they also received cash wages—on the Cairon farm in Bretteville-l'Orgueilleuse, as early as the late fifteenth century.[41] The farmer could give the servants a low wage when they started—low relative to what would be appropriate given their skill and aptitude—and then raise their pay once they had proved themselves. Over time he might come to a better appreciation of their probity, effort, and ability; that, too, would merit a further raise until servants eventually earned their marginal product, or what they were worth. But if the servants failed when first hired, or if their effort slackened later on, the farmer could cast them out.

What about the hired hand, the plowman, or the milkmaid who served such a master? If they failed to work hard, the risk was being fired and never getting the raise. He or she would have to seek a new master and perhaps even start over again at a low wage. The raise might justify making an effort, but what if the farmer reneged on the implicit promise of rewarding the diligent? After all, if the farmer were unscrupulous, he might get the servant to work assiduously by promising a raise and then, at the end of the season, say he was unsure and put off the raise until after yet another period of trial and low pay. He might thus defer the raise for a couple of years. Such conniving might of course seem farfetched, but Old Regime masters did try to cheat agricultural servants out of their pay.[42]

In such a situation, the servant's recourse would be to quit. Other masters would offer, at the very least, the same low starting wage, and they might well be honest and keep their promises about future raises. In addition, if the servant waited until the end of the season to leave, then other masters would presumably realize that the servant had quit and had not been fired. They would deduce that he or she was trustworthy and hardworking and might pay accordingly. The servant might even be able to switch employers without a great loss of pay. In any case, the very threat of quitting might dissuade the unscrupulous master from cheating his servant of the raise. The master would lose a servant who had demonstrated worth and he would be forced to start anew with a fresh hired hand, one who might be just as untrustworthy as the conniving master. Also, the other servants might cease believing the master's promises of future raises, tainting him with such a reputation for dishonesty that honest hands would spurn his employ. For the master, it might have been best to accord the raise when it was due and thus retain a proven servant.

Such speculation may of course seem a bit removed from the reality of Old Regime farms, but it merely generalizes the advice given farmers and landlords in treatises on agriculture. Despite his suspicions, the abbé Rozier urged rewards for trustworthy servants, and he was not alone. A similar sentiment lurks behind the nostalgic portrait of rural life in Rétif de la Bretonne's *La vie de mon père*. There, too, diligent servants were to be cherished, and presumably rewarded.[43] The speculation about masters and servants also fits what little we know about the actual workings of rural labor markets. Farmers did fire workers, and even more frequently servants quit—just what we would expect if masters were slow to offer a raise, whether from a lack of scruples or from doubts about the hireling's true value. In all likelihood, quitting was facilitated by the numerous *louées*, or hiring fairs, that brought masters and servants together at critical times of the agricultural year.[44] At the hiring fair, a servant could leave one master and readily find another. Perhaps he could even keep his reputation for diligence intact and win a higher wage, since the fairs were by and large local.

In one of the rare instances in which we can follow the servants' pay—on the Cairon farm—it does seem that servants who remained in the family's employ received raises, just as our speculation would suggest. We can follow the servants thanks to two journals kept by the family, one from the late fifteenth century and the other from circa 1700.[45] Between 1473 and 1485, for instance, the family hired over eighty-one different male and female farmhands for a season or a full year. Some thirty-one of them repeated, and those who did averaged a 31 percent raise.[46] The case of Ma[t]hieu Donesnel was typical. When he was first hired in 1479 to work from the Feast of Mary Magdalene (July 22) to early November, he earned 35 sous. He stayed on through the winter and into the next year and got his raise: in 1480 his pay for the period from Magdalene until November was 47.5 sous. By 1481 it was higher still—a full 50 sous.[47]

The fifteenth-century journal also suggests that servants taken on at local fairs managed to keep their reputations for diligence intact and earn higher wages. We do not know the precise dates of the local fairs in the late fifteenth century, but the Cairon journal suggests that they took place near the Feast of Mary Magdalene in the early summer, and again in early November, either on All Saints' Day (November 1) or on Saint Martin's Day (November 11). Most of the Cairon servants began work on these dates, and their terms of employment (whether for a full year or a portion of a year) were always scheduled to end on one of these dates too. Presumably, hands who began work at other times of the year did not come from the hiring fairs: they arrived at a time when little hiring was being done. The Cairon could thus reasonably suppose that they had been fired by their previous employer. After all, they had not quit at the end of their contracts and sought the Cairon out at a hiring fair. We might therefore expect them to receive a lower wage, unless the Cairon were having trouble finding an off-season replacement. And the wages of these new employees were in fact lower than the other workers'—10 percent lower on average.[48] Having lost their reputation, they presumably had to build it up again.

Two centuries later, the Cairon were still giving raises to servants, but with a few slight differences. Now farmhands were hired for the entire year, as was the custom throughout France by the eighteenth century, apparently for legal reasons.[49] A second difference was that servants were more likely to be recruited locally. In 1473–85, farm workers had come from an average of 11.3 kilometers from Bretteville. Two centuries later, in the years 1691–1705, they arrived in Bretteville from an average of only 3.5 kilometers away. They were more likely to be from near Bretteville (say less than 10 kilometers away) and less likely to be from afar (over 50 kilometers). The greatest difference in 1691–1705, though, was the special treatment accorded servants who had traveled longer distances. In the late fifteenth century, all the new hirelings, both those from near and afar, went through the ordeal of the raise. Two centuries later, only those from far away did. They were the only ones whose earnings jumped if they remained on the farm. The locals' wages remained stable.[50]

The Cairon, one might surmise, now knew the local servants well enough to sift the diligent from the lazy. Or perhaps the hiring had pushed them into repeated dealings with local families. Such repeated dealings were apparently common, both in Bretteville and in the other villages. Typically, they might involve hiring the young adults in a family as servants, employing older family members as day laborers, lending the family money or plowing their fields in return. Servants from such families, one would expect, would exert themselves to preserve their relationship with the Cairon, a relationship that was one of clientage, or *fidélité*. Hiring in the labor market—a seemingly modern institution—could thus underwrite personal relationships. The Cairon were, in any event, not the only employers to indulge in such behavior. North of Paris, for instance, on a large tenant farm recently analyzed by Jean-Marc Moriceau and Gilles Postel-Vinay, the farmers seemed to use a similar strategy. Although precisely how they accorded raises is not clear, they did pay servants recruited from afar a lower wage. Local hands earned more. Presumably their virtues as servants were well known, coming as they did from families repeatedly involved with the farmer.[51] Similarly, near Lyon, successful servants on a farm belonging to the city's Hôtel-Dieu saw their wages rise with experience, just as on the Cairon farms.[52]

There were still other problems with agricultural labor markets—arranging to have enough labor at the harvest crunch, for instance—and other tactics to ensure the loyalty and diligence of farm servants. Using family labor was one way to avoid the difficulties with servants, for family members would presumably work without nearly as much supervision. The problem was having enough children who were old enough to work, particularly during the harvest. Given high rates of child mortality, it might be a long time before enough children reached their teens and were able to help out on the farm. Extended families might provide enough labor, but they were rare and surprisingly difficult to hold together. Even where they did exist, they did not rule out the use of servants.[53]

In describing the relationship between masters and servants, we have stressed suspicion and mistrust. They were motives lurking behind the strategy of raises that the Cairon and other farmers adopted. But under the Old Regime, master-servant relations were supposed to be based on quite different feelings. Ideally, they were to be governed by the notions of loyalty and reciprocity that colored so many dealings under the Old Regime.

Often, the servant's loyalty to the master was marked by a ritual when the servant was hired. The master would give the servant some wages in advance as a mark of trust, and the two would drink wine together, a sign of the bond of faithfulness that henceforth bound them together.[54]

Yet there is really no incompatibility between the ideals of the Old Regime service and the strategies based on suspicion and mistrust. The Cairon's strategy of giving raises to the best servants and firing the worst, for instance, was perfectly compatible with the Old Regime ideals. The servant who passed the test and stayed on for several years (before marrying or inheriting property) might well become a faithful client and send his or her own children to work for the family. If the servant was recruited locally, his or her family was probably already one of the employer's clients, tied by exchanges of goods and services.

The trick was transforming a short-term deal between master and servant into a long-term relationship. Fragile short-term dealings encouraged pernicious behavior on both sides. Long-term relationships favored cooperation—effort by the servants, rewards by the master, and exchanges that tended toward clientage. The practices of the rural labor market nurtured such cooperation and clientage. The existence of the labor market is thus entirely consistent with the traditional ideals of loyalty and reciprocity, even though the ideals themselves derived from hierarchical notions of fidelity peculiar to the culture of the Old Regime. Indeed, the labor market's existence even makes clear how such ideals could coexist with the diametrically opposed sense of suspicion and mistrust that also characterized master-servant relations. It is easy to see how such disparate attitudes could survive together. On the farm, at least, suspicion and mistrust were unavoidable, because the reality of farming made it too easy for a servant to shirk. But a farmer could ferret out the diligent servant in a variety of ways—by following the strategy of raises, by playing upon clientage, or by recruiting his domestics from nearby. Once discovered, the diligent, loyal, and honest servant deserved universal praise. He or she was one among many, the ideal amidst the real. The praise each then received was the sort so redolent of the Old Regime.

THE RENTAL MARKET

In France, then, few peasants owned enough property to keep themselves fully occupied. Much of the land was in the hands of the privileged, who often lived far away, in cities or at court. Such absentee ownership had deep roots in the medieval past, but it grew ever more pervasive because of the honors attached to holding land and the early modern tax system, which encouraged the privileged to hold land rather than to sell it to peasants. Yet because of the inconvenience of supervising labor from afar, few of the absentee owners hired servants to till their holdings. Rather, they rented the land out, much as wealthy landlords in developing countries do today.[55] For the landlords, renting would seem, at least at first glance, to be a panacea. Tenants would shoulder all the risk of farming and free the landlords from the task of supervision. The landlord's only duty would be to pocket the rent.

Alas, tenancy had its own vexations, as evidence from throughout early modern Europe makes clear. Even a fixed-rent tenant might neglect buildings or ignore problems with ditches that might cause flooding or erosion long after his lease had run out. He might cut vines too short, which would boost the yield during his tenure but reduce productivity thereafter. And when his lease was up, he might return the "land tired and exhausted, like rented horses."[56] Worst of all, he might go broke and not pay his rent. Default by tenants was a real concern, as manuals for landlords and records of property administration demonstrate. Landlords were told to avoid insolvent tenants and cautioned against raising the rent too high, lest the tenant go bankrupt and not pay his rent. A bankruptcy might cost the landlords far more than they would gain from a slight increase in the annual rent. They would have to find a new tenant, who, after a long and ruinous delay, would only take on the farm at lower rent. They might also become entangled in expensive legal disputes with the tenant's other creditors.[57]

Landlords could (and often did) demand that tenants furnish guarantors, who would be responsible if the tenant failed to pay the rent. Getting the guarantors to settle up, though, required at least the threat of legal proceedings, which cost a great deal and could ultimately prove fruitless.[58] Landlords could also investigate a prospective tenant, renting to him only if he seemed solvent and had, as one eighteenth-century landlord put it, a "good reputation." The abbé Rozier advised landlords to visit the farm that the prospective tenant was currently working, talk to his former servants (even those who had been fired), and see whether he haunted the local cabarets. Similar advice had been given since the sixteenth century. Solvency was a particular worry, from at least the sixteenth century onward. Rozier urged landlords to pay close attention to the capital a tenant could furnish—the livestock, equipment, and seed. It would help ward off disaster and could be attached in the case of default. When landlords found a solvent and reputable tenant, they were urged to keep him.[59] As for the tenant, he clearly had reason to preserve his reputation, in order to remain the sort of renter whom landlords preferred. Some landlords even drafted letters of recommendation for tenants. In 1750, for instance, the Cairon received such a letter, concerning a farmer named Mauger. Written by a property owner who knew Mauger well, it traced Mauger's history as a tenant, stressing that Mauger had never been fired and that landlords were always happy with him, for he was a "very good man, hard working, thrifty, and to my belief, quite solvent."[60]

When a tenant was solvent and possessed enough capital to take on a large farm, he posed less of a risk for landlords. As one knowledgeable eighteenth-century observer (the abbé Tessier) noted, when landlords rented to wealthy tenants, "They are assured of being well paid, of getting their revenue rapidly and of being able to use it at their discretion. Nor do they have to put up with delays or interruptions in years when some calamity has ruined or diminished the income from their crops."[61] Landlords might even allow wealthy tenants to fall into arrears, knowing full well that their livestock and equipment served as collateral for their debts. Clearly, such tenants were advantageous for a landlord, but because they were difficult to find, they paid less per hectare for the large farms that they alone could rent. As Tessier noted, big farms rented "less dearly" than undersized ones because fewer tenants had the resources to take the large leases on.[62] The lower rents were offset by the reduced risk of default.

At least in theory, a landlord might dismember a large property and then rent out the pieces to small-scale farmers. The small-scale tenants would pay more per hectare, but the higher rent was simply a risk premium that compensated the landlord for the greater chances of default. When landlords in the *généralité* of Soissons divided up their farms and rented them to smallholders, they did get higher rents. Yet as the local intendant observed, in the end they often "did not get paid and were foiled in their hopes of deriving more revenue from their fragmented property."[63] A tiny parcel of land could also be rented to a substantial tenant farmer, yet even that would carry risks beyond those entailed in leasing an entire farmstead. True, the substantial tenant was more likely to remain solvent, and he had collateral to secure his loan. But his collateral was usually livestock and grain on a farm he rented. If he went broke, the owner of the farm itself would have first claim to the collateral, not the landlord of the tiny parcel. In short, the landlord of a minuscule plot risked having only a junior lien on a substantial tenant's assets. Hence he would charge even a big tenant a risk premium.[64]

What we have here is the basis for an oft-noted phenomenon of the Old Regime rental market: the high rent on little parcels of land and the corresponding low rent on sizable farms. As the observations of contemporaries make clear, the rent charged on little parcels included a risk premium, which compensated for the losses of renting such crumbs of land to tenants both big and small. It compensated for the shakier claims to a big tenant's assets. It compensated as well for the greater likelihood that a small-scale tenant would fall into arrears or default, with no collateral to pay his back rent.[65] Why, though, were tenants willing to pay such elevated rents? A substantial tenant might do so to round out a farm. As for the small fry, their motives perhaps derived from the costs of supervising hired labor and the harsh uncertainties of agriculture. On a tiny patch of land, worked only with family labor, there would be no time spent supervising hired hands. The savings in supervision might offset any inefficiencies of size and allow a small-scale tenant to pay high rents, particularly if he specialized in labor-intensive crops. In addition, he might wish to rent the tiny lot as a means of coping with the uncertainties he faced as a net buyer of food. If he worked part-time as an agricultural laborer, some of his pay would be in kind, but the rest was likely to vary little in nominal terms, at least in the short run. In early modern Europe, cash wages rarely kept pace with the feverish short-term changes in the price of grain, which, as the major part of the diet, dominated popular budgets.[66] In real terms, an agricultural worker's wages were thus likely to vary inversely with the price of grain. If he were land-less, in times of dearth his income would plummet.

If he rented a little land, though, the agricultural laborer might avoid such a fate. If fortune blessed him and his own crops survived, he could eat. Better yet, he might conceivably even profit from the high price for food. Indeed, given the inelastic demand for agricultural goods and rents fixed for the short run in nominal terms, his profits might soar. If, on the other hand, his crops were destroyed, he had little to lose, as the intendant of Soissons noted, by not paying his rent.[67] After all, he possessed no assets that could be seized by the landlord. The rented plot might well let the land-poor agricultural worker recoup at least a part of the decline in his real wage. Owning land would be better, but renting might still serve as a hedge against a plunge in his income that could push him and his family to the edge of starvation. In the jargon of finance, the rented plot provided a return that was not perfectly correlated with his real wage. It was, in effect, a form of insurance, imperfect insurance to be sure, but insurance worth the price of higher rent.

Historians, it should be noted, tend to favor two very different explanations for the rent differential. One simply ascribes the high rent on minute plots to the "land hunger" of the small-scale peasant. His noneconomic motives would lead him to bid up the price of tiny parcels far beyond what a profit-maximizing farmer would pay, particularly when the population was rising and land was growing scarce. The second explanation has as its focus the low rent on large plots, with historians attributing it to the power of the substantial tenant farmers in the village rental market. Such tenants dominated villages and could exclude competition in the bidding for leases, forcing even mighty landlords to accept lower rents. They and their families held on to farms for generations. As long as they leased, rents would remain low. The argument here, it must be admitted, is certainly plausible. In any given village, the land rental market might only involve a few great tenants. Furthermore, in some parts of France large-scale tenant farmers did undeniably wield such power. George Lefebvre described such farmers in the department of the Nord, who, via a custom known as *mauvais gré* (collective ill will) or *droit de marché* (right of occupancy), barred landlords from evicting them and from raising the rent; and the Nord—near the Belgian border—was not the only region where tenants exercised such power.[68]

Which explanation is then correct? Was the rent differential the result of mauvais gré or land hunger? Or was it a risk premium, with customs such as mauvais gré relegated to being something of a marginal phenomenon? Contemporary literature on land management was certainly not obsessed with mauvais gré. The authors were so concerned with retaining good tenants that they almost never bring up problems involved in evicting overweening ones. But perhaps the best way to settle the issue is to look at what actually happened when farms were rented. One ideal place to look is the Paris Basin—the region around Paris. Its large arable farms made tenant power and land hunger conceivable, and customs such as droit de marché did creep over its northern borders.[69]

In the Paris Basin, we can actually put the various explanations to the test, thanks to an extraordinary sample of leases, which, later on, will also help us measure agricultural productivity. The leases come from the records of the Cathedral of Notre Dame in Paris. Like other major religious institutions in early modern Europe, Notre Dame owned a staggering amount of agricultural property—in particular, scores of farms and tracts of land scattered throughout the Paris Basin. The cathedral's papers, housed today in the French National Archives, describe those holdings, record the sometimes poignant details of their management, and preserve the leases that tenants agreed to, typically every nine years. As one might expect, the documents are voluminous. The index alone, compiled by an obsessive eighteenth-century archivist, comprises thirty-three manuscript volumes in a squat Latin hand, and for property after property one encounters strings of leases running from the late Middle Ages to the end of the eighteenth century. Thanks to the index, the leases themselves, and property descriptions compiled during the Revolution, we know the makeup of the properties and whether they changed over time. We also know whether the leases included rights to collect the tithe and seigneurial dues.[70]

Fortunately, Notre Dame's leases suffer from few of the problems that sometimes afflict early modern rental contracts. The cathedral did occasionally use unnotarized *contre-lettres* to modify a lease, but the contre-lettres, which are preserved among Notre Dame's papers, never revised the rent. Another virtue is that few of the leases included extensive rights to collect the tithe and seigneurial dues. We can cast aside the rare ones that do in order to focus on farming and the operations of the land rental market.[71] We end up with 809 leases drawn up between 1450 and 1789. The leases form 39 series, each one concerning a separate property in one of 25 different villages scattered throughout the Paris Basin (figure 3.2). The properties lay on the average a little less than 40 kilometers from Paris, the closest being only 5 kilometers and the farthest 96 kilometers from the city center. Most were rented along with only minor rights to collect the local tithe or local seigniorial dues, and none changed significantly in size. (If the size did change appreciably, I began another series of leases for what I considered to be a different holding.) As a whole, the properties ranged from a minuscule plot measuring only 0.26 hectare (roughly two-thirds of an acre) to an enormous farm of 278 hectares, or roughly 700 acres; they averaged 67 hectares. As one might expect, they were devoted overwhelmingly to grain production: only 1.4 percent of the land was vineyard and 4.8 percent natural meadow. Although they do not form a random sample, there is nothing peculiar about them, and the rental trend they trace out differs little from that elsewhere in the Paris Basin. One might of course worry that a large and powerful ecclesiastical institution like Notre Dame could squeeze more from its tenants than other landlords. But the rental trend is much the same on the holdings of other property owners, whether they were ecclesiastics or laymen, powerful or powerless.[72]

Notre Dame's larger properties did indeed rent for less per hectare. The rent of course depended on land quality and location, and it was buffeted as well by changing prices and the trials of warfare. To determine precisely how much lower rents were on big farms, we should filter out all these other factors that affected the amount tenants would pay. We can do so statistically, by regressing the rent per hectare on property characteristics and the other variables that influence the rent.[73] If we include the size of the property as one of the explanatory variables in the regressions (in other words as one of the variables that explain the variations in the rent), then its coefficient will measure the decline in per-hectare rent on larger farms.

Table 3.1 displays the regression.[74] The dependent variable is the rent; both it and several of the explanatory variables are measured as logarithms. (In table 3.1 and elsewhere, the "Ln," or the "ln," means the natural logarithm: thus ln(rent) is simply the logarithm of the rent.) Besides having certain statistical advantages, the logarithms make it easy to interpret the regression coefficients in terms of percentage changes, but the results would have been similar had logarithms not been employed. According to the negative coefficient of the property area, the per-hectare rent declined 8.5 percent when the property size doubled, an effect that the corresponding t statistic suggests was not a chance result. But the same regression tends to undercut the argument about the power of tenant farmers. If powerful tenants held down the rent, we might expect lower rent when leases remained in the same tenant's hands. Such repeat tenants would presumably be the sort who could wield market power. We might therefore expect

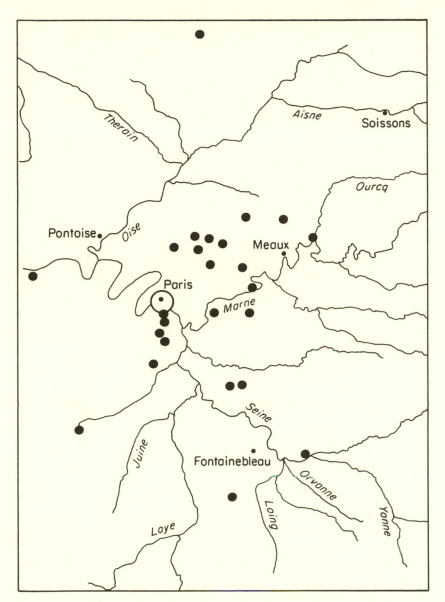

Figure 3.2 Location of Properties in the Notre Dame Sample

TABLE 3.1
Rent Regression, Notre Dame Leases, 1464–1788

Independent Variables	Dependent Variable
	Ln(Rent)
Constant	−11.23
	(−16.69)
Dummy: years 1775 and after	0.075
	(0.60)
Dummy: war years, 1589 to 1597	−0.097
	(−0.71)
Percentage of meadow	0.39
	(2.09)
Percentage of vineyard	0.0018
	(0.005)
Dummy: good soil	0.0050
	(0.09)
Ln(distance to Paris in kilometers)	−0.27
	(−6.24)
Dummy: tenant holdover from previous lease	0.021
	(0.42)
Time (units of 100 years)	0.91
	(23.11)
Ln(property area in hectares)	−0.085
	(−3.42)
Observations	652
R^2	0.57
Standard error	0.63
Mean of dependent variable	2.70

Source: See text, Chapter 3, and Appendix A, part 14.
Note: Rent is in livres per hectare, with in-kind payments converted to cash. For details, see Appendix A, parts 1 and 8. T statistics are in parentheses.

a negative and statistically significant coefficient for the dummy variable that is 1 when tenants are holdovers from the previous lease. The coefficient, though, is actually positive. In other words, there is no sign that holdover tenants paid lower rent. Much the same is true if we ask whether tenants were relatives of the previous renters.

Even stronger evidence emerges from another regression, this one involving the rate at which rent increased on each property when the lease was renewed. If powerful tenants depressed the rent, then rent increases would have been significantly lower when the same person renewed a lease and significantly higher when an outsider was finally installed. But the sample of leases suggests that the rent did not behave in such a fashion. We can see this if we regress the rate at which the rent increased from lease to lease on various factors that should have affected the rental value of farm-land. Among such factors, we can include the effect of tax increases, which would cut into the rent, and changes in local agricultural prices, wages, and the cost of agricultural capital, which would influence the prosperity of farming and the amount of rent that could be paid.[75] In the regression, all the explanatory variables have coefficients with the appropriate sign: higher agricultural prices, for example, boosted the rent, while more expensive labor and agricultural capital cut it. As for retaining the same tenant, that depressed the rent by only a microscopic and statistically insignificant amount (table 3.2, regression 1). If a relative of the old tenant renewed the lease, the result was just as small. There is thus little evidence of tenant market power, at least among Notre Dame's tenants.[76]

A related regression points in the same direction. With tenant market power, we might expect lower increases in the rent on the sizable tracts of land that powerful tenants were likely to lease. If we add a measure of property area to the regression with the rent increases, it should sport a coefficient that is negative, significant, and sizable. That would be all the more likely if we restrict ourselves to periods when the rent was increasing, such as the eighteenth century, for then, presumably, the powerful tenants could prevail against the trend of higher rents. Yet if we add the logarithm of the property area to the regression, its coefficient, though negative, turns out to be small and statistically insignificant, particularly for the eighteenth century (table 3.2, regressions 2 and 3). Once again, a regression fails to turn up firm evidence of tenant market power.

Evidence of a different sort also casts doubt on the market power of tenants in the Paris Basin. Substantial tenants in the region commonly switched farms during their careers. Their mobility fit a world in which landlords had no difficulty introducing new tenants from other villages. The tenants also had large families, and while one could perhaps imagine collusion between two or three tenant patriarchs in order to depress local rents temporarily, the collusion would in all likelihood break down once the patriarchs tried to establish their numerous children on farms. They would compete with one another to settle their children, and their heirs would do the same. Collusion, even if it existed, would have been hard to maintain.[77]

In addition, landlords seemed to have little trouble dislodging mediocre tenants in favor of better ones—or at least this was so for Notre Dame. In 1762, for example, the cathedral easily replaced the Labour family, who had leased their farm in Dampmart since the beginning of the century. It brought in the widow Vernois and her son from a village 10 kilometers away, hiking the rent considerably. The cathedral's agent, Monsieur Thezzier, who was seeking replacement tenants before the Labour's lease expired, urged one prospective renter named de la Place to approach the

TABLE 3.2
Regressions with the Growth Rate of Rent: Notre Dame Sample

Independent Variables	Regression Numbers		
	1	*2*	*3*
	Periods Covered		
	1524–1788	*1524–1788*	*1701–1788*
	Dependent Variables		
	Rent Growth Rate (percent per year)	Rent Growth Rate (percent per year)	Rent Growth Rate (percent per year)
Constant	1.23	1.74	1.12
	(5.78)	(3.88)	(1.86)
Growth rate, agricultural price-cost ratio	0.16	0.16	0.13
	(7.26)	(7.26)	(3.95)
Growth rate of taxes relative to rents	−0.0044	−0.0045	−0.13
	(−0.11)	(−0.11)	(−2.04)
Dummy: war years, 1589 to 1597	−4.14	−4.16	—
	(−4.85)	(−4.87)	
Dummy: tenant holdover from previous lease	−0.17	−0.17	−0.070
	(−0.58)	(−0.57)	(−0.19)
Ln(property area in hectares)	—	−0.14	−0.0037
		(−1.29)	(−0.03)
Observations	648	648	249
R^2	0.086	0.088	0.076
Standard error	3.69	3.69	2.87
Mean of dependent variable	1.10	1.10	1.00

Source: see text, Chapter 3, and Appendix A, part 14.

Note: All growth rates equal the rate of change of logarithms calculated from lease to lease, in percentage per year. The price-cost ratio is calculated with local prices and wages; it is explained in detail in Chapter 4 and Appendix A, parts 5 and 9. The growth rate of taxes relative to rents is explained in Chapter 4 and Appendix A, part 13. *T* statistics are in parentheses.

Labour in 1761 and see if they might leave early. Thezzier did not want de la Place to go to the Labour family directly, but his concern was probably to get the Labour to abandon their lease early on favorable terms. In any case, while discussing the pros and cons of coming to the farm with de la Place, Thezzier never mentioned the sort of threats against new tenants that one might expect in the regions of mauvais gré.[78]

Regression analysis also casts doubt on land hunger, belying the argument that small-scale tenants behaved differently in the rental market. Again the idea is to add the property area to the regressions with the rent increases, for its coefficient will reveal any difference between small and large properties. If small-scale tenants did act differently, if they bid up the rent on the tiny parcels they typically rented, then rent increases should be higher on little properties. As in the case of tenant market power, the coefficient of the property area should then be big, negative, and statistically significant. Yet as we know, the coefficient is scarcely different from zero and statistically insignificant (table 3.2, regression 2). The other coefficients are unchanged. There is, in short, no firm evidence that small-scale tenants acted differently from their more prosperous colleagues. One might object that they would only do so when the population was increasing. Only then, the argument would go, would their hunger for land drive rents past what a substantial tenant would pay. In that case, the coefficient should be negative, big, and statistically significant if the regression is restricted to a period of population increase such as the eighteenth century. But here too, as we know, it is small and insignificant (table 3.2, regression 3). The results are much the same during another period of population increase, the late fifteenth and sixteenth centuries. In the Notre Dame sample, the tenants who rented crumbs of land behaved no differently than their brethren who rented larger portions.

Perhaps the only evidence for land hunger in the sample derives from a comparison of rents and population. If land-hungry peasants were bidding up leases, we would expect the rent to rise more in villages where population growth outstripped the norm. There, the burgeoning group of smallholders would be competing for land. The result would presumably be a positive correlation between population growth in villages and rent increases on local farms, although the same correlation might arise for other reasons, such as local agricultural prosperity. If we take rent increases from the Notre Dame properties and population growth for the corresponding villages in the 1720s and the 1780s, then a faint correlation does appear (figure 3.3). But it is far from convincing, and it fades into insignificance if we use the 1710s as our initial period instead of the 1720s.[79] Again, the evidence for land hunger seems weak.

Needless to say, not all landlords necessarily behaved like Notre Dame. Nor was the Paris Basin all of France. Yet if Notre Dame's behavior as a landlord had been exceptional, rent on its properties would presumably have diverged from the pattern observed elsewhere near Paris. But as we know, that was not the case. Furthermore, despite the Paris Basin's peculiarities—its large farms and extensive commercialization—it is not the only region where the evidence argues against land hunger and tenant market power. Leases from the western province of Brittany, for example, suggest much the same. The leases there concern three agricultural properties 20 kilometers east of Nantes: a tiny *bordage* of 3.5 hectares, and two *métairies* of 7 and 48 hectares, respectively.[80] With these leases, we can perform the same sort of analysis that we did with the Notre Dame leases: regress the

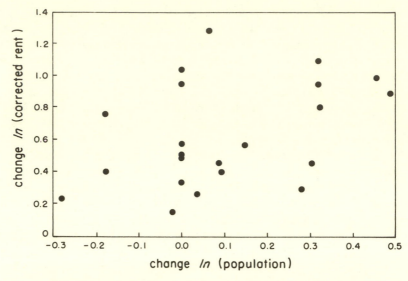

Figure 3.3 Change in Ln(Population) and Ln(Rent): Paris Region, 1720s to 1780s. Rents here are corrected for location, land type, and soil fertility, using the method outlined in Chapter 4.

rent increases on changes in taxes and local agricultural prices and costs. If we add to the regression a measure of property area, it will reveal whether land hunger influenced the rent, for with land hunger its coefficient should be negative and statistically significant. The coefficient, though, actually turns out to be positive, a result inconsistent with the smallholders' bidding up the rent on tiny properties (table 3.3). One might object that the years involved (1651–1790) were a period of declining population in the region, but the evidence for land hunger still seems to be lacking.

In the same sample, the case for tenants' market power is also weak. Again, if tenants or their families held down the rent, then the rent increases should be lower when tenants or their relatives were repeat renters, and higher when unrelated newcomers took over the properties. To detect such an effect, the regressions include a variable indicating when a tenant was a newcomer and unrelated to the previous lessee. Its coefficient is negative, suggesting that rent increases were perhaps lower when newcomers took over. But the coefficient could easily be a chance result. Furthermore, the coefficient of the property area is not the sizable negative number we would expect with market power: the rent did not lag on the larger properties that the substantial tenants would presumably control. Evidence from other parts of France points in the same direction.[81]

The sales market for land furnishes one final rebuttal to the claims about land hunger and market power. If land hunger or market power did explain

TABLE 3.3

Regression with the Growth Rate of Rent: Three Properties near Nantes, 1651–1790

Independent Variables	Dependent Variable Rent Growth Rate
Constant	0.75
	(0.76)
Growth rate of taxes relative to rents	−0.61
	(−3.61)
Growth rate, agricultural price-cost ratio	−0.31
	(−1.17)
Dummy: tenant new and unrelated to previous lease	−1.55
	(−1.25)
Ln(property area in hectares)	0.032
	(0.10)
Observations	38
R^2	0.30
Standard error	2.28
Mean of dependent variable	0.47

Sources: See text, Chapter 3, and Appendix B, part 2.

Note: All the growth rates equal the rate of change of the logarithm from lease to lease in percent per year. The agricultural price-cost ratio is calculated using local prices. It does not equal the analogous ratio in table 3.2. For an explanation, see Chapter 4, Appendix A, parts 5 and 9, and Appendix B, part 2. The growth rate of taxes relative to rents is calculated using local rents; it, too, is not the same as in table 3.2. See Chapter 4 for details. *T* statistics are in parentheses.

the higher rent on tiny parcels, we would expect that tiny parcels would always sell for more per hectare as well, for the higher rent would not merely compensate for the risk of default. If small peasants drove up the rent on minuscule plots, their land hunger would inevitably push up the sales price too. Similarly, if market power reduced the rent on big tracts, it would drive drown the sales price. If, on the other hand, the rent differential were merely a risk premium, the per-hectare sales price of large and small parcels would normally be the same. The one exception would be if sellers of land granted mortgages to buyers, for a mortgage on a little plot could be just as risky as a lease. A poor peasant buying a little piece of land might have no collateral to secure the mortgage besides the land itself, and a substantial peasant's assets might be subject to senior liens. Depending on the frequency of such mortgages, per-hectare sales prices might thus be either higher on tiny parcels or the same. By contrast, if land hunger or market power were at work, sales prices on tiny patches of land could only be higher; they could never be the same.

The records of land sales, though, simply do not fit the arguments about land hunger and market power. Per-hectare sales prices are sometimes higher on smallholdings and sometimes the same—a pattern consistent with the argument about the risk premium but incompatible with land hunger and market power. In the Beauce near Paris and in Lorraine in eastern France, little properties rented for more per hectare than larger ones, but they did not fetch a higher price per hectare when sold.[82] Much the same was true near Albi in southwestern France and near Cavaillon in the southeast. Yet in other samples—all in areas where mortgages by sellers were common—both sales and leases displayed the same premium for tiny plots.[83] The pattern in England was probably similar.[84]

Historians should therefore hesitate before invoking land hunger, for in many cases small-scale renters behaved no differently from their larger colleagues. As for tenant market power, it certainly existed but it was hardly ubiquitous. Admittedly, it can never be ruled out completely, because on a given farm the incoming tenants may have paid off the departing leaseholders for rights to the lease, with not a trace of their action surviving in the historical record. Still, it does seem to have been confined to specific areas, such as the northern portions of the Paris Basin or the Belgian frontier, where rights such as mauvais gré had taken root and achieved a certain notoriety. In many other places (much of the rest of the Paris Basin, for example) it was not a force, leaving landlords free to raise the rent.[85]

In many parts of France, then, landlords could set rents so as to maximize their profits. That at least appeared to be Notre Dame's policy. Before replacing its tenant and boosting the rent in Dampmart in 1762, Notre Dame estimated the tenant's revenues and costs. Having discovered that the tenant was enriching himself, Notre Dame increased the rent. Similar calculations in 1746 preceded rent increases in La Grande-Paroisse. When consolidating its properties, Notre Dame asked whether the operation would pay for itself in higher rent or reduced upkeep. Similarly, the decision to invest in a larger barn in Viersy in 1757 hinged on whether the increased rent would yield an investment return greater than that available from perpetual annuities (*rentes*).[86] The rent was of course limited by what the market would bear. When one of Notre Dame's farms in La Grande-Paroisse lay deserted in 1618, the cathedral had to cut the rent in order to attract tenants. On another occasion when it had difficulty attracting takers, it put up posters to attract interested parties, but it also cut the rent.[87]

There were, to be sure, some exceptional landlords who set their rent low. One could find some even in the Paris Basin, though the anemic rental might well have reflected the peculiarities of their property and the virtues of retaining tenants who always paid on time.[88] As contemporaries noted, it was in any case unprofitable to push the rent so high that tenants teetered on the verge of default. When, in 1693, Notre Dame debated exchanging farms with the Hôtel-Dieu, its agent noted that the Hôtel-Dieu was charging too much in rent. He suggested a cut from 1,200 livres per year to at most 1,000. Otherwise, the farmer "will not be able to keep on paying the rent" and "you will end up making a mistake."[89] Here, it is worth noting the argument (made by the knowledgeable abbé Tessier) that renewing a tenant's lease would ultimately yield higher rent, provided of course that the tenant was a good farmer and paid his bills. The possibility of renewal would give the tenant an incentive to work hard and to invest his own capital in the farm. Switching tenants at the end of every lease, he argued, would cause rents to stagnate.[90]

While our regressions do not necessarily support Tessier's views, it is true that Notre Dame showed an increasing tendency to retain tenants or their relatives, as did landlords in certain other parts of France.[91] In 1500–25, only 40 percent of Notre Dame's tenants were holdovers or the relatives of previous tenants; by 1775–89, the figure had risen to 81 percent. The increase was hardly smooth, as it undoubtedly derived more from the accidents of the weather and from France's political and economic history than from anything Notre Dame did. The number of tenants who repeated or took over from relatives dropped during the Wars of Religion (1562–98), in the aftermath of the Fronde (1648–53), and then again during the difficult years at the end of Louis XIV's reign (1715). All were times of civil unrest, heavy taxes, or plunging farm incomes, when tenant defaults typically soared.[92]

Although Notre Dame was not responsible for the growing number of its tenants who repeated, it undoubtedly wanted to offer the possibility of a lease renewal. Such a policy might not push rents higher, but it would help Notre Dame to retain those tenants who paid their rent on time. It would have also discouraged tenants from abusing the property (particularly at the end of their lease) and facilitated their cooperation in long-term improvements. For similar reasons, Notre Dame—and it was not alone here—might offer to rebate part of the rent in return for a tenant's contribution to capital improvements.[93] It might do the same when an unforeseen calamity struck, even though its leases stipulated that disasters gave tenants no rights to rent reductions. Given the problems of finding reliable tenants, such gestures, which might at first glance smack of clientalism, were certainly compatible with a concern for profits. Indeed, English landlords used identical tactics, even in the rack-renting eighteenth century.[94] And such gestures would find theoretical support in work by economists on multiperiod contracts and repeated games of moral hazard.[95]

Notre Dame was certainly not the only French landlord concerned with profits. At first glance, one might think that a wealthy banking and mercantile family such as the Gadagne of Lyon had abandoned the profit motive when they bought seigneuries and rural properties in the sixteenth century, stuffing their newly acquired châteaux with expensive furniture and works of art. Yet their management of their rural properties shows every mark of a concern with profit. They made a great effort to round out their agricultural holdings, as if they were concerned about the economies of scale in supervising tenants, and they invested considerable money in converting mediocre grainfields to more profitable vineyards. They did seek honors, but a taste for honor certainly did not blind them to monetary gain. Similarly, Alexis Chorlon, a seventeenth-century magistrate in Guéret, might dwell at length on the beauty of his rural estate, but he also devoted considerable attention to its costs and to the revenues it brought in.[96]

Elsewhere, landlords auctioned leases to the highest bidder if they thought rents were low—an unimpeachable sign of a concern for profits.[97] Public auctions of leases were long a common practice, one required of certain institutional landlords since the sixteenth century. Often landlords would hold an auction, yet retain a trustworthy old tenant provided he matched the highest bid.[98] Retaining tenants could thus march hand in hand with competitive rents and a quest for profits.

But was the search for profits more thoroughgoing in the eighteenth century? It is certainly a possibility. The century of the Enlightenment and seigneurial reaction may well have given landlords and their agents the tools they needed to gauge a farmer's earnings and, where necessary, jack up the rent. It is perhaps telling that the surviving estimates of tenant earnings in Notre Dame's archives all date to the eighteenth century. On the other hand, the scraps of paper on which such estimates were scribbled would have been the first records to have been discarded. Unlike leases, the calculations themselves were not worth preserving in order to establish property rights. And with changing prices, the calculations were swiftly outmoded.

Moreover, Notre Dame and its agents seemed able to appraise a farmer's profits, and decide whether its rents were low, without formal calculations (or least surviving ones). They did as much when they considered the exchange of farms with the Hôtel-Dieu in 1693. Clearly, local rents would help reveal when rents were low. So, too, would competition among prospective tenants, who would be attracted by the putting up of posters. The key was the short length of leases in France: generally nine years or less, except during the recovery after the Hundred Years' War. By the middle of the sixteenth century, if not before, the longer leases that served to repair the war's damage were far less common. Taxes and the law also discouraged longer leases.[99] Henceforth, French leases were short, although the same family of tenants might repeat. Here, the contrast with England is striking. Until customary tenures were eroded and replaced by short-term leaseholds—a process not complete until well into the eighteenth century—leases in England ran much longer. Renegotiation was much less frequent. Indeed, customary tenures such as copyhold gave the holder almost as much security as ownership, at least in the seventeenth century. With leases turning over slowly and renegotiation rare, it is not surprising that English landlords were slow to learn how to evaluate rents. Nor is it startling that rents in England had a greater tendency to lag behind the true value of the land.[100]

What if a landlord could not find tenants willing to pay a fixed rent? What if prospective tenants seemed insolvent, lacked the necessary capital, or hesitated to shoulder the risk? The landlord could divide his property and lease the pieces to tenants who would combine farming with day labor. He could also furnish some of the capital himself, although doing so would mean more time spent monitoring the tenant. Otherwise the capital—livestock in particular—might be mistreated. Another possibility would be to let the property on shares. According to Olivier de Serres, sharecropping might in fact be easier and more profitable than charging a fixed rent. In his opinion, whereas the renter "will take on the responsibility at his own loss or profit," a sharecropper "does not risk everything up front as he only contracts to cultivate the land on shares." As he noted, the fixed rent tenant might demand a large reduction in the rent in return for taking on all the risk. He might demand an even greater reduction in rent if he furnished all the seed, livestock, and other inputs.[101] Shifting from fixed rent to a share contract had the further advantage of reducing the chances of default, for with the sharecropping contract the landlord could collect his rent simply by going to the property at harvest time and taking his due.[102]

Sharecropping obviously seemed quite advantageous, for many landlords let their rural holdings on shares. Indeed, though apparently little known in most of France in medieval times, sharecropping seems to have spread there in the sixteenth and seventeenth centuries, just as it had earlier in northern Italy. In the west of France, for example, in the region known as the Gâtine Poitevine, share contracts rose from less than 5 percent of leases in the 1580s to over 90 percent one century later. By the late eighteenth century, they remained rare only in the north and east of France.[103]

Here, economic theory can help explain sharecropping's appeal—in particular, recent applications of principal agent models to agrarian economies. The theory seems all the more appropriate since it fits the arguments made by de Serres and other contemporary observers.[104] As de Serres suggested, tenants willing to take on the risks of fixed rent frequently demanded compensation in the form of lower rent. If there were tenants who could forgo such compensation—risk-neutral tenants—then the landlord was obviously better off leasing it to them for a fixed rent. His earnings would not fall, and the lease would give the tenants an incentive to farm efficiently, making it possible for them to pay the high rent. But if the tenants demanded a large reduction to take on the fixed rent contract—if, in other words, they were quite risk averse—then a share contract might prove attractive. The share contract reduced the risk the tenant faced, a virtue that de Serres noted. With it the landlord would share the burden of bad harvests or low prices.

In principle, the tenant could do just as well by working for a fixed wage and renting a smaller piece of land for a fixed rent. That combination would reduce his risk just as much as a share contract. But the landlord might well prefer one share contract to a mix of fixed-rent leases and wage labor. The reason was simple: wage labor, as contemporaries well knew, required nearly constant supervision. Admittedly, the sharecropper would require monitoring too. Because he received only a portion of what he produced, the sharecropper had reason to shirk his duties and leave the farm under-supplied with labor. As with a hired hand, the landlord would be hard-pressed to tell whether the reduced harvest was an accident of the weather or the result of the sharecropper's lack of exertion. Still, the sharecropper did require less supervision than a wage laborer. After all, if the sharecrop-per did nothing, he earned nothing in return. By contrast, if a wage laborer could get away with doing nothing, his wage would remain the same.

The share contract thus gave the sharecropper an incentive to exert him-self—less of an incentive than a fixed-rent lease, but some incentive none-theless. It thus required less monitoring than a wage contract, though more than a fixed-rent lease. Contemporary leases tend to support this point: rental contracts in early modern France invariably contained fewer stipula-tions detailing what the tenant had to do than sharecropping agreements.[105] As for the even greater cost of supervising wage labor, it suffices to recall the measures embodied in Rozier's panopticon farm. The landlord thus faced a trade-off between the costs of monitoring, on the one hand, and the rent reductions that risk-averse tenants might demand, on the other. Fixed rentals cut supervision to a minimum, but they might involve considerable compensation for risk. Wage contracts involved no risks for the hired hand but entailed extensive supervision. Sharecropping, which was somewhere in the middle, was likely to be an ideal compromise.

Why then was sharecropping more appealing in certain parts of France, and why did it spread? One possible cause involves variations in the ability to shoulder risk. Relevant here, perhaps, is the evidence from developing countries, where studies suggest that peasants are somewhat risk averse, though not extraordinarily so. Their risk aversion does vary, and it seems reasonable to assume that wealthy peasants are less averse to risk than poorer ones. The same assumption would seem reasonable under the Old Regime. In addition, apart from any differences in risk aversion, wealthy peasants in early modern France had means of coping with calamities that remained out of reach for the poor. They had savings that could tide them over a disaster and collateral that could facilitate borrowing in times of distress. Their savings and their credit would make the risk of a fixed-rent contract less frightening, as would lower-risk aversion.[106] They would be the ones most likely to take on fixed-rent leases.

One might worry whether risk aversion would actually vary enough to explain the popularity of fixed-rent leases in some regions and of share-cropping in others. The theory of sharecropping, though, can be recast in terms that have nothing to do with risk aversion. When recast in this way, the link between peasant wealth and fixed-rent contracts is still preserved. The critical observation is that wealthy peasants had the capital needed for farming—the livestock and seed. Poorer ones lacked that capital, and since they had few assets it was probably more difficult for them to borrow in order to purchase or to rent all the assets they needed. Why lend money to a peasant with no land and no livestock so that he could purchase a team of horses? Anyone who would do so would be highly unusual, like Rétif de la Bretonne's idealized father, in the novel *La vie de mon père*, whose gener-ous loans to the insolvent robbed him of any profit from his sales of live-stock.[107] Obviously, landlords could advance some of the necessary capital, as they often did in early modern Europe, particularly with sharecropping contracts.[108] But the limits to the tenant's own capital would affect the sort of lease that the landlords would prefer to offer. Wealthier tenants would receive fixed-rent leases and provide all of the capital themselves. Poorer tenants would get sharecropping contracts, requiring some supervision to ensure that they worked hard enough. And with the poorest tenants, the landlord would have to supply an enormous share of the capital and take an enormous share of the crop as compensation. The tenant's portion of the output would be so low that he would have little incentive to work. At some point, the landlord would be better off supplying all the capital and simply hiring the tenant to work for a fixed wage.[109]

Whatever the effect of peasant wealth—whether it meant having more farm capital, less risk aversion, or a greater ability to borrow and thus to cope with disaster—the implication is the same: wealthy tenants would end paying a fixed rent, poorer ones would sharecrop, and the poorest of all might work for a wage. We might also expect a pattern of differences among landlords. Landlords who could supervise tenants or workers at lower cost would be more likely to adopt share contracts, and, in the ex-treme, to hire wage laborers. For them, it would be easier to supervise a sharecropper than to find a tenant who could furnish the capital and take on the risks of a fixed-rent lease. A landlord whose property was planted with vinestock, for example, would have to journey to his property to inspect his vines even if his tenant paid a fixed rent. Vines were a capital investment requiring frequent inspections no matter what the terms of the rental con-tract were. Since the landlord had to be at the property anyway, it would cost him relatively little to judge what his tenant was doing. His costs of supervising a sharecropper (or even a wage laborer) would thus be lower. Other sorts of long-lived capital requiring inspections would give a landlord a similar cost advantage.[110]

So would living close to a rural property. If a landlord resided on his property or lived close by, he could monitor tenants and laborers at lower cost. As Olivier de Serres and other contemporaries stressed, distant properties were more expensive to administer, and for that reason alone de Serres all but ruled out wage labor unless the landlord resided on his farm. If he lived away from the property (particularly if he lived far away), then de Serres argued that he should lease his property for shares or for a fixed rent. Presumably, the fixed rent would be most appropriate for distant properties, where the cost of supervising a sharecropper was prohibitive.[111] On properties far from the landlord's residence, we would thus expect practically no wage labor and less sharecropping than leases for a fixed rent.

Evidence from the French countryside bears out our analysis. In the Lyonnais, both sharecropping and fixed-rent contracts were common. There was even some use of wage labor recorded in notarial registers. A sample of local notarial records during the years 1563–1633, for example, turned up eighty-three contracts concerned with the management of rural properties. Of these forty-seven were rentals, thirty were shares, and six were contracts hiring wage laborers. As expected, a vineyard increased the likelihood of sharecropping relative to renting; it also raised the chances that the landlord hired wage labor. Consider, for example, the odds of a landlord's sharecropping rather than leasing for a fixed rent. All other things being equal, the presence of vineyards on a property increased his odds of doing so by 232 percent. The odds of sharecropping or employing wage labor also rose if the landlord resided near his property. In the sample, the average landlord lived 39 kilometers away from his land. If he resided on the property, the odds of his sharecropping rather than renting jumped by 88 percent.[112]

What all the evidence points to is an explanation for the spread of sharecropping in early modern France. Absentee ownership increased during the sixteenth and seventeenth centuries, as higher taxes encouraged the country's privileged elite—its nobles, officeholders, and even wealthy bourgeois—to buy up land from the impoverished, taxpaying peasants. The privileged enjoyed tax exemptions and escaped taxation on much of their rural property. To exploit their land, though, they did not engage wage laborers. They lived too far away to supervise hired hands. Instead, they rented their property out. If it had vineyards or similar capital, it might be rented for shares. The same was true if they lived relatively close to their property, or if it proved difficult to find a tenant willing to pay fixed rent. In any event, we would expect to see an increase not only in fixed-rent tenancy but in sharecropping as well.[113]

We can also venture a tentative explanation for sharecropping's strength in particular regions. Crop differences were part of the story, for crops such as vines favored sharecropping, by reducing the cost of monitoring tenants. Some crops may have posed greater risks than others, rendering sharecropping even more attractive, at least to the tenant. The second factor would be wealth differences. Where tenants were poor, it would be more difficult to get them to pay a fixed rent, either because they would have more trouble dealing with risk or more trouble raising the necessary capital. Unfortunately, it is difficult to link the wealth of peasants to the type of rental contracts they signed, even with evidence from nineteenth-century censuses. But knowledgeable observers such as the abbé Tessier did note the poverty of sharecroppers and their lack of agricultural capital. So did foreign experts such as Arthur Young. And for what it is worth, the evidence on the physical heights of men (and other indicators of wealth, such as literacy) only underscores the evidence for poverty in the districts where sharecropping prevailed. In southwestern France, where sharecropping predominated, men were more likely than in the northeast to be short and illiterate—both signs of poverty.[114]

Sharecropping, it is true, has often been blamed for the stagnation of the French rural economy. But if it accompanied poverty, it in all likelihood did so not as poverty's cause but as its consequence. Sharecropping was a method of administering property when tenants possessed little land or capital. It was a way of coping with indigent tenants, not the reason for their destitution. Landlords funneled capital to their sharecroppers and invested in their rural holdings. Evidence from developing countries is perhaps relevant here. Studies of sharecropping in developing countries have by and large failed to detect significant inefficiencies on sharecropped farms, and there is little evidence that sharecroppers in the Third World are slower to innovate. Much the same appears to have been true in early modern France. Indeed, two regions where sharecropping was firmly implanted—the Beaujolais and the Albigeois—witnessed what was perhaps the most rapid productivity growth of any part of France under the Old Regime.[115]

CREDIT AND REPUTATION IN THE LOCAL ECONOMY

Early modern villages formed part of a tiny economy. Farmers hired servants from their own community and neighboring villages. Landlords contracted with tenants to work their farms. Such dealings linked the villagers and their neighbors in a web of economic transactions. In 1479, for example, the Cairon family in Bretteville-l'Orgueilleuse hired Yvonne Le Goupil as a servant. Previously, they had lent money to her father. In 1474, they paid a portion of Guillaume de Vic's wages to his father—

presumably to extinguish an earlier debt. Two centuries later, the family's relationship with its servants was little changed. Both in Bretteville and elsewhere, paying the domestics still meant more than just handing over money. It could entail the offer of grain, clothing, or the services of the Cairon's plow to prepare the servant's fields. In any case, there was no distinction between the money and the payment in kind, which was always converted to a cash equivalent and charged against wages due in periodic settling of accounts.[116]

Exchanges with tenants could be equally complex. When Jean de Cairon settled his accounts with Michel Le Peinteur in 1709, the tenant acquitted his entire debt by furnishing goods and services. That Le Peinteur provided the Cairon with cider, eau-de-vie (a fruit brandy), and the use of his carts and work animals is hardly surprising. But he also carried messages to the intendant and paid Jean de Cairon's bills to roofers, bailiffs, and the tax collector. Here, too, dealings were converted to money of account in periodic settlements, typically several times a year. The same was true elsewhere, even when the rent was in kind or the tenant was a sharecropper.[117]

The local economy was alive with still other transactions as well. If a farm worker with little or no land was lucky enough to possess a horse, he rented it out with his own labor. The practice was fairly routine, no doubt because renting draft animals without a master risked mistreatment and other problems of moral hazard.[118] In Bretteville, Jean de Cairon hired the local farrier, Jean Oriau, to shoe his horses and maintain their harnesses. He leased him land and loaned him grain as well. The two acquitted their debts to one another roughly once a year, taking into account all their complicated dealings. At the beginning of 1696, for instance, Oriau owned Cairon 62.5 livres; by the end of the year, his debt had fallen to 26.5 livres.[119]

In effect, Cairon was making loans to Oriau. Their trade was not the simultaneous exchange of objects or services that we would qualify as barter. Rather, it amounted to sales of goods and services, paid for by loans and periodic settlings of accounts. The practice was ubiquitous. Servants, for instance, were not paid in advance, for that would only encourage them to run off. They might receive room and board and occasional advances, but the bulk of their pay came in periodic clearings of accounts. In effect, they were lending their services to their employers. Landlords also settled up periodically with tenants. In the middle of the seventeenth century, a landlord in Brittany, Georges Tirel, settled what was owed once or twice a year with day laborers who worked for him regularly and sometimes rented his land. The Sire de Gouberville did much the same in sixteenth-century Normandy. Dealings with sharecroppers were similar. They, too, involved annual or semiannual settling of accounts, with the landlords typically making a variety of loans to the sharecroppers—advancing them capital or paying their taxes—until the rent was paid.[120]

The local economy, in short, ran on credit. There were long-term loans—the perpetual annuities known as *rentes*—that might finance purchases of land. There were medium-term loans (*obligations*) as well, which, in the countryside, usually lasted several months or even several years. Typically they paid for a draft animal or tided a person over in a time of dearth. Or they might consolidate and formalize the debts of a borrower who teetered on the verge of default. Whatever the purpose, the obligations were common. In the late sixteenth century, in the southern village of Grillon, the local notary registered some forty of them each year, all in a village of only six hundred inhabitants.[121]

Beyond the rentes and obligations there were also a host of informal advances that made possible exchanges of goods and services. They crop up repeatedly in journals and account books. In the late fifteenth and early sixteenth centuries, for instance, the Cairon's journals make it clear that they lent money in the spring in return for work on the harvest the following summer. Elsewhere such loans paid the tax bill or facilitated trade when coins were scarce. Lenders ranged from city dwellers, landlords, and seigneurial agents to wealthier peasants and rural entrepreneurs.[122]

Probate records provide us another glimpse of informal credit. It is a glimpse at the moment of death, to be sure, when economic activity may have been at a low ebb, but it is still illustrative. In a sample of fifty-one probate inventories from the village of La Grande-Paroisse, southeast of Paris, some thirty-seven bothered to list money owed by and to the deceased or his spouse. On average, each estate was due 82 livres and owed 493 livres, a sizable sum relative to the 1,286 livres of personal property (the inventories omitted real estate) that the average estate possessed. Nearly all of the lending involved informal credit extended by the villagers and their neighbors in adjacent communities.[123] The money was due servants and tax collectors, carters, horse traders, and sellers of fodder. It was even owed to farm laborers, such as Bonnaventure Barat, who in 1740 was due 30 livres for straw sold to a Sieur Lacaille, the "steward of Mylord Bolingbrock."[124]

In the local economy, such loans swelled the volume of trade well beyond what barter and the meager stock of coins made possible. Coins were frequently in short supply under the Old Regime. Barter required a highly unlikely coincidence of wants—in other words, that each party to a trade had the goods or services that the other desired at the precise moment of exchange. Trade would have remained limited had it not been for the loans, which allowed purchases of goods or services without payment in coins or an immediate exchange of goods and services.

This insight can in fact be formalized in an economic model.[125] Although the model itself may seem a trifle alien to early modern France, it has the great virtue of capturing the essential features of the local economy. In the model, we imagine that villagers meet periodically to trade goods and services with one another and with the members of neighboring villages as well. The goods and services might encompass labor, the rights to land, and agricultural commodities. Each villager is paired up with a trading partner, who changes randomly from period to period. The partners can barter, make purchases with money, or finance purchases with loans, which can be repaid when the partners meet again. Under the right conditions, it turns out that the possibility of offering loans expands trade and improves the lot of the villagers.[126] Trading partners make loans, which finance trade. One might expect borrowers to renege on their loans, but they prefer to repay, for if they fail to do so, they risk being denied credit and opportunities for trade in the future. If conditions are right, these losses in the future more than outweigh the momentary gains of reneging on their loans. Trade thus grows, and it will wax even greater if partners can pass one another information about previous credit dealings—a reasonable assumption for a village where everyone knows everyone else. That way villagers will swiftly learn who has defaulted on loans and who should be cut off from further credit and trade. The punishment for default will grow more severe, while repayment becomes more attractive. Trade will increase in turn.

To function well, this mechanism assumes that the economy is small. If it is large, the problem is that borrowers rarely meet their old trading partners. Future trades with a given partner are therefore rare, and a borrower suffers little loss by defaulting on his loans. As a result, the sort of behavior the model describes would do little to inflate trade in a large economy. But in a village, or in a small group of villages, the model seems to parallel what we have observed. In particular, it sheds light on the common practice of settling accounts periodically. In the model, accounts are settled periodically in cash in order to reduce a borrower's incentives to default in future transactions. Having paid off a loan, the borrower faces less of a temptation to renege in the future. That seems a reasonable motive for the practice we observed.

The model also suggests that a villager's reputation—his past history of credit dealings—would be enormously important.[127] In the model, one mistake, one default, denies a villager credit in the future. Real life may not have been so merciless, but a reputation for honoring debts did assume enormous importance in early modern society. Without a good reputation, the model suggests, one would have a difficult time gaining access to credit in the local economy. Similar reasoning might well apply to dealings between farmers and their employees: Why, after all, hire a servant known for dishonesty? It would certainly fit the agricultural rental market as well. In an era in which landlords traded letters of recommendation for their tenants, why rent to one who had misused property or defaulted on his rent?

Reputation, it is true, is normally discussed in anthropological terms, at least in traditional societies like early modern France. It is usually a matter of honor, of respect, of status, and of the community's moral code. But reputation also had an economic dimension, one bound up with paying debts, working hard, and behaving responsibly as a tenant. In short, it involved probity and rectitude in economic transactions. Such virtues were not mere creations of the triumphant nineteenth-century bourgeoisie. They were at work in local economy (and in city neighborhoods as well) in the early modern period, as one can gather by the very meaning—in French as well as English—of the heavily laden word, "credit." Among several definitions of the French word "credit," perhaps as early as 1481, was that of a reputation of solvency, a meaning that unites an older sense of "credit" as trust or repute and a newer financial sense of the word as a loan or debt. The English word "credit" also linked reputation and financial strength in the early modern period.[128] Credit in the local economy, as one might gather, was thus quite personal—the economic model, with loans between pairs of individuals who know one another well, suggests as much. Paying off debts, as we can infer from older meanings of the word "pay" (again in both English and French), involved restoring or maintaining a personal relationship. It meant satisfying or making peace with a person[129] It was not simply an anonymous trade of money for goods and services previously rendered.

The economic dimension of a villager's reputation emerges quite clearly in stories told by Rétif de la Bretonne in *La vie de mon père*. Rétif's father, a paragon of virtue, always counseled those who sought his advice to pay their debts, for doing so was apparently essential to rural morality. Furthermore, the father's considerable reputation derived, at least in part, from his scrupulous probity in commercial transactions. He was even honest when he sold horses, an anomaly at a time when a horse trader might burn a horse's teeth, dye its hide, or weave in a false tail in order to disguise the beast's age and condition. Equally illustrative is the tragic tale Rétif tells about the owner of a wine press, who discovered that his press leaked. Unable to fix it quickly, he captured the leaking wine in a vase hidden underneath his press and then secretly returned what had leaked to his client's stock. He kept all of this hidden "in order not to discredit his business," but a peasant discovered the vase and assumed—wrongly—that the press owner was a cheat. The peasant complained to the authorities, but before the press owner could be cleared, his mother, "an honorable woman," died of grief, presumably because her family's reputation had been ruined.[130] Whether true or not, Rétif's story speaks volumes about the economic dimension of village honor. Obviously, honor had other dimensions as well—from sexual to religious—but it was at least in part economic.

A similar picture emerges from court records recounting what happened when debts were unpaid and reputations tarnished.[131] South of Paris, in the village of Brétigny-sur-Orge, the local nobleman Alexandre de Fregré went to a tavern in 1619 to settle a debt owed to the tavern keeper, Guillaume Desanclos. An argument broke out between the two over precisely how much was owed—1 écu or 11 sous; in any case, a relatively small sum. Fregré rose to leave, believing the debt had been paid, but Desanclos's wife ran outside after him, insulting him and screaming that he was a "thief." Responding in kind, Fregré drew his sword and attacked the innkeeper. An assault with a sword was perhaps how one would expect a nobleman to respond to an insult, but the insult itself was at least in part an attack on Fregré's financial reputation: a public announcement, in the streets outside the village tavern, that he was a thief and unworthy of trust. Interestingly, the court ordered Fregré to pay a large sum (48 livres) in damages to Desanclos, a judgment undoubtedly embarrassing for a nobleman. He also had to acknowledge that Desanclos and his family were in fact "good and honorable persons." Although they had insulted a nobleman, the lenders were honorable, because all that they had demanded was repayment of the loan that was their due.[132]

As the court records demonstrate, loans were not always repaid. Yet there is no doubt that repayment was expected, and repayment in full. South of Lyon, in the village of Saint-Genis-Laval, Claude Rocher offered only 6 of the 20 sous he owed the local innkeeper, Roman Tignat, and his wife. Rocher asked them to be patient, but Tignat and his wife flew into a rage, cursing and swearing that by "God's death and blood" Rocher would pay all that he owed. Along with their partner—a woman named Gallet— they jumped Rocher and beat him until he was bloody.[133] As this and other incidents like it suggest, arguments over debts could unleash violence, particularly in the rougher sixteenth and seventeenth centuries. They could also provoke family feuds. In Brétigny one Sunday in 1624, the vintner Gilles Brunet and his wife were set upon outside their home by their neighbors, the Pinson. Brunet and his wife were gravely injured. The origins of the attack reached back to a tiny debt of 10 sous owed to the Pinson.[134]

In the long run, borrowers gained if they cooperated with their lenders and paid what was due. The problem was that they sometimes failed to honor their debts. Such uncooperative behavior, even if it is only occasional, is not inconsistent with the economic model of local credit. Thoroughgoing cooperation by borrowers who always repay their loans is the best outcome of the model—in technical terms, the Pareto optimal equilibrium, which does the most to expand trade. But there are other possible outcomes; in technical terms, there are multiple equilibria.[135] The other outcomes would involve periodic defaults by borrowers and retaliation by lenders. In the model, retaliation takes the form of refusing both trade and loans in the future (so-called "grim trigger strategies"); but in real villages, retaliation could go much further. Which outcome any two villagers got—which equilibrium—depended on the peculiarities of their relationships, relationships that were constantly being renegotiated in the local tavern, the streets, or the public square.

Here, paradoxically, the threat of violent retaliation might have actually encouraged cooperation, by raising the penalty for borrowers who defaulted on their debts. Yet borrowers might find ways to parry such a threat. They could seek refuge in local alliances or move to another community. Both maneuvers were possible in the early modern countryside. The outcome would then be more defaults by borrowers and frustrated retaliation by lenders.

It was not just among borrowers and lenders that relationships could go awry in a variety of ways. Dealings between farmers and servants and between landlords and tenants could be equally volatile; here, too, we are dealing with economic models (repeated games) having multiple equilibria. Farmers and servants might cooperate, with the servant working hard and the farmer rewarding him via prompt payment of his wages or periodic raises. But the farmers might mistreat or misjudge their servants, just as servants might sometimes loaf and cheat their employers. Or there might be a misunderstanding about the salary paid. In Auvergne in 1661, the shepherd Simon Vergnes demanded his back pay, while his former master, Claude Teyssedre, maintained that Vergnes owed him rent equal to his wages. Vergnes tried to seize one of Teyssedre's sheep and beat up his wife. Teyssedre then retaliated in kind.[136]

Cooperation could also fail in the repeated interactions linking landlords and tenants. In Brétigny in 1630, for example, the tenant farmer Pierre Briberon felt wronged by his landlord, the local seigneur. Briberon denounced him bitterly in public and attempted to sue him outside the seigneurial court.[137] In the Beaujolais in 1620, the tables were turned, with the landlord—the Sieur de Varennes—suffering the wrong. He had leased his farm and seigneurie of Laye to Claude Rabbin, who laid waste to the property while de Varennes was away. Rabbin's behavior in fact shocked local tenant farmers. He let ditches silt up, stole tiles that the landlord had purchased for repairs, and cut down and burned expensive trees in order to bleach hemp. De Varennes did not learn of the damage until his farm and château were practically in ruins.[138]

So far the discussion has been driven by economics, which is not the usual discipline historians invoke when analyzing a peasant economy and its social and cultural ramifications. Typically, historians look elsewhere for inspiration. They turn to classic social thinkers such as Karl Polanyi or Marcel Mauss, or to works that arose out of the old debate over the use of economics in anthropology, such as Marshall Sahlins's *Stone Age Economics*. They do so not just in European history, but in fields as distant as colonial New England. Political scientists do the same.[139] Yet the recourse to such works may not be entirely appropriate. Sahlins's book, for example, despite its undeniable virtues, concerns egalitarian tribal societies. Whether it should be applied to early modern peasant societies, with all their inequities, is another matter. Perhaps it would be better to consult one of the many recent works in economic anthropology, which provide a different perspective from that of Sahlins.[140] But historians rarely cast their eyes in that direction.

Obviously, there are sharp differences between the literature on traditional economies that historians favor and the economic models used here. Perhaps the starkest is the tendency to interpret the exchange of goods in a traditional economy as an engine of harmony. In both Polanyi and in the sort of anthropology historians usually cite, exchange is viewed as reinforcing a group's identity and creating a sense of community. In other words, exchange serves some transcendent interest or purpose of the group as a whole, be it a village or an extended family. That purpose might be moral or religious or it might be material, such as group survival.[141]

The economic models—of credit and of dealings in the labor and rental markets—provide a radically different perspective. They do allow for the repeated and highly personalized dealings between economic agents that were characteristic of the local economy: a servant who stays on and becomes his master's client, or a borrower who repays his loan only to borrow from a lender again. They also admit harmony, at least in the sense of mutually beneficial cooperation. By working hard, for instance, the servant helps his master and at the same time earns a raise. Similarly, by repaying, the borrower cooperates with the lender and at the same time gains access to additional trade. And the tenant who invests in long-term improvements shares in the profits when his lease is renewed.

Yet the economic models never posit any transcendent group interest. The notion is by and large foreign to economics. This may of course seem like a drawback when it comes to analyzing the countryside of traditional Europe, for medieval Christianity had certainly tried to inculcate a sense of group interest in villages throughout Europe. On the other hand, it is not at all clear that Christianity continued to do so after the Reformation and the Counter-Reformation, for the various types of Protestantism and even Counter-Reformation Catholicism were far more individualistic.[142] In any event, inside the strife-torn villages of early modern France, group interest was practically invisible and harmony often nonexistent. The economic models hardly seem out of place. And there is no reason why the behavior they describe could not coexist with the lingering ideals of late medieval Christianity. Max Weber to the contrary, religion and the economy can live independently: they need not be forced into a shotgun wedding to ensure the consistency of cultural values.

The economic models have another advantage as well. While they allow for cooperation, they have more than one possible outcome, more than one equilibrium. The other outcomes involve at least periodic storms of strife and retaliation. That possibility certainly fits what we have seen in early modern France, and it fits what historians have discovered in other parts of Europe as well. Once again, one cannot simply assume that cooperation automatically prevailed in early modern villages and that it was reinforced by dealings within the local economy.[143] Although local trade could bind up social relations within a village, it could also rub them raw.

What the economic models suggest is that we avoid drawing too sharp a line between the local economy and the modern economy. There were differences to be sure, but it is wrong to explain everything in terms of a simple contrast—a contrast between a traditional world of cooperation, reciprocity, and face-to-face dealings and a modern world of anonymous competitive markets. Despite face-to-face dealings, strife abounded in traditional villages. By the same token, we certainly encounter face-to-face transactions in the modern world—among brokers in London's City, for example. And transactions today are still not all channeled through anonymous markets. Indeed, taking a cue from Ronald Coase, we need only note the economic dealings that take place far away from markets, in the interior of modern corporations.[144]

The local economy thus lacked some of the characteristics of a stereotypical traditional economy. In some ways, it was not all that different from certain economies today. But in at least one other respect it was still quite distinctive: the transactions it generated rarely left a narrow geographic area. Credit in the local economy was particularly unlikely to stretch over long distances. In the southeastern village of Grillon, at the end of the sixteenth century, 57 percent of the loans recorded in notarial archives linked parties living within Grillon itself, and the average distance between borrower and lender was slightly over 3 kilometers. Near Paris, as shown among the seventeenth- and eighteenth-century probate inventories from La Grande-Paroisse, the distance was just over 2 kilometers, even though the villagers occasionally used the seemingly more mobile endorsable promissory notes (*billets de commerce*), particularly after 1700.[145]

To reach further required a different sort of credit, based not on local reciprocity but on intermediaries who could link the local economy and more distant markets. Suitable intermediaries were not unknown under the Old Regime: notaries, entrepreneurs in rural industry, middlemen in the grain trade, or even prosperous farmers.[146] Yet they did not extend credit everywhere, and where they did offer it, their services might be costly or inaccessible for some individuals. That left local credit. Its geographical limits in normal circumstances are in any case easy to understand. With local credit, the lender had to know the borrower well, know his reputation and his collateral. Such knowledge was unlikely at greater distance, and distance, our model suggests, would only increase a borrower's incentives to default.

Intermediaries who operated over greater distances would confront an even graver dilemma. They, too, preferred borrowers who had become familiar, either through repeated dealings or local contacts. But because their business reached beyond the confines of the local economy, they had to deal with partners whose creditworthiness was unknown. Getting them to lend to such ciphers would nonetheless be difficult. And linking the intermediaries themselves in a network of long-distance finance and trade might well prove impossible.

To the extent that trade depended on credit, the difficulties of arranging loans limited the sale of goods over long distances. The geographical hurdles to long-distance credit restricted the reach of trade, compounding the high transportation costs of the Old Regime. Unfortunately, the economic penalties were severe. Because credit could not easily extend across regions, and because transportation costs hemmed in trade, it was difficult for producers to profit from regional specialization based on soil, climate, and location—in short, from comparative advantage. That was one of the foremost barriers to economic growth in Old Regime agriculture.

The obstacle here, it should be stressed, was not the local economy itself, with its ingrained habit of face-to-face dealings, or the stress it placed on reputation. Such customs were merely a solution to the problem of trust—or in the jargon of economics, moral hazard—inherent in extending credit. The solution was easiest within the local economy. It was far harder when trade stretched over longer distances. Nor was this problem peculiar to the market for credit. As we saw, it also arose in dealings between farmers and servants and between landlords and tenants. It afflicted other markets as well—for instance, the sales market for land.[147] But if moral hazard plagued economic exchange, the methods of coping with it varied enormously. In the rural labor market, masters watched over their servants and gave the diligent ones raises. In the rental market, landlords adjusted the type of leases they offered, demanded a premium of tenants likely to default, and monitored their tenants' behavior. Both landlords and employers sought reliable agents. Both rewarded trust with repeated business. Still other solutions were possible in different historical contexts, each with distinctive social and cultural ramifications.[148]

If we compare the solutions adopted in the early modern countryside with those prevailing in other preindustrial societies, we can draw upon an important contrast established by Avner Greif in his work on medieval trade.[149] The contrast distinguishes between individual and collective remedies for problems of moral hazard. It revolves about the sanctions imposed on those who violate trust—the borrower who defaults, the servant who steals, or the tenant farmer who falls behind in his rent. At the very least, the punishment for such misbehavior involves the loss of future opportunities—future loans and trade for the borrower, future employment at an elevated wage for the servant, future tenancy and a low rent for the farmer. If the only loss is the chance of doing business with the person who has suffered from the misbehavior, then the sanctions are individual, as in the case of a servant who can never work again for the employer he has wronged. But if the losses extend to future business with other partners as well, then the punishment is collective. That would be so, for instance, if the servant could never work again for any local employer. Similarly, if all a defaulting borrower lost was the chance to trade with the lender he had cheated, he would face individual sanctions. But if no one in the village would trade with him or lend him money in the future, then his punishment would be collective.

Obviously, collective sanctions are more powerful. The lost opportunities are larger, and the threat of collective punishment makes it harder for a cheat to take advantage of one person and then to move on to a new victim. If individual sanctions are the only ones available, though, potential victims will presumably seek additional remedies. They might demand additional security, such as pledges from relatives. They might wish to bring in the courts; and to facilitate legal intervention, they might insist upon costly formal contracts, such as a tenant's lease or a borrower's notarized obligation.[150] They might intertwine transactions with a potential cheat, raising the stakes for misbehavior. Lenders, for example, might rent land to a borrower and hire his services too, as Jean de Cairon did with the farrier Jean Oriau. Or they might interact repeatedly with the same persons (what we might take as a form of clientage) and avoid the short-term transactions that would be a temptation to misconduct. And if they were cheated and had no other recourse, they might well resort to violence.

Collective punishment, by contrast, would permit simpler transactions, with less formality and fewer repeated dealings, and presumably a reduced threat of violence. Yet it might be difficult to sustain. The question then arises: Where on this spectrum from collective to individual did the economy of the early modern countryside lie? Was it collective or individual or were there pockets of both? What determined the local pattern of sanctions? Was it the idiosyncracies of local culture, or was local culture merely the reflection of politics and the local economy? Finally, if individual sanctions predominated in a particular village, did they really bring in their wake additional remedies, from use of the courts to violence and clientage?

The answers, unfortunately, are not yet clear. Only further research will tell, research that has the potential to reunite material wants and cultural ideals and effect a rapprochement between economics and history. Our model of the local economy permitted both collective and individual sanctions, and in the confines of an early modern village it would be reasonable to assume that everyone knew the cheats and would shun them in future dealings. The importance of reputation points in the same direction. After all, if a tenant's reputation could be spread by letter from landlord to landlord, an untrustworthy tenant might never rent again. Much the same would hold for borrowers and servants—indeed, for nearly everyone. Still, we cannot be certain. There was enough mobility and enough divisiveness to thwart collective sanctions. Tenants moved far away. Servants journeyed in search of new masters. Neighbors did not always share the history of their commercial misfortunes, and instead of warning a neighbor whom they hated, they might secretly gloat when he was cheated.

CHAPTER FOUR

Agricultural Productivity in France, 1450–1789

FOR MOST HISTORIANS of early modern Europe, economic stagnation in the countryside is a comforting point of departure, a secure base camp for forays into grand historical explanation. After all, outside certain exceptional regions—chiefly England and the Low Countries—there seems no doubt that early modern agriculture failed to advance. So persuasive does the evidence seem (despite all the questions raised in Chapter 1) that many scholars swiftly accept it and hurriedly glide on to the more pressing issue of explaining rural backwardness. For some of them, the lack of advance can be attributed to runaway population growth, which fragmented farms and impoverished the peasantry. For others, it is rural isolation or rustic mentalities, which discouraged specialization and investment. Still others blame the class structure, the legal system, or property rights. And sometimes the accused are, paradoxically, the very victims of economic stagnation—the subsistence peasants themselves—whose minuscule holdings, recalcitrant institutions, and obsession with self-sufficiency supposedly precluded economic growth.

France, as was shown in Chapter 1, is no exception in this regard. Ever since the writings of Marc Bloch, historians have made the slow pace of economic change in the French countryside the focus of arguments about class relations, the political structure, and the nature of the peasant economy. But is the evidence behind their arguments actually justified? Do we really know that economic growth crept to a halt in the French countryside? Before we explain economic stagnation, ought we not first measure the performance of early modern French agriculture and verify that it was always slow?

Measuring economic performance means assessing productivity: gauging what farms could produce from a given amount of land, labor, and capital and doing so in a way that permits comparisons across regions and even countries. Some historians, of course, might object that the very idea of productivity is a modern obsession, one anachronistically forced on the past. Others might dismiss its significance. But in a country long haunted by food riots and subsistence crises, greater agricultural productivity was obviously important, for it and perhaps it alone could deliver the kingdom from the specter of want. Contemporaries—physiocrats, agronomists, and government officials—knew as much, at least by the eighteenth century, and although their concepts were not the same as ours, they too wished to wring more sustenance from France's meager stock of resources.[1]

Studying productivity demands a very different historical register. It requires manipulating productivity indices and immersing oneself in the stark details of measurement and data. This chapter creates new productivity indices for much of France, beginning with the Paris Basin. It explains the new method of measuring productivity, justifies it in great detail for the Paris Basin, and then turns more rapidly to other regions of France and to a judgment of French agriculture as a whole and a comparison with other countries. Throughout, the data consist of leases and series of prices, which, it turns out, can shed considerable light on agricultural productivity. Under the proper conditions, evidence from the leases can be combined with product prices and the costs of the factors of production to give a measure of productivity. The measure of productivity here is not merely the partial productivity of land or of labor—how much is grown per acre or per farm worker—but total factor productivity (TFP), the ratio of outputs to inputs that takes into account all the factors of production used in farming: land, labor, and capital. Agriculture leases have previously been employed in this way to study the productivity of early modern English agriculture, and though using them may at first seem a picaresque adventure in pseudo-statistics, they ultimately furnish us with firmer evidence than the shaky figures we have for crop yields and output per worker. And it is evidence of considerable importance, for it reveals whether agriculture was in fact shackled by organizational and technological rigidities, as so many historians assert, or whether, even under the Old Regime, certain farms could extract more output than other farms from the same amount of land, labor, and capital and thereby achieve economic growth.

Inevitably, the answers here involve trekking through issues of statistics and method. In this chapter, the first step is to criticize the usual measurements of Old Regime agricultural productivity. I then propose my method, explain its virtues to readers unversed in economics, and illustrate it in detail via the example of the Paris Basin. To employ it in the Paris Basin, I first demonstrate that certain key assumptions hold, and then discuss what the method reveals. After applying the same method to the rest of France, I finally judge French agriculture as a whole.

Using Leases and Prices to Measure Productivity

How do we calculate the productivity of Old Regime agriculture? Today, we measure the productivity of agricultural labor by dividing the quantity of goods produced by the number of workers. Performing a similar computation for the Old Regime, however, is a treacherous undertaking. The first problem is determining the size of the agricultural labor force, a calculation that, even when based on nineteenth-century census records, is fraught with difficulty. How does one know what fraction of the rural population worked in farming when many denizens of the countryside toiled in cottage industry? For the nineteenth century, it is true, the somewhat meager evidence suggests that the labor force did not vary as a proportion of the rural population. The same relationship continues to hold if the labor force is adjusted for the fact that individual workers divided their time between agriculture and industry. But one can only assume that this relationship reaches back into the Old Regime, and even if it does, there remains the vexing problem of estimating what farms produced.[2]

It is equally difficult to trace the evolution of the productivity of land. To be sure, we can derive grain yields from a variety of documents, and the yields measure the productivity of land used in grain farming. The problem is that the French evidence is always scanty, making comparisons of yields over time a treacherous venture. Grain output per hectare varied drastically from year to year and from one end of a farm to another, casting doubt on any comparison between, say, a sixteenth-century yield taken from a lone probate description of a particular field and a nineteenth-century yield calculated from a census average for the surrounding *arrondissement*. Worse, even seemingly reliable averages can be deceiving. If wheat supplants crops of lesser value (such as rye) on poorer soil, then average yields for wheat can stagnate or decline, even though the value of output per hectare and physical yields themselves (on soil of a given quality) are rising.[3]

If following grain yields over the centuries seems intractable, one might hope (as many historians have) that the tithe could be used to track land productivity, provided that it was levied on fields of a fixed size.[4] But tithe records suffer from a host of problems. Beyond the well-known difficulties of collecting the tithe during the Wars of Religion—masked men absconded with the tithe in the village of La Grande-Paroisse, for example—there are other, more serious, but largely unacknowledged complications. Perhaps the worst is that the tithe series are likely to omit output from innovations such as artificial meadows and from new crops such as turnips. From the voluminous tithe records of the Cathedral of Notre Dame, for instance, one learns that Notre Dame went to court in 1603 because it was unable to collect the tithe on land recently put into cultivation and sown with turnips in the village of Louvres. In 1713 to 1716 it lost the tithe on new artificial meadows in the village of Dampmart to the local curé, who claimed the right to tithe such novelties. Stories of this sort are are in fact common and hardly peculiar to Notre Dame. In Normandy, the tithe was lost when land was converted from arable to more productive pasture. It is thus conceivable that the tithe records favored by historians—such as the records of large ecclesiastical institutions like Notre Dame—could even register a decline at a time of agricultural improvements, either because the tithe rights to new crops belonged to the local parish priest or because the tithe was simply no longer due when crops changed. And a flat graph of the tithe derived from such records might mask growing productivity and thus gravely mislead us.[5]

We therefore cannot easily compute labor productivity or extend yields and other measures of land productivity back into the past. And none of those figures gives us total factor productivity: even when reliable, they furnish only partial productivities of land or of labor and usually only for a single crop, such as wheat. What of agricultural capital, especially livestock, which could boost yields and reduce the need for agricultural labor? And what of the farm products that the tithe series often skip, such as wool or meat, which were far from negligible even in grain-growing regions?[6]

What we need, of course, is a new source of information, preferably one that lets us measure not just the productivity of one output or of one factor but total factor productivity. That is what leases allow us to do. When combined with prices and wages, the rental values in the leases yield a measure of total factor productivity that, while itself open to objections, seems much more reliable than the dubious physical measures of output per worker or even output per hectare. Using prices and rents in this way was first suggested in economic history by Donald McCloskey, in an analysis of English enclosures. More recently, Robert Allen has successfully employed the same method to examine the productivity of enclosures and of English agriculture in general in the early modern period.[7] What McCloskey and Allen rely on is the fact that total factor productivity can be calculated with prices and rents in place of the actual physical measurements of the products and factors of production. Behind their calculation lurks a relatively simple intuition: higher productivity—producing more with less—also means producing at lower cost. In farming, the lower costs may initially mean higher profits for more productive farmers, but they should eventually lead to either higher rents for landlords, higher wages for farm workers, higher payments for agricultural capital, or lower prices for farm products. It should thus be possible to deduce levels of total factor productivity from the relationship of rents, wages, and prices.

The definition of total factor productivity (TFP) here is a standard one. It gauges the effectiveness of farm production and is defined—roughly speaking—as the average product of all the inputs to farming. Its rate of change equals the speed at which farm production is growing less the rate at which use of the factors of production is increasing, with each product weighted by its share in total revenue and each factor by its share in total cost. In mathematical terms, the rate of growth of TFP is

$$\sum_{i=1}^{m} u_i \dot{y}_i - \sum_{j=1}^{n} v_j \dot{x}_j = \sum_{j=1}^{n} v_j \dot{w}_j - \sum_{i=1}^{m} u_i \dot{p}_i \qquad (1)$$

Here the y_i's are the outputs produced; the p_i's and u_i's are the corresponding output prices and output shares in total revenue; the x_j's, the factors of production used; the w_j's and v_j's, the corresponding factor prices and factor shares in total cost; and dots refer to growth rates. The expression on the left is simply the definition of the growth rate of TFP, measured in terms of physical units of inputs and outputs; under conditions specified below, it will equal the expression on the right, which is measured in terms of prices.

If we also assume, as Allen does, that the product and factor shares remain constant over time (an assumption that turns out to be very reasonable for early modern agriculture), then we can integrate equation (1) with respect to time to get a formula for TFP:

$$TFP = \frac{w_1^{v_1} \cdots w_n^{v_n}}{p_1^{u_1} \cdots p_m^{u_m}} = (r+t)^s \frac{C}{P} \qquad (2)$$

Here, r is nominal rent per hectare; t is taxes per hectare; s is the factor share of land; C is an index (geometric) of the costs of the other factors of production weighted by their factor shares; and P is an index (geometric) of the price of agricultural products weighted by their shares in total revenue. We have made the reasonable assumption that the burden of taxation falls on land, so that the cost of land equals rent plus taxes, or $(r+t)$. In nonmathematical terms, TFP is high if a property manages to support high rent and taxes despite high costs for the other factors of production and low product prices.[8]

To calculate TFP, it thus suffices to know product and factor shares, the prices of agricultural products, and the cost of the various factors of production, including land. We can measure TFP either as a weighted ratio of output quantities produced divided by factor quantities utilized, or, equivalently, as a weighted ratio of factor costs divided by product prices. The point is that more efficient techniques and organization not only increase physical outputs for a given level of inputs but also depress product prices relative to factor costs and ultimately show up in the form of higher profits and rents, once we correct for the level of prices and payments to the other factors of production via the indexes P and C. If a clever farmer discovers how to increase his productivity—perhaps he manages to squeeze more wheat from the same plot of land, the same amount of capital, and the same amount of toil—then he will reap higher profits as well, profits that will eventually fund higher rent payments to his landlord. After all, in the countryside it will be hard for him to hide his success from his landlord. It will be even harder to hide his methods from other farmers. If they imitate him, the price of wheat may fall, but TFP, which is a weighted ratio of factor costs divided by product prices, still increases. On the other hand, a mere shift in rents, wages, and prices in response to population change or price inflation will not affect TFP. If the population increases, for example, rents may rise relative to agricultural prices while wages fall. Yet the index of TFP, if properly estimated, will remain the same.[9]

It all sounds quite logical, a historian unfamiliar with the concept might say, but how is total factor productivity actually calculated? A hypothetical example can illustrate the computation. Suppose that we are interested in measuring the total factor productivity of a hypothetical farm at two different dates—say 1750 and 1775. Suppose as well that we can estimate likely costs and revenues on the farm, either from actual accounts for the farm itself (perhaps at some third date) or from a description of a similar farm. From the costs and revenues we can estimate the product and factor shares of the farm—in other words, what fraction of the farm's annual revenue came from the various products it sold (the product shares) and what fraction of its annual costs were paid to land, labor, and the various forms of capital (the factor shares). For the sake of simplicity, let us assume that the hypothetical farm yields only two products: wheat and mutton. Other commodities, from wool to oats, are either negligible or are used up in the production of wheat and mutton: the oats, for example, are fed to horses. In producing the wheat and mutton, the hypothetical farm uses land, labor, and capital, such as horses, sheep, seed, and equipment. To avoid complications, we shall ignore equipment in this example, and take wheat output net of seed so as to ignore seed as well. The factors of production (in this example only) are then land, labor, sheep, and horses. The cost of land will include rent and taxes, while the cost of labor will encompass wages, food consumed on the farm, and any profits that the farmer earns. As for horses and sheep, theirs will be the rental cost—in other words, the cost of using the livestock for a year.[10]

If the costs and revenues yield the product and factor shares shown in table 4.1, and if these shares apply to the farm in both 1750 and 1775, then an index of total factor productivity is easy to compute. We simply raise the price of each factor of production to the power of its share, multiply the resulting numbers, and then divide by the analogous product of the product prices. In 1750, for instance, total factor productivity is

$$\frac{(1^{.48})(35^{.37})(32^{.08})(1^{.07})}{(10^{.79})(.2^{.21})} \tag{3}$$

or 1.12. In 1775, as readers may check, it is 1.23; in other words, it has grown by 10 percent. It has increased—at least in this example—because rent and payments for agricultural capital have jumped. Wages have not changed, and the prices of wheat and mutton have risen, which would

TABLE 4.1
Hypothetical Calculation of Total Factor Productivity, 1750–75

Product or Factor of Production	Product or Factor Share	Price in 1750	Price in 1775
Labor (livres/day)	0.48	1.00	1.00
Land (livres/ha)	0.37	35.00	55.00
Horse rental (livres/year)	0.08	32.00	52.00
Sheep rental (livres/year)	0.07	1.00	2.00
Wheat (livres/hl)	0.79	10.00	11.00
Mutton (livres/livre)	0.21	0.20	0.30
Index of total factor productivity		1.12	1.23

Source: See Chapter 4.
Note: The prices and shares here are not taken from real data and are used only to illustrate the calculation of TFP.

tend to depress the index of TFP. But the jump in rent and payments for capital more than compensates for the rise in prices, yielding a higher index of TFP.

Expression (3) provides another vantage point for understanding the index, at least for readers who recall a little economics. The denominator in (3) is just our index P of the price of agricultural products. If we substitute P for the denominator and do a little algebra, we get:

$$\left(\frac{1}{P}\right)^{.48} \left(\frac{35}{P}\right)^{.37} \left(\frac{32}{P}\right)^{.08} \left(\frac{1}{P}\right)^{.07}$$

Each of the terms is the cost of a factor of production divided by the price P of the farm's products: the first term is the wage divided by P, the second term is the cost of land divided by P, and so on. Under the right conditions—the same conditions that make our index a measure of TFP—each of these terms will equal the marginal product of the associated factor of production; in other words, how much additional farm output one more unit of the factor would produce. The first term, for instance, will be the marginal product of labor: what one more unit of labor would produce in wheat and mutton. The second will be the marginal product of land; the third, the marginal product of horses; and the fourth, the marginal product of sheep. The marginal products are simply a measure of the productivity of each factor of production. Taking each to a power and multiplying them is simply a way of combining the productivities of all the factors of production so as to gauge the total productivity of the farm—that is to say, our TFP.

Since expression (3) produces only indices, it makes sense only when there are two numbers to compare. The same sort of calculation, though, could be applied to two different farms—for instance, two neighboring farms in the same year. In that case, the two farms would face the same prices and wages, and only the difference in rent would distinguish them. With real data, of course, productivity computations may be more complicated and entail additional products or factors of production, from seed to oats and wool. But the principle behind the calculations would remain unchanged.

CALCULATING TFP: THE EXAMPLE OF
THE PARIS BASIN

To see how the method works with real data, let us calculate TFP for agriculture in the Paris Basin. We can take the necessary per-hectare rents from the sample of Notre Dame leases, which shed so much light on the rental market in the Paris Basin. The sample, given in Chapter 3, comprised thirty-nine series of leases, each series concerning a separate property in one of twenty-five different villages scattered throughout the Paris Basin. Nearly all the leases in the sample were intended to last nine years. Among the most ancient—those dating to the early sixteenth century or before—a few had been drawn up for longer periods, or even for the life of the tenant. Far more common, though, were leases brought to a premature end because of a tenant's death or bankruptcy. Given such interruptions, it is not surprising that the lease series do not run unbroken from 1450 to 1789, monotonously casting up a new contract every nine years. Some of the series did not begin until well after 1450; others terminated when properties changed. And in several instances leases proved unusable. Still, the series seem nearly continuous: between the first and the last usable contract for each property in the sample, the gaps between leases average nine and a third (9.4) years.

The Notre Dame sample is of course not random—few of the properties lie west of Paris—but it does seem representative of open-field agriculture near the city. It also lets us track a large number of identical properties over three and a half centuries, something previous researchers have never accomplished. The sample has another advantage as well: we know each property's characteristics—the area, the location, the nature of the crops, the identity of the tenant, and so on. We can therefore relate variations in agricultural productivity to those characteristics and do so more precisely than ever before.

Also in favor of the sample is one of its virtues uncovered in the previous chapter: the Notre Dame leases suffer from few of the problems that afflict early modern leases—seigneurial dues that seriously distort the rent, for example, or *contre-lettres* that secretly revise it. It was thus relatively easy to derive per-hectare rents from the sample for each decade from 1450 to 1789 (table 4.2).[11] Most authors limit themselves to simple averages, but because rent depended on land quality and location, I have also adjusted the rent averages for variations in quality as properties jump in and out of the sample. Columns two and four of table 4.2 display the results of the adjustment, which uses the regression of ln(rent) on property characteristics and other variables affecting rent in table 3.1.[12]

The net adjustment is relatively minor and does not affect the overall trend in land rent. Other methods of correcting for quality differences have an equally small effect. So, too, does averaging the rent in a different way: weighting all the leases in force in each year by area, under the assumption that each lease remained valid for nine years or until renewed (table 4.2, column three). The difference with the second method is that it weights leases by area and counts not only leases signed in a given year but all those from previous years that had not overrun their nine-year lives and expired.

The only discrepancy between the two methods appears when crises strike or when rents are growing. During crises, averaging over all the leases in force exaggerates somewhat the rent that was actually paid; during rent inflation, it lags behind the true value of the land. The difference may of course seem small, but it can disturb the calculation of productivity, which requires an up-to-date figure for rent—ideally, what land would fetch if leased to the highest bidder. Given the slight problems with averaging over all the leases in force, I therefore eschew it in favor of the average over the leases in the sample; that is, only the leases signed in any period. In other words, columns two and four in table 4.2 are preferred to column three.[13]

This rental series, it turns out, matches the evidence for the Paris Basin unearthed by other historians. Plotting the numbers in table 4.2, column two, against the rents for the outskirts of Paris published by Béatrice Veyrassat-Herren and Emmanuel Le Roy Ladurie yields startling agreement (figure 4.1). The same chorus of agreement rings out if we compare the series with leases from the Hurepoix, to the south of Paris, or from the Beauce, to the city's southwest, and it holds whether the properties were large or small, whether the landlords were laymen or clerics, nobles or bourgeois, and whether the leases were drawn up in the sixteenth, seventeenth, or eighteenth century.[14] Although such harmony may detract from the novelty of the Notre Dame numbers, it lends credence to what they say. Indeed, what they reveal about productivity is likely to hold not just for the properties of Notre Dame but for the Paris Basin as a whole.

TABLE 4.2
Nominal Rent (Livres/Hectare) and Agricultural Price-Cost Index: Paris Basin

Decade	Leases in Sample	Nominal Rent			Ln(Rent)	Price-Cost Index
		(1)	(2)	(3)	(4)	(5)
1450–59	2	0.70	0.76	0.57	−0.29	—
1460–69	3	0.72	0.80	0.67	−0.23	—
1470–79	3	0.73	0.94	0.62	−0.07	—
1480–89	4	0.68	0.69	0.79	−0.69	—
1490–99	5	0.94	0.97	0.81	−0.07	—
1500–09	4	1.23	1.33	0.98	0.28	—
1510–19	6	1.74	1.76	1.40	0.50	—
1520–29	11	2.14	2.24	1.82	0.57	0.62
1530–39	14	3.01	2.96	2.23	0.79	0.69
1540–49	13	3.66	4.12	3.11	1.36	0.72
1550–59	20	5.07	5.15	4.72	1.58	0.74
1560–69	13	6.55	7.34	5.86	1.92	0.77
1570–79	23	9.09	8.74	7.28	1.99	0.86
1580–89	24	12.43	10.98	10.40	2.27	0.81
1590–99	26	12.02	12.86	11.92	2.13	1.14
1600–09	31	12.81	11.64	10.53	2.21	0.95
1610–19	35	10.85	11.05	8.96	2.25	0.87
1620–29	38	13.54	13.16	11.61	2.35	0.96
1630–39	38	20.78	20.26	15.79	2.84	1.19
1640–49	32	20.91	20.54	17.40	2.83	1.05
1650–59	27	23.07	22.28	19.14	2.84	1.22
1660–69	33	26.42	26.53	19.55	3.11	1.13
1670–79	25	18.78	17.92	17.12	2.79	0.95
1680–89	24	19.92	19.75	15.88	2.86	1.04
1690–99	26	21.27	21.58	17.49	2.96	1.10
1700–09	35	25.44	23.97	20.83	3.06	1.06
1710–19	31	23.79	23.54	19.12	3.06	1.12
1720–29	30	30.34	27.81	20.55	3.24	1.07
1730–39	32	25.01	23.35	22.17	3.10	1.09
1740–49	32	25.73	25.29	19.03	3.17	1.16
1750–59	29	27.41	27.14	21.20	3.25	1.12
1760–69	27	31.90	28.95	23.75	3.32	1.12
1770–79	19	43.74	43.07	32.44	3.73	1.32
1780–89	30	49.46	47.91	38.40	3.83	1.16

Sources: Sample of leases from Notre Dame; other sources are listed in Appendix A, part 14.

Note: Column (1) is the average rent for the leases in the Notre Dame sample; column (2) is the average of quality-adjusted rent for the leases in the sample; column (3) is the area-weighted average of quality-adjusted rent for all leases in force; column (4) is the average of quality-adjusted ln(rent) for the leases in the sample; and column (5) is the agricultural price-cost index (mean equals 1). The quality adjustments rely on the regression in table 3.1 and begin by correcting ln(rent) lease

TABLE 4.2 *(cont.)*

by lease. Column (4) is the decennial average of the following: $z = \ln(\text{rent}) - a_1 x_1 - a_2 x_2 - a_3 x_3 - a_4 x_4 - a_5 x_5$, where a_1 through a_5 are the coefficients of percentage of meadow, percentage of vineyard, good soil, ln(distance to Paris), and ln(area) in table 3.1, and x_1 through x_5 are the corresponding variables measured as deviations from their means. The variable z is quality-adjusted ln(rent); because the quality adjustment is linear, we would get the same answer if we first averaged ln(rent) over each decade and then applied the quality adjustment. Column (2) is the decennial average of e^z for each lease; because exponentiation is not linear, column (2) will not be precisely the same as what we would get by exponentiating the values in column (4). Column (3) averages the area-weighted rent for all the leases in force; it involves the same quality adjustment, except that x_1 through x_5 are now measured as area-weighted averages. Column (5) is P/C, the ratio of agricultural prices to the costs of the factors of production other than land, where each price and each cost is weighted by its share in total revenue. Shares are from the Bernonville farm. See Appendix A, parts 1, 3, 6, and 9, for details.

Assumptions

The whole method of calculating TFP with leases and prices is of course open to certain objections. Some are technical and are discussed elsewhere.[15] More important and far more interesting are the assumptions underlying the whole exercise, which may raise some questions among both economists and historians: that the agricultural cost and product shares for the Paris Basin can be described with some precision for a period of three centuries, that agricultural markets existed, and that the local land-rental market was competitive. These assumptions obviously deserve detailed scrutiny.

The first is that we know the agricultural technology in the Paris Basin well enough to calculate the factor and product shares that enter into the formula for TFP. One might suppose that the shares could be recovered from clever regressions with rents, prices, and wages, but such a tactic is doomed to failure even with the most drastic simplifications.[16] The alternative is to derive the shares from the records of a typical farm in the Paris Basin. I have done so for the farm of Bernonville, located some 150 kilometers north of Paris near the town of Saint-Quentin. When its accounts for the year 1765 were published in 1767, Bernonville was described as an average large farm, by no means exceptional. And although it lay farther from Paris than any of the properties in the Notre Dame sample, its technology differed little from what one finds elsewhere in the grain-growing regions of the Paris Basin. In the Brie, to the southeast of Paris, in the Beauce, to the southwest, on the plains north of the city, and to its immediate south, farmers grew the same crops, hired similar numbers of workers, and used nearly the same number of animals—and their farm accounts yielded similar product and factor shares. In Bernonville, for instance, 80 percent of the revenue came from grain crops; on a farm in the Brie in the 1730s, 77 percent did. The factor share of land in Bernonville was 27 percent; in the

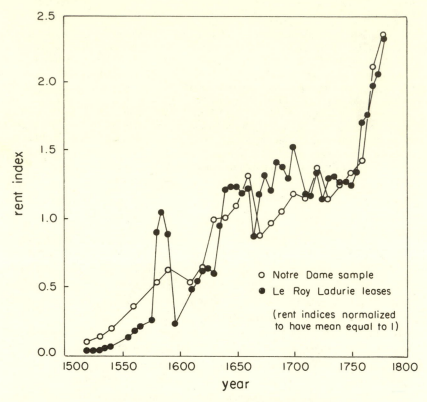

Figure 4.1 Nominal Rent Indices for Notre Dame Sample and for Le Roy Ladurie Leases

Brie, 31 percent. And on another farm, located some 20 kilometers north of Paris and investigated by J. M. Moriceau and Gilles Postel-Vinay, the numbers are much the same.[17]

Factor and product shares thus seem to have varied little from farm to farm near Paris, and the Bernonville shares would appear to fit the agricultural technology of the properties in the Notre Dame sample very well, at least in the eighteenth century. One might worry, though, that factor and product shares changed over time—that they were quite different in the sixteenth and seventeenth centuries. Modern economic growth has accustomed us to increases in the factor share of labor, and in early modern Europe whole regions—western England, for example—were transformed by the coming of a pastoral economy, which diminished the product share of grain.

Such was not the case, however, near Paris during the period under study. The occasional share tenancy contracts we have from other landlords, in which tenants paid a portion of the output as rent, point to similar factor and product shares in the seventeenth century. Death inventories imply that the use of labor and livestock had not changed significantly from as far back as the sixteenth century. The number of plowmen hired may have declined somewhat during the eighteenth century, but the overall effect on the labor factor share was small. Furthermore, if the two most important factor shares, those of land and labor, had shifted drastically, we should be able to detect it from demographic data, but no such shift is apparent in the sixteenth and seventeenth centuries. In fact, the land and labor shares seem not to have shifted at all before the late eighteenth century.[18]

Nor do product shares in total revenue seem to have changed. Farmers did plant new crops such as sainfoin in little artificial meadows that added to the supply of fodder, but the effect on the overall proportion of outputs was small. Near Paris, farmers had specialized in grain production as early as the late Middle Ages; they continued to do so into the nineteenth century. What animal products they produced—such as wool from the sheep that fertilized the arable—derived from grain production, and relative prices never shifted in favor of acquiring additional livestock. Indeed, because much specialization in early modern Europe was driven by the effect of transportation costs on relative prices—farmers hundreds of miles from cities might raise easy-to-transport livestock, while those nearby tilled fields of wheat—it is no wonder that our farms, all near Paris, never abandoned grain.[19]

While the assumption of constant product and factor shares appears reasonable, it would be prudent to check the sensitivity of the results to variations in the share values. To do so, I relied on an alternative set of product and factor shares from the Chartier farm north of Paris, whose accounts were analyzed by Gilles Postel-Vinay and Jean-Marc Moriceau. Although the Bernonville and the alternative shares resemble one another, there are a few differences, for the Chartier farm had specialized to a certain extent in the production of oats and fodder crops and the available records are not as detailed. Nonetheless, as shown below, the alternative shares yield similar estimates for TFP.[20] In the end, the TFP calculation is simply not all that sensitive to changes in the product and factor shares.

The formula for TFP also assumes the existence of rudimentary markets in which the factors of production can be purchased and farm products sold. We must be able to measure prices in those markets to calculate the indexes C and P in equation (2) for TFP. Not all of a farmer's dealings need have passed through the product and factor markets—merely a portion. It would not matter, for example, that a farmer employed some family members, provided he also hired servants. Nor would it matter that he consumed some of his crops, provided he also sold a portion. As long as he had some involvement in the markets, though, it would be fair to say that the costs and the prices he faced equaled those dictated by the market, once we allowed for the costs of transportation and of market preparation.

Here, again, we may raise some historians' hackles, for Old Regime farmers, we know, are often considered self-sufficient and thoroughly isolated from markets. But as Chapter 3 demonstrated, self-sufficiency was largely a myth, particularly in the Paris Basin. Nearly all the peasants in the region either cultivated wine for sale, worked on the side as farm laborers, or rented land in a tight land market. By no stretch of the imagination were they self-sufficient.

There remains the practical problem of measuring wages. Ideally, we would like to have the wage of farm labor, preferably unskilled. Farm wages, though, are difficult to appraise: domestics were often paid a considerable portion of their earnings in kind, and salaries varied from season to season and task to task. Even for a given task, as was shown in Chapter 3, the salary might vary considerably because of differences in strength, skill, reliability, or tenure with the same employer.[21] The only alternative, it seems, is to use urban wages for unskilled building workers. Calculating the mode of the observed wages would capture what the average unskilled building worker earned and allow us to overcome differences in strength and skill. One might object that urban and rural wages were different, but fifteenth- and sixteenth-century evidence from the region around Paris suggests that wages for unskilled day laborers in the city differed little from those prevalent in the countryside, at least during the harvest, when farmers hired day laborers from the city. "In the sixteenth century, the wages of two laborers, one working in the fields and the other in the city, were identical," stated Micheline Baulant, who studied wages around Paris—and her data support that assertion. An unskilled urban helper earned 2.5 *sous* a day in 1500 to 1505 and 10.4 sous a day in 1594 to 1598; a *hotteur* (basket carrier) in the grape harvest earned 2.5 sous in 1500 to 1505 and 10 sous in 1594 to 1598.[22] Evidence from the seventeenth and eighteenth centuries, albeit meager, points in the same direction. And even if there were sometimes differences between city and country wages, the trend of pay for the unskilled was nearly everywhere the same, and it is that trend, not absolute prices, that we need in order to establish changes in our cost index C and thereby in our formula for TFP. For nearly all unskilled occupations, both within the city and without, wages in cash and in kind moved in parallel—or at least this is what the evidence from the Paris region suggests.[23]

Of course, we should not jump to the conclusion that a national labor market existed. Since labor was mobile, labor markets did extend beyond the local economy. Still, they were only regional, though the one around Paris was undoubtedly large enough to embrace the localities from which our leases were drawn. Similarly, we should not overlook evidence that the labor market was segmented, with farmers in certain places and at certain times able to hire cheap labor at a cost that bore only a slight relationship to the wages paid in Paris. There is some evidence for such segmentation, but it is as yet neither overwhelming nor convincing. Differences in remuneration were not large, and they may simply have reflected the heterogeneity of labor, the complexities of in-kind pay, and variations in the cost of living. It is in any case difficult to argue for complete segmentation in the face of the enormous mobility of labor in the Paris Basin during the Old Regime. Parisian workers, we know, helped take in the harvest. Domestics quit the farm for the city, as did paupers fleeing rural poverty. And whole families moved in and out of the small towns surrounding Paris, presumably in search of work. Given such mobility, it seems unlikely that the regional labor market was partitioned into isolated and mutually exclusive compartments.[24]

As it does for agricultural labor, our method also requires the existence of markets for agricultural capital—in particular, livestock. Fortunately, long-distance markets for horses, cattle, and sheep reach far back into the past, and though price series for livestock are skimpy and we must be careful of differences between breeds, it is possible to assemble the necessary series of cost trends—or at least gross averages for twenty-five-year periods, which (along with interest and depreciation rates) is all that is necessary for our cost index C in the formula for TFP. There are of course still other forms of capital, such as clearing, drainage, and other improvements to the soil. But these improvements would be counted in the rent.

For the price index P in the formula for TFP, we need prices of agriculture outputs, and here it is grain that poses the most daunting problems. The price of grain was terribly volatile. Taking long-run averages can adjust for the price volatility, but it is not clear over what period one should average. Furthermore, the cost of transporting grain was high enough to drive a wedge between the farm-gate price and the market price that enters into our agricultural price index P. If the wedge were large enough, or if it varied considerably, it could distort our index of TFP.[25]

But the difficulties here are far from insurmountable. Although we cannot be absolutely certain about what years to average prices over, employing the current year and the previous eight (in other words, averaging over the outgoing lease) seems concordant with contemporary practice. We shall therefore calculate P and C using the Bernonville shares and Paris prices averaged over the outgoing lease. Table 4.2 displays the resulting decennial averages of the price-cost ratio P/C, which is all we need to calculate TFP. Of course, we can check the sensitivity of our results to this process of averaging by using prices from a radically different set of years in the indexes P and C. We shall do so, using prices averaged over the life of the new lease—or in other words, over the current year and the next eight years. This alternative set of prices makes strong demands of our tenant farmers (namely, that they be able to see eight years into the future), but as we shall see, it does not change the index of TFP greatly.[26]

As for transportation costs, though they drove a wedge between grain prices in distant markets, the long-run average price trends—all that is necessary for our price index P—tended to move together, as long as the markets were not too far apart. Away from Paris, for instance, grain prices in local markets were lower and more volatile than within Paris in the sixteenth, seventeenth, and eighteenth centuries—yet price trends in markets as far as 100 kilometers away tended to follow the trend of the Paris price, particularly if we examine averages, which smooth out local crises. Such parallel movement should hardly be surprising in view of the considerable evidence that merchants and large-scale farmers carried out what amounted to intermarket arbitrage in the sixteenth, seventeenth, and eighteenth centuries. With individuals buying and selling once price gaps widened, it is no wonder that grain prices, though different in absolute terms, exhibited similar trends. I therefore used Paris grain prices in general, though I kept track of the gap of the price in the city and the price out on the farm.[27]

The last assumption I need is that untaxed profits from farming eventually went to landlords—in other words, that the land rental market was competitive, with no barriers to tenant entry. In the short run, it is clear, that was not always the case, for it might take a landlord time to renew a lease or even to realize that more could be squeezed out of a property. What concerns us, though, is the long run. Unlike the markets for labor, livestock, and agricultural products, which swarmed with hundreds of minuscule actors, the land rental market in any given village might involve only a small number of tenants, who could conceivably drive rents down and thereby retain some of the profits of farming even in the long run. In some parts of France—areas of so-called mauvais gré or droit de marché—tenants wielded such power, but as we know from Chapter 3, mauvais gré was unknown throughout much of the area where the farms from the Notre Dame sample were located.

Admittedly, there is some evidence that can be construed as a sign of tenant market power—the lower rents per hectare that big farms fetched both in the Notre Dame sample and in general throughout much of France. But as Chapter 3 suggested, the lower rents for big farms simply reflected the risk premium that landlords demanded when renting small parcels. That was apparently the case with the Notre Dame sample, which showed few signs of tenant market power. Chapter 3 also argued that in the long run it would be difficult for tenants to maintain market power outside the regions of mauvais gré. Without mauvais gré, unsatisfactory renters could eventually be replaced, for tenants were mobile and leases short. Competition for leaseholds was in fact stiff, particularly when large-scale farmers were trying to establish their numerous progeny on farms. With few barriers to entry, tenants could not long siphon off profits.

One might of course debate the normal entrepreneurial profits due to tenants. Our assumption is that in the long run the competitive rental market would have driven these down to zero, leaving tenants no more than what they would earn in the labor market and making the cost of the entrepreneurial input equal to the wage rate. This assumption, it should be stressed, does not mean that the tenants were paupers, for in addition to the compensation for their labor, our calculations include a return on the capital they furnished, which, in the Paris Basin, would typically consist of the livestock, equipment, seed, and animal feed. The revenue from it would amount to 4 to 6 livres per hectare or more in the middle or late eighteenth century. On a large farm—such as the 420 hectares worked by François Chartier in the 1740s—a tenant might earn over 3,000 livres per year from his capital and his labor, plus additional revenue from whatever land he possessed. If he owned roughly 50 hectares of land, as Chartier did, we might thus expect an income of 5,000 livres a year.[28]

What did such tenants *actually* earn in the Paris Basin? François Chartier's earnings in the 1740s were much larger—on the order of 12,000 livres a year, according to Moriceau and Postel-Vinay. Some of the difference (perhaps another 1,000 livres) might be attributed to the relatively low rent he paid, but 6,000 livres in profits would still remain. Furthermore, to judge from estate records, François Chartier was not unique, for the fact is that tenants in the Paris Basin were thriving in the mid-eighteenth century. The important point, though, is that tenants had not always fared so well. In the late seventeenth and early eighteenth centuries, for instance, their fortunes were at low ebb. At that point Chartier's ancestors were earning less—less probably than normal earnings due Chartier for his labor and capital—while other farmers in the Basin were going bankrupt.[29] The families that survived as tenants, like Chartier's, did earn relatively high returns by the 1740s. However, landlords such as Notre Dame eventually discovered these higher profits and raised the rent, which brought entrepreneurial earnings back to normal.[30] In short, while there were times when entrepreneurial earnings diverged from what we have assumed, over the long run the assumption of zero entrepreneurial profits is probably fairly close to reality. The only effect on our calculations of total factor productivity would be a bit of short-run error—error that would disappear over the course of several leases.

One might still worry that the short-run error would be enough to distort the trend of total factor productivity or to disturb our calculations (in particular our regressions), but statistical tests suggest that such worries are unwarranted. In the end, the assumption of zero entrepreneurial profits appears quite reasonable. The evidence for competition in the rental market runs in its favor; so too does the short life of French leases—nine years or less versus a much longer duration in early modern England. Also supporting the zero profits assumption is an eighteenth-century analysis of farm earnings: it suggests that entrepreneurial profits were too small on average to affect our calculations.[31]

Although the use of prices and leases to calculate TFP may now seem reasonable, a reader might still like some reassurance that an index of TFP based on prices would really yield reliable results. In one instance where, thanks to an unusual set of farm accounts, we can compare physical quantities produced and factors employed for a real eighteenth-century farm in the Paris Basin, the method of calculating TFP described here gives extraordinarily accurate results. The farm is the Chartier's; its productivity can be compared in the 1740s and again in the 1780s. Using physical quantities, we find that productivity on the farm rose 9.79 percent between the 1740s and the 1780s. If instead we use the method adopted throughout the rest of this chapter—with shares that came from the Bernonville farm—we get very nearly the same thing, 9.03 percent. Neither the assumption of constant product and factor shares nor the use of prices in place of physical quantities seems to be misleading.[32]

Results for the Paris Basin

What then do the leases reveal about the Paris Basin? The place to begin is with the evolution of TFP. From equation two, TFP equals $(r + t)^s C/P$, where r is rent per hectare; t is taxes per hectare; s is the factor share of land; and C and P are the indexes of agricultural costs and prices. We do not know t precisely, but if we ignore taxes for the moment—an assumption soon to be corrected—then TFP will be very nearly equal to $r^s C/P$. Of perhaps greater interest is the logarithm of TFP, whose graph will more accurately depict percentage growth in productivity. It will be very close to $s\ln(r) - \ln(P/C)$, which we can average across properties for different periods. We can then chart, at least roughly, the changes in TFP, and we can hone the accuracy of the graph by adjusting $\ln(r)$ for variations in land quality via the procedure used in table 4.2.

Figure 4.2 plots such an average for twenty-five-year periods. It also charts average values of TFP computed with the alternative factor and product shares and with the alternative prices in the indexes P and C—prices that are averaged over the newly signed lease instead of over the outgoing one. All three curves are corrected for variations in land quality and location.[33] The alternative shares and prices shift the graph of TFP somewhat but do not disturb the overall trend. The alternative shares tip the curve upward a bit—largely because the land share s is higher—but TFP still traces out the same peaks and valleys. The pattern with the alter-

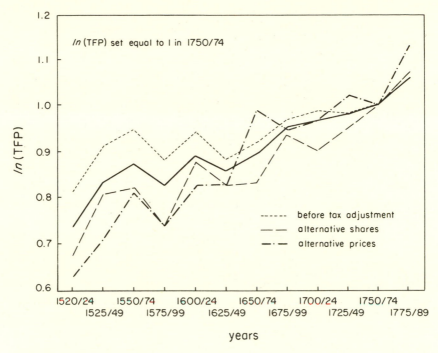

Figure 4.2 Notre Dame Sample Ln(TFP): Tax Adjustment and Alternative Prices and Shares

native prices is also similar, except in 1650–74 and 1775–89, when its behavior may well be an aberration.[34] Overall, TFP follows essentially the same path, whatever the shares and prices.

Built into figure 4.2 is an adjustment for having omitted taxes in the calculation of TFP. Without such a correction, TFP growth would be understated, because of the increasingly heavy fiscal burden that the monarchy imposed on the land. The size of the resulting error, though, turns out to be relatively small. Figure 4.2 plots TFP both before and after the tax adjustment for the Bernonville shares and for prices averaged over the outgoing lease. The graphs of TFP with alternative shares and prices include tax adjustments of a similar magnitude.[35]

The years from 1450 to 1519 have been excluded from figure 4.2, because the prices needed for the indexes C and P become less reliable and the number of usable leases dwindles. As is well known, this earlier period witnessed a recovery from the devastation wrought by the Hundred Years' War. Tenants reoccupied abandoned farms, rebuilt walls and barns, and cleared fields overgrown with weeds. The process of reconstruction swept on well into the sixteenth century, particularly in villages that were cursed with poor soil or situated far from Paris. As late as 1545, for example,

Notre Dame was still clearing land in the village of La Grande-Paroisse, 77 kilometers to the southeast of Paris, where one of its tenants, Jean Godet, reclaimed 9 hectares of briar-choked meadow. Godet also had to enclose the meadow with ditches to keep wandering animals out, evidence that the process had extended beyond mere rebuilding to become one of general improvement to the land.[36]

If the wave of improvements persisted well into the sixteenth century, it might explain the relatively high levels of TFP we observe in 1550–74 (figure 4.2). Investment hidden in improvements would boost rents and thereby appear—somewhat erroneously—as higher TFP. It would also explain the rapid pace of TFP growth. Between 1520–24 and 1550–74, TFP grew between 0.3 and 0.4 percent a year, a brilliant achievement by early modern standards and, as we shall see, one that compares favorably with the English performance even two centuries later.[37]

In all likelihood, however, the cause of the higher productivity in 1550–74 lies elsewhere than in recuperation and improvements after the Hundred Years' War. In the first place, information contained in the leases often allows us to deduct the portion of the rent that reflects improvements, at least when buildings are concerned. When it is deducted, the rent and consequently the TFP estimates hardly change. One could argue that clearing and other investments in land would not leave a trace in the leases, but clearing was unlikely to have continued after 1550, particularly on properties close to Paris, where the TFP increases in the middle of the century were largest. The farms near Paris had suffered much less during the Hundred Years' War, and they would in any case have been rebuilt during the fifteenth century, not as late as 1550 nor even after 1525.[38] Evidently, some other force was pushing TFP upward in the mid-sixteenth century, a force that waxed stronger near Paris. Perhaps it was the opportunities offered by proximity to a large city—a point to which we shall return in the next chapter.

After the heights of 1550–74, TFP plummeted during the Wars of Religion of the late sixteenth century. If we compute the growth rate of TFP from lease to lease and average it across properties, we see that it too dropped, confirming the dismal picture at the close of the 1500s.[39] Between 1550–74 and 1575–99, TFP fell 5 percent or more, depending on which shares and prices we employ.

The cause of the collapse was undoubtedly war. The decline was steepest during and immediately after the years 1589 to 1594, the period of most intense fighting in the Paris Basin, when undisciplined armies traversed the region sowing devastation in their wake. During these accursed years soldiers wreaked the greatest havoc. Not content to trample crops, seize livestock and grain, and burn farm buildings to the ground, they resorted to extortion and kidnapping and completely disrupted trade. Understandably, many a farmer fled, abandoning his farm to weeds or to pillage. Notre Dame's tenant Bernaye quit his lease in La Grande-Paroisse in 1594 because of attacks by soldiers, and warfare left Notre Dame's farm in Dampmart abandoned and ruined in 1597. During the worst period of anarchy and plunder, TFP dropped by perhaps 25 percent.[40]

Such were the heavy consequences of war. To be sure, the index of TFP might seem ill-suited for gauging the effects of such transitory events, as it was designed to measure only long-term trends. Yet the evidence suggests that the plunge of TFP during the Wars of Religion was in fact real. What pushed TFP down in the 1590s was not a decline in rent but a sharp upswing in agricultural prices (table 4.2). Those leaping prices were a direct result of markets disrupted and products destroyed.[41]

Productivity growth increased sharply in the peaceful opening years of the seventeenth century. Then, in the second quarter of the century, TFP again declined (figure 4.2). The drop probably resulted from the heavy taxes imposed to fund the kingdom's involvement in the Thirty Years' War (1618–48). Our TFP figures were of course adjusted for taxes, but the adjustment concerned only that portion of the farm profits or surplus that went to the fisc instead of to the landlord. Skyrocketing taxes also could have wreaked havoc by disrupting the agrarian economy. Tax increases, after all, pushed peasants into debt and led to the frequent seizure of livestock and other agricultural capital for the payment of back taxes. Along with troop movements during the Fronde and a series of disastrous harvests in the early 1630s, the tax-provoked disruptions fit the chronology of declining TFP in 1625–49 and no doubt lay behind it.[42]

The following century witnessed a recovery and then slow growth. At least a part of the apparent gains in the century after 1650 was in fact a mirage, reflecting a decline in transportation costs rather than increased agricultural productivity. The cost of transport, we recall, drove a wedge between farm gate prices and Paris prices for bulky commodities such as grain and thus progressively reduced rents on land farther from the city. Because our calculation of TFP is based on Paris prices, and because the measure of TFP combines low local rents with high Paris grain prices, we undoubtedly underestimate the absolute level of TFP for farms distant from the city. The reason again is the simple fact that local rents adjust to transportation costs and local prices, not to the higher prices prevailing in Paris.

As long as local grain prices moved in parallel with Paris prices—the usual pattern—there would be no cause for worry. Although absolute levels of TFP might err slightly, trends in productivity and rates of productivity growth would be the same. But over the course of the late seventeenth and early eighteenth centuries, local prices in markets such as Pontoise and Soissons rose slightly to approach those prevailing in Paris, and the gap between the Paris price and the local prices closed.[43]

What was happening was that transportation costs were dropping. The increase in local prices relative to the Paris price was more pronounced the farther markets were from Paris, just as we would expect if the cost of transportation were falling. Such declining costs were themselves a mark of increased productivity, but in transportation rather than in farming.[44] Unfortunately, our measure of TFP would mistakenly confound the two. Rents would increase as local grain prices converged to meet the Paris price, but as we would be judging rents relative to a Paris price index P, it would seem as if TFP were rising, particularly on distant farms where the effect of declining transportation costs was most conspicuous. It was precisely on such farms that the productivity gains in the late seventeenth century seemed largest.

Prices in markets outside of Paris can therefore reveal how much of the TFP growth between 1650–74 and 1750–74 actually resulted from declining costs of transportation and from the concomitant rise in local prices. Let us consider, for instance, a market far from Paris, where the shift in grain prices relative to those in Paris was large. Soissons provides a perfect example: at nearly 100 kilometers from Paris, it was farther away than any of the properties in the Notre Dame sample. Not surprisingly, the increase of grain prices in Soissons relative to Paris accounts for an 8.3 percent rise in our measure of TFP between 1650–74 and 1750–74, roughly three-quarters of the 11.3 percent gain we observe if we compute TFP with the Bernonville shares and with prices averaged over the outgoing lease.[45]

Closer to Paris, the convergence of local prices and the Paris price has much less effect on our measurement of TFP. At a market such as Pontoise, approximately 30 kilometers from Paris, the convergence of prices explains only a 3.6 percent increase in the same TFP measure over the same period. Clearly, Pontoise provides the example relevant to the Notre Dame properties, for they lie on the average a little less than 40 kilometers from the city, not 100 kilometers away. Between 1650–74 and 1750–74, then, true agricultural TFP grew by perhaps only 7.7 percent—the other 3.6 percent we measure resulted from better transportation. Improved transportation should not, of course, be slighted: it helped feed the growing city of Paris as much as did more efficient farms.

After the century of slow growth, TFP finally accelerated in the late eighteenth century (figure 4.2). Between 1750–74 and 1775–89 TFP vaulted 6.5 percent, measured with the Bernonville shares and outgoing prices. The spike at the end of the Old Regime is even more pronounced if we look at rates of growth. They averaged more than 0.3 percent a year between 1750–74 and 1775–89 and reached a peak of more than 1 percent—rates comparable or superior to those achieved across the English Channel. Indeed, in the early eighteenth century, when TFP growth in English agriculture seemed to crest, it was gaining 0.6 percent annually, according to N.F.R. Crafts; later in the century, he estimated, the growth rate was only 0.2 percent. Robert Allen's work on the English Midlands points to a similar range: between 0.2 and 0.3 percent over the seventeenth and eighteenth centuries.[46] Agriculture in the Paris Basin was thus hardly lagging behind England; in fact, its performance seems positively buoyant.

But was the late eighteenth-century increase in TFP in the Paris Basin illusory? Did it, at least in part, mirror declining transportation costs, as did the slow growth in the years before 1750? The answer this time is no. In the first place, after 1775 our index of TFP rose no faster on distant properties than on those near Paris—the opposite of what one would expect given declining transport costs. Local prices, moreover, had by 1750 ceased rising relative to the Paris price, and their movement no longer accounted for any of the increase in TFP. Prices in Soissons explain perhaps a 1.8 percent increase in our measure of TFP between 1750–74 and 1775–89; those in Pontoise—the ones relevant to the Notre Dame sample—explain none at all.

It is true that the measure of TFP used here may lag a bit behind reality in the late eighteenth century. It took time to renew a lease, time to determine that a tenant was thriving and that the rent could be ratcheted upward. A wise landlord might wait before demanding more from his tenant, lest the tenant go bankrupt and the landlord receive nothing. Notre Dame, for example, investigated several tenants in the late 1750s, discovered that they were profiting, and ruled out the prospect of bankruptcy. Only then did it raise the rent. If such a pattern were general, the increase in productivity could have begun earlier than the graphs suggest.[47]

Here, historians might wonder whether it was in fact more feverish competition among tenants, not greater productivity, that drove up rents and hence our measure of TFP. Or perhaps it merely reflected tighter estate management by Notre Dame, estate management that grew out of the oft-discussed seigneurial reaction in the eighteenth century. Conceivably, better management might have allowed Notre Dame to squeeze more from its tenants and thus jack up the rent. The problem with such arguments, though, are numerous. First, increased competition among tenants or excessive pressure from landlords would presumably lead to faster turnover among tenants, but nothing of the sort happened among Notre Dame's tenants in the late eighteenth century. Second, the focus of the tighter seigneurial management was typically seigneurial dues, but they were unimportant in the Notre Dame sample. Finally, pressure on tenants was not confined to the late eighteenth century, and while Notre Dame's management perhaps improved in the eighteenth century, the improvements did not mean pressing tenants to the wall. As we saw in Chapter 3, Notre Dame, like most landlords, was too fearful of tenant bankruptcy to do that. For Notre Dame, better management may have simply meant greater accuracy in estimating rents, accuracy that could just as well cut the rent as increase it, for fear that a tenant might fail.[48]

On Notre Dame's properties at least, the eighteenth-century TFP increase seems real, and nothing suggests that the jump in TFP was peculiar to our sample. Nominal rent increases of 79 to 120 percent between the 1730s and 1780s were common in Ile-de-France, in the Hurepoix, in Picardy, and in the Beauce. On the Notre Dame farms the increase was 105 percent (table 4.2, column two). Because the trend of prices and taxes was similar throughout the environs of Paris, TFP must have grown by a like amount on farms throughout the region.[49]

Regression analysis based on individual leases corroborates this three-century story of productivity change in the Paris Basin and helps us refine our results. The regressions let us measure the effects of war, for instance, with much greater precision, and they assure us that the TFP changes are unlikely to be chance results. In the regressions the dependent variables are the logarithm of TFP and its growth rate, both calculated lease by lease (tables 4.3 and 4.4). Here ln(TFP) is computed from equation (2) using Bernonville shares, prices averaged over the outgoing lease, and rent without an adjustment for land quality. Alternative prices and shares yield similar results, and we can correct for land quality and for the use of Paris prices by including quality and locational measures among the explanatory variables.[50]

The regression with ln(TFP) confirms that TFP plunged during the worst phase of the Wars of Religion. The coefficient of the dummy variable for the terrible years from 1589 to 1597 (the period of most intense fighting around Paris plus the following three-year crop cycle) translates into a 25 percent drop in TFP, and the t statistic is too large for it to be a fluke (table 4.3, regression 1). Similarly, TFP really does jump after 1775—by 6.6 percent, if we judge from the coefficient of the variable for the years after 1775. As for the rest of the three centuries, the coefficient of the year, which averages TFP growth outside the periods from 1589 to 1597 and from 1775 to 1789, is certainly consistent with our story of rapid gains in the early sixteenth century, a sharp recovery after 1589 to 1597, a crisis in 1625 to 1650, and slow growth for the following century.[51]

Like the analysis of farm gate prices in the seventeenth and eighteenth centuries, the regressions also argue against interpreting the increase in our TFP index exclusively as a decline in transportation costs. If falling transportation costs alone were to explain all the growth of our index of TFP, then the rate of change of TFP would seem higher farther away from Paris. It would be on the distant properties that local prices would rise the most, and rents would follow in their wake. We would therefore expect to measure higher rates of TFP growth on distant properties and hence a positive coefficient for the logarithm of the distance to Paris in the regressions with

TABLE 4.3
Regressions with Ln(TFP): Notre Dame Sample

Independent Variables	Regression Numbers	
	1	2
	Dependent Variables	
	Ln(TFP)	Ln(TFP)
Constant	0.079	0.11
	(0.42)	(0.60)
Dummy: years 1775 and after	0.064	0.056
	(1.97)	(1.80)
Dummy: war years, 1589 to 1597	−0.29	−0.28
	(−8.08)	(−8.30)
Percentage of meadow	0.16	0.11
	(3.25)	(2.51)
Percentage of vineyard	0.014	0.15
	(0.13)	(1.50)
Ln(distance to Paris in kilometers)	−0.067	−0.070
	(−5.94)	(−5.76)
Dummy: good soil	0.00093	0.0041
	(0.06)	(0.28)
Dummy: tenant holdover from previous lease	0.019	0.026
	(1.42)	(2.01)
Time (units of 100 years)	0.061	0.063
	(5.49)	(5.82)
Ln(property area in hectares)	−0.024	−0.050
	(−3.68)	(−7.46)
Ln(area per property parcel)	—	0.043
	—	(6.91)
Observations	638	581
R^2	0.31	0.37
Standard error	0.17	0.15
Mean of dependent variable	0.79	0.80
Condition number of single-value decom- position	93.46	92.83

Sources: Notre Dame sample of leases and property descriptions; additional sources are described in Appendix A, part 14.

Note: Years before 1520 are omitted; t statistics are in parentheses. The TFP figures are adjusted for taxes.

the rate of change of TFP (table 4.4, regression 1). Yet such is not the case. The coefficient is insignificant and negative, and while transportation was growing more efficient, farming did the same.

Overall then, agricultural TFP in the Paris Basin climbed by 39 percent between the periods of 1520–24 and 1775–89, if we use the standard shares

TABLE 4.4

Regressions with the Growth Rate of TFP: Notre Dame Sample

Independent Variables	Regression Numbers	
	1	*2*
	Dependent Variables	
	TFP Growth Rate (percent per year)	*TFP Growth Rate (percent per year)*
Constant	0.46	0.45
	(1.32)	(1.09)
Growth rate of taxes relative	−0.041	−0.044
to rents	(−2.00)	(−2.10)
Growth rate of Paris population	0.24	0.23
	(6.16)	(5.88)
Dummy: years 1775 and after	1.04	1.03
	(3.48)	(3.35)
Dummy: war years, 1589 to 1597	−2.44	−2.25
	(−5.85)	(−5.19)
Dummy: repairs	−0.31	−0.56
	(−0.85)	(−1.39)
Dummy: tenant holdover from	−0.085	−0.041
previous lease	(−0.64)	(−0.29)
Ln(distance to Paris in kilometers)	−0.074	−0.083
	(−0.71)	(−0.70)
Ln(property area in hectares)	−0.024	−0.012
	(−0.43)	(−0.18)
Ln(area per parcel)	—	−0.022
	—	(−0.34)
Observations	648	593
R^2	0.20	0.19
Standard error	1.68	1.68
Mean of dependent variable	0.13	0.13
Condition number	14.34	16.63

Sources: As in table 4.3.

Note: All growth rates here, both for the dependent and the independent variables, equal the rate of change of logarithms calculated from lease to lease; they are all measured in percentage per year. The TFP growth rates are not adjusted for taxes, but as is shown in Appendix A, part 13, the lack of a tax adjustment will not affect the regression coefficients because the growth rate of taxes relative to rents figures among the explanatory variables. Years before 1520 are omitted; *t* statistics are in parentheses.

and prices, and by as much as 64 percent, if we calculate with the alternative prices. Some of the increase reflected more efficient transportation, but only a fraction—perhaps as little as 3 or 4 percent. What the greater productivity implied for the food supply must wait for a moment. So must explaining what it resulted from: higher yields, new crops, or savings of labor and capital. The task for the moment is to survey agricultural productivity in the rest of France.

PRODUCTIVITY TRENDS ELSEWHERE IN FRANCE

The same method applies equally well to other parts of early modern France, as long as the assumptions still hold. Having explained the method at length for the Paris Basin, we can move through the evidence with greater speed, though given the idiosyncracies of the French countryside— idiosyncracies that social historians cherish—each TFP series and each region will still demand individual attention. Unfortunately, the method will not take root everywhere, and the places where it does bear fruit are not a random sample of French farms. Nonetheless, the method still has considerable merit. Perhaps its greatest virtue is that it paints the clearest picture ever available of the potential for growth in the Old Regime countryside. With it, we can locate those regions and periods that witnessed growth and determine what caused their good fortune and what spared them from stagnation. We can compare the French results with the English and the German experience, and if we have enough evidence, we can judge French agriculture as a whole. We can estimate whether agricultural output kept pace with the population or whether output per agricultural worker lagged far behind England.

Applying the method does involve dealing with certain recurrent problems. In some parts of France, of course, the available evidence is rickety; other regions lack the necessary prices, wages, or usable leases. In much of the southwest, for example, sharecropping predominated, making it impossible to know precisely what rent was paid. The same held true for parts of Provence.[52] And even where land was leased out, private agreements— contre-lettres—to revise a lease could also obscure the true rent. Elsewhere the requisite assumptions break down. We must beware of areas where mauvais gré or droit de marché makes the rental market uncompetitive. Mauvais gré, for example, rules out use of the leases diligently compiled for the Cambrésis by Hugues Neveux, and it clouds the results from other border territories—Flanders and Hainaut—where Old Regime agriculture was reputedly thriving.[53] There are also difficulties when crops and products vary widely, for we have assumed that the shares of the various farm products in total revenue remained constant. If, for example, a farmer raises livestock where he once grew grain—as in parts of Normandy in the seventeenth and eighteenth centuries—the portion of his revenues coming from livestock will swell enormously. An analogous shift would take place when vineyards spread, as in the Beaujolais or in parts of Provence.[54]

More insidious problems crop up when the evidence wears thin. The ideal of course is a large collection of leases, one that tracks the same properties over a long period, like the Notre Dame sample, but that is not always possible. In some regions, only a small number of properties can be followed. Are the productivity trends then mere statistical mirages? In others, rents must be averaged over different farms and plots of land, a practice that can mask subtle shifts in property characteristics and easily lead the calculations astray. If arable is converted to pasture, for instance, the surviving leases of arable will concern only fields unsuitable for conversion. Their rent might point to flat or declining productivity, despite the gains from the shift to grass and livestock. Similarly, in areas where common rights were extensive, as near the Alps or in parts of western France, access to the commons would affect land rents—and thus productivity calculations—in ways that have nothing to do with productivity itself. Barring a tenant farmer from the local commons, for example, would cut the rent he could pay and yet leave not a trace in the lease.

Still, these problems can be circumvented quite easily with a dash of historical imagination. If we cannot follow the same properties through time, regression analysis will weed out the effects of changing property characteristics. It will also help detect tenant market power and reveal whether the productivity trends are mere statistical mirages. If the problem is changing output, then the shares can be averaged before and after the new crops are planted. Once the averages shares are inserted in equation (2), they will provide an excellent estimate of TFP, making the method applicable to the new vineyards in the Beaujolais and to the Norman fields that were converted to pasture.[55] We can thus gauge the productivity gained from new crops. Some of the gains from new crops will involve true technological innovation—for example, sowing a novel crop such as maize. But at times they will simply reflect specialization, or what economists call comparative advantage, with no new techniques whatsoever. Farms may simply shift to an old technology that suits them best: raising livestock in Normandy, for example, or planting vineyards in the Beaujolais. Such specialization does allow farmers to produce more with less, and while it may not qualify as true technical change, it still counts as increased productivity.

The method of measuring productivity with prices and rents is thus worth pursuing throughout France because of the light it sheds on long-term economic growth in the French countryside. And it can be extended into a number of different territories, thanks to samples of leases from both published and archival sources. I have in fact managed to apply it to twenty-two additional localities scattered throughout France, plus, for the sake of comparison, one site in England and another in Germany (table 4.5, figure 4.3). The leases and rental figures come from a number of French archives and, to an even greater extent, from an abundant set of printed sources.[56] To use this evidence, I have by and large followed the same procedure as with the Notre Dame leases. I first constructed trends in rent and regional wages and prices, I next weighted the prices and rents via input and output shares, and I then calculated TFP lease by lease via equation (2). For each different locality I have derived a suitable set of input and output shares. They come from local farm accounts, and if local farms accounts are lacking, from nineteenth-century agricultural censuses or from farms in regions that have similar technologies.[57] Once I have calculated TFP for each lease in a locality, I average it across all the properties in the locality to yield a trend.

As with the Notre Dame sample, it is obviously worth trying alternative shares for each locality and alternative methods of averaging the prices that enter the TFP calculation. I have done so for nearly all the sites where I measure TFP (table 4.5), but in practically every case the alternative shares and alternative prices averages yielded a similar TFP trend.[58] I have therefore drawn my graphs and run my regressions using only one set of shares and prices. Adding the others would clutter the graphs without changing matters greatly.

For each locality, I verified that shares remained constant and that transportation costs did not greatly change farm-gate prices. I also sought evidence that the local rental market was competitive and entrepreneurial profits small (table 4.5). Once again, in nearly every instance, the evidence supported my assumptions, as I explain in Appendix B, part 2. Where there were doubts, I noted them in the text or the appendix and tried to assess their impact on my measurement of TFP. As for taxes, I corrected the TFP figures for the tenant's tax burden, using either actual village taxes or the method employed with the Notre Dame sample (for details, see Appendix B, part 2). And when necessary, I applied regression analysis to the TFP indices, both to estimate the rate of TFP growth and to determine whether the productivity trends were real or mere statistical mirages.

Each of the twenty-two localities has its own peculiarities that demand a modicum of individual attention. Although economic historians may wish to jump over such details and skip immediately to the next section, social historians (and particularly the skeptics among them and those who know rural France well) will want to linger over the details of each site. Let us therefore tour the various sites one by one and begin by pushing out toward the edges of the Paris Basin—south toward the Orléanais and north toward Amiens (figure 4.3). From there, we can sweep first east and then west and later descend to the south of France.

TABLE 4.5
Treatment of the Evidence Used in TFP Calculations: Sites Other Than the Notre Dame Sample

Site	Number of Leases or Figures for Value of Land	Were the Same Properties Followed Over Time? (If So, the Number of Properties Is in Parentheses)	Were Alternative Shares Constructed for the Site?	Were Alternative Price Averages Used for the Site?	Was It Possible to Check for the Effect of Short-Term Entrepreneurial profits?	Are TFP Figures Corrected for Taxes?
Orléanais	23	yes (1)	yes	yes	no	no
Near Amiens	288	yes (34)	yes	yes	yes	yes
Lorraine	12 twenty-five-year rent averages	see note	yes	no	no	no
Plain of Caen: Bretteville-L'Orgueilleuse	155	no	yes	yes	yes	yes
Plain of Caen: Cheux	22 annual rent averages	no	yes	yes	yes	yes
Plain of Caen: Rots	18 annual rent averages	no	yes	yes	yes	yes
Normandy: Caux	95 annual rent averages	yes (16)	no	yes	no	no
Normandy: Auge	see note	no	yes	not necessary	not necessary	correction not necessary
Near Nantes	54	yes (3)	yes	yes	yes	yes
Near Angers (two properties)	50	yes (2)	yes	yes	yes	yes
Near Angers (eight farms)	88	yes (8)	yes	yes	yes	yes
Near Le Mans	60	yes (10)	yes	yes	yes	yes
Ille-et-Vilaine	56	yes (12)	yes	yes	yes	yes
Gâtine Poitevine	36	yes (3)	yes	yes	yes	yes

TABLE 4.5, *(cont.)*

Near Marseille	11	yes (2)	yes	yes	no	correction not necessary
Near Avignon: Grange de la Sacristie	11	yes (1)	yes	yes	no	correction not necessary
Cavaillon	19 annual land-sale figures	no	yes	yes	no	no
Grillon	113 land sales	no	yes	yes	no	no
Albigeois	45 land sales	no	no	no	no	no
Near Béziers	172	yes (6)	yes	yes	yes	correction not necessary
Salers	see note	see note	yes	not necessary	not necessary	correction not necessary
Beaujolais	see note	no	yes	not necessary	not necessary	correction not necessary
North German Coast	rental averages; see note	no	yes	no	no	no
Hertfordshire (England)	rental averages; see note	no	yes	no	no	yes

Sources: See Chapter 4 and Appendix B, part 2.

Note: In Lorraine the evidence is taken from a published series concerning some fifty farms (gagnages), but it is not clear that the gagnages are always the same. In the Auge and the Beaujolais, the calculations involve changes in land use; entrepreneurial profits, tax corrections, and prices other than the value of land are unlikely to affect the calculation. In both cases, all that is necessary is evidence about the price of land before and after conversion, which is taken from average rental figures. In Salers, the calculations were based not on prices and rents but rather on physical evidence; it was therefore unnecessary to worry about price averages, tax corrections, or entrepreneurial profits. In other instances, where a tax correction was unnecessary, it was because taxes were paid by landlords and were included implicitly in the rent. For the sources and for the German and English calculations, see Chapter 4 and Appendix B, part 2. Appendix B also discusses—site by site—the evidence in favor of constant shares and a competitive rental market. Among the tests for constant shares was a plot of population trends alongside the ratio of rent to wages. This test was possible for the Lorraine and the sites near Nantes, Anjou, and Béziers, and it always supported the assumption of constant shares. It was possible to test for rent increases after tenants changed near Nantes and Avignon; here, the evidence supported the assumption of a competitive rental market. So did the tests for short-term entrepreneurial profits, which were conducted via regressions of ln(TFP) on the rate of increase of crop prices, as with the Notre Dame sample. In every instance, the regressions suggested that entrepreneurial profits were small. For further details, see Appendix B, part 2.

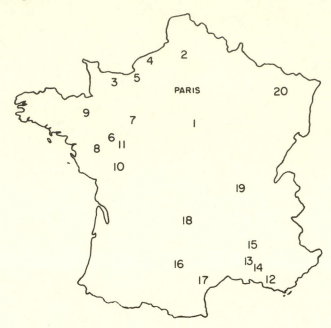

Figure 4.3 Sites of Other TFP Calculations in France.
1. Farm of Châtillon-sur-Loing in Orléanais 2. Farms near
Amiens 3. Plain of Caen in Normandy: Villages of Brette-
ville-l'Orgueilleuse, Cheux, and Rots 4. Normandy: Caux 5.
Normandy: Auge 6. Properties near Angers: Sample of Two
Properties and Sample of Eight Farms of the Hospital of
Angers 7. Farms near Le Mans 8. Holdings near Nantes 9.
Properties in Ille-et-Vilaine 10. Properties in Gâtine Poite-
vine 11. Farm of Chavais 12. Properties near Marseille
13. Grange de la Sacristie near Avignon 14. Cavaillon 15.
Grillon 16. Albigeois 17. Properties near Béziers 18. Salers
19. Beaujolais 20. Lorraine

In the Orléanais, on the farm and seigneury of Châtillon-sur-Loing, TFP
growth was practically indistinguishable from that observed closer to Paris.
The only difference was that warfare wreaked even greater havoc in Châtil-
lon than on the average Notre Dame farm. The disparities loom somewhat
larger near Amiens, where we can follow 288 decennial rent observations
for thirty-four farms belonging to the Hôtel-Dieu of Amiens (figure 4.3).
TFP there does display the same weakness in the early seventeenth century
that we noticed with the Notre Dame sample—a weakness accentuated by
the Spanish troops who invaded the region in the 1630s.[59] But in contrast
to the Notre Dame index, TFP remains utterly listless in the late eighteenth
century (figure 4.4).

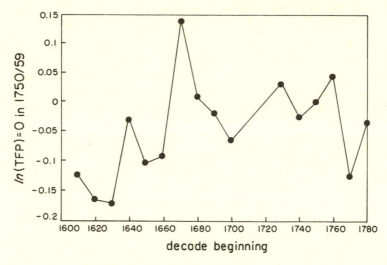

Figure 4.4 Ln(TFP) by Decade near Amiens: Thirty-four Farms. Ln(TFP) is calculated with standard shares and prices and is corrected for taxes. It is normalized to equal 0 in 1750–59 for each farm.

The torpor after 1750 might be more apparent than real, for it probably reflected a growing local problem with mauvais gré, which held down rents and masked productivity growth.[60] If not, then productivity growth near Amiens was weak indeed. We can estimate it (even if it was biased downward by mauvais gré) by regressing ln(TFP) on a constant and the decade; the coefficient of the decade in the regression is then the growth rate of TFP over the seventeenth and eighteenth centuries. Obviously, the regression should also control for the differences among the various Amiens properties, which might affect the coefficient. One way to do so is to include property characteristics in the regression, much as we did with the Notre Dame regressions. The problem, though, is that we know less about the Amiens properties than about the Notre Dame farms. An alternative strategy is to adjust the way we compute TFP, by measuring the rent on each Amiens property relative to its level in 1750–59, when rental prices are available for every farm. Measuring the rent relative to this sort of common base period filters out each property's idiosyncrasies—the richer soil or more favorable location that would otherwise boost the rent and hence our index of TFP. It leaves behind only the trend of TFP, precisely what is of greatest interest. Such a technique in fact seems ideally suited to the Amiens properties and to most of our other lease samples. Not only do we know relatively little about the properties involved, but the rental series themselves are relatively short. Because they are short, we can more easily find a common base period for relative rents—a near impossibility with the

Notre Dame sample. We have therefore computed TFP using the relative rents both in figure 4.4 and in the regressions (table 4.6). We shall use the same technique for all the other sites where the same properties can be followed through time (table 4.5).[61] In the case of the Amiens properties, the regressions with relative rents confirm that TFP growth was slow; indeed, it did not even reach a feeble 0.1 percent per year.

Mauvais gré keeps us from sampling rents north of Amiens, but we can find usable leases for parts of the northeast and the northwest of France. In northeastern France, for instance, there are the prices and rental rates gathered for Lorraine over a century ago by Charles Guyot. Guyot's rents concern some fifty farms (*gagnages*), and he collected the numbers with considerable care, showing remarkable concern for issues such as variations in land quality. The local rental market appeared competitive, justifying the use of prices and wages to calculate TFP. Unfortunately, given Guyot's method of using twenty-five-year averages, there is no way to correct the calculations for taxes.[62] As for factor and product shares, usable farm accounts are not available, but evidence reaching as far back as the sixteenth century suggests that the shares resembled those in the Paris Basin, the major difference being the lower grain yields in Lorraine. We have therefore relied upon the Parisian shares, adjusting them for the lower yields.

Figure 4.5 graphs ln(TFP) in Lorraine for several different yield assumptions. The graphs that assume the lower yields (9.2 hectoliters/hectare) or the medium yields (13.5 hl/ha) are probably more realistic, the higher yields (17 hl/ha) representing an unusual upper limit to what was possible. The shares do not appear to have changed in Lorraine, but it is possible that the lower yields prevailed in the sixteenth century and the medium ones in the eighteenth and early nineteenth centuries. If yields did in fact shift from 9.2 to 13.5 hectoliters per hectare in Lorraine, then TFP would have grown at a respectable rate of 0.2 percent per year between the middle of the sixteenth century and the late eighteenth century, and perhaps even more if we could correct for taxes. Alas, over a generation had to be wasted repairing the appalling devastation of the Thirty Years' War, which ravaged Lorraine and caused TFP to plunge in the middle of the seventeenth century. And although growth overall was respectable, the rural economy stagnated after 1750, in stark contrast to the Paris Basin.[63]

In northwestern France, TFP follows a different path. In the province of Normandy, for example, we can assess what happened to TFP on the fertile plain between Caen and Bayeux (figure 4.3). There farmers did not convert their fields to pasture, as in other parts of the province. They continued to grow grain, as in the Paris Basin, and evidence from notarial records and local farm accounts suggests that the local rental market was competitive and that factor and product shares were stable.

TABLE 4.6
Overall Growth Rates of TFP from Regressions: Selected Sites

Sample	Years Covered	TFP Growth Rate (Percent per Year)	Number of Observations
Near Amiens	1610–1789	0.04 (2.91)	288
Caux	1695–1789	–0.28 (–6.30)	95
Ille-et-Vilaine	1676–1790	–0.24 (–4.45)	56
Near Angers: two properties	1655–1785	–0.18 (–5.22)	48
Near Angers: eight farms of hospital	1640–1709	0.13 (2.39)	56
Near Le Mans: ten farms of Hôtel-Dieu	1660–1719	–0.38 (–3.86)	60
Gâtine Poitevine	1655–1782	–0.05 (–0.98)	36
Near Nantes	1645–1790	–0.21 (–6.96)	43
Farm of Chavais: western shares	1655–1790	–0.26 (–6.35)	26
Farm of Chavais: Moriceau–Postel-Vinay shares	1655–1790	–0.12 (–2.62)	26
Métairie of La Chapelle-aux-Moines: without vineyard	1699–1789	–0.35 (–4.22)	10
La Chapelle-aux-Moines: with vineyard	1699–1789	–0.03 (–0.23)	10
Grillon: full sample	1580–1745	0.22 (3.00)	113
Grillon: sales before 1700	1580–1699	0.70 (4.34)	89
Albigeois	1705–88	0.34 (3.13)	48
Near Béziers: six farms	1589–1750	–0.31 (–8.05)	110

Source: See text, Chapter 4.

Note: The TFP growth rates are estimated from regressions. In each regression, the dependent variable is ln(TFP), calculated with the standard shares and prices averaged over the current year and the previous eight. The coefficient of the year then gives the TFP growth rate in percent per year. To correct for the differences among the properties in each sample, the TFP figures for samples with multiple properties are computed with rents measured relative to a common base period for each property; the only exceptions are the Caux sample, where I used a rent index for all the properties, and the Grillon and Albigeois samples, where, because the properties were all distinct, I corrected for property differences via rent regressions. All the TFP figures are corrected for taxes except for Caux, Chavais, La Chapelle-aux-Moines, Grillon, Albigeois, and Béziers. For Béziers, the lack of a tax correction does not matter because taxes there were paid by landlords rather than tenants. For La Chapelle-aux-Moines, the regressions are restricted to a common set of years for which all the necessary data are available. The numbers in parentheses are t statistics.

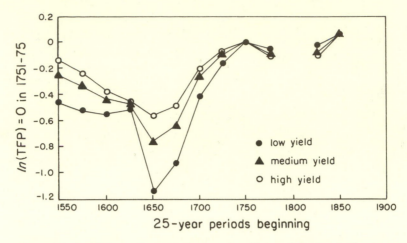

Figure 4.5 Ln(TFP) on Gagnages in Lorraine. Shares differ by yield assumption.

In the village of Bretteville-l'Orgueilleuse, where the large hedged fields of the Cairon family reminded Marc Bloch of English enclosures, TFP surged ahead at an annual rate of 0.4 percent in the sixteenth century; it apparently grew most rapidly on the village's enclosed fields. By the seventeenth century, however, TFP collapsed (figure 4.6). The causes perhaps were the heavy taxes levied early in the century and the havoc wreaked in suppressing the Nu-Pied tax revolt of 1639. As with the Notre Dame sample, the Bretteville figures adjust for the portion of profits that went to pay taxes, but not for the economic disruption of having livestock seized and tax revolts put down by force.

We cannot follow the same properties in Bretteville and must rely instead upon a sample of 155 leases of distinct properties—leases culled from notarial records, family papers, and religious archives. The sample tends to overlook large properties, and because it dwindles in the late sixteenth century—there is only one lease between 1580 and 1619—it cannot shed light on the Wars of Religion. It also wears thin again in the late eighteenth century, and its shallowness casts some doubt on the path graphed in figure 4.6, as do problems with the local prices that enter into the indexes C and P. Still, the evidence from Bretteville cannot simply be dismissed out of hand. It is comforting to note, for instance, that TFP apparently took a similar path in the nearby village of Cheux. There, too, it rose in the sixteenth century, only to be dashed after 1600; and while TFP in Cheux recovered in the eighteenth century, it did not surpass the levels of two centuries before. The TFP indices for Rots, another nearby community, do not extend back to the sixteenth century, but they too suggest a nadir in the second half of the seventeenth century. Local yields and tithe

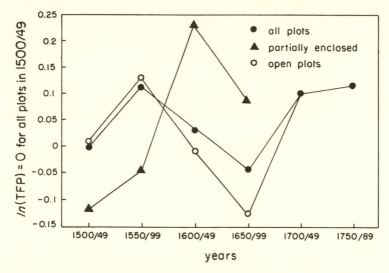

Figure 4.6 Ln(TFP) in Bretteville-l'Orgueilleuse: Open and Partially Enclosed Plots. Partially enclosed plots are at least 50 percent enclosed.
Open plots have no enclosure at all.

series, which would be unaffected by any errors in *C* and *P*, only reinforce
this story. Yields were already high at the beginning of the seventeenth
century, as we would expect after the explosive growth of the preceding
century. As for tithe series, though fragmentary, they trace out a depression
in the seventeenth century, just like the graphs of TFP.[64]

Furthermore, regression analysis tends to confirm the story told by the
Bretteville leases, even though the sample appears relatively small. If
ln(TFP) in Bretteville is regressed on time (and on one of the chief property
characteristics, the fraction of the property that was enclosed), then overall growth from the sixteenth century to the French Revolution is nearly
flat, just as figure 4.6 would suggest (table 4.7). But if the regressions
are instead performed century by century, they substantiate both the rapid
TFP growth in the sixteenth century and the equally swift decline after
1600 and suggest that neither part of the roller-coaster ride was a statistical
fluke.[65]

In the eighteenth century, productivity growth in Bretteville seemed
flabby indeed, although the size of the sample counsels against undue certainty here. In at least one other corner of Normandy—the territory of
Caux—productivity was also flaccid after 1700: there, it appeared to decline at a 0.3 percent rate in the eighteenth century (figure 4.3 and table
4.6).[66] But there were also parts of Normandy where arable was converted
to pasture, a prime source of productivity growth in early modern agriculture. Conversion to pasture not only played upon comparative advantage

TABLE 4.7
Regressions of Ln(TFP) in Bretteville-l'Orgueilleuse: Various Periods

Independent Variables	Ln(TFP) for Leases[a]				
	1520–1776	1520–1599	1600–1699	1700–1776	1520–1776 (All leases— Alternative Specification)
Constant	1.20	–5.42	8.34	3.08	1.39
	(2.08)	(–1.69)	(3.72)	(1.01)	(2.34)
Time (units of 100 years)	0.00	0.44	–0.43	–0.10	–0.01
	(0.14)	(2.11)	(–3.18)	(–0.56)	(–0.20)
Percentage of property enclosed	0.14	–0.25	0.31	—	0.09
	(2.07)	(–1.25)	(4.18)		(1.16)
Houses per acre	—	—	—	—	0.09
					(0.69)
Percentage of pasture	—	—	—	—	–0.08
					(–0.88)
Ln(area in acres)	—	—	—	—	0.02
					(1.15)
R^2	0.04	0.24	0.25	0.02	0.06
Number of observations	104	21	65	18	104
Condition number	56.88	165.35	185.50	172.12	65.78

Source: See text, Chapter 4.

Note: The dependent variable in each regression is ln(TFP), which is calculated with the Moriceau–Postel-Vinay shares and prices averaged over the previous lease. It is corrected for taxes. The numbers in parentheses are t statistics, and the coefficient of time is the growth rate of TFP in percent per year. None of the eighteenth-century leases involved enclosed property; hence, the percentage enclosed was omitted from the eighteenth-century regressions. The alternative specification will be discussed in Chapter 5; it adds a measure of farmhouses per acre, percentage of pasture, and area. The areas here are in the local measure and do not equal modern acres.

[a] TFP could not be calculated for leases before 1520.

in areas where climate or distance from markets favored stock raising; it could also boost grain yields on whatever arable fields remained. And in the portion of Normandy known as the Pays d'Auge, the conversion was pushed further than in nearly any other part of Old Regime France (figure 4.3). Farmers and merchants in the Auge region raised livestock and fattened animals born elsewhere—cattle from Brittany, Maine, and Poitou, for example. The animals were then sold to local merchants and to buyers from Rouen and Paris. The demand, especially from Paris, was so strong that farmers in the seventeenth and eighteenth centuries converted much of their arable to pasture, relying for grain supplies upon nearby regions such as the plain near Caen. Exactly how much land was converted one can only guess, but a reasonable estimate is that arable dropped from 70 percent of the farmland in 1600 to only 35 percent in 1830, with pasture rising accordingly.[67]

What was the effect on TFP? Knowing precisely would involve knowing prices, rents, and factor and product shares for a property actually converted to pasture, and it would require the information both before and after the property was turned into pasture. We would then calculate TFP from equation (2) both before and after the conversion, using the average of the shares from when the property was arable and when it was pasture. The ratio of TFP after the conversion to TFP before would be the productivity increase. Unfortunately, it is simply impossible to find all the evidence needed for such an exacting calculation. But we can grope toward an upper bound for the TFP increase by looking at prevailing rental rates for arable and pasture. If arable could be turned into pasture rapidly and at little cost, then a farmer would face the same prices and wages after conversion as before. Except for rent, the prices and wages in equation (2) would be no different before than after the conversion. If we assume that the conversion would not change the fraction of rent going for taxes—a reasonable approximation—the TFP increase would reduce to $(r_{after}/r_{before})^s$, where r_{after} is the average rent after conversion, r_{before} the rent before, and s the average of the factor shares of land before and after conversion. In nonmathematical terms, TFP would rise if conversion increased the rent. The only flaw is that the TFP figure here is an upper bound—something of an optimistic guess—because it ignores the resources expended in transforming arable into pasture, and because some of the conversion may merely stem from a shift in prices with no change in productivity whatsoever.[68]

If we perform such a calculation for the Auge, though, the results are disappointing. Even with generously optimistic assumptions about the size of the rent increase and the pace of conversion to pasture, TFP for the Auge as a whole only creeps along at a rate of less than 0.1 percent per year. For an individual field, the results could admittedly be dramatic: a TFP increase of nearly 70 percent was perhaps the outer limit of what was possible.[69] But for the Auge as a whole, the dramatic effects were muted. The process of conversion to pasture stretched out over decades, and even in the Auge, one of the most specialized examples of Old Regime agriculture, too much land remained frozen in grain production to allow conversion to have a large impact.

Elsewhere in the west of France, we have 344 rental prices from properties near Le Mans, Angers, and Nantes, and from eastern Brittany and the Gâtine Poitevine as well: decennial rent observations for ten farms of the Hôtel-Dieu of Le Mans and eight farms of the Saint-Jean Hospital of Angers; and leases on two additional properties near Angers, three holdings east of Nantes, twelve in the Ille-et-Vilaine in eastern Brittany, and three in the Gâtine Poitevine (figure 4.3). Discussing them all in the same breath

might spark some objections, but agriculture throughout these western territories had long shared certain common characteristics. Much of the area
was *bocage*, a landscape of fields enclosed by hedges and trees, which gave
travelers the impression of forest "sprinkled with isolated clearings."[70]
Here livestock predominated over cereals. Some fields were of course
sown with grain—typically several harvests of rye and perhaps oats or
buckwheat—but they were then left to grow over, perhaps for years, with
grass or furze, on which animals grazed. Arthur Young remarked upon the
common characteristics—the immense expanses of wasteland, the seemingly backward crop rotation, and the farms that produced little more than
livestock—when he toured Brittany, Maine, and Anjou on the eve of the
French Revolution. The same similarities emerge from the reports of the
royal intendants in the seventeenth and eighteenth centuries and from the
statistics of the first prefects at the dawn of the nineteenth century.[71] Crop
rotations and outputs were alike; so was the use of agricultural capital.
When in 1710 Laurent Ripocheau and his partner René Babonneau fell
behind in the rent due on the *métairie* of La Chapelle-aux-Moines, 23 kilometers east of Nantes, a court-ordered sale revealed that they used almost
the same amount of livestock as farmers 50 kilometers southeast in the
Gâtine Poitevine.[72]

The parallels do not mean that factor and product shares were everywhere identical: that much is apparent from a comparison of eighteenth-
century farm accounts from the Gâtine and from near Laval, which lay
roughly halfway between Le Mans and the city of Rennes in eastern Brittany. The labor factor share in the Gâtine (.36) is smaller than near Laval
(.52), and the land share correspondingly larger. But the output shares are
fairly close, and, more important, the differences in factor shares are not
great enough to shift the trend of TFP. Because both sets of shares trace out
similar paths for productivity growth, we shall use the Gâtine shares as our
standard for estimating TFP.[73]

For all the western samples, the indexes *C* and *P* will be based on a
single set of prices. Certainly, it would be preferable to use different prices
for regions as distant as say, the Gâtine and the Ille-et-Vilaine. Ignoring
price differences between such regions may add a bit of uncertainty to our
results, as will certain gaps in the price series themselves. In the end, however, the price differences are likely to have little impact on the TFP calculations, because prices throughout the west tended to run in parallel. This
was clearly true for livestock, which was transported across the region as
part of a trade that reached as far as Paris. The same was true for animal
products such as meat and even butter, and probably for labor as well, since
it too was mobile. But the parallelism held for grain as well: prices in Angers and Rennes, for example, moved together, and their ratio showed no
trend. We can in any case minimize the effect of regional price differences

by taking the price of grain from a market such as Angers, which was roughly in the middle of our western properties. And we can recalculate TFP with grain prices from other markets to see if the productivity trend is disturbed: it turns out to be practically the same.[74]

In the west, the samples follow the same properties through time (table 4.5). To correct for differences among the various properties, we therefore measure rents relative to a common base period for each sample, just as with the Amiens farms. Taxes are adjusted for, as with the Notre Dame leases. Figure 4.7 (parts A and B) displays the resulting trend of ln(TFP) for each of the western samples. Except for the eight farms near Angers and the ten farms near Le Mans, where the evidence stems from decennial rent observations, ln(TFP) is averaged over twenty-five-year periods. Unfortunately, although the rental series extended back to the beginning of the seventeenth century for some of the samples, the fragmentary price data made it impossible to push the TFP calculations back before the 1640s.

Overall, the trend is grim, almost uniformly so. All across the west, TFP remains flat or drops, sometimes sharply. The agrarian economy seems particularly dismal in the eighteenth century, when TFP dips below the levels of the late 1600s; even in the late eighteenth century productivity seems weak or in decline. Regressions confirm the bleak trend. If ln(TFP) is regressed on a constant and time, the coefficient of the year—the TFP growth rate—is only positive for the eight farms near Angers, a sample that does not reach beyond 1700–1709 (table 4.6). Even then the growth rate is only a feeble 0.1 percent per year. Elsewhere it is even worse—flat or negative. The same dismal story repeats itself no matter what the shares and no matter how prices are averaged. Taking grain prices from Rennes rather than Angers makes little difference either.[75] Nothing, it appears, can shake this story: neither changing the shares, nor the prices, nor the way they are averaged.

One might hesitate perhaps before accepting this tale of woe. One might worry that the rental figures, particularly if they are taken from published sources, omitted additions to the rent that were common in the west: additions such as entry fines, seigneurial dues, in-kind payments that were difficult to convert to cash, and rent increases specified in secret contre-lettres. Yet it is unlikely that omitted rent led to an underestimate of TFP. Every bit of the rent is included for the farms in the Gâtine and for the métairie of La Chapelle-aux-Moines near Nantes, and yet their productivity still sloped down (figure 4.7A and, see later, figure 4.9). And on the other farms near Nantes and the holdings in the Ille-et-Vilaine, the additions to the rent could not have been large enough to change the trend of TFP.[76]

Conceivably, the decline in productivity could reflect diminishing access to the west's abundant commons—the woods and the abundant wasteland on which livestock grazed. As we know from Chapter 2, conflict broke

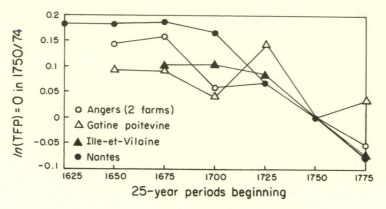

Figure 4.7A Ln(TFP) in the West: Twenty-five-Year Averages for Se-lected Sites. Ln(TFP) is corrected for taxes, calculated with standard shares and prices, and, for each site, normalized to be 0 in 1750–74. The sites are the two properties near Angers, the properties in the Gâtine Poitevine, those in the Ille-et-Vilaine, and those near Nantes.

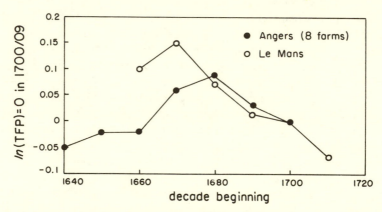

Figure 4.7B Ln(TFP) in the West: Decennial Averages for Selected Sites. Ln(TFP) is corrected for taxes, calculated with standard shares and prices, and, for each site, normalized to be 0 in 1700–1709. The sites are the eight farms of the Hospital of Angers and the farms near Le Mans.

out in the west over access to the commons, and in some instances the local commons was plowed under for conversion to arable. That was particularly likely in the eighteenth century, when the state was encouraging land recla-mation. The loss of access to grazing land could have reduced both the rent and our estimate of TFP, even though actual productivity would remain unchanged. Yet we should not exaggerate the effects of land reclamation.

The three farms near Nantes suffered absolutely no loss of access to commons, but their productivity still dropped sharply (figure 4.7A). Furthermore, very little acreage was actually reclaimed from the commons, and what was reclaimed was often cultivated for only a short time, after which it returned to its original state. All in all, it seems unlikely that the loss of the commons can explain the dismal trend of productivity in the west of France.[77]

Painting the agrarian economy in such broad strokes may perhaps upset social historians who know western France well; for them, lumping together properties from different parts of the west may well pose a problem. Not all the west was bocage, they might say, and agriculture could vary within minuscule regions—in some instances from village to village—as farmers adapted to the local terrain. The diversity was perhaps greatest in the province of Anjou, the area about Angers. Much of the province was bocage, but in parts of southeastern Anjou the bocage gave way to open plain and to rich farms resembling those in the Paris Basin. Elsewhere in Anjou agriculture was labor intensive—given over to vines, for example. Vineyards were also important near Nantes, where they spread in the eighteenth century in response to foreign demand from Dutch merchants in Nantes, bringing prosperity in their wake.[78]

The effect of such differences, though, was small. The reason is that it is hard to find individual properties in our western samples that escaped from the general trend—farms whose rent rose dramatically, while others fell. Conceivably, the wrong shares might be leading the calculations astray: farms that did not fit the western pattern might have different shares and hence a different index of TFP. The farm of Chavais might be such an example. One of the properties in Anjou, it lay southeast of Angers, on the very edge of the region where farming reminded observers of the prosperous arable in the Paris Basin (figure 4.3). Since Chavais straddled the border between bocage and plain, it ought perhaps to be treated as an arable farm and its productivity recalculated using different shares—for instance, the shares from the Chartier farm in the Paris Basin. But if we do so, we find that the path of TFP changes little and then only after 1750 (figure 4.8). True, TFP no longer dips as sharply, but the overall trend is still down, with TFP declining at a 0.1 percent annually instead of 0.3 percent (table 4.6).[79]

The effect of the vineyards near Nantes also appears limited. The métairie of La Chapelle-aux-Moines—one of the three farms near Nantes—included some vines, but if we recalculate TFP by incorporating them into the shares, the farm's productivity does not suddenly shoot skyward (figure 4.9 and table 4.6).[80] Instead of declining, it simply flattens out. And on La Chapelle and the other two neighboring farms, TFP growth is not any faster on the farms where vines are grown.[81] Despite the vines and the

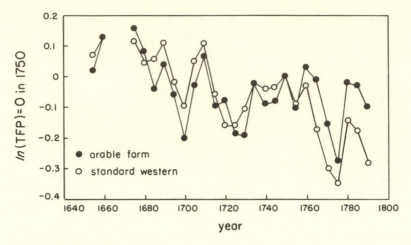

Figure 4.8 Ln(TFP) on the Farm of Chavais: Arable Shares versus Western Shares. Ln(TFP) is calculated with the standard western shares and with shares from the Moriceau–Postel-Vinay arable farm. The same prices and price averages are used in both cases. Neither calculation involves a correction for taxes.

patches of prosperous arable, despite all the local varieties of western agriculture, productivity in the west undeniably was stunted. The TFP curves are of course not the only evidence of western agricultural stagnation. Indeed, tithe records paint much the same picture of a precipitous fall from a peak late in the seventeenth century.[82]

In southeastern France, the story is not so uniformly bleak. There we can pursue TFP at a number of locations in what is now the departments of the Bouches-du-Rhône and the Vaucluse: near Marseilles in the Bouches-du-Rhône; in the vicinity of Cavaillon and Avignon in the Vaucluse; and in the village of Grillon further north in the same department (figure 4.3). Near Avignon, on the Grange de la Sacristie, TFP apparently grew rapidly in the seventeenth century (0.5 percent per year) and then declined with nearly equal speed (0.4 percent) a century later (figure 4.10, part A). The TFP indices include no correction for taxes, but none is needed, for here and in the surrounding region it was landlords rather than tenants who paid the tax bill.[83] True, the graph plots a mere eleven leases for the farm and only three for the seventeenth century—too feeble a basis for any sort of conclusion. But an analogous pattern emerges from an analysis of 113 land sales contracts from the village of Grillon in the northern Vaucluse, where TFP seems to rise over the course of the seventeenth century, only to decline after 1700 (figure 4.10, part B).[84] Obviously, the sales contracts cannot track the same properties over time, but the TFP calculations do correct for varying property characteristics. The high variance of land

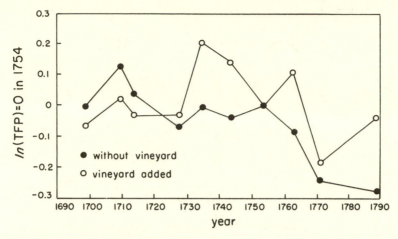

Figure 4.9 Ln(TFP) on the Métairie of La Chapelle-aux-Moines near Nantes: With and without Vineyard. The standard western shares are used to compute Ln(TFP) without the vineyard, and they are modified to include the costs and revenue from the vineyard. There is no tax correction.

prices may raise questions about the trend in Grillon, but there is little doubt that TFP rose over the seventeenth century. Regressions reveal that the increase—a rapid 0.7 percent annually between 1580 and 1699—was not a statistical aberration (table 4.6), and fiscal documents from neighboring regions also argue for thriving agricultural productivity in the seventeenth century.[85]

In Grillon, as on the Grange de la Sacristie, TFP does seem to fall in the eighteenth century, although the sample contains far too few eighteenth-century contracts to lend credence to such a conclusion. It is true that TFP seemed sluggish in other parts of the southeast after 1700. Regional land-sale prices collected by Jean-Laurent Rosenthal for the region about Cavaillon point to stagnant TFP in eighteenth-century Provence (figure 4.10, part B), as do leases gathered by René Baehrel for two properties near Marseilles. All imply TFP growth rates of no more than 0.1 percent per year after 1700.[86]

Because of the prevalence of sharecropping, usable leases grow rare in southwestern France, but forty-five land-sale contracts do permit a calculation of TFP for the Albigeois (figure 4.3), where TFP apparently grew at a rapid pace during the eighteenth century—some 0.3 percent per year (table 4.6). Although the regression suggests that the growth rate is not a fluke produced by the small sample, the figure is still not completely trustworthy. The price data are simply too tattered, and there is unfortunately no way to correct the TFP index for the burden of taxes or to test its sensitivity to alternative shares and price averages.

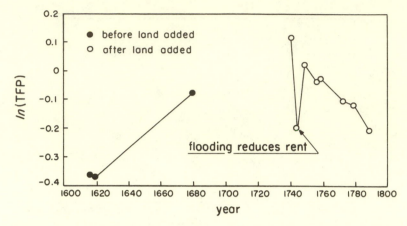

Figure 4.10A Ln(TFP) in Provence: The Grange de la Sacristie near Avignon. In the eighteenth century, the farm was leased along with additional land, making it impossible to compare the TFP figures from the seventeenth century with those after 1700.

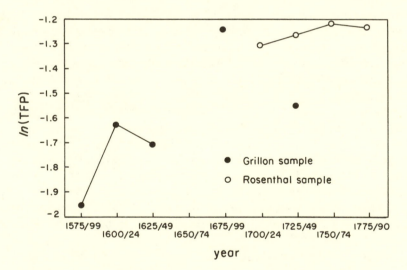

Figure 4.10B Ln(TFP) in Provence: Grillon and Rosenthal's Unirrigated Samples. It is not possible to compare results from the Grillon sample with those from the Rosenthal sample because the units are different. The TFP measurements are not adjusted for differences in land quality and location.

In between the Albigeois and the properties in the southeast, we can estimate TFP for agriculture near Béziers in southeastern Languedoc (figure 4.3), where 172 leases survive for six properties, ranging from a parcel of roughly 3 hectares to a giant farm of 154 hectares. TFP for the six properties can be computed using local prices and shares from local farm accounts. To adjust for differences among the properties, the rents are measured relative to a common base period, as with the Amiens farms. There is no need for a tax correction because near Béziers it was the landlord rather than the tenants who paid the fisc.[87]

Once TFP is calculated for the Béziers properties, the results are bleak indeed, for TFP stagnates in the late sixteenth and seventeenth centuries and then collapses after 1680. From start to finish, TFP near Béziers fell at a 0.3 percent annual rate (table 4.6 and figure 4.11). Conceivably, the dismal results near Béziers are the fault of our sample. Although it begins with six properties, there are really only two that remain from 1690 on. Furthermore, although the farms in the sample are assumed to grow some grapes, they may have failed to profit from a shift to wine production that brought prosperity to the area in the eighteenth and nineteenth centuries. Still, the specialization in wine production was limited under the Old Regime, and our method would undoubtedly have detected any gains from the extension of vineyards, which would show up in higher rent. In addition, other sources tell the same story: the records of the tithe, for example, and the portrait drawn by Emmanuel Le Roy Ladurie in *Les paysans de Languedoc*. They only confirm the grim picture of an agricultural crisis late in the seventeenth century.[88]

For certain parts of France, TFP estimates are still missing. We lack them where sharecropping prevailed, as in the southwest, and where the soil was covered with vines. They are also missing for the vital stock-raising areas of the Alps, the Pyrenées, and the Massif Central. There, common property rights rule out the use of prices and wages to compute TFP, for no document records what the grazing land actually cost. Worse, when leases exist in these regions, they are often of little value.[89] But for one location in the Massif Central—near Salers in the department of the Cantal (figure 4.3)—we can calculate TFP, thanks to physical evidence that James Goldsmith has gathered. In a territory where cheese was the major product realized from herds of cattle, Goldsmith demonstrates that cheese production per cow increased 31 percent between 1705–20 and 1775–89. That can be translated into TFP growth at the expense of certain assumptions, which can be pushed to extremes to yield an upper limit of productivity growth. We can borrow product shares from early-nineteenth-century census records and make them as large as possible so as to exaggerate TFP growth. We also suppose that the cheese was produced with no additional land, labor, and capital—an overly optimistic assumption, given that more

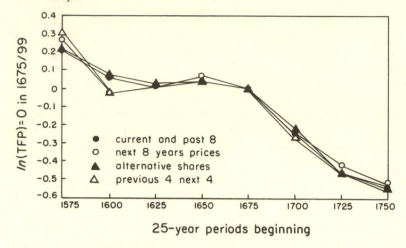

25-year periods beginning

Figure 4.11 Ln(TFP) near Béziers in Languedoc: Twenty-five-Year Averages for Six Farms. Ln(TFP) has been calculated with alternative shares and price averages. The price averages include the current year and the previous eight years; the current year and the next eight; and the previous four years, the current year, and the next four years. Because landlords paid taxes, there is no tax correction.

cheese probably did involve the use of some additional resources. Even under these assumptions, TFP grew at a modest 0.1 to 0.2 percent annually—hardly a stunning pace—and in all likelihood, the lower figure is closer to reality.[90]

Estimating TFP is also possible for one important region of viticulture, the Beaujolais, where much arable was converted to vineyard in the early modern period (figure 4.3). Conversion swept through the eastern reaches of the province in the seventeenth century, reaching western Beaujolais by the 1700s. In western Beaujolais it was driven by newly felt demand from Paris, and it depended on the creation of a network of merchants and transporters, who shipped the wine overland to the Loire river and then through the Canal de Briare and the Canal du Loing to Paris.[91] We can estimate the resulting TFP increase via the same method we used to compute productivity growth for conversion of pasture in the Auge; we need only the fraction of land converted, the rental value of arable and vineyard, and the factor share of land before and after conversion. Again, the estimate will exaggerate TFP growth somewhat, for it ignores the resources expended in planting vineyard and overlooks the possibility that some of the shift to viticulture may have been a simple response to prices, with no change in productivity. But we reduce the error by taking only lower values for the rental value of vineyard. Depending on shares and rental rates used and on the amount of land actually converted, TFP growth rate in western

Beaujolais forged ahead at between 0.3 and 0.4 percent per year in the eighteenth century, a rapid rate indeed.[92] Unfortunately, the growth affected only a small area—roughly what is today the arrondissement of Villefranche. As in the Auge, the benefits were not widespread.

The TFP figures we now have are unlikely to lead us too far astray in judging Old Regime agriculture, despite the gaps in the list of sites. While the sites are not random, there do seem to be enough of them to represent three major farming regions: the southeast, the western bocage, and the northern arable, from Normandy through the Paris Basin to Lorraine. For these regions, at least, we have enough data to estimate long-term TFP growth rates. For the Paris Basin and Lorraine, we can perform the necessary calculations using the twenty-five-year averages derived from the Notre Dame sample and the Lorraine rental series. For arable farming in Normandy, we can pool the evidence from the three sites near Caen (Bretteville, Cheux, and Rots) and regress the logarithm of TFP on the year and on dummy variables for each site. As in table 4.6, the coefficient of the year will yield an overall growth rate of TFP, while the dummy variables correct for the idiosyncracies of the individual site—its location, its soil quality, or the different units used in measuring local rents. And we can perform similar regressions for our sites in the west and the southeast.

Table 4.8 displays the results. It includes a separate and somewhat hypothetical calculation for the late eighteenth century, under the assumption that TFP growth rose in the Paris Basin, while remaining the same in Lorraine, Normandy, the west, and the southeast. Since our discussion suggests that TFP growth probably slackened in these four regions in the late eighteenth century, the figures in the rightmost column probably err on the side of optimism outside of the Paris Basin.

Before we discuss the significance of the figures in table 4.8, we might also try combining them to estimate productivity growth for French agriculture as a whole. While such an exercise will be shrouded in uncertainty, it can at least suggest a range of possibilities for the evolution of TFP. The key to the exercise is to divide France up into regions for which average agriculture rent levels are known. We then impute to each region a likely range of TFP growth figures, using the evidence from our sites. These regional TFP estimates can then be translated back into growth rates of regional rents relative to the local prices in the indexes P and C. The growth rates of rent imply a rise in average rental levels for each region, which allows us to calculate the increase in rent (relative to prices) for France as a whole. That in turn yields a crude estimate for the evolution of TFP on a national level.

Where, though, do we get average rent levels for various regions of France? There are no censuses that compile farm rents until the middle of

TABLE 4.8
TFP Growth Rates, Major Regions

| | | TFP Growth Rate (Percent/Year) | |
| | | Overall | Late Eighteenth Century |
Region	Years Covered	Overall	Late Eighteenth Century
Paris Basin	1520–1789	0.13	0.31
Northeast (Lorraine)	1550–1789	0.13	0.13
Normandy (near Caen)	1520–1785	0.01	0.01
West	1611–1790	–0.16	–0.16
Southeast	1580–1790	0.21	0.21

Sources: Notre Dame sample (Paris Basin); Lorraine rent index; Bretteville, Cheux, Rots leases and rental series (Normandy); leases and rental series from near Nantes, Angers, Le Mans, the Ille-et-Vilaine, and the Gâtine Poitevine (west); rental and sales figures from near Marseille, Avignon, Grillon, and Cavaillon (southeast).

Note: All calculations are done with standard shares and price averages. Growth rates for Paris Basin and Lorraine are calculated from twenty-five-year averages. For the other regions, they are calculated by pooling the observations and running regressions on the year and on dummy variables for each sample. For the late eighteenth century, I assumed that TFP growth remained the same in Lorraine, Normandy, the west and the southeast, while for the Paris Basin I calculated it from the difference between TFP in 1750–74 and TFP in 1775–89. The TFP figures are not corrected for changes in transportation costs in the Paris Basin, but they are corrected for taxes there, in Normandy, and in the west.

the nineteenth century. The only data available for the entire country (or at least for most of it) are the figures Arthur Young collected on the eve of the French Revolution. Young divided France into regions based on soil types and estimated the areas and average rents for each of his regions. Certainly, his evidence is far from unimpeachable. But it is far from worthless, and the errors involved are probably small in a process that is itself only a rough approximation.[93] I have therefore relied on Young's rental figures and assigned TFP growth rates to his regions, using the evidence from tables 4.6 and 4.8. His loam district, for instance, covered much of northern France plus much smaller portions of the southwest and the Massif Central. Since it included Normandy and most of the Paris Basin, I assigned it their TFP growth rates as a low and high possibility. TFP growth rates were imputed to the other regions for similar reasons. The result is a range of possibilities for French agriculture as a whole, both over the long run and for the late eighteenth century (table 4.9).

Perhaps the most obvious flaw is the lack of evidence for the mountains, the southwest, and the sort of gardens and vineyards that our lease samples omit. The lack of evidence, though, is unlikely to change the results very much. It is hard to imagine, for instance, that the stock-raising farms in the

TABLE 4.9
Estimated TFP Growth, France

Young's Regions	Weight (from Young's Area)	Young's Rent 1789 (Livres/Sterling per Acre)	TFP Growth (Percent/Year)	
			Overall	Eighteenth Century
Loam	0.24	1.19	0.01/0.13	0.01/0.31
Mountain	0.24	0.88	−0.31/0.21	0.21
Stony	0.17	1.08	0.13	0.13
Chalk	0.14	0.34	−0.16/0.13	−0.16/0.31
Heath	0.21	0.81	−0.16/0.00	−0.16/0.00
Overall TFP growth			−0.08/0.12	0.04/0.19

Sources: Tables 4.6, 4.8, and Young, *Voyages en France*, 2:600, 837.

Note: The regions are Young's. I have left out two additional regions, which covered only 9 percent of the country. For each of his regions I assume a range of TFP growth rates based on overall growth rates in tables 4.6 and 4.8. For the loam region, I used TFP growth in Normandy and the Paris Basin. For the mountain region, I used the southeast and the sample near Béziers for the overall growth rates, and the southeastern figure only for the eighteenth century because the Béziers sample does not extend past 1750. For the stony region, I used Lorraine. For the chalk, I used the west and Paris. For the heath, I used the west, with an alternative assumption that the western figures were biased downward and that TFP was actually constant. I translated these TFP growth assumptions into rent increases (relative to prices), using Young's rents and then weighted by his areas to get a national rent increase, which then implied a growth rate of TFP.

mountains would yield a TFP growth rate higher than what we found in Provence, or lower than that recorded near Béziers. As for the southwest, the real difference there would presumably be the new crop, maize. Could it have pushed the Old Regime's TFP upward, with help from the vineyards, the gardens, and the specialty crops that our samples omit? We can hazard a guess by examining the 1852 agricultural census. In 1852, the area devoted to maize, vineyard, gardens, potatoes, and industrial crops amounted to about 12 percent of French farmland. If the percentage were the same under the Old Regime (in all likelihood, it was smaller), then even rapid productivity growth in gardens, vineyards, or fields of maize would leave little mark on French TFP as a whole, for the area involved was too small. Suppose that the TFP were advancing at a rapid 0.4 percent a year in vineyards, gardens, and maize fields—the same torrid pace achieved in the Beaujolais. Then, even under the most generous assumptions, the addition to TFP for France as a whole would be less than 0.05 percent a year.[94] The vineyards, gardens, fields of maize, and industrial crops simply cover too small an area to make much of a difference. The calculations for all of France are perhaps more robust than one would imagine.

JUDGING FRENCH AGRICULTURAL GROWTH

A score of TFP growth rates now lies on our palette, but the picture the rates paint of the agrarian economy is not exactly the familiar one. Usually, the agrarian economy in early modern France is portrayed in somber and unvarying hues: its technology was rigid and its productivity static, at least until 1750. This same dismal picture, as we saw in Chapter 1, colors the great syntheses of French rural history, and it haunts comparisons of England and France as well, from the eighteenth-century efforts of Arthur Young to the more recent treatment by Robert Brenner.[95] Given such enduring technological stagnation, it is hardly surprising that the history of the rural economy in France has so often been depicted in Malthusian terms, with the population growth pressing against fixed resources and disastrous crises whenever the population ventured too high. It is only after 1750 that the picture finally brightens, when the countryside finally experiences "true growth."

To be sure, this portrait of rural France has not gone unchallenged. Michel Morineau, for example, has denied that growth finally spurted after 1750. In his view, although agricultural production fluctuated wildly, even as late as 1840 it had not surpassed technological limits in place since the late Middle Ages.[96] As for our TFP indices, they paint a picture that is different still, one that is far more complex. In the first place, they suggest that productivity did grow after 1750, but that the growth was restricted to a limited number of regions: certainly the Paris Basin, and probably the Albigeois and the Beaujolais as well. Elsewhere—in the west, in the southeast, in Normandy, and in Lorraine—productivity stagnated or even declined in the 1700s. And in the sixteenth and seventeenth centuries—periods of supposed universal stagnation—growth was also possible, at least in certain regions. In the sixteenth century, TFP advanced rapidly in the Paris Basin and in Bretteville in Normandy, and during the seventeenth century it did so in the southeast.

What about the overall picture? Is it as dismal as the consensus would have it, at least for the years before 1750? Answering such questions requires a comparison with productivity growth in other countries, particularly England. The comparison with England would be more than a numerical curiosity, for it would help resolve the long-standing debate about the relative merits of agriculture in the two countries, a debate ignited in the eighteenth century by agronomists such as Duhamel du Monceau, La Salle de l'Etang, and of course Arthur Young.[97] A full comparison should involve not just productivity growth rates but absolute levels of TFP as well, for it would make little sense to demand growth of a country or a region that was already highly productive. It has long been argued, though, that levels of agriculture productivity were lower in France than across the English Channel. Furthermore, the historical consensus maintains that growth was sluggish or nonexistent in France, at least before 1750. It thus seems reasonable to begin with a comparison of TFP growth rates in various regions of early modern France, England, and Germany as well. We can then move on to examine French agriculture as a whole and then consider levels of productivity.

Was growth then impossible in France? Was the rural economy practically inert? Obviously not everywhere. In the Paris Basin, we know, growth rates could soar high by early modern standards: 0.3 to 0.4 percent per year in the sixteenth century, 0.3 percent per year or more at their peak in the late eighteenth century, depending on which shares and price averages are fed into the calculations. Other regions witnessed equally rapid change. TFP increased at 0.4 percent per year during the sixteenth century in Bretteville, at 0.5 to 0.7 percent per year during the seventeenth century in the southeast, and at better than 0.3 percent per year if we trust the figures from the Beaujolais and the Albigeois. Such growth matched the performance of farmers in England, and it could approach the best that could be achieved in early modern Europe—in the Netherlands or on the German North Sea coast, for example, where TFP forged ahead at perhaps 0.8 or 1.0 percent annually in the sixteenth century and perhaps (though this is less certain) at 0.7 percent annually in the late eighteenth century.[98]

The problem was that the French could not sustain their productivity advances. In the Paris Basin, for example, the gains in the early sixteenth century were dashed by the Wars of Religion; the recovery in the early seventeenth century was sapped by military taxes and the Fronde. In the end, agriculture near Paris suffered grievously from those setbacks. Whereas in the English Midlands farmers maintained productivity growth rates of 0.2 to 0.3 percent per year over a full two centuries, in the Paris Basin they managed only 0.13 percent over the long haul (table 4.8). They could push their farms at better than 0.3 percent per year for fifty or even seventy-five years, but an exogenous crisis would soon cut short their advances. Ultimately, it took them three centuries to accomplish what the English did in two.[99]

Outside the Paris Basin progress was equally erratic. In Bretteville, TFP gains halted in the seventeenth century, while in the southeast, the 1700s ushered in stagnation and decline. The TFP increases did maintain a 0.2 percent annual pace for over a century in the southeast, and in Lorraine as well, but in every other region the growth rate of TFP over the long run was lower, even dipping into the negative in the west and near Béziers (tables 4.6 and 4.8). Admittedly, we lack data for several regions where agriculture was undoubtedly thriving—regions of intense cultivation, such as Flanders—but adding them would not alter the story. In place after place, despite moments of considerable glory, TFP repeatedly faltered and receded, most noticeably in dire moments of crisis and war. As a result, the overall performance of French agriculture was disappointing, even under optimistic assumptions (table 4.9).

Such halting long-term progress had unpleasant implications for population growth and the standard of living. The growth rate of TFP, after all, measures the rate at which farm production expands relative to the land, labor, and capital used in farming. Given the TFP growth rates and guesses about increases in the supply of land, labor, and capital, it is possible to derive the speed at which farm production rises. In mathematical terms, equation (1) implies that total farm production Y will increase at a rate

$$\dot{Y} = \dot{T} + v_K \dot{K} + v_L \dot{L} + v_C \dot{C} \tag{4}$$

where T is TFP; K, L, and C are, respectively, the land, labor, and capital employed in farming; the v's are the corresponding factor shares; and the dots refer to rates of growth.[100] In other words, the food supply—what farms produce—will expand at a rate that reflects productivity change and the amounts of land, labor, and capital harnessed in agriculture. The greater the productivity growth and the more resources devoted to agriculture, the more food will be available.

If one calculates how fast the food supply was increasing from equation (4), the results are intriguing both for France as a whole and for the Paris Basin in particular. For the kingdom as a whole, we can imagine both an optimistic and a pessimistic scenario. The pessimistic estimate begins with the lower TFP growth rates for France in table 4.9; the optimistic estimate takes the higher rates. As for the supply of land, labor, and capital, the amount of land farmed may not have changed at all, but the optimistic scenario allows for an increase based on eighteenth-century rates of land reclamation. The agricultural labor supply can be derived from calculations made by Anthony Wrigley, leaving only growth of capital left to estimate. If we restrict capital to livestock and equipment, then the supply varied little over the long run.[101] There was, of course, additional capital in buildings and improvements to the soil—terracing, ditches, and so on—but that would be reflected in higher rents and hence find its way into our estimates for TFP.

The calculations are crude, but they imply that the food supply grew by less than 0.22 percent per year in the early modern period (table 4.10). At best, it almost doubled between 1500 and 1800. Meanwhile, the French population—depending on the estimates used—rose at the same or perhaps a slightly faster rate: 0.21 to 0.32 percent per year. With the food supply failing to edge ahead of the population, and perhaps even lagging behind, we have all the ingredients for food crises or, at the very least, a static

TABLE 4.10
Growth Rates of Population and Food Supply (Percent per Year)

| Place and Period | Growth Rate of Population | | Growth Rate of Food Supply (Estimated Range) |
	City of Paris	France	
Paris Basin			
1450–1789	0.57	—	0.20–0.36
1750–1789	0.39	—	0.46–0.53
France			
Circa 1500–circa 1800	—	0.21–0.32	–0.01–0.22
Circa 1700–circa 1800	—	0.30–0.35	0.15–0.33

Source: See text, Chapter 4.

Note: The range of population growth rates for France as a whole reflect varying estimates and different starting points (1450 or 1500). Food-supply growth rates are calculated using equation (4) with the factor shares from the Chartier farm; the Bernonville shares lead to similar results. The smaller food-supply growth rate is the pessimistic estimate, and the larger food-supply growth rate is the optimistic estimate. TFP growth rates are taken from table 4.8 for the Paris Basin and table 4.9 for France as a whole. The land supply is assumed to be constant, except in the optimistic scenario for France as a whole, which assumes growth at 0.08 percent per year. The supply of capital is constant as well, except in the Paris Basin, where the calculations assume either no capital growth or, alternatively, growth at 0.5 percent per year. Labor-force growth rates for the Paris Basin are 0.31 percent per year (1750–89) and 0.14 to 0.32 percent per year (1450–1789); for France as a whole, they are 0.14 percent per year (1500–1800) and 0.23 percent per year (1700–1800).

standard of living. And if the estimates are redone for the eighteenth century, the story remains much the same (table 4.10). The gap perhaps narrowed, so that subsistence crises ebbed away, but the standard of living stagnated. Food prices climbed, and real wages, even if they did not perform as miserably as historians once thought, failed to keep up. Only landlords had reason to be gleeful, as rents soared under the pressure of the population.[102]

The conclusions are equally grim if we use table 4.10 to sketch the evolution of output per worker, or agricultural labor productivity. The figures in the table imply that for France as a whole, agricultural output per worker rose by less than 27 percent between 1500 and 1800 and less than 10 percent during the eighteenth century. Despite all the uncertainty, the numbers are not preposterous, for Anthony Wrigley has arrived at similar increases by analyzing demographic data: 23 percent between 1500 and 1800 and 8 percent during the eighteenth century. Wrigley's estimates do suggest that the truth lies closer to the larger of our values for the evolution of the food supply, but even with the larger figures, the performance of French agriculture seems disappointing. Indeed, while labor productivity on French farms gained perhaps 27 percent between 1500 and 1800, in England, by Wrigley's method, it almost doubled.[103]

Here, the interpretation may begin to sound a bit too much like the consensus, with its gloomy refrain of near universal stagnation. It is true that table 4.10 resembles what has been proposed by consensus historians, at least for the eighteenth century, for which they are willing to make precise estimates. Joseph Goy and Emmanuel Le Roy Ladurie, for instance, have argued from tithe returns that the output of cereals grew between 0.28 and 0.42 percent per year in France during the eighteenth century, and they believe that the lower end of this range is most likely. The values in table 4.10—0.15 to 0.33 percent per year—are similar, though they do suggest that growth in the 1700s may have been even slower than Goy and Le Roy Ladurie imagined.[104] If the truth lies closer to 0.33 percent per year, as Wrigley's work implies, then we have a remarkable concordance between three different methodologies—Wrigley's, Goy and Ladurie's, and my own.

Yet, despite this agreement, there are still major differences between my story and the historical consensus. The consensus sees a break in 1750. So do I, but only in certain places. It views the sixteenth and seventeenth centuries as times of flat productivity and minimal output growth; for me, they were just as likely to achieve growth as the eighteenth. But the greatest difference between my story and the consensus lies in the role accorded temporal and regional variations in growth. The consensus historians—particularly Le Roy Ladurie—have certainly chronicled the devastating effects of warfare and crises on the temporal pattern of growth, and they have noted the variations in growth rates from region to region. But they have relegated these regional and temporal variations to a subordinate role in their overarching story of long-term stagnation followed by a 1750 breakthrough. I consider the variations far more important, so important that they make nonsense of the consensus account and confound most generalizations about France as a whole. I thus disagree with them, and I differ with the major critic of the consensus account, Michel Morineau, as well. While he acknowledges the regional and temporal variations, he too banishes them to a secondary role in his tale of enduring stagnation. For me, the regional and temporal variations were paramount. The task is in fact to explain why growth favored some periods and not others; why it visited some regions and spurned their neighbors.

Among the various regions, the one where the history of growth seems most intriguing is undoubtedly the Paris Basin, because it had an enormous city to feed. We can glimpse the problem by estimating the increase in the food supply available from Basin farms. We can then compare the Basin's food supply with the city's population in order to see if the hinterland could feed the capital.[105] If we consider the late eighteenth century, there is no doubt on this score: while the food supply jumps ahead at a rate of 0.46 to 0.53 percent per year, the city's population advances at only 0.39 percent per year (table 4.10). But if we look instead at the long run, at the sixteenth, seventeenth, and eighteenth centuries as a whole, then the tables are turned. Over this long period the local food supply could simply not have kept pace with the rapid expansion of Paris. The local food supply perhaps tripled between 1500 and 1789, but the city's population nearly quadrupled. Apart from the periods of crisis, it would have been in the years 1650–1750 that the shortfall would have been most severe, for TFP in agriculture itself—rather than transportation—was particularly sluggish and the local food supply was increasing at less than 0.1 percent per year. Over the long run, and particularly between 1650 and 1750, the city's demand simply forced merchants to fan out even farther in their search for supplies. Fortunately, it was precisely in these years that transportation costs fell and Paris began to draw upon a wider and wider area for provisioning.[106]

So far, the focus has been upon growth and stagnation. But stagnation can have a very different meaning if productivity is already high. Such high-level stagnation may seem unthinkable in early modern France, but it was a distinct possibility in certain regions. Consider, for example, the farms in Bretteville-l'Orgueilleuse and the surrounding region. Productivity there, we recall, grew rapidly in the sixteenth century but not thereafter. Yet if the local agrarian productivity stagnated, it did so at a very high level. At the end of the eighteenth century, grain yields in this region of arable farming equalled those in the Paris Basin and in other regions of rich soils and prosperous farming. Since grain was the major farm product, the productivity of land equaled that around Paris, despite the grievous setbacks of the seventeenth century. The number of workers per hectare at the end of the eighteenth resembled that around Paris as well, and because grain was the major product and grain yields were the same as those around Paris, output per worker—or labor productivity—must have been at the level of the Paris Basin, too. The productivity of capital must have been on a par with the Paris Basin as well, because the capital used per hectare— chiefly livestock—was the same as around Paris.[107] And since the productivities of land, labor, and capital were high, so was TFP.

The fragmentary physical evidence suggests that productivity in Bretteville had been elevated for a long time—indeed, ever since the spurt of growth in the sixteenth century. At the dawn of the seventeenth century, local grain yields surpassed yields in England, and the productivity of labor and capital also seemed high.[108] Agriculture near Bretteville had apparently reached elevated levels as early as 1600—productivity on par with that attained in the Paris Basin in the eighteenth century.

We could reach a similar conclusion by looking at rents, wages, and prices. If we calculate TFP for a farm in Bretteville and a contemporaneous farm in the Paris Basin, then our formula for TFP—equation (2)—will give us the relative productivities of the two farms. All we have to do is to measure our prices, wages, and rents in the same units and, if the product and factor shares are different, perform our calculations with the average shares for the two farms. The only other concern is that we take into account all of the factors besides productivity that influence the rent: factors such as the soil fertility, the farm size, and the distance to the market that provide the prices in the index P. After all, it would not do to compare a fertile piece of land just outside Paris with a stony patch of ground that was miles from where crops were sold.[109] Fortunately, the soil quality near Bretteville was similar to that near Paris. Furthermore, we can use the rental regressions for the Notre Dame sample (table 3.1) to calculate the rent for a hypothetical farm in the Paris Basin, one that was as large as an average property in Bretteville and that lay as far from Paris as Bretteville did from relevant Norman markets in Caen and Bayeux. If we do all this and then compute the relative productivities for fifty-year periods, we see that TFP in sixteenth-century Bretteville was indeed high: in fact, it surpassed productivity in the Paris Basin in the last half of the century by nearly 15 percent (figure 4.12). Agriculture near Paris more than caught up in the following century, a period of crises in Normandy, but in the eighteenth century, when the effects of the crises had been repaired, agriculture in both places was on a par.[110] Once again, productivity in Bretteville may have stagnated after 1600, but it was stagnation at a high level of productivity.

The same calculations can be repeated for other regions as well, provided we adjust for all the factors affecting the rent. If we compare TFP in the Paris Basin with TFP in Grillon in the southeast, it appears that agricultural productivity in Grillon lagged behind that in the Paris Basin by perhaps 31 percent at the beginning of the seventeenth century. After productivity surged in Grillon in the seventeenth century, the gap closed to roughly 3 percent by 1675–99; but by the second quarter of the eighteenth century, the Paris Basin was again 26 percent ahead. Whatever the doubts about these numbers, we should note that a comparison of this sort would be unthinkable if we were limited to physical evidence. The only physical evidence we have for Grillon are yields, which were lower there, at least in the late eighteenth century.[111] Yields, though, are only one bit of evidence, and it is impossible to assemble the rest of the physical evidence needed for a comparison. It is impossible to compare the productivities of labor and capital and impossible to take into account the crops other than grain— crops that were far more important in Grillon than near Paris.

The productivity gap between Grillon and the Paris Basin was thus large,

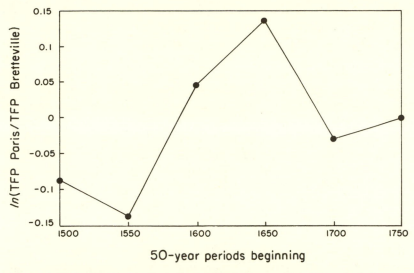

Figure 4.12 Ln(TFP in the Paris Basin/TFP in Bretteville). The calculation corrects for differences in wages, grain prices, property areas, and distance to market, but it assumes that livestock and meat prices are the same.

but an even wider one separated the Paris Basin and the west of France. If we compare the Basin and the three farms near Nantes—the western properties for which we have the most information—we find that agriculture there lagged behind the Paris Basin by an even larger amount than in Grillon. The TFP near Nantes trailed the Paris Basin by a considerable margin: by perhaps 19 percent in the late seventeenth century, and then, in the late eighteenth century, after productivity had collapsed in the west and surged ahead near Paris, by nearly 60 percent. Again, the comparison cannot claim any extraordinary precision, but the gap between the Paris Basin and the west is undeniable. It is in fact borne out by the lower yields in the west and by similar comparisons of prices and rents using nineteenth-century census results from other parts of the west.[112]

The same technique applies to comparisons between different countries. Again, we need only measure prices in the same units and correct for the various factors besides productivity that affect the rent. The appropriate exchange rate is not a problem: it simply drops out of the calculations because both the product and the factor shares add up to one. The country to choose is obviously England. Certainly, if we consider England as a whole, there is little doubt it bested France, at least in the eighteenth century. In the first place, agricultural labor in England seemed much more productive. If we trust the evidence assembled by Anthony Wrigley, then by the end of the eighteenth century it took only forty English farmers to feed one hundred people. The French needed nearly sixty. Grain yields in France were inferior too. Arthur Young surveyed both countries in the late eighteenth century, and although his results have to be corrected for his personal biases and for the peculiarities of his sample, there is no doubt that the yields were lower throughout much of France. And the same could undoubtedly be said for the production of meat, wool, and dairy products.[113]

Yet, given the diversity in France and the great variations of productivity across the realm, the proper comparison is not between the two entire countries but between analogous regions. After all, the productivity of France as a whole could simply be dragged under by the miserable performance in regions such as the west, while the results for more buoyant parts of the country—the Paris Basin or the part of Normandy near Bretteville—could be completely different. Here, two comparisons are both appropriate and feasible, given the available data: between the Paris Basin and the English arable, and, better yet, between the Paris Basin and a comparable region of productive farms outside London, the county of Hertfordshire. The comparison with Hertfordshire relies on late-eighteenth-century rents and prices; the comparison with English arable, on eighteenth-century physical evidence. One might of course object that English arable as a whole is too large for comparison, but it was long reputed to be highly productive, with advanced crop rotations and high grain yields.

How then does the Paris Basin measure up to the English arable? As far as grain yields in the Basin are concerned, they were certainly on a par with those achieved on English arable farms; the same was in fact true for the other fertile parts of northern France. Arthur Young's observations imply English wheat yields of 23.8 bushels per acre. His estimates for northern France—numbers more trustworthy than others he collected—suggest an average that is nearly the same: between 21.6 and 23.5 bushels per acre, depending on how one revises his observations.[114] The difference in grain yields is simply too small to be meaningful.

Grain was of course the major product of the Paris Basin, but the region apparently produced as much meat, wool, and cheese as arable farms in England. The Basin had a similar number of animals per hectare as in England, and unless the French animals were smaller and less productive—something that will never be known—they would have produced the same amount of meat, wool, and cheese per hectare.[115] With the same output per hectare of grain and animal products and a comparable number of animals per hectare, the output per animal must have been similar too. And because animals constituted the major form of capital, the productivity of capital in the Paris Basin must have resembled that in England. As for labor productivity, the Paris Basin had about as many workers per hectare as the number per comparable area found on English arable farms. There were about the same number of plowmen, and harvesting took the same number of hands.[116] Again, by implication, output per worker must have been the same as well.

The physical evidence argues that the Paris Basin was as productive as the English arable. But how did it stand relative to Hertfordshire? The comparison is certainly appropriate. Hertfordshire was close to London, and it had a fair amount of arable farming. Soils were similar to the Paris Basin, and most important of all, Hertfordshire is hardly a weak example: agriculture there was advanced and crop rotations quite complex. Happily, we have what we need to compare TFP using rents and prices. Rents for Hertfordshire were collected by Arthur Young in 1768–71, and local prices and wages are also available. It is possible to make a reasonable guess at local factor and product shares as well. For the comparison, we can take Paris Basin rents from the Notre Dame sample in the 1760s, along with the corresponding prices and factor and product shares. The exercise does raise certain doubts, because of the different tax regimes in the two countries, and difficulties with certain prices—in particular, the price of agricultural capital. But we can experiment with tax burdens and prices for capital to determine if such problems are insurmountable.[117]

As we vary taxes and the price of capital, the results vary greatly, but they do at least suggest that TFP was higher in the Paris Basin. The ratio of TFP in Hertfordshire to TFP in the Basin ranged from 0.42 to 1.00 according to our estimates. The estimates never exceeded 1.00. If we make the comparison with the Paris Basin in the 1780s, when local agriculture was even more productive, the strength of the Paris Basin becomes overwhelming: Hertfordshire's TFP runs between 0.39 and 0.82 of the Basin's. The results are only slightly more favorable to England if we compare the Basin with another appropriate English county, Buckinghamshire. At best, Buckinghamshire is 7 percent more productive than the Paris Basin in the 1760s, but by some estimates it trails the Basin by over 54 percent.

Conceivably, the odds could be stacked against England because leases there lasted so long that rents lagged well behind the true value of the land. Using the rental values that Arthur Young collected, Robert Allen has argued that rents on open fields would have to be two and a half times higher before they would drive profits to zero. But if we multiply Young's rents for Hertfordshire by 2.5, or use Allen's figures for the profits retained by tenants, Hertfordshire still fails to dominate the Paris Basin. The ratio of TFP in Hertfordshire to TFP in the Basin still ranges from 0.59 to 1.21, evidence that the best Hertfordshire could claim was equality with the Basin.[118]

Agriculture in the Paris Basin was therefore as productive as it was across the Channel, whether we look at the English arable as a whole or at a region of advanced farming such as Hertfordshire. On this, both the physical evidence and the prices and rents agree. Despite all the criticisms

heaped upon French farmers by agronomists and historians, they had reason for pride, at least in the Paris Basin. So too did their counterparts in
other regions of advanced productivity in France, such the plain of Caen
near Bretteville, which was just as productive as the Basin. And it was not
just England that Bretteville and the Paris Basin could rival. Yields in
Bretteville and the Basin exceeded what was achieved in the bulging gra-
naries of eastern Europe, and the French farmers there managed to out-
produce the East Europeans using fewer workers on their farms.[119]

Yet Bretteville and the Paris Basin were not all of France. The country
also endured regions of low productivity, regions where TFP actually declined, such as the west. There, farmers could not rival their counterparts in
England—or in the Paris Basin, for that matter. And even where productivity was high, as in the Paris Basin, it suffered frequent reverses, particularly
during moments of warfare and political crises. In contrast to what most
historians believe, the Old Regime countryside was not immobile, and the
rural economy was hardly static and unchanging. Indeed, at times the rural
economy proved all too flighty, as it danced about to a rhythm set by a
variety of forces.

The task now is to delve behind the growth rates and see what they mean,
for economic growth is more than a ballet of numbers. What accounts for
the alternation of growth and decline—the fragmentation of holdings, the
rise of urban markets, or the actions of the monarchy, including its crises
and wars? Where growth did occur, did it reflect higher yields, new crop
rotations, increased specialization for markets, or greater efficiencies in the
use of agricultural labor and capital? And which obstacles, whether political, ecological, or material, explain what was, in the long run, a disappointing performance by so much of French agriculture? The answers will vary
from region to region and from century to century; so too will their implications for the larger questions of rural economy and society.

CHAPTER FIVE

Explaining Productivity in a Traditional Economy

UNDER THE Old Regime, one source of abundance—agricultural capital—remained nearly constant, at least as we measured it, although it should be stressed that our measurement was confined to livestock and equipment. That left one path to a plentiful food supply: higher productivity, or more precisely higher total factor productivity (TFP). Why then did TFP rise to imposing levels in some regions of France, while in other sections of the country it remained mired in a rut? Part of the difficulty in answering this derives from the notion of productivity growth itself. The concept is always a bit obscure, for it masks precisely how more can be produced with less. Yet ultimately, elevated productivity must always be imbedded in new techniques or new capital. In the countryside of preindustrial Europe, higher productivity might reflect increased yields or more efficient use of labor and agricultural capital, such as buildings and livestock. It might result from something as simple as different organization, made possible perhaps by a larger farm and the skills (or in the jargon of economics, the human capital) of a clever tenant farmer. Or it might amount to true technical change, albeit at a glacial pace by modern standards: the scythe that here and there replaced the sickle and reaped grain in a half or a third the time, or a novel crop such a maize, which spread from village to village in a haphazard way in the centuries after its arrival from the New World. As we computed it, productivity would increase with specialization—specialization that allowed farmers to grow the crops that suited them best, whether it was grapes in the Beaujolais or grass for pasturing animals in the Auge. And productivity gains might derive from the sweat and toil invested in buildings, ditches, fences, and the drainage and terracing of fields. Although such improvements actually constituted a form of capital, they boosted rents and so counted in our measurements as higher TFP.

Productivity growth in agriculture depends on what is happening in the rest of the economy: the weight of taxation, the cost of transport, the strength of middlemen, and the impact of urban demand. It is affected by the nature of property rights and by political decisions—whether to build roads or to seek glory in war. But in a traditional society such as early modern France, productivity growth in the countryside raises issues that reach far beyond the customary bounds of economic history and touch upon what Karl Polanyi called the great transformation: the violent remaking of peasant culture that gave birth to the modern world.[1] For Polanyi, for social thinkers such as Weber and Marx, and for many historians as well, as we know from Chapter 1, productivity gains in peasant agriculture presuppose a drastic transformation of the peasantry, of their village communities and their very patterns of thought. The same is true of economic growth in general in traditional societies. The assumption is not simply the obvious one about the inevitable consequences of growth: that it draws peasants to cities or drives them off the land. Rather, it is that growth confronts a formidable obstacle in the peasantry; until they are swept away, growth will be held in check. Their mentality, it is claimed, is too resistant to change; their farms, too small and too isolated from markets. What must take their place are large capitalist farms, farms that hire wage labor, produce for the market, and can innovate because of their size.

Behind such beliefs lurk a number of concerns, ranging from the role of markets and family labor to the powers of the village community and the nature of peasant mentalities. But perhaps the most palpable is the belief that large capitalist farms are absolutely essential for growth. Large farms have always been the crux of the matter for scholars who view the peasantry as a barrier to growth, and small farms have long been considered the bane of the peasant economy. Such opinions have a long pedigree, particularly in French history. They reach back to the eighteenth century, when physiocrats such as François Quesnay and agronomists such as Arthur Young blamed much of what they considered the weakness of French agriculture on tiny farms. From Marc Bloch to the present, two generations of historians have repeated the same refrain, arguing that only large capitalist farms could save French agriculture.[2]

Here, what is surprising is that most scholars agree on this point, despite violent differences on other issues. Historians who favor demographic explanations blame population growth for small peasant farms; their assumption, of course, is that such farms were unproductive. Their adversaries, the most notable being Robert Brenner, refuse to reduce economic change to demography; but most of them begin with the same assumption: small farms are unproductive. For Brenner, for example, it was class relationships not demography that explain the failings of French agriculture, but the problem with the French class structure is that it cursed France with small and unproductive peasant farms.[3]

The same arguments echo back and forth, with few dissenting voices.[4] Large farms in England were capital intensive. Small farms in France were unproductive. Worse, they discouraged the sort of enclosures that seemed so essential to English agriculture. In this chorus of agreement the only hollow note is the absence of evidence demonstrating the higher productivity of large farms. It is always assumed that they were more efficient than the small farms of early modern France, but the point, curiously, is never proven. Here, though, our samples of leases can settle the matter. They can put the claims about large farms to the test, and they can weigh the other factors affecting productivity growth, from the impact of enclosures to the effects of urban demand. The results are not what one would expect.

EXPLAINING PRODUCTIVITY GROWTH IN THE PARIS BASIN

To shed light on the somewhat shadowy concept of productivity growth—at least in the early modern French countryside—let us begin with the Paris Basin, where the evidence is most illuminating. What then explains the slow growth of TFP that we saw in the Basin during the years between 1650 and 1750—or the rapid increases we observed in the sixteenth century, the early seventeenth century, and again after 1775? Part of the gains in the Paris Basin between 1650 to 1750 reflected improved transportation, and the surge in the early seventeenth century signaled a recovery after the Wars of Religion. But what of the other periods of rapid growth? The answer does not lie with a social or technological revolution, for nothing of the kind happened before 1789. No wave of enclosures depopulated the countryside, and no mechanical revolution or drastic change of crops transformed farming, even at the end of the eighteenth century. What change there was probably reflected the opportunities made possible by the proximity of Paris and its growing market. The evidence thus fits the story, told by several historians, that stresses the growth of urban markets in explaining agricultural gains before the technological upheavals of the late nineteenth century.

By using the sample of leases from the Cathedral of Notre Dame, we can begin to see how local agriculture benefited from proximity to Paris and from the resultant opportunities for trade that transportation costs would rule out in other, less urbanized areas. Admittedly, such a claim is a bit difficult to make for the productivity growth in the sixteenth century, because this early growth remains a bit obscure. It probably involved improvements to the soil and buildings, or modified crop rotations, which let farmers sow more of the valued wheat.[5] Whatever the precise cause, though, it was no accident that growth waxed stronger near Paris.

About the productivity gains in the seventeenth and eighteenth centuries we can say much more. The higher productivity achieved in the 1600s and even more so in the 1700s did not necessarily stem from dramatically higher yields—evidence about the evolution of yields in the Paris Basin is in any case unclear—but it does seem to have been at least in part a response to the increasing animal population in the city. The horses that pulled the newly invented carriages of the privileged and brought food to the officials of the growing state drove up the price of forage and encouraged the production of additional animal feed on grain farms close to the city. Early on, farmers planted pulses (vetch, peas, or beans) and artificial meadows of sainfoin (a perennial herb grown for forage) to nourish their own livestock; they then carted their oats, straw, and hay to Paris. They might then return with loads of manure to spread on their fields, releasing them from the terrible constraint that the lack of fertilizer had imposed on traditional agriculture and boosting their grain yields. These changes all tended to be piecemeal and accomplished on a small scale—in the corner of a field here, on an enclosed parcel of land there—rather than on entire farms. Thus, they did not upset the agricultural technology. Nonetheless, they sufficed to push TFP upward.[6]

Regression analysis with the Notre Dame leases substantiates the important role played by proximity to Paris and by the city's growth. Multicollinearity precludes adding the population of Paris to the regressions with the logarithm of TFP, but the growth rate of the urban population appears to have had a large effect on the growth rate of TFP (table 4.4). In the early seventeenth century, for example, when the population of Paris was gaining by 1.3 percent annually—rapid growth by contemporary standards—it added 0.3 percent to the rate of increase of TFP, also a large amount in the early modern world.[7] It is of course conceivable that rising TFP made possible a larger urban population and not vice versa, but the evidence is at least consistent with the city's being a motor of agricultural growth.

Because small farm size has been invoked repeatedly to explain the failings of French agriculture, it is important to know whether any of the TFP growth in the Paris area resulted from increases in farm size or from the related process of consolidation—the merging of scattered outbuildings and parcels of land into compact farmsteads. Large size (as measured by the logarithm of property area) actually diminishes rent and thus our measure of TFP, but the effect, we have argued, is merely the risk premium demanded with small parcels (table 4.3, regression 1). If we add to the regression a somewhat crude measure of consolidation (the logarithm of the number of hectares per property parcel), it does seem to boost the level of TFP, but the coefficient could be an artifact of multicollinearity (table 4.3, regression 2). More convincing, perhaps, are growth rate regressions, where multicollinearity poses no problems. There, neither the size of the property nor its consolidation seems to affect TFP's advance (table 4.4, regressions 1 and 2).

Yet we must be careful here. All that the growth rate regressions really imply is that no long-run obstacles blocked the enlargement or amalgamation of properties. To understand why, we must realize that properties were frequently combined and consolidated by tenants who rented land from different landlords. Although the properties were distinct, the tenant operated them together. When André-Paul Hanoteau and his wife leased Notre

Dame's 30-hectare property in Tremblay-lès-Gonesse in 1784, for example, it was not the only land they farmed. Indeed, they worked a total of several hundred hectares in Tremblay-lès-Gonesse and its environs.[8] After the late seventeenth century such mergers—known as *cumul de baux*—grew increasingly common and seemed to capture economies of scale. The practice allowed a tenant to economize on buildings, equipment, and certain tasks. He could operate what had once been two farms with only one set of buildings, one shepherd, and perhaps fewer plowmen.[9] And most important of all, he could spread his skills as an overseer—an important part of early modern farming—over multiple properties.

Notre Dame had so much land that it could occasionally effect a merger by leasing two of its own properties to the same tenant. The record for mergers of this sort reveals some failures but also some striking successes, as in La Grande-Paroisse in the early seventeenth century, where TFP gained 6 percent.[10] Further evidence emerges from surviving rural tax rolls, which by the late eighteenth century routinely carried information about the total acreage a tenant farmed. Taxes were generally paid by tenants rather than absentee landlords, and the assessments in any given year turn out to be very nearly proportional to the total acreage the tenant worked. Assessments can thus serve as a proxy for the amount of land under the tenant's direction. If we compare various tenants' tax assessments for two fixed periods, the change in assessment will give a relative measure of the increase in the scale of their farming operations. To be sure, the overall tax rate would have changed over the intervening period, but the assessment increase would still yield a relative measure of how much more land a tenant farmed. If he took on additional hectares via merger, his assessment would rise faster than the tax rate. If not, the assessment would merely keep pace with the tax rate.

This ability to employ changes in tax assessments as a proxy for changes in farm scale lets us use the tax rolls from the 1740s, when, at least near Paris, taxes still seemed proportional to the area a tenant farmed even though the areas themselves rarely appeared on the rolls. For a small number of properties, we can find tenants' assessments in both 1740–41 and 1783–89. If we plot how much the tax assessment changed for each property between 1740–41 and 1783–89 on a logarithmic scale versus how much the logarithm of TFP changed for the same property over the same period, the relationship between the scale of a tenant's operation and the TFP stands out clearly, even though we are dealing with only seven properties (figure 5.1).[11]

Again, the overall tax rate per hectare had shifted between 1740–41 and 1783–89, but the change in taxes for a given property still yields a relative measure of how much more land the later tenant farmed.[12] In Tremblay-lès-Gonesse, for example, the scale of the tenant's operation grew appre-

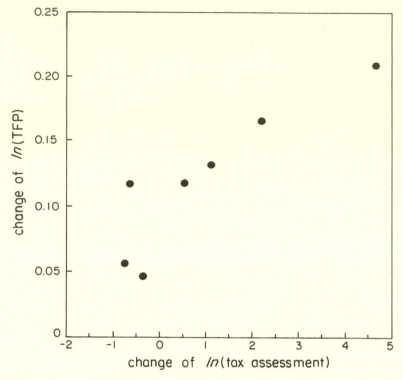

Figure 5.1 Ln(TFP) Change of Ln(TFP) versus Change of Ln(Tax Assessment), 1740–41 to 1783–89

ciably between 1740–41 and 1783–89. Until 1741, a struggling Mathieu Bignon had been farming Notre Dame's property in Tremblay, along with roughly 30 hectares of his own. But by the early 1780s, we know, the property was farmed by André-Paul Hanoteau, who worked much more land. The increased acreage had boosted the tenant's *taille* assessment in the intervening years, and the TFP of the property marched in step, climbing 14 percent.[13]

Apparently mergers via *cumul de baux* did increase productivity: evidence that farm size mattered. The fact that our measures of property size and of property consolidation had no noticeable positive effect in the regressions merely implies that the mergers encountered few obstacles, at least in the eighteenth century. Otherwise, the large properties, which had no need of a merger, would have enjoyed a great advantage, and the coefficients of property size and property consolidation would be large and positive in the TFP growth rate regressions. To operate a larger farm, tenants simply combined properties and did so without difficulty, so that the distribution of the true farm size was independent of the distribution of property size. Under such conditions, property size would not be expected to play a significant role in the TFP regressions, even if there were increasing returns to scale in farming.

Size and consolidation thus mattered, but near Paris, at least, there were few obstacles to achieving the appropriate scale. That scale did increase over time, particularly in the late seventeenth and eighteenth centuries.[14] Attempts to amalgamate properties earlier had often failed. Perhaps the skills needed to run a large farm had been scarce in the earlier centuries, when few farmers could mobilize the necessary capital or keep the requisite farm accounts. For the farmer with the requisite skills and capital, though, nothing blocked the way. Communal property rights were no barrier to amalgamation; neither was the village community, at least in the Paris Basin. Had they in fact hindered amalgamation, as historians frequently claim, the coefficients of property size and property consolidation would have been positive in the TFP growth rate regressions.

Weighing the various factors that boosted TFP in the Paris Basin is treacherous, but we can at least advance some crude guesses for the eighteenth century, for which more information is available. Between 1725–49 and 1775–89, TFP climbed roughly 9 percent, if we compute TFP with the Bernonville shares and with prices averaged over the outgoing lease. Some 1 percent resulted from improved transportation, leaving 8 percent that reflected the growth of agricultural outputs relative to the factors of production.

Practically none of the 8 percent derived from the sort of capital improvements that our method would ascribe to TFP: drainage, buildings, or land reclamation. Of the remaining forms of agricultural capital, the number of animals per hectare perhaps rose, but any increase would be offset by a corresponding shift in animal outputs, leaving TFP essentially unchanged apart from any effect the larger herds had on crop yields.[15] As for the final factor of production—labor—the Chartier farm accounts analyzed by Gilles Postel-Vinay and Jean-Marc Moriceau suggest that the amount of agricultural labor employed fell by perhaps 6 to 13 percent in the Paris Basin between 1725–49 and 1775–89, probably because of farm consolidation. The more efficient use of labor accounts for a 2 to 5 percent TFP gain, with the lower figure being more likely.[16]

On the output side, it was grain that mattered most, because the net contribution of animal products was probably nil. Unfortunately, the evolution of grain output between 1725–49 and 1775–89 is uncertain. On the one hand, Jean Meuvret and others have suggested that there was no increase in yields near Paris in the eighteenth century. On the other, George Grantham has proposed a 15 percent rise in wheat yields between 1750 and 1800, which translates into a 6 percent TFP gain over our period. Grantham's estimate fits the numbers proposed by other recent scholars, and if we accept it, then together with the likely 6 percent decline in the use of labor we can account for nearly all the eighteenth-century progress of TFP in the Paris Basin.[17]

Even if we side with Meuvret rather than Grantham and assume that yields were stagnant, crop outputs were still likely to have risen in value. In part, the reason was that farmers outside Paris had improved their techniques for storing grain and preparing it for market. They were also replacing their remaining fields of maslin—a wheat-rye mix—with more valuable pure wheat. The timing and location of this change cannot be pinned down precisely, but where wheat did supplant maslin TFP was likely to have been pushed up a small amount—perhaps 2 percent. There were other, more important ways to augment the value of crop output as well. Some farmers apparently sowed strains of wheat that yielded more straw, which could be sold in Paris, as on the Chartier farm. Others planted pulses or artificial meadows, which released oats and fodder crops for the Paris market. That, too, brought in additional revenue and hence boosted TFP. On the Chartier farm, for example, the sales of straw, oats, and fodder crops contributed more to TFP growth in the eighteenth century than did a greater output of wheat, and as Jean-Michel Chevet's research suggests, the Chartier farm was hardly unique.[18]

In all likelihood, the truth probably lies somewhere between Grantham and Meuvret. In some parts of the Paris Basin, grain yields increased by relatively small amounts between 1725–49 and 1775–89, but maslin disappeared, while increasing amounts of oats, straw, and fodder were shipped to Paris. Elsewhere, grain yields grew 15 percent, explaining all of the TFP increase not accounted for by greater efficiencies in the use of labor. The precise outcome undoubtedly depended on commercial opportunities on each individual farm.

One mystery, though, remains: what boosted grain yields in the parts of the Paris Basin where they did rise? Several possible answers suggest themselves, answers that will be explored in greater detail below. First of all, farmers in the Basin may have done more to prepare their soil before sowing. Soil preparation boosted yields in England, and the same may have happened near Paris, at least on a small scale.[19] Farmers also did a better job of cleaning and selecting seed.[20] In addition, they may have added more fertilizer to the soil, which was starved for nitrogen and other nutrients. One source of nitrogen may have been the pulses and the new artificial meadows. Both—so it has been argued—would add nitrogen to the soil and so boost grain yields. As we shall see, there is evidence against such an argument, but the artificial meadows may have still fertilized crops indirectly. They released straw that had been used as animal feed, allowing farmers to make more effective fertilizer by adding straw to manure. They also permitted farmers to raise more animals, or if not more animals, larger ones. The result would presumably be more manure for fertilizer.[21] Finally, there is one source of fertilizer about which we can be much more certain: the city of Paris itself. Farmers from the Basin who carted manure back from Parisian stables had an obvious source of fertilizer to increase their yields. Feed lots near the city probably played a similar role.

Assessing the Role of Large Enclosed Farms

In the Paris Basin, larger farms enjoyed higher productivity; in that sense, farm size mattered. But did farm size have the same effect elsewhere in France? How important was it really in explaining agricultural growth and stagnation? How precisely did larger farms increase productivity? Did they make possible more efficient use of labor, or did they boost yields as well? Did they facilitate the planting of artificial meadows and the sale of oats and fodder crops? And how can we disentangle increases in farm size from the related processes of consolidation and enclosure?

Finding answers to such questions is no easy matter, at least for Old Regime France. French historians lack the sort of detailed surveys that, in Robert Allen's hands, have shed such light on the effects of farm size and enclosure in England—works such as Arthur Young's accounts of his tours through the English countryside. True, Young did report at length on his journeys through France in 1787–89, but his French travels omit the abundant statistical evidence gathered during the English tours: evidence about the size of farms, the number of farmhands, and the amount of agricultural capital.[22] Worse yet, the documents that might fill the breach, rural probate inventories, are rare or of little use in certain parts of France, and where they are abundant (and contain the necessary information) they have yet to attract the army of researchers they have in England.[23] Indeed, for French agriculture it is difficult even to determine the actual size of farms before the late nineteenth century. The first agricultural census to measure farm size—as opposed to land ownership—dates to 1862, but for accurate statistics one has to wait until the end of the century, when the countryside had been completely transformed.

The only recourse is to fall back on a smaller number of local records: selected tax documents, a limited number of probate inventories, and the archives of property management. One particularly illuminating set of such records comes from the Norman village of Bretteville-l'Orgueilleuse, where, in Marc Bloch's opinion, the consolidation of farms (and agricultural practices in general) had "progressed to an extent undreamed of" in other parts of France. In Bretteville, we know, productivity did grow rapidly, at least in the sixteenth century, and the growth was accompanied by the consolidation of the village's scattered fields into large enclosed blocks

TABLE 5.1

Consolidation and Enclosure in Bretteville-l'Orgueilleuse, 1479–1666

Property Characteristics	Entire Village		Cairon Family Holdings	
	1479–82	1666	1479–82	1666
Total area (hectares)	586.00	586.00	88.00	299.00
Number of parcels of land	1,386	640	194	155
Area per parcel (hectares)	0.42	0.92	0.46	2.11
Area enclosed (hectares)	32.00	131.00	14.00	114.00
Average size of enclosed parcels (hectares)	0.86	4.24	2.28	6.33
Percentage of total area enclosed	6.00	22.00	16.00	35.00

Sources: AD Calvados, F 1757, H 3226, H 3229, H 3351; M. Boudin, "Du laboureur aisé au gentilhomme campagnard: Les Perrote de Cairon, de Bretteville-l'Orgueilleuse," *Annales de Normandie* 13 (1963): 237–68.

Note: All figures have been rounded. The total village area, which is smaller than that of the village today, was taken from a 1687 land survey, which I assumed was more accurate than the preceding ones. The total area in 1687 may actually have been slightly different in 1479–82 and 1666 because of the inclusion of an additional 27 hectares of land in 1687. The total area differs from the figure in Boudin, because he failed to notice that the land surveys did not use the customary local acre equal to 0.6078 hectares but rather an acre of 0.6753 hectares. Enclosed land was here defined to include only land with hedges or ditches on all four sides. The definition omits property that may have been very nearly enclosed—say with hedges on three sides. The Cairon family includes all owners with the surname Cairon or Perrote and all owners known to be in the family, as determined from family trees.

surrounded by hedges and ditches—a transformation so dramatic that it reminded Bloch of the English enclosures.[24] The effects of this transformation can be glimpsed in surveys conducted in 1479–82 and again in 1666. Between these two dates, the number of parcels of land in Bretteville dropped by half, as enclosures multiplied and the size of the average parcel more than doubled (table 5.1). But even more striking than the numbers are the watercolor maps drawn for the 1666 land survey. With hedges and trees often planted along their borders, the enormous blocks of land loom out amidst the remaining fragmented parcels (figures 5.2 and 5.3).

Behind the consolidation in Bretteville stood the Cairon family, the provincial nobles whose journals revealed the workings of the Old Regime labor market. Beginning in the late fifteenth century, they feverishly bought, sold, and exchanged parcels of land, gradually freeing themselves of scattered strips and welding what remained into large, contiguous lots. In 1666, for example, François de Cairon owned the walled and hedged Clos de la Perrelle, its nearly 22 hectares planted not only with grain but with sainfoin grass to form an artificial meadow (figure 5.2). In 1482 the same property had formed not one enclosed field but over forty-seven sep-

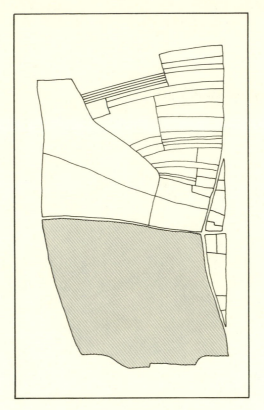

Figure 5.2 François de Cairon's Clos de la Perrelle and Surrounding Parcels of Land in
Bretteville-l'Orgueilleuse, 1666–67. The Clos
de la Perrelle is shaded on the map. Walled and
hedged, it was planted not only with grain but
with sainfoin grass to form an artificial meadow.
Source: AD Calvados, H 3229, p. 403.

arate parcels, only six of which belonged to members of the Cairon family.
In figure 5.3, the large block in the Delle des Grands Champs was also
François de Cairon's; in 1482, it was shattered into fifty-three separate
strips. The holdings of other family members bore the same imprint, so that
by 1666 property in hands of the Cairon was much more likely to be consolidated and enclosed than other land in the village (table 5.1).[25]

As in the Paris Basin, consolidation in Bretteville seems to have boosted
productivity. We cannot match TFP measurements from Bretteville with
evidence of tax records as we did for the Notre Dame farms, but some of the
effects of consolidation can be derived from the Cairon journals and their

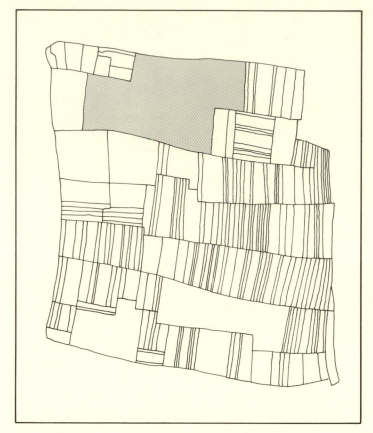

Figure 5.3 François de Cairon's Large Block in the Delle des Grands Champs, 1666–67. Shaded on the map, Cairon's block contrasts with the narrow strips in the nearby open fields. *Source*: AD Calvados, H 3229, pp. 448–49.

estate records. We know how much property family members owned in the late fifteenth century and again in 1666. The journals shed light on the family's farming operations in the late fifteenth and early sixteenth centuries and again two hundred years later. Probate inventories are rare in Normandy, but we have a few for the Cairon.[26] To be sure, such records are far from perfect, for they force us to generalize from a single probate list or to guess at how much land the Cairon farmed themselves and how much they leased out. But if we interpret the documents so as to exaggerate the impact of consolidation, then we can at least place an upper boundary on the effect consolidation had on productivity growth.

Whether consolidation let the Cairon family employ less capital and less labor overall is unclear. Between the end of the fifteenth century and the end of the seventeenth century, the amount of livestock per hectare—the major form of agricultural capital—remained about the same, although the estimates are subject to considerable uncertainty. It is even more difficult to determine whether total labor use changed. We do not know how much family labor the Cairon themselves supplied in the late fifteenth century, when local nobles such as the Cairon might well dirty their hands in certain tasks of farming. Nor do we know how many of their domestics in the late seventeenth century were actually household servants rather than farm-hands.[27] But if we concentrate on a particular type of capital and labor—horses and plowmen—then it does seem that the consolidation led to greater efficiency. Back in 1525, it seems, Nicolas de Cairon had to harness twelve or more farm horses for every 100 hectares he farmed, but by 1673, his descendant Jean de Cairon apparently needed only ten horses to work the same area, a decline of 17 percent or more. Presumably, the number of plows and plowmen also diminished by about the same percentage, the explanation being, one might guess, that consolidation facilitated the plow team's arduous task. There was little doubt that Jean de Cairon's holdings were more compact than those of his ancestor in 1525: Jean de Cairon's property had an average parcel size of nearly 3 hectares, versus less than half a hectare for the family's holdings in 1479–82, the date closest to 1525 when we can measure property size.[28] The concentration of the family's holdings reduced the time wasted in moving the plow team from parcel to parcel and, if the shape of the parcels was right, in turning the plow around at the end of each furrow. A similar decline in the number of plowmen accompanied the amalgamation of farms near Paris.[29]

Although the evidence here is obviously fragmentary, there are other documents that tell the same story—in particular, tax records from Bretteville and from surrounding towns. In 1735, the tax roll for Bretteville included the total amount of land farmers worked (both property they owned and property they rented), the number of horses they possessed, and whether they hired someone else to plow their land. The number of horses can be divided by the farm size to yield horses per hectare, and it can in turn be regressed on the total number of hectares farmed to see if it declined with farm size, as the Cairon records would suggest.

In performing the regression, we must of course beware of certain problems. To begin with, the size of a farm is not precisely the same as consolidation, although the two were obviously related. We must also keep in mind that it was common to have one's land plowed by others, and, worse yet, smallholders often earned money from horses they owned by hiring them out. Fortunately, the tax records indicate if land was tilled by hired draft teams, allowing us to include a dummy variable in the regressions to correct, at least in a crude way, for the use of other horses. We can take the further precaution of eliminating all farmers without horses, who must have had other villagers plow their land. As for the smallholders who rented out the services of their horses, we can restrict the regressions to properties over 5 hectares. As we know, anyone working less than 5 hectares must have spent much of his time off his own land, whether it was renting out his horse or his own labor. Furthermore, it was about at 5 hectares that ownership of a horse becomes nearly universal. The statistically minded might worry, of course, that such restrictions would disturb the regressions, but they do not seem to.[30]

The regression points to a decline in the number of horses per hectare on larger farms, a decline that cannot be the result of a different relative price for horses since all the farmers presumably faced roughly the same costs for draft teams (table 5.2). Admittedly, the number of cases is small, and one might still worry about the smallholders renting out their horses or about the possibility of a systematic misstatement of the number of horses by farmers eager to lessen their tax burden. But more accurate tax roles for three nearby villages lead to similar results. Like Bretteville in many respects, the three villages grew the same crops, and at least one of them—Rots—had experienced the same process of consolidation as Bretteville. The three villages also had extraordinarily accurate tax roles, prepared as part of a campaign to reform local tax assessments. The role for Rots, for example, was prepared under the supervision of a royal officer who spent twelve years in the village.[31] The roles even estimated what fraction of each horse's time was spent working away from its owner's farm, making it possible to adjust for smallholders who rented out their horses. If we perform the same regression for the three villages—once again limiting it to farms with horses and over 5 hectares in size—the number of horses per hectare once again declines with farm size (table 5.2). Furthermore, the relationship seems much too strong to be a statistical fluke.

The number of horses used thus declined with farm size, as did plows and plowmen. Consolidation would probably bring about a similar decline, giving consolidated farms greater productivity of the capital and labor tied up in draft teams. Much the same was apparently true near Paris, according to evidence gathered for various localities by Jean-Michel Chevet; there, too, big farms had fewer draft teams (table 5.3).[32] Enlarging farms also increased labor productivity in the English Midlands, although the process at work there was apparently different and perhaps more important. In the Midlands, the huge farms employed more specialists and fewer unskilled workers such as women. Nothing of the sort, though, happened in Bretteville. In 1473–85, before the consolidation of holdings in Bretteville, 26 percent of the Cairon's hired servants were women. In 1691–1705, after consolidation was finished, the percentage had hardly changed: women still constituted 24 percent of the servants who appeared to be working at agricultural tasks.[33]

TABLE 5.2
Livestock Regressions, Plain of Caen

	Dependent Variable		
	Horses per Hectare Farmed		Weighted Units of Livestock per Hectare
Independent Variables	Bretteville- l'Orgueilleuse 1735	Three Nearby Villages[a] 1740	Four Nearby Villages 1740
Constant	0.23	0.18	0.40
	(9.82)	(18.82)	(17.45)
Total hectares farmed	−0.39	−0.18	−0.18
(units of 100 hectares)	(−3.77)	(−3.81)	(−1.75)
Dummy variable: farm	−0.05	—	—
plowed by another person	(−1.60)		
Observations	11	72	80
R^2	0.64	0.17	0.04
	Mean Dependent Variables		
	0.15	0.15	0.37

Sources: AD Calvados 2 C 1174, 2 C 1191, 2 C 1193, 2 C 1317, 2 C 1345.

Note: Regressions are run for farms over 5 hectares and only for those possessing some horses or some livestock. As a result, the total number of animals per hectare is likely to be exaggerated here. Unfortunately, the tax rolls omit information on farms worked directly by tax-exempt individuals, such as some of the Cairon properties. The 1735 tax roll for Bretteville does not specify units for the acre used; internal evidence suggested it was the same as in Rots, or 0.9725 per hectare. If not, the results would not be greatly changed. The three nearby villages are Carpiquet, Cheux, and Rots. The fourth village of Secqueville-en-Bessin is added for the livestock regressions; it is omitted from the horse-per-hectare regression because the tax roll does not correct for the number of horses used off the farm. The livestock weights are contemporary measures of the amount of manure produced by different animals, with each horse and each head of cattle counting for one, each pig for one-sixth, and each sheep for one-eighth. The numbers in parentheses are t statistics.

[a] In this regression only, the number of horses is corrected for use off the farm.

Whatever the mechanism, we should take care not to exaggerate the effects of increases in farm size and consolidation. In the English Midlands, greater farm size explains only a portion of the TFP increase in the early modern period.[34] The same was true in France. Even in Bretteville, where consolidation had been taken to such extremes, it resulted in at most a 17 percent drop in the number of horses, plows, and plowmen, according to the Cairon accounts. That translates into only a 7 percent increase in TFP, even if the savings on oats and of equipment such as harnesses are included, and it pales by comparison with the total TFP growth in Bretteville, at least when the process of consolidation was most rapid.[35] After all, between 1520 and 1599—before productivity collapsed in the seventeenth

TABLE 5.3
Horses and Livestock per Hectare, Near Paris

Farm Characteristics	Farm Size (hectares)			
	10–25	25–50	50–100	over 100
The Hurepoix, South of Paris, 1539–1672[a]				
Number of farms	14	11	13	3
Number of horses per 100 hectares	17.1	10.0	7.5	3.0
Number of head of live-stock per 100 hectares	44.6	29.4	33.5	5.9
Enquête, Election of Melun, 1717				
Number of farms	28	40	72	33
Number of horses per 100 hectares	14.3	10.8	6.8	5.3
Number of head of live-stock per 100 hectares	52.1	47.4	33.3	28.5
Evidence from Twenty Parishes near Paris, circa 1750				
Number of farms	13	8	17	18
Number of horses per 100 hectares	16.6	10.3	7.4	6.7
Number of head of live-stock per 100 hectares	41.1	31.2	29.5	33.5

Source: Chevet, "Le marquisat d'Ormesson," 2:670–72. His calculations for the Hurepoix are based on Jacquart, La crise rurale, pp. 355–57.

Note: Chevet restricts himself to farms over 10 hectares in size with livestock. His weighting scheme for counting livestock differs slightly from that used in table 5.2.

[a] Determined from probate records.

century—TFP in Bretteville apparently rose 0.44 percent per year, or 42 percent overall.

To be sure, the figure for overall TFP growth here derives from a regression and could well be in error. It might conceivably be smaller—perhaps as low as 12 percent. If so, then consolidation would of course play a greater role. Still, the 42 percent figure does seem a fairly plausible estimate of how much TFP grew in Bretteville between 1520 and 1599.[36] If 42 percent is correct, then there is still a 33 percent TFP increase to account for. Some might be due to economizing on buildings, as in the Paris Basin, but a generous estimate indicates that the lower building expenses, whether in Bretteville or in Paris, would explain at most another 3 percent of TFP growth, and probably much less.[37] The lion's share—nearly

30 percent or more, if we trust the overall TFP growth numbers—remains unaccounted for.

It is possible that the larger and more productive farms in Bretteville economized not just on plowmen but on other sorts of labor as well. As we noted above, a bigger farm could spread an overseer's skills over a greater enterprise. It might also stretch the services of a shepherd over more sheep. But efficiencies of this sort would presumably reward sheer size rather than consolidation, and in Bretteville they do not seem to have been at work, at least on the Cairon farms we have been comparing. The Cairon farms, after all, were no bigger in the late seventeenth century than they had been two hundred years before. Though consolidated and far more compact, they had grown no larger and they did not use any fewer shepherds and overseers. Nor is it likely that the remaining productivity gains in Bretteville reflected more efficient use of sheep—the other major form of agricultural capital besides horses.[38]

The only explanation for the remaining productivity gains is that farmers in Bretteville accomplished quite early what their counterparts in the Paris Basin would achieve after 1750. Either they increased their output of oats, straw, and fodder, or they raised their grain yields. Oats, straw, and fodder, though, can safely be ruled out. Although the Cairon diaries are incomplete, they do mention the sale of straw, but it is apparently a minor matter. Furthermore, while the Cairon repeatedly sold wheat, they do not seem to have sold oats. Indeed, on occasion they even bought oats. It hardly seems likely therefore that they grew rich selling animal feed. Furthermore, eighteenth-century descriptions suggest much the same, for they make it clear that the whole region about Bretteville—the Plain of Caen—was devoted overwhelmingly to the production of wheat. According to tax records, the region did not fatten animals for the nearby market in Caen either.[39]

That leaves only an increase in grain yields in Bretteville. While the data are meager, local yields do seem to have increased over the sixteenth century, and there is much stronger evidence that they had reached elevated levels by 1600, just as one would expect after a surge in productivity.[40] What, though, caused them to rise? Conceivably, the elevated yields were themselves the fruit of consolidation or increases in farm size. One might assume, as Arthur Young did, that large, consolidated farms had more livestock per hectare, livestock that fertilized the grain crops more abundantly. The documents, though, argue to the contrary. The Cairon did not appear to possess any more livestock per hectare after they consolidated their holdings, and according to local tax rolls, large farms had no more livestock either. Indeed, using the same sort of tax roles that shed light on the number of horses and plowmen, we can calculate the number of animals per hectare and then weight the number of animals by each species' production of manure. If we then regress this index of animals per hectare on farm size, it appears to be no bigger on larger farms, for the coefficient of farm size is not the large and positive number we would expect if big farms actually had more animals per hectare (table 5.2). Counts of animals from the vicinity of Paris (table 5.3) and from England lead to the same conclusion: in France as in England, large farms simply did not fertilize their grain more abundantly than did their smaller counterparts.[41]

There is also direct evidence against higher yields on large consolidated farms. It comes from Cheux, a village some 5 kilometers from Bretteville, where the Abbey of Saint Etienne collected a seigneurial levy on grain, the *champart*, which amounted to one fourteenth of the crop. In the early seventeenth century, the abbey recorded the collection of the champart in unusual detail. Instead of merely indicating the total collected, the abbey actually noted the number of sheaves of grain due on each parcel of land. Given the rate of the champart and the area of the parcel, which the abbey also took down, one can calculate grain yields for each parcel, and it is precisely such a calculation, based on the champart documents from Cheux, that reveal the elevated yields near Bretteville in the early seventeenth century. Admittedly, the levy was collected on only some 10 percent of the land in Cheux, but the parcels subject to it were scattered almost randomly over the village's fields. It seems reasonable to assume then that the champart parcels were representative of land throughout the village and that they were larger on consolidated farms.

If so, and if crops actually grew more bountiful after consolidation, then yields should be higher on larger parcels, and regressions of the wheat yield on parcel area ought to produce a large, positive, and statistically significant coefficient. Yet the regressions argue to the contrary (table 5.4, regressions 1 and 3). Based on champart records from 1603 to 1608, these regressions adjust for the annual vicissitudes of the harvest, and regression 3 takes into account variations in microclimate and soil fertility from one part of the village to the other. Whatever the form they take, they demonstrate that consolidation failed to boost the yield of grain.[42]

Neither did increases in farm size, the proof coming, once again, from the champart records. They nearly always mention the farmer who paid the levy, and if the parcels subject to the champart were randomly scattered through the village, then the total area on which any farmer owed the champart should provide a good index of the size of his entire farm. Were yields to rise with farm size, they would presumably be greater whenever this index were higher, or, in other words, when the farmer of the parcel operated a larger farm. A regression of the yield on the value of the index for each parcel should then reveal a large, positive, and statistically significant coefficient. Once again, though, the regressions prove disappointing: the relevant coefficients are small and statistically insignificant (table 5.4, regressions 2 and 4). Even if we trust the coefficients, the effect of farm

TABLE 5.4
Wheat Yield Regressions, Cheux, 1603–8

Regression Statistic	Correcting for Annual Yield Variations		Correcting for Annual Yield Variations and Differences in Micro-climate and Soil Fertility	
	Regression Numbers			
	1	2	3	4
Coefficient of parcel area	−0.77		−1.43	
(hectares)	(−1.30)	—	(−1.61)	—
Coefficient of area worked	—	0.07	—	0.08
by farmer (wheat only, in		(0.70)		(0.61)
hectares)				
Degrees of freedom	340	340	220	220
R^2	0.04	0.03	0.12	0.11
Mean of dependent variable	18.33	18.33	18.33	18.33
(hectoliters per hectare)				

Source: See text, Chapter 5.

Note: In each regression, the dependent variable is the wheat yield (in hectoliters per hectare) calculated from the *champart* records. To calculate yields in hectoliters per hectares from the champart figures, which are in sheaves (*gerbes*) per local acre, I followed Pavard, "Productions et rendements céréaliers à Cheux," and assumed that one hectoliter of wheat equaled 33 gerbes. The rate of the champart was one-fourteenth, and the local acre was 0.675 hectares. As Pavard points out, the number of gerbes of wheat per hectoliter could have varied; it is equally reasonable to suppose that it was as low as 22.5 gerbes per hectoliter. In that case, average wheat yields on the champart parcels would be much higher: nearly as high as 27 hectoliters per hectare. Whatever the average wheat yields, though, the argument about parcel size and farm area still holds: neither has a large effect on yields.

For some of the parcels of land used here, the champart was collected with the tithe, causing the champart to double. Following Pavard, I have therefore assumed that all champart figures of 45 gerbes or more per acre have to be divided by 2 because they include a tithe at the same rate as the champart. Making a similar correction at 40 gerbes per acre or omitting the correction altogether leads to similar results. All the regressions include a constant term and dummy variables for the years 1604–8 in order to correct for annual variations of the wheat yield. The regressions that correct for microclimate and soil fertility use additional dummy variables for the parcel location, as is explained in the text. I have omitted the co-efficients of the constant term and all the dummy variables from the table. Finally, the area worked by each farmer is actually only the total of the area the farmer had planted in wheat subject to the champart during the years 1603–8. Since the area planted in wheat was typically a third of the arable, it should still provide a good index of farm size. *T* statistics are in parentheses.

size seems minimal. Indeed, magnifying the tiniest farm in Cheux until it equalled the biggest agricultural enterprise in the village would explain only a fraction—something less than 3 percent—of the enormous variation we see in yields.[43]

What then was the legacy of the vaunted consolidation and enlargement of farms near Bretteville, the legacy of what Marc Bloch considered the most dramatic agrarian metamorphosis of the Old Regime? Sadly enough, it was only a moderate increase of TFP. Consolidation and greater size did not boost yields, and both in Bretteville and near Paris, the larger arable farms did not monopolize the livestock fertilizer that made elevated yields possible. The same held true in England, where years of work with probate inventories has failed to link farm size and bountiful harvests.[44] If Bretteville is any indication, the gains from consolidation boiled down to savings on plowmen and the associated capital costs of plows and horses—economies that were far from overwhelming. Enlarging a farm—as opposed to merely consolidating it—may have permitted additional savings on shepherds and supervision. All of this was certainly important. Yet much of the productivity gain—in particular, higher yields—was independent of farm size.

That was the case not just in Bretteville, but in the Paris Basin as well, at least in the eighteenth century. Near Paris, it is true, we must consider more than just grain yields, for there were also the farms growing oats, straw, and fodder for the Paris market. Yet one of the essential crops grown on such farms clearly did not involve economies of scale: the artificial meadows. As Jean-Michel Chevet has discovered, the artificial meadows near Paris were in fact more prevalent on small farms than large.[45] On the other hand, there was one procedure on farms near Paris that consolidation did favor: sheepfolding (*parcage*), the practice of confining sheep in temporary pens on different parts of a field each night. Folding offered a number of advantages, particularly to the farmer peddling straw and fodder in Paris. It spared the straw litter used to collect sheep dung in barns—straw that could be sold to stable owners—and it reduced the number of sheep needed to fertilize a field, thereby increasing the amount of fodder that could be marketed. It also spread mineral-rich sheep manure efficiently. Clearly, it was easiest when a farm was consolidated.[46]

Yet, even if folding worked to the advantage of large consolidated farms in the Paris Basin, most of the productivity gains there were independent of farm size. The evidence from the tax rolls—evidence displayed in figure 5.1—suggests that even tripling the size of a farm would increase TFP by slightly less than 3 percent in the eighteenth century. Mergers in the Paris Basin did double or even triple the size of the largest farms in the late seventeenth and early eighteenth centuries, but what happened to average farms was less dramatic, as were the changes of scale later on, in the years

1725–49 to 1775–89, that interest us most.[47] Indeed, if we actually examine the rare villages in the Paris Basin where we can measure the change in average farm size between 1725 and 1789, it turns out to be much smaller—on the order of roughly a third, which translates into a TFP increase of a bit less than 1 percent. In all likelihood, then, the productivity gains from larger farms lay under 3 percent and probably closer to 1 percent. Compared with the 8 percent productivity increase we measured between 1725–49 and 1775–89—an additional 1 percent deriving from improved transportation—such a gain of 1 to 3 percent seems small. It fits the 2 percent TFP increase we attributed to more efficient use of labor, but the remaining 5 to 7 percent had to be independent of farm size.[48]

Whatever the effect of farm size on productivity, we know that few obstacles stood in the way of reaching the appropriate farm size, at least in the Paris Basin. As the regressions with the Notre Dame sample demonstrated, the initial size of a property did not raise the rate of TFP growth. Apparently, Notre Dame's tenants merged properties leased from different landlords and did so without difficulty. Agricultural stagnation in the Basin cannot be blamed therefore on minuscule property holdings or on barriers to farm amalgamation: tenants simply combined properties from different landlords to realize all the economies of scale. The same point, it should be stressed, can be established for certain other parts of France. For four other lease samples—the farms near Amiens, Béziers, Nantes, and in the Gâtine Poitevine—we can regress the rate of change of TFP on property size. Again, if farm size mattered greatly, and if tenants could not easily merge smallholdings, then larger properties would enjoy a great advantage, and property size would have a large, positive, and significant regression coefficient. In all the regressions, though, the coefficient of property size is statistically insignificant, and only for the Gâtine is it large (table 5.5). Although the pastoral farming in the Gâtine might have involved economies of scale beyond the reach of the poor local sharecroppers, the regression coefficient could well be a fluke. In the other samples, the coefficients imply that even tripling the size of a farm would add less than 0.1 percent to the rate of TFP growth.

Logically, there seem to be only two possibilities here: either farm size had only a modest effect on TFP, or tenants could easily assemble the farms of the appropriate size. Certainly, the samples here do not cover all of France. They omit the southwest and, worse yet, the eastern provinces such as Lorraine and Burgundy, where severe fragmentation may well have made it nearly impossible to put together a large farm. There, a tenant eager to assemble a large farm would have to deal with too many landlords—landlords worried about whether he might act against their interests. Or if he sought to exchange leasehold land to enlarge his farm, he would have to bargain with too many other tenants. As for a landowner

TABLE 5.5
Regressions with the Growth Rate of TFP: Various Lease Samples

Independent Variables	Sample of Farms near				
	Amiens (with Area)	Amiens (with Area per Parcel)	Béziers	Nantes	Gâtine Poitevine
Constant	−0.181	−0.249	0.435	−0.197	−0.818
	(−0.41)	(−0.51)	(0.50)	(−0.24)	(−0.21)
Ln(property area)	0.056	—	−0.143	0.060	0.312
	(1.06)		(−0.67)	(0.22)	(0.24)
Ln(area per property parcel)	—	0.017	—	—	—
		(0.15)			
Weather: days delay in southern French grape harvest, year of lease	—	—	0.093	—	—
			(2.04)		
Dummy: tenant new and unrelated to previous lessee	—	—	—	0.149	—
				(0.14)	
Ln(distance to Montdidier)	0.0009	0.056	—	—	—
	(0.01)	(0.41)			
Growth rate of taxes relative to rents (percent per year)	−0.192	−0.159	—	−0.040	−0.327
	(−5.44)	(−3.59)		(−0.30)	(−2.19)
Number of observations	249	143	99	38	33
R^2	0.11	0.09	0.05	0.004	0.14
Mean dependent variable (percent per year)	−0.04	−0.04	−0.46	−0.03	0.04

Sources: The weather variable is from Le Roy Ladurie, Les paysans de Languedoc, 2:749–50. The other variables are taken from price series, lease samples, and property descriptions in Appendix B.

Note: T-statistics are in parentheses. The growth rate of TFP is calculated from lease to lease using the standard shares for each region and prices averaged over the current year and the previous eight. The TFP growth rates are not corrected for taxes, but as is shown in Appendix A, part 13, the lack of a tax adjustment will not affect the regression coefficients, because on the farms near Béziers the tenants did not pay taxes and in the other regressions the growth of taxes relative to rents is one of the explanatory variables. The dummy variable for tenants was available for the Nantes properties only, and the area per parcel for the Amiens properties only. For the Amiens properties, therefore, the regression was run first with ln(property area) and then with ln(area per property parcel). The weather variable was relevant to the Béziers properties but not to the others. Finally, the logarithm of the distance to Montdidier corrects for the use of prices from Montdidier rather than from Amiens for the Amiens property.

who sought to create his own large farm, he would face too many costly land sales or exchanges—or so nineteenth-century evidence suggests.[49] Agricultural productivity may have suffered consequently in eastern France, though by how much it is impossible to say, since we lack any reliable evidence about the size of farms there. Outside these eastern regions, though, the conclusion still holds: ultimately, farm size did not matter a great deal. And if we believe the evidence from Amiens and the Notre Dame sample, in the long run farm consolidation had an equally small effect on TFP (tables 4.4 and 5.5, regressions with area per parcel among the independent variables).

Another key to productivity growth in the eyes of eighteenth-century agronomists and the historians who repeat their ideas was the introduction of new crops and novel crop rotations: clover and turnips, pulses such as vetch and peas, and the artificial grasses such as sainfoin, which had proved so important near Paris. That was the opinion of eighteenth-century agronomists from Duhamel du Monceau to Arthur Young, and a host of modern historians repeat the same refrain.[50] Once again, Bretteville seems a perfect example. Pulses had sprouted there since the late fifteenth century; by the 1570s they may have covered as much as 12 percent of the cropped land. Although they were initially little more than a substitute for spring grains such as oats, by the early seventeenth century they were cultivated as part of a complex new crop rotation. As for artificial grasses, as early as the 1660s sainfoin was growing behind the enclosures both in Bretteville and in neighboring villages.[51] All these new crops, we know, were supposed to fix nitrogen in the soil and increase the supply of manure.

If new crops and crop rotations were the key, then it was perhaps the enclosures that were the ultimate cause of productivity growth in Bretteville. Eighteenth-century observers certainly lamented the lack of enclosures in the arable districts of France: for them, enclosures were essential for any change in traditional crop rotations.[52] At least until recently, most historians agreed. For Marc Bloch, for example, it was only enclosures that could break the shackles of traditional cropping patterns; without them, new crops would be destroyed or simply rendered impossible by fallow grazing rights and restrictive communal crop rotations. Unfortunately, such arguments have been by and large demolished—at least for France—by the late Jean Meuvret, who demonstrated that fallow rights and communal regulations rarely limited a farmer's freedom to innovate. But even Meuvret believed that enclosures could protect pasture and natural meadow—and even more so new artificial meadows—from marauding animals. In Bretteville, that was precisely what the enclosures did: their hedges and ditches sheltered sainfoin, as in François de Cairon's Clos de la Perrelle. Artificial grasses like sainfoin could easily be damaged, particularly by sheep, and there were clearly instances when such artificial meadows came under attack. The problem was particularly severe when meadow and arable were mingled and fields scattered, as in Lorraine. There, a patch of sainfoin might suffer repeated incursions, as in Gorze, a small city near Metz, where in 1787 the widow Ladoucette's sainfoin was invaded six times in a week.[53]

It would be wrong, though, to exaggerate the importance of the new crops and the enclosures that protected them—wrong for a number of reasons. First of all, if evidence from England is to be believed, the pulses and the artificial grasses had no effect on grain yields. They undoubtedly sustained livestock and raised the amount of fodder that could be sold, but they did not boost grain output.[54] Second, whatever their benefits in France, it is clear that the artificial grasses could be cultivated without enclosures. Sainfoin, for instance, was grown on open fields in the Paris Basin, albeit in limited quantities. In the Basin—to generalize from the court records of La Grande-Paroisse—the sainfoin apparently suffered few incursions, but it even sprouted on the scattered fields of Lorraine.[55] Conceivably, the meadows of sainfoin and other artificial grasses would have spread more widely in provinces such as Lorraine had enclosures been easier, but the effect of two royal edicts in 1767–68 argues to the contrary. Passed at a time when the government was multiplying similar efforts to improve agriculture, the edicts allowed farmers in Lorraine and the neighboring Trois Evêchés to disregard grazing rights and to fence in their open meadows. The edicts were followed by a number of enclosures, but the acreage involved remained rather small—not what one would expect if grazing rights and open fields had been the obstacle to productivity growth. Finally, even when enclosures existed they might fail to protect the crop if property rights themselves were under dispute. In Gorze, widow Ladoucette's sainfoin was enclosed, but those who wanted access to her meadow—including a mayor of Gorze—simply knocked down her fence. According to the municipal government in Gorze, the problem was not enclosures, it was the negligence of the guards who policed the fields and the low fines they could impose for violations. If fines could be set equal to the damage done, the municipality maintained, incursions would disappear and sainfoin could be cultivated on open fields.[56]

Even where the enclosures were far more extensive, as in Bretteville, their effect was limited. We can gauge their impact by including the fraction of the property that was enclosed in the Bretteville TFP regressions. The corresponding coefficient enclosed will then measure the boost that enclosure gives to TFP. If we restrict ourselves to leases from the years 1520–99, when TFP was growing, the coefficient actually turns out to be negative (table 4.7). The negative coefficient may well be a statistical fluke or a result of multicollinearity, and perhaps therefore we ought to turn to the entire sample of leases, where multicollinearity poses no problem. Yet there, too, the coefficients are far from overwhelming. In one of the regressions with an entire sample, the coefficient is not statistically significant, raising the possibility that enclosure had no real effect at all. In the other, admittedly, the coefficient is significant and also larger: it is 0.14, which suggests that enclosure raised TFP by about 15 percent. But even the 15 percent increase following enclosure is far from dramatic. Such a boost was undoubtedly enough to defray the costs of enclosing an individual field—the costs of planting sainfoin and of maintaining hedges—but overall it added little to TFP in the village. Bretteville went from 6 percent enclosed to 22 percent enclosed between the late fifteenth century and the 1660s (table 5.1). Even if all this enclosure had taken place in the sixteenth century, and even if each field were in fact 15 percent more productive, the total addition to TFP would be scarcely 2 percent. Like consolidation, enclosure, too, fails to account for the productivity growth in Bretteville. It simply affected too little of the village.

Yet enclosures should not be dismissed altogether. In the first place, the evidence from Bretteville may well underestimate the effect of enclosure. The reason is that the land which remained open may have been (to use Donald McCloskey's words) "especially suited to openness."[57] Presumably, enclosure would proceed until it no longer produced any benefits. The remaining open fields would then show no sign of lower productivity. To detect the effect of enclosure, we would need to follow the same piece of property, measuring its TFP before and after enclosure, rather than comparing open and enclosed land simultaneously.

There is another reason why the evidence from Bretteville may understate the consequences of enclosure as well. In Bretteville, after all, the enclosures involved little more than hedging and ditching around individual artificial meadows—artificial meadows assembled via a process of voluntary exchange. Elsewhere, enclosures could be far more drastic. They could consolidate all the land holdings in a village and completely reshape the layout of the fields, as with La Galaizière's project in the villages of Roville and Neuviller in Lorraine, where all the plots of land and even the roads were rearranged.

Such general enclosures might be the only way to amalgamate property in regions of extreme fragmentation, such as Lorraine and Burgundy. As was shown in Chapter 2, the general enclosures in Roville and Neuviller did improve access to parcels by remaking the roads. Most important of all, they greatly improved drainage, which boosted yields and allowed artificial meadows to thrive. The rent increase that followed the general enclosures in Roville and Neuviller translated into at least a 15 percent increase of TFP, and this is evidence that deserves our trust, since it derives from the rent increase on what was essentially the same farm. Given the nature of the improvements in Roville and Neuviller—better access and especially better drainage—it is reasonable to assume that these benefits spread out over the entire two villages. English evidence supports such an assumption: after enclosure led to drainage of clay soils in England, TFP rose by 12 percent throughout entire communities.[58]

By the standards of the Old Regime, such a jump in TFP was enormous, particularly when whole villages were concerned. Yet surprisingly, general enclosures were rarely tried. Indeed, the French countryside apparently witnessed perhaps only eight of them in the eighteenth century, and they remained highly unusual throughout the nineteenth century as well. Difficulties with drainage and fragmented holdings were much discussed and afflicted hundreds of communities.[59] Why, then, was the remedy of general enclosure so extraordinary?

It was not the cost, for if La Galaizière's project is any indication, the rent increase following a general enclosure was easily enough to cover the expenses and yield a handsome profit as well. Figures from the nineteenth century suggest much the same.[60] The consensus historians would of course maintain that the general enclosures foundered on the opposition of subsistence peasants, but the subsistence peasants, as Chapter 2 demonstrated, were not the problem for Galaizière's project. Rather, it was the large landowners, who, unlike the subsistence peasants, could not easily be bullied. And by threatening to sue, they held La Galaizière's project up for ransom in order to extort a disproportionate share of the profits.

General enclosures were thus rare for reasons that were at least in part political. The barrier was the structure of property rights and the legal system. La Galaizière could only pursue the completion of his general enclosure with the unanimous consent of all the property owners, in particular the other large landowners. Even he—the intendant and the local seigneur—had no powers of eminent domain. The difficulty of getting unanimous consent was aggravated by another institutional obstacle: the disconcerting lack of finality in the Old Regime legal system. Overlapping jurisdictions covered France, and if opponents could not stop a general enclosure in the first court they tried, they could always, even years later, file suit in another jurisdiction and threaten the profits the enclosure had created. La Galaizière himself, we know from Chapter 2, faced such a disabling suit ten years after his project had been completed. It cost him not only substantial legal fees but also cut the revenue from his farm.

Overcoming such political obstacles was practically impossible under the Old Regime. Overlapping jurisdictions were the backbone of the Old Regime legal system; it took the French Revolution to eliminate them. Worse yet, there was no way to discourage the strategic behavior that bedeviled La Galaizière's general enclosure. Here, the contrast with eighteenth-century England is striking. In England, landowners wanting to enclose their land could seek a private act of Parliament, which typically let owners of four-fifths of the land in a village override minority opposition. The proponents of an English enclosure (typically, large landowners) could easily promote a private enclosure bill, often by influencing friends on parliamentary committees. Their opponents were often tenant farmers unaccustomed to such lobbying, and the structure of Parliament facilitated the bill's passage. Common by the 1760s, the private acts kept opportunists from blocking reform projects in an effort to appropriate a share of the gains. They also protected enclosures from the sort of unending suits that plagued La Galaizière and that had once troubled English enclosures, too, for once the Parliamentary bill was passed the enclosure was secure from legal challenge.[61]

Lacking anything like the English acts of enclosure, French landowners had no way to circumvent strategic behavior and no way to defend general enclosures against disabling suits. There were, to be sure, edicts permitting the division of a village's common grazing land. There were also decrees (as in Lorraine) allowing landowners in various provinces to enclose meadows. But there was nothing to facilitate the general enclosure of an entire village. The explanation is partly ideological: though theoretically absolute, the French crown by the eighteenth century was quite leery of disturbing private property, particularly real property. Interfering with it violated beliefs that were fundamental to the Old Regime polity, especially when (as was inevitable) some of the property was wrapped in privilege and belonged to powerful absentee owners.[62] Furthermore, any legislative attempt to facilitate enclosures would have run afoul of powerful organized interests: tithe collectors, intendants fearful of civil disorder, agents who leased out grazing rights on the royal domains, and seigneurs who enjoyed a large share of the local commons. Opponents of this sort emasculated edicts permitting division of the commons and individual enclosure of meadow; they would have gutted general enclosures too.[63]

Finally, even if general enclosure had been permitted, there would still be the judicial problem of disabling suits. France had no sovereign legislature or centralized court system whose decrees would halt legal challenge. In theory, the monarchy could have permitted general enclosure by decree, but in the eighteenth century the crown was limited by divisions within the government and by the claims of the powerful and privileged. It would never have attempted such a bold step. And village assemblies simply lacked the power to undertake a general enclosure. They would have had to get the approval of the intendant, and their undertaking would never be secure from attack in the courts. In such a situation, a general enclosure could only take place when one individual had enough power to overcome the opposition and enough land to make it worth his while to do so—the extraordinary situation prevailing in La Galaizière's Roville and Neuviller.[64]

Similar problems afflicted irrigation and the drainage of marshes, sapping agricultural productivity both in Provence and along the coast of Normandy, as Jean-Laurent Rosenthal has demonstrated.[65] The Revolution put an end to the suits that plagued irrigation and drainage of marshes, rendering both much easier. But it did not remove the unanimity requirement for general enclosures. The reasons, according to George Grantham, were multiple. Villages still lacked the authority to carry out general enclosures on their own, and the benefits of general enclosure—rent increases—were spread among a large number of landowners, making it difficult to organize support for enclosure legislation. Most important of all, the state had only limited powers to tamper with private property, and any extension of state power over property rights would have faced widespread opposition. Unlike most of western Europe, France therefore lived without general enclosure legislation—and without large numbers of general enclosures—until the twentieth century.[66]

What, then, was the loss to French agriculture from these political obstacles? A precise answer eludes us. Clearly, much of France could do without general enclosures. Where property was already consolidated, large landowners could drain their own property and not worry about their neighbor's consent; they would not need a general enclosure to drain and consolidate their land. That was in fact what happened in the department of the Seine-et-Marne in the middle of the nineteenth century.[67] But where fields were scattered and drainage a problem—drainage being the essential public good that general enclosure furnished—that is where a general enclosure would be necessary. In the middle of the nineteenth century, it was estimated that 34 percent of France's farmland needed drainage. Some of this was undoubtedly marshy wasteland; hence, the fraction of arable needing drainage was presumably less. How much of the watery arable lay in areas of scattered fields is impossible to say, but it was undoubtedly a problem in Lorraine. There, it was estimated that one sixth of the arable needed drainage in the 1860s. If so, and if the drainage there necessitated a general enclosure, then TFP in Lorraine as a whole could have been increased slightly under 3 percent. The real TFP increase, of course, might have been lower still. Some land would have been too costly to drain, even with technologies that went far beyond what La Galaizière utilized: pipes and underdrains, for example, which first appeared in France in the middle of the nineteenth century. In any case, the net addition to TFP would have been small, even in Lorraine.[68] Even there, where problems of drainage and scattering were severe, removing the political obstacles to enclosure would have done little for productivity.

CITIES, MARKETS, AND THE PATTERN OF TFP GROWTH

While enclosures might revolutionize an individual village, over wider regions their impact was muted. The effect of enlarging or consolidating farms was also diluted. But what then explains the pattern of TFP growth we see across early modern France? Obvious possibilities are urbanization and access to city markets. Urbanization, of course, has always been a consequence of economic growth, as peasants are driven off the land or drawn to jobs in cities. But urbanization has also been invoked as a cause of growth. Given high transportation costs, the concentrated demand near a city can widen the scope of the available market and thereby facilitate specialization. Cities can also serve as fertile grounds for new ideas and new technology. They provide what economists call positive externalities, helping new technologies spread, be it the craft of printing in fifteenth-century Mainz in Germany or the modern skill of circuit design in today's Silicon Valley in California. Not surprisingly, historians have long debated the economic role of cities in early modern Europe. Sometimes they condemn early modern cities as parasites, as with the Castilian capital, Madrid. Sometimes they extol their virtues, as with London, whose astonishing growth seems to have transformed English agriculture.[69]

Paris could proudly advance similar claims. In the Paris Basin, we recall, regressions linked the city's population to increases in agricultural productivity. Admittedly, the influence here could have flowed from productivity to urbanization and not the reverse: the higher productivity in local agriculture could itself have led to the growth of Paris, by releasing peasants to work in cities or by feeding urban migrants. One might hope to decide the matter by further statistical analysis, but the statistical tests are unfortunately inconclusive.[70] Still, the bulk of the evidence points to urbanization being a cause of agricultural productivity gains, not a result. When productivity in the Basin rose in the middle of the sixteenth century, it climbed most rapidly near Paris itself, as if farmers near the city could take advantage of opportunities that were unprofitable farther away. And the technological changes that fueled the productivity gains of the eighteenth century were intimately bound up with city trade: farmers who planted artificial meadows and then sold their extra fodder to feed the growing number of urban horses, farmers who on the return trip took urban horse manure back to their fields, or farmers who sowed wheat instead of maslin to suit urban demand and then strove to enhance their wheat yields.

Did other cities in France exert such an influence? The evidence suggests not, although it too is far from conclusive. We can certainly repeat similar regressions for other parts of France. All we need to do is to regress the growth rate of TFP for properties on the rate of population increase in the largest nearby city. To calculate TFP growth with any accuracy, though, we must be able to follow the same properties over time; otherwise, we may confuse increases in TFP with variations from property to property. The regressions also require population figures for the relevant cities, which we can reasonably take to be the largest city within a long day's journey for a farmer transporting grain (45 kilometers).[71]

Only five of our samples can meet such requirements—one near Avignon and four others in the west. If we perform the regressions for the five

TABLE 5.6

Regression of TFP Growth Rates on Urban Population Growth Rates: Selected Results from Pooling Five Lease Samples

Regression Statistic	Value
Coefficient of urban population growth (percent per year)	0.25
T statistics	1.50
Degrees of freedom	49
R^2	0.049
Mean of dependent variable (percent per year)	0.44

Sources: TFP was calculated using lease samples described in Chapter 4 and Appendix B. Population figures were taken from the series *Paroisses et communes de France. Dictionnaire d'histoire administrative et démographique*, ed. Jean-Pierre Bardet and Claude Motte. The volumes I used were *Ille-et-Vilaine*, ed. Claude Renard (Paris, 1990); *Sarthe*, ed. René Plessix (Paris, 1983); *Maine-et-Loire*, ed. François Lebrun (Paris, 1974); and *Vaucluse*, ed. Roland Sicard (Paris, 1987). For Nantes, I derived population figures from the graph in Dupâquier, *Histoire de la population française*, volume 2, figure 39.

Note: The regression involved pooling together five samples of leases. In each sample, all the properties lay within 45 kilometers of one of the following cities: Nantes, Rennes, Le Mans, Angers, and Avignon. Each sample followed the same properties over time, and the growth rate of TFP, which was calculated from lease to lease, was regressed on the growth rate of the population in the city within 45 kilometers of the sample properties. The regression also included dummy variables for each sample; the coefficients of the dummy variables are omitted. The dates for which I could calculate both TFP and urban population growth differed from sample to sample. Overall, the regression data ranges from 1640 to 1790. In matching TFP and urban populations, I assumed that the population figures were constant for each decade.

samples, the coefficient of urban population growth is large and positive, just as we would expect if urbanization boosted productivity (table 5.6). Indeed, the coefficient is about the same as with the Notre Dame sample. The problem, however, is that it could well be a statistical fluke; it simply does not merit much confidence, as a scatter plot suggests (figure 5.4). The relationship between urbanization and productivity withers even further if we attempt another exercise: plotting average productivity increases for each sample versus population growth in the largest nearby city. Using averages overlooks differences among individual properties, but we can perform such a calculation for a much larger number of samples, particularly in the eighteenth century. Unfortunately, once the data are plotted, the

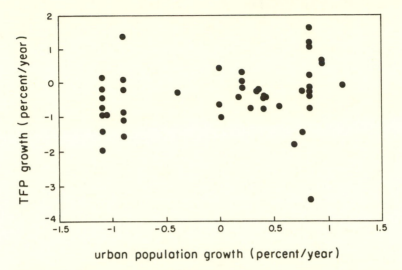

Figure 5.4 Growth Rates of TFP and of Urban Population: Nantes, Rennes, Le Mans, Anjou, Avignon. TFP growth rates are calculated from lease to lease for each of the five samples. The years involved vary from sample to sample and range from 1640 to 1790.

relationship disappears (figure 5.5). Looking at urbanization in the first half of the century, or the preceding fifty years, does not change matters, and statistical tests cast doubt on existence of any credible relationship.[72] Leases from other regions—the vicinities of Bordeaux and of Lille immediately come to mind—might lead to a somewhat different conclusion, but among the numerous cities covered by our samples, only Paris stimulated the countryside.

The mystery is what made Paris and other large cities such as London so exceptional.[73] In some cases, of course, it is easy to understand why a city might have little effect on local agriculture: a port city, for instance, might expand simply by importing food from afar. The French port of Nantes followed such a course. Its booming trade with the French colonies had some effect on the local vineyards, but in general Nantes drew only meager amounts of agricultural produce from the surrounding countryside, or, for that matter, from the entire Loire valley. To provision the colonies, it actually imported butter, canvas, and salted beef from Ireland, rather than from its own hinterland.[74] Yet the example of Nantes still does not explain why Paris behaved so differently from other French cities.

Resolving this enigma requires making clear what precisely was the contribution large cities made to early modern agriculture. It was not that their enormous market for food in and of itself permitted specialization or economies of scale in agriculture, for then as now farms were minuscule relative

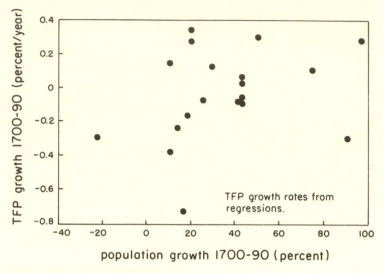

Figure 5.5 TFP Growth versus Population Growth in the Largest City within 45 Kilometers, 1700–90

to the size even of village markets. A large urban market would presumably mean more farms of the same size and sown with the same crops, not bigger farms or more pronounced specialization. Nor does it seem likely, at least in early modern Europe, that cities facilitated the spread of new agricultural techniques. True, city life did help pass knowledge among early modern craftsmen—from metalworkers to printers, for instance, or among the first printers themselves—but it is difficult to see how it could do the same among farmers. They were scattered in the countryside, and unlike urban artisans they did not rub shoulders with one another in guilds and city neighborhoods.

It is conceivable that the extraordinary demand near large cities like Paris compelled nearby farmers to innovate.[75] If so, then we might expect more innovation as Paris grew and hence find a link between agricultural productivity growth and the city's population. There is perhaps some evidence for such a process in the Paris Basin. Innovation, one might argue, should be reflected in a narrowing of the range of the TFP growth rates: if farmers were forced to innovate, only the best would survive, and TFP growth rates might close in on one another, as weaker tenant farmers were replaced by dissatisfied landlords. Statistically, one could measure the range of TFP growth rates by calculating their standard deviation for, say, twenty-five-year periods. In the Paris Basin, this standard deviation would presumably decline as the Paris population rose.

If we graph the standard deviation of the TFP growth rates on the Paris Basin properties, it does decline as Paris grows; it seems to dip as well

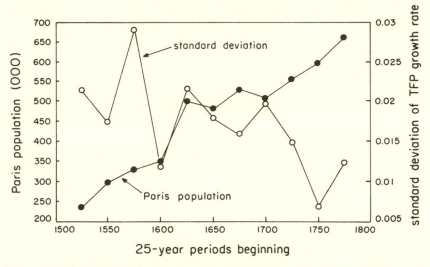

Figure 5.6 The Population of Paris and the Standard Deviation of the TFP Growth Rate in the Paris Basin. The standard deviations are calculated for twenty-five-year periods.

during most periods of productivity growth—in 1600–25, for example (figure 5.6). Yet, even in this graph the relationship seems weak. Worse yet, more refined calculations—standard deviations averaged by decade, for example—argue against any close relationship between the size of the Paris population and the range of TFP growth rates. Furthermore, the narrowing of the TFP growth rates in the long run—particularly between 1650–75 and 1750–75—might have little to do with innovation. It might simply reflect the decline in transportation costs in the Paris region, a decline that would tend to level rent differences and push TFP growth rates together. Finally, even if there were a relationship between innovation and the Paris population, why would similar relationships not prevail in the vicinity of smaller French cities? Unfortunately, the lease samples from other regions are too small to let us calculate the standard deviation of TFP growth rates with any confidence, but urban demand about smaller cities would presumably have the same effect as about Paris.

Although the effect Paris had on innovation remains murky, the city did influence agricultural productivity growth in a more visible way, for it was Parisian demand that made the artificial meadows profitable. Despite all the attention paid to artificial meadows in the eighteenth century, they were in fact likely to be unprofitable in much of the east, west, and south of France: in other words, the regions from which most of our lease samples derive. The argument here has been advanced by George Grantham on the basis of evidence from the first agricultural census in 1840. But Grantham's findings apply equally well to the end of the Old Regime. In part, his argument is that soil and climate excluded the artificial meadows from much of France—in particular, from most of the south and west. The other part of Grantham's case is that the artificial meadows proved unprofitable in most of France, too. Indeed, the only places where they earned a profit in 1840 was in the Paris Basin, in parts of Normandy, and in the heavily urbanized north. Even then the profit was likely found only on land with the best loam rather than, say, soils of clay.[76]

No census exists that would let us repeat Grantham's calculations for the Old Regime, but we can at least project his figures back for three of his regions for which we have necessary price series: Lorraine, the west, and the Paris Basin.[77] The point is to compare what fodder from an artificial meadow cost with what it was implicitly worth when fed to animals on the farm. If artificial meadows were profitable, then the value of the fodder they yielded—in other words, the fodder's implicit price—would exceed what it cost to produce. To calculate the costs and implicit prices, we simply project Grantham's costs and implicit prices back, using available price and wage series (table 5.7).

The whole procedure assumes, as do Grantham's original calculations, that artificial meadows are simply used to feed livestock on the farm; it ignores what the meadows may have added to grain yields by fixing nitrogen in the soil or by increasing supplies of manure from livestock. Under such assumptions, what made the artificial meadows profitable were high prices for meat or, equivalently, high prices for livestock and animal feed. Obviously, any such calculations are subject to considerable uncertainty, but they suggest—as do Grantham's original numbers—that prices were not high enough to turn a profit in Lorraine or in the west. Of the three regions, it was only near Paris that the meadows would apparently make money, for only there did urban demand for livestock and animal feed exert a sufficient force.

Contemporaries near Paris would of course have agreed. Ever since the late sixteenth century Parisian observers had noted the city's enormous demand for animal feed, a demand that the artificial meadows helped satisfy. Although our calculations concern only the late eighteenth century, we know that some farmers near Paris had been planting artificial meadows in order to release livestock feed for the Paris market for ages—since at least the middle of the seventeenth century, if not before.[78] We might reasonably presume then that as the city expanded, the prices of meat and of livestock feed grew higher and higher, making the artificial meadows more profitable and the farms that sowed them more productive. Hence, this demonstrates at least one of the links between the size of the Paris population and productivity growth in the Paris Basin. By contrast, in most of the other regions we examined—Normandy is probably an exception here—

TABLE 5.7
Hypothetical Costs and Prices of Fodder from Artificial Meadows, 1775–89

| Area | Cost of Sowing Artificial Meadow (Livres/Quintal) | | Implicit Fodder Price (Livres/Quintal) |
	Loam	Clay	
Paris Region	1.68	2.14	1.99
Lorraine	1.04	1.44	0.88
West	1.82	2.03	1.33

Sources: Grantham, "The Diffusion of the New Husbandry" (costs and implicit fodder prices in 1840); Husson, *Les consommations de Paris*, pp. 217–18 (wholesale prices of beef per livre in Paris, 1775–89); D. Zolla, "Les variations du revenu et du prix des terres en France au XVIIe et au XVIIIe siècles," *Sciences politiques* 9 (1894): 214 (price of meat in Le Mans, 1780–85); Henri Hauser, *Recherches et documents sur l'histoire des prix en France* (Paris, 1936), pp. 268–72 (oat prices in Angers, 1775–89); *SA 1840* (the prices of oats, wheat, and beef in 1840); and *SA 1852* agricultural census (rural wages in 1852). Other prices and wages for 1775–89 were taken from the same series used to construct productivity indexes for the west, Lorraine, and Paris in Chapter 4; they are described in Appendix B.

Note: The calculations here simply project Grantham's costs and implicit fodder prices (from 1840) back into the eighteenth century. Grantham's implicit fodder price is pg/rw, where p is the price of meat per kilogram, g is the weight gain per day in kilograms, w is the average live weight in kilograms, and r is the feeding ration per day as a percent of w. I took Grantham's median fodder prices for oxen and cows and projected them back under the assumption that the ratio g/rw remained constant and only p changed. In other words, I assumed that although animal weights might vary, weight gain as a fraction of food consumed did not change. In the absence of any evidence about animal weights, this seemed a reasonable assumption.

I also projected Grantham's costs per quintal backward. To do so, I assumed that Grantham's costs of tillage and haymaking per hectare of meadow would be proportional to the change in wages, that his costs of wheat foregone per hectare would be proportional to the price of wheat, and that his costs of seed and fallow grazing per hectare would be proportional to an index of the price of oats. I then used prices and wages in 1775–89 and 1840–52 to project the costs per hectare backward; I converted the costs per hectare to costs per quintal under the assumption that Grantham's fodder yields did not change. The prices I used to project the costs backward come from the 1840 agricultural census for Grantham's regions, save for Lorraine, where I used my own figures from 1825–49. Since the 1840 census does not mention wages, I used the 1852 census for wages, save again for Lorraine. For 1775–89, my Paris region prices were for Paris itself. My 1775–89 prices for the west included grain prices and wages from the Maine-et-Loire and Brittany, which were not in Grantham's west; evidence from the 1840 census suggests that the addition should not matter greatly. For Lorraine, I used the costs and implict prices that Grantham gives for a larger region including Lorraine, which he calls Champagne.

there would be no such relationship between productivity and the local urban population. Artificial meadows would be ruled out in those regions from the start by infertile soil, a hostile climate, and feeble urban demand.

If Parisian demand stimulated artificial meadows, the city also supplied agriculture with something essential as well, forging yet another link between agricultural productivity and the city's population growth. What Paris had to offer agriculture was fertilizer—the horse manure that was carted back to farms from urban stables, or the fertilizer from feed lots and dairy cattle. Given the rate at which eighteenth-century farmers applied manure to their fields, there was probably enough from the city's horses alone to fertilize all the farms within a 15-kilometer radius of the city. By the late eighteenth century, the use of urban manure on local farms had become common.[79]

Other cities were of course also endowed with horses and feed lots, but Paris undoubtedly had far more. In part the reason was simply that Paris was far larger than any other French city: at 660,000 souls in 1790, it dwarfed its closest rival Lyon, which was far behind with a population of only 146,000.[80] Furthermore, its wealthy population could better afford the luxuries of horse-drawn carriages and meat. With far more animals in Paris, manure would presumably be far cheaper than in other cities. It would be cheap enough to buy after delivering goods to Paris, and cheap enough for a farmer to fill his wagon and then haul the manure back to spread on his fields. And it would be cheap enough for him to buy when a stable owner dispatched a servant to his farm with a wagon of manure to sell and an order to purchase oats. For farmers from outside most other cities, though, the urban manure would be too costly. Buying it after a trip into town would not be worthwhile, for it would be less expensive to acquire animals in the countryside and simply let them defecate on the fields. Indeed, outside most cities, the cost of urban manure would be prohibitive for arable farming or agriculture that mixed livestock and grain. It would be too expensive for anything but vineyards and market gardens lying just outside the city walls.

Unfortunately, evidence concerning the redolent traffic in urban waste hardly exists; in particular, we will never have price series for urban manure. We cannot therefore compare the price of urban manure for farms outside Paris with its price for those outside other cities. Nor can we confirm that only in the Paris Basin (and perhaps in the heavily urbanized north of France) did it pay to import urban manure. Yet the argument is coherent, and it fits nineteenth-century evidence as well.[81] It forges yet another link between the growth of the population of Paris and agricultural productivity, for as Paris grew, so did the supply of manure. The price of the manure then fell, making it possible to utilize more of it on arable farms. The cheap manure in turn raised yields and productivity. In other cities, by contrast, the urban manure supply would never reach the threshold of profitability in arable farming. Its use would never spread beyond periurban vineyards and market gardens. As a result, we would never see a relationship between urban populations and local agricultural productivity except in large cities like Paris.[82]

Paris had other unique advantages as well, advantages that may well have facilitated the traffic in manure and the sowing of artificial meadows. For political and military reasons, the capital profited disproportionally from the road building that began under Jean-Baptiste Colbert (1619–83), the controller general of finance. Road construction in the eighteenth century also showered Paris with a lavish share of the benefits.[83] The improved roads made it possible for farmers to use larger carts and perhaps to ship goods greater distances overland, cutting the cost of shipping livestock feed to Paris and of bringing urban manure back in return. The lower costs could only hasten the adoption of artificial meadows and the use of urban manure. Near cities less well endowed with roads than the Paris Basin—in France that would include much of the west and south—the higher costs of transportation would be yet another obstacle to sowing artificial meadows or to initiating the traffic in urban manure.[84]

The better roads near Paris benefited the trade in wheat as well. But what did more to cut the cost of shipping wheat was the reorganization of the grain trade. In the seventeenth century, for example, a farmer might take wheat to market in Paris in his own small wagon and sell it to a baker. The baker would then ship it to a miller, whose mill often lay outside the city, to be ground into flour and then returned to Paris. But by the eighteenth century the miller himself might purchase the wheat in the fields, grind it outside Paris, and then have the flour shipped directly to the bakery. The baker and miller would spare themselves a superfluous shipment to the mill outside Paris, and they would also economize by transporting flour much of the way, instead of bulkier grain. And if they were not buying from one of the big tenant farmers who now had large efficient wagons, they could hire specialists to cart the grain at low cost.[85]

This reorganization is what explains much of the decline in the cost of shipping grain that we detected in the Paris Basin between 1650 and 1750. Here, Paris seemed far ahead of other cities in France. The practice of shipping flour, for instance, was well advanced near Paris by the beginning of the eighteenth century; near other French cities it had to await the 1760s.[86] Whether, as a result, the cost of transporting wheat dropped further around Paris than around other cities is, unfortunately, impossible to say. An answer would require parallel series of grain prices reaching well back to the early seventeenth century, not just for the other cities but for their hinterland towns. Such series simply do not exist. But in Paris, wheat did go from dear in the seventeenth century to relatively cheap in the eighteenth—relative, that is, to most other French cities—and that evidence is at least consistent with a greater decline in the cost of shipping wheat in the Paris Basin.[87]

The lower costs for shipping wheat undoubtedly raised farm gate prices, and the higher farm gate prices made it profitable to sow wheat for sale in Paris instead of more robust maslin and rye, which were the staples of rural consumption. Lower shipping costs would also encourage seed selection, improved storage, and soil preparation before sowing grain. The result in any case would be increased productivity, which once again would be far more pronounced in the Paris Basin than in the hinterland of other towns.

One should not conclude, though, that the Paris Basin was the only region where cheaper transportation boosted agricultural productivity. Inexpensive transportation was in fact a major impetus behind productivity growth in early modern agriculture, because it encouraged trade and specialization. Contemporaries recognized as much. According to Sébastien le Prestre de Vauban, the famed military engineer, once one moved away from economical water transport, "the regular market for farm products disappears; one grows only for subsistence, or, at best, for local demand; and crops provide a farmer with only a scant return on his costs of cultivation."[88] As with the Parisian grain trade, the source of cheaper transportation was usually organizational changes. Apart from improving roads and building canals, there was little else that could be done in the centuries before railroads. Unfortunately, the organizational changes had their limits, limits that in many cases had already been attained. In some parts of France agricultural trade was already efficiently organized, and the available benefits had already been squeezed out of trade and specialization, leaving no room for productivity growth.

Such was the case in much of the west, where agriculture had long revolved about the breeding of cattle and sheep for sale in markets as far away as Paris. The clearest example comes from the Gâtine Poitevine, where in the sixteenth century landlords planted hedges, plowed under vines, and consolidated farms, in large part to expand herds of cattle and sheep. The cattle were sold to merchants from Brittany or from as far away as Paris. The sheep went to Paris and Bordeaux, while their wool fed a rural textile industry. The shift toward the breeding of such livestock suited a region where soil and climate favored natural meadows, and where distance from cities ruled against specialization in arable farming. Had our TFP series for the Gâtine reached back deep into the sixteenth century, it would in all likelihood have registered a jump in TFP. The transformation reached its limit, though, early in the seventeenth century, a limit largely set by inadequate transportation and the consequent need to continue growing some grain for local consumption.[89] Hence, the stagnant productivity that we encountered after 1650–74.

Elsewhere in the west specialization rarely reached so far, despite a soil and climate that favored livestock. In the seventeenth and eighteenth centuries, it is true, the Auge witnessed a sizable conversion of arable to pasture, a change driven by Parisian demand. What made such a transformation possible, though, was the existing specialization in cereals in the nearby Plain of Caen. The two parts of Normandy traded with one another, with the Plain shipping grain in return for livestock from the Auge. If Bretteville-l'Orgueilleuse is any indication, the Plain could have furnished the Auge with abundant grain as early as the sixteenth century. Yet even in the Auge, as we know, specialization had a muted impact on productivity, because the conversion to pasture proceeded slowly and much of the land remained frozen in grain farming. As for other parts of the west, they were in a still worse situation. They usually lacked a nearby source of cereals, and with poor yields, even more land had to remain in arable than in the Auge. The area's roads were often bad and trade was stunted. Under such conditions, it was difficult to extend trade beyond levels that had been reached well before the eighteenth century. One should not be surprised that the TFP figures in the west failed to grow.[90]

It is true that in the west the indices of TFP did not simply fail to grow; they actually declined. Perhaps western agriculture suffered from more than just a lack of trade. Perhaps the soil was so poor and so easily exhausted that it could not produce much until chemical fertilizers became available.[91] Perhaps the trade the west did have—notably, in livestock—faced fiercer competition, which might have cost the west some of its existing opportunities for specialization.[92] Or perhaps, as Chapter 4 suggested, the TFP indices in the west were biased downward, and agricultural productivity was actually stagnant rather than declining. In that case, conditions of trade and transportation suffice as explanations.

If the cost of transportation and the available opportunities for trade can account for stagnation in the west and the peculiarities of Normandy, they can also explain the most rapid cases of productivity growth we observed. In the Beaujolais, for example, the connection is obvious. The productivity gains there derived from the conversion of arable to vineyard, a conversion driven by Parisian demand. Establishing the trade with Paris was in part a matter of better water transportation—namely, the opening of the Briare and Loing canals, which linked the Loire and the Seine. But it also reflected a number of demanding organizational changes: in particular, the creation of a network of merchants and specialized transporters who could purchase the wine, cart it overland to the Loire river, and then ship it by boat (via the Loire, the canals, and the Seine) to Paris.

The network built upon existing traffic between the Mâconnais (an area to the north of the Beaujolais) and Paris. Because wine from the Mâconnais was barred from the Lyon market to the south by internal tariff barriers, the

Mâconnais had developed a trade in high-priced wines with more distant Paris—high-priced wines that could defray the cost of transportation. The problem was getting the wine over the hills of the Mâconnais to the Loire. By an accident of geography, one of the easiest routes led south to the Beaujolais, then overland to the Loire. Paris wine merchants took the wine from the Mâconnais south and hired local farmers' ox carts to ship it overland in the off season. They also organized storehouses so that the four- to five-day journey overland could be broken up into one-day trips. That way none of the farmers would have to make a costly stay overnight. But once this network was organized, it could easily be adapted to transport wine from the Beaujolais. The Beaujolais lay along the way to Paris, and even cheap wine from the Beaujolais could be shipped to Paris at a relatively low marginal cost once the network was in place. The result was rapid productivity growth of 0.3 to 0.4 percent a year in the Beaujolais.[93]

It seems likely that improved transportation explains the brisk TFP growth (0.3 percent per year) in the eighteenth-century Albigeois as well. Maize had already spread throughout the area by the beginning of the century, yet it was not the source of the productivity gains that we measured. The key was probably the extension of roads, giving the Albigeois access to the Canal du Midi. That cut transportation costs, allowing local farmers to specialize further in wheat production.[94]

Finally, the fastest productivity growth we encountered—the 0.8 to 1.0 percent per year achieved in the sixteenth century along the western coast of Schleswig-Holstein in northern Germany—also stemmed from the establishment of trade. There, farming profited from a burgeoning trade in dairy products for markets in Hamburg, Bremen, and the Netherlands. Elsewhere in the region (and in neighboring parts of Denmark and the Netherlands as well), it was the traffic in cattle that thrived. Both sorts of commerce required organization, but both permitted specialization—specialization that suited the soil, the climate, and local costs of transportation. The result was higher productivity.[95]

It would be tempting to extend the argument to other regions: to landlocked Lorraine, for example, where productivity growth faded after 1750, or to Provence and southeastern Languedoc, where it languished throughout the entire eighteenth century. Yet the argument should not be stretched too far. Compared with the rest of northern France, for instance, roads in Lorraine were fairly well developed, and there were even hints of specialized transporters early in the 1700s.[96] Evidently, the cause of Lorraine's problems lies elsewhere. As for Provence and southeastern Languedoc, although they lacked sufficient roads, their waning productivity in the eighteenth century had other causes. Legal barriers to irrigation, which would have boosted productivity, shackled one source of productivity growth, while erosion gnawed away at the productivity already attained. And part of the disappointing performance derives, quite simply, from the peculiarities of the properties we sampled. In both Provence and southeastern Languedoc, our samples lacked properties that underwent conversion from arable to vineyard. They therefore omitted a transformation that, on other properties in the region, undoubtedly boosted productivity in the eighteenth century.[97]

Still, transportation costs seem to explain much of early modern productivity growth, not just in France, but in Germany and England as well.[98] When transportation costs fell, trade and specialization flourished, and agricultural productivity eventually did the same. When transportation costs could fall no more, productivity growth ground to a halt. Of course, that is hardly surprising in an era before the reaper, chemical fertilizer, and scientific agronomy. In the countryside, one of the few sources of productivity gains lay with trade and comparative advantage. Since the major obstacle to greater trade was the high cost of shipping crops over long distances, anything that lowered transportation costs (and more generally, the costs of transactions at a distance) was a boon to agriculture.[99]

Had the government built more roads or dug more canals, its efforts might have reaped a handsome dividend in the form of increased agricultural productivity. Precisely how much is impossible to say, for in the rare instances when the government undertook such public works—the building of the Canal du Midi, for example—we lack the local farm leases or the evidence about the physical quantities transported that would let us calculate the impact on agriculture. In any event, a large project like the Canal du Midi would probably not be the appropriate one to investigate. Its aims were more grandiose than ameliorating local agriculture, and although it cut local transport costs for grain drastically, it might have represented a far larger investment than was necessary.[100]

To be sure, expecting the government to spend more on roads and canals would be naive. In early modern Europe, taxes funded not transportation but the spiraling costs of warfare, and it would have been difficult for the scattered landowners who benefited from the roads and canals to lobby in unison for better transportation. As for private entrepreneurs who sought to improve roads and canals, in France they faced they same thicket of privileges and legal obstacles that, as Jean-Laurent Rosenthal has demonstrated, blocked the construction of irrigation canals.[101]

In any case, in early modern France—England was hardly different—cheaper transportation often resulted from organizational changes, not from the roads or the canals themselves. One thinks of how the grain trade was reorganized around Paris, or of how the network of merchants and farmers arose to ship wine from the Beaujolais. Not that the organizational changes cut a unique path to cheaper transportation and commercialization. Depending on local prices and momentary opportunities, the organizational structures could vary from place to place and century to century. The Paris Basin provides an illuminating example. In the nineteenth century, farmers there sold less fodder and devoted more resources to sheep. Repeated dealings in manure and fodder crops—so important a century before—now vanished without a trace.[102]

THE TRANSFORMATION OF THE COUNTRYSIDE: MYTH AND REALITY

Unlike farm size and enclosure, cheaper transportation thus mattered a lot. But it was not the only factor influencing agricultural productivity. Low agricultural prices could discourage investment in improvements such as ditches, vinestock, and soil preparation. Maintenance could suffer as bankrupt farmers prepared to abandon their leases. The result would be stagnant or even falling TFP. Such a process might have been at work in Languedoc at the dismal end of the seventeenth century, or in the Paris Basin during the years of slow growth from the middle of the 1600s to the early eighteenth century. In both places, farmers were in trouble.[103]

Taxes and the fiscal system also had a role to play in explaining the variations of TFP, albeit a largely negative one. Blaming the excesses of the fisc for shortcomings of the French economy has of course been customary at least since the smug observations of Sir John Fortescue in the late fifteenth century. Although the per-capita tax burden in France was actually lighter than in England in the eighteenth century, that was not necessarily the case a hundred years before.[104] And even in the eighteenth century, one might ask whether French agriculture, by taking on more than its share of taxation, ended up laboring under an unusually heavy fiscal load. As a fraction of agriculture rent, royal tax levies varied greatly in France. On seven of Notre Dame's farms, the assessment of tenants in 1789 ranged from 18 to 35 percent of the rent, with an average of 28 percent. Near Bretteville in 1727, taxes ran to perhaps 19 percent of the rent, although they might have been a bit higher a century before. On farms across the English Channel, taxes did bear down more lightly, but not dramatically so. A typical English land-tax assessment circa 1740 might have amounted to 18 percent of the rent, to which the tithe and potentially heavy parish rates would have to be added. A farmer in France would owe the tithe seigneurial dues as well, but except in areas with heavy seigneurial levies—parts of Burgundy, for example—it is hard to argue that his tax burden was extraordinary. Taxes on agricultural capital in France also seemed low. By the eighteenth century, when tax assessments were frequently linked to the number of acres farmed and the amount of livestock owned, the marginal tax rate on livestock in Normandy amounted to merely 1 or 2 percent of the beasts' rental value.[105]

The problem with the fisc, though, was not the weight of taxation. It was the incentives the fiscal system created and the way taxes were levied, particularly before the reforms of Colbert. Among the worst abuses was the seizure of livestock when taxes fell in arrears, a practice that was all too common in the first half of the seventeenth century, especially among the hapless peasants charged with collecting their villages' taxes. The effect on agriculture was devastating. When sheep were seized, it meant the loss of essential fertilizer; when horses and oxen were taken—in spite of laws protecting draft animals—fields went unplowed. The peasants might also be cast into prison, and in extreme cases (as during a tax revolt) troops would be dispatched to hold the entire village responsible, wreaking havoc on the village economy. The fisc was particularly rough on wealthier peasants, and by penalizing their initiatives, the tax system encouraged them to direct their investments away from agriculture, or so Jean Meuvret has argued. It is true that the nefarious consequences of tax collections disturbed Colbert; the worst abuses subsided as a result of his reforms in the late seventeenth century. But the fisc still caused considerable damage in the first half of the century, when numerous villages fell into debt to pay huge tax levies and to keep the troops away. It thus seems likely—certainty is impossible here—to blame the tax system (along with troop movements during the Fronde and a series of disastrous harvests in the early 1630s) for the slow TFP growth in the Paris Basin during the second quarter of the seventeenth century. The charge would apply equally well to the slump in seventeenth-century Bretteville. In addition to bad harvests and bouts of the plague that frightened surviving farmers away from the market, the region endured crushing taxes, the repression of a major fiscal revolt, and repeated imprisonments and seizures of livestock.[106] Even if we allow for the hyperbole natural to any complaint about taxes, there remains a good deal of truth in the claim that the fisc's seizures had depleted local herds of livestock in 1661 and that the fear of imprisonment had driven farmers away from market.[107]

The real evil of the fiscal system was then the uncertainty it created, and the havoc it wreaked with trade, capital, and property rights. War had the same disastrous effect, at least in the sixteenth and seventeenth centuries, and while the argument about the tax system must remain tentative, about the effects of warfare there is no doubt. Outside Paris, fighting during the Wars of Religion cut TFP by 25 percent. TFP suffered when Spanish troops swept near Amiens in the 1630s, and it collapsed when the Thirty Years' War ravaged Lorraine. Civil war sowed chaos; so did rebellions such as the Fronde, albeit on a lesser scale. Even mobilizing royal troops could damage the rural economy, for given the lack of discipline common in early modern armies, it made little difference whether the troops were friend or foe. Both practiced arson, extorsion, and the theft of livestock and grain.[108]

Some of the damage was easy to repair. If warfare frightened farmers and merchants away from the market, as in Dauphiné during the Wars of Religion, peace would bring a revival of commerce.[109] On the other hand, if trade involved repeated dealings among farmers and merchants, as with wine or the longer distance traffic in grain, then the revival might require more time, to reknit commercial networks and reestablish reputations of trust. South of Paris, for example, the Wars of Religion interrupted the flow of grain from the Beauce; shipments did not fully recover until well into the seventeenth century.[110] Similarly, if war drove off tenants, it might take landlords months or even years to find reliable replacements: east of Paris, after the Wars of Religion left the farm of Dampmart vacant and in ruin, it took over fifteen years to replace Pierre Vacuet. If animals were seized, buildings put to flame, or fields left to grow over because of the fear of attack—if, in short, capital goods were damaged—then recovery might also be long delayed. Clearing away the brush and small trees that sprouted on abandoned fields was a particularly slow and arduous task; it might continue for years. And if farmers lost their savings to soldiers, rebuilding could last a full generation.[111] In the long run, farmers might even shy away from investments that risked attracting the military. Early modern armies, for instance, commonly requisitioned draft animals, which might be injured or not returned at all. With troops repeatedly pummelling Lorraine, requisitioning drove farmers to starve their horses in order to produce animals so small and so weak that the soldiers would not be tempted to seize them.[112]

It is thus easy to understand why agricultural productivity recovered only slowly after war or rebellion. If a political crisis unleashed rapacious tax collectors, the wounds might be just as slow to heal. Near Paris, in what was one of France's richest agricultural regions, it was no surprise that productivity growth repeatedly faltered because of the Wars of Religion and the crises of the seventeenth century. Although local agricultural productivity was on a par with that in England by the late 1700s, it had taken farmers in the Paris Basin three centuries to reach this level, a task that the English had accomplished in only two. The century the French had wasted was the price paid for warfare and political disaster.

Beyond warfare, taxes, and prices, beyond urban markets and farm size, there are still other explanations that historians have advanced to account for the successes and failures of early modern agriculture. Among them is the claim—common since the eighteenth century—that blames French landlords for their country's agricultural failings. While in England landlords resided on their farms and zealously improved them, in France they lived away from their property and displayed little direct interest in farming. In England they were said to cooperate with their tenants in investments and the pursuit of better farming; in France their focus was short-run gain, at the expense of growth. For example, the Saulx-Tavanes, landlords in Burgundy, devoted themselves to squeezing higher seigneurial dues from their peasants. Investment in agriculture was not their concern. Similarly, the predilection French landlords showed for sharecropping seemed linked to agricultural stagnation.[113]

This matter our leases cannot settle definitively, because they nearly all concern absentee landlords. One can certainly invoke the Cairon family, who long resided on their property and took a deep interest in agriculture. Their farms, to be sure, were highly productive, but the leased properties of Notre Dame were just as efficient, and Notre Dame actually cooperated with its tenants in making investments in outbuildings and improvements to the soil.[114] Obviously, a few examples are a meager basis for judging the issue, and the reasonable tack here is perhaps to edge away from a final judgment concerning the landlords' share of the blame. On the one hand, there were obviously landlords, such as the Saulx-Tavanes, whose obsession with seigneurial dues—a matter of pure redistribution—undercut growth and did nothing to spur investment. On the other, English landlords were not the paragons of economic virtue as is usually assumed.[115] Furthermore, much of what French landlords did is readily understandable and had little effect on productivity.

Absentee landlordship in France, for instance, was fueled by the tax system and by the political and social rewards of residence in Paris or at the court.[116] While absentee ownership imposed additional monitoring costs on property administration, there were nonetheless clear signs that French landlords and tenants were forging the same sort of cooperative relationships that prevailed in England, and such cooperative relationships would have reduced the burden of monitoring. Manuals for landlords encouraged such relationships as early as the sixteenth century, and we can see them developing in the Paris Basin and various other parts of the country—despite claims by historians to the contrary. Perhaps the best sign of the growing cooperation among tenants and landlords was the increasing tendency of families to repeat as tenants and to remain on the same farms for longer and longer times. In the Notre Dame sample, for instance, tenant families had been on their farms for an average of only eleven years in 1525–49; by 1775, the figure had risen to an all-time high of thirty years. The increase was not uniform: although high in 1550–74, 1650–99, and 1725–49, the tenure of families dropped during bad harvests and war. The overall trend, though, was up. Although the same was not true of the farm of the Sacristie near Avignon, a similar trend was apparent on our three properties near Nantes.

Yet what is important for our purposes is that these cooperative relationships apparently had little or no effect on productivity. If we use the length of time a tenant family had stayed on a farm as a measure of landlord-tenant cooperation, it accounts for practically none of the productivity growth near Nantes and Avignon, and in the Paris Basin. With the Notre Dame sample, for instance, the family's tenure in a leasehold has a negative and insignificant coefficient if added to the regressions with the growth rate of TFP. If added to the regressions with the level of TFP, its coefficient is positive and significant, but so small that it explains only a 0.2 percent increase in TFP between 1725–49 and 1775–89. On the farm of the Sacristie and the properties near Nantes, results of regressions are the same: long tenure by a leasehold family never has a strong positive effect on TFP. Lack of cooperation thus seems unlikely to explain France's agricultural failings. As for sharecropping in early modern France, Chapter 3 demonstrated that it was simply a response to problems of monitoring and risk. Although our fixed-rent leases do not let us test its effect on growth directly, evidence from the regions where it prevailed suggests that it did not throttle growth. And as we saw in Chapter 3, both economic theory and data from developing countries support the same conclusion.

One final explanation for France's agricultural failings can also be put to the test: the widespread belief that economic growth presupposes a drastic transformation of the countryside. The argument, again, is that growth faces a formidable obstacle in the subsistence peasantry; until they are swept away, growth will be held in check. The subsistence peasants' mentality and their village communities are too hidebound and too resistant to change; their farms are too small and too isolated from markets. What must take their place are large capitalist farms, which hire wage labor, produce for the market, and innovate because of their size.

Our story casts doubt on such assumptions, at least in early modern France. In the first place, the very picture it draws of the rural economy— the self-sufficient peasants, cut off from markets—is largely a myth, as shown in Chapter 2. In early modern France, farmers did produce food for their own consumption and hire family labor, because transportation costs and the difficulties of monitoring servants made doing so highly rational. But markets (markets that had their peculiarities to be sure) were nearly everywhere. Most peasants simply owned too little land to be self-sufficient. They had to lease land in a tight rental market or hire themselves out as servants and day laborers.

As for peasant mentality as an obstacle to growth, one should note that the whole notion glosses over the enormous differences among the denizens of the countryside, and it seems sadly demeaning to them. The belief that such a peasant mentality existed, and worse yet, that it discouraged growth and innovation, derives, of course, from a variety of sources—from the historian Lucien Febvre or from figures such as Karl Polanyi. Yet—to focus on Polanyi for a moment—it is clear that his work rests upon a number of assumptions of dubious value in early modern Europe. Polanyi, after all, posited a society untouched by the market, a society whose goal was collective subsistence and in which everyone cooperated to ensure the group's survival. It was a society of near-idyllic reciprocity, where even minimizing one's effort was unthinkable.[117] If such a society ever existed, it was certainly not in the countryside of early modern France, with its villages riven by jealousies and strife. Although cooperation was not absent from the early modern French countryside, it sprouted, ironically, precisely where Polanyi would have least expected it: in the local markets for credit, land, and labor, with their repeated dealings between lenders and borrowers, landlords and tenants, farmers and hired hands.

Furthermore, although Polanyi drew upon the history of early modern Europe and particularly England, his argument is hard to reconcile with actual peasant farming practices at the time, whether one looks at France, Germany, or even England. Most of the peasants' technology did seem to minimize costs and effort. The first plot to get manure, for instance, was the garden outside the peasant's home, not some distant field. Similarly, if peasants usually reaped their wheat with a seemingly inefficient sickle, it was because the scythe posed technical problems and required costly skilled labor.[118] As for cooperative efforts to ensure their survival, the peasants' tactics were individualistic, not collective. Their commons rarely provided any social insurance, and they did not store grain for the entire village or pursue other strategies of collective security. If Donald McCloskey is correct, they simply scattered the location of their fields to protect against disaster, a tactic that benefited individuals and their families, not entire villages.[119] Had they been fully altruistic, they would never have needed to scatter their fields.

True, early modern Europe did witness a cultural shift from an ideal of reciprocity to one of individual gain, a shift that ended, one might argue, with the smug liberalism of the modern age. Yet in its early stages this shift was largely independent of social and economic change. It began with humanism, with the Reformation and the Counter-Reformation, with the quest for individual justification instead of the fraternal charity of the medieval Church. In rural France, it left its mark upon confraternities, upon churches, and upon gifts fervently inscribed in wills. Yet where we can follow it in detail—in the Lyonnais and the Beaujolais, for instance—it bore absolutely no relationship to economic activity.[120] It cannot be reduced to a mere result of economic growth, or fashioned into a prerequisite for productivity gains. To do so, as Polanyi did and as so many historians continue to do, would be to confuse culture and the economy, which, at least in early modern Europe, were two largely independent spheres.

Culture and peasant mentality return us to large capitalist farms, the crux of the matter for the consensus historians and for social thinkers who consider the peasantry an impediment to be swept away. Here, despite great differences on other issues, nearly everyone seems to agree. The consensus historians blame population growth for the minuscule peasant farms; their assumption, of course, is that such farms were unproductive. Their opponents, such as Robert Brenner, begin with the same assumption. For Brenner, the French class structure cursed France with small and unproductive peasant farms. Farm size was in fact the touchstone (along with a cooperative relationship between landlords and tenants) of his comparison of England and France. In his view, French landholdings were fragmented even in advanced regions like the Paris Basin, and he believed that was one of the principal reasons why the peasant agriculture of France—even in the Paris Basin—suffered by comparison with the large, enclosed capitalist farms in England or, for that matter, with the great German estates east of the Elbe.[121]

Part of the problem with Brenner's argument is a simple historical mistake. When Brenner compared landholdings in England with those in the Paris Basin, he confused *propriété* and *exploitation*, the amount of land owned and the amount of land farmed. The statistics he cited did reveal a large number of peasants who owned small amounts of land. But they were part-time workers, not full-time farmers, and were the counterparts to cottagers in England. Actual farms in the Paris Basin were in fact much larger, for they might well unite land rented from a number of different owners. Indeed, the working farms in the regions were probably about the same size as those across the English Channel.[122]

A much more grievous error is the assumption that farm size determines productivity, an error common to both Brenner and his opponents. We found that farms in the Paris Basin (and near Caen as well) were just as productive as English farms and far more productive than East German estates. Farms elsewhere in France lagged behind, but their size usually had little to do with their poor performance. Increases in farm size explained only a portion of the high productivity near Caen and Paris, and with the possible exception of eastern France, there seemed no barriers in the long run to achieving the optimal farm scale.

Here, one might reject the evidence, arguing that since it derives from leases it does not paint a true picture of the peasantry. Peasants, one might object, did not lease their land; for all intents and purposes, they owned it. Their costs of capital and labor were thus quite different. Now it is true that the leases omit mention of such small peasant owners. But we should not exaggerate their numbers, for only a few peasants owned enough land to be self-sufficient. Most of the others were part-time farmers. They worked in the labor market and rented what capital they used from *laboureurs*. They may have specialized in labor-intensive crops such as grapevines, where the labor required considerable supervision, but it would be hard to maintain that they faced wildly different prices for capital and labor. And, as we know from Chapter 3, their behavior in the land rental market seemed little different from that of their brethren with larger holdings.

It should be stressed, too, that not all the evidence came from leases. For instance, there was physical evidence suggesting that yields did not rise with farm size. The physical evidence demonstrates that large farms were not more capital intensive: they had no more livestock per hectare. And it shows that large farms had no monopoly over agricultural innovation either. Southeast of Paris, for example, the innovative use of artificial meadows was in fact more common on small farms than on large ones.[123] As for the other hallmark of large farms—enclosures—they proved important in individual villages, but overall their role was slight, even in Lorraine.

The story was not all that different across the English Channel, according to Robert Allen. Neither enclosures nor even large farms explained the bulk of England's agricultural success. Instead, the credit should go to peasant farmers. Ironically, they and not absentee landlords were responsible for most of England's growth. Evidence from developing countries sketches the same picture. There, too, small farms do not lag technologically. Indeed, they actually prove to be more productive than their larger counterparts.[124]

At bottom, there is little reason why farm size should greatly influence productivity. In early modern Europe, large farms did spare some labor. But the size of a farm was ultimately determined, one could argue, by the nature of the crops and by difficulties of supervising laborers, who, on an enormous farm, might spend most of their day toiling in far-off fields. Relative to grain, vines required enormous amounts of labor, and hence vineyards were relatively small, whereas grazing livestock required vast amounts of land. A region or a country that specialized in livestock—England, for instance—would tend to have large farms relative to France, with its vineyards and more labor-intensive crops. Similar arguments still prevail today, and they explain why the most efficient farms are still family enterprises. Even today, in most parts of the world, large corporate farms enjoy little advantage when it comes to productivity.

In the era before scientific agronomy and mechanical invention, what drove most agricultural productivity growth was not farm size, although increases in farm size did explain some of the heightened efficiency. Neither was it any one of the other verses in the historians' usual refrain: demography, the class structure, landlord-tenant relations, or the obstacles raised by peasant mentalities and the village community. Rather, it was taxes and prices; and even more so, peace, demand from large cities, and access to trade. When a country was at peace, farmers could invest in livestock and improvements, and trade in their produce in security. They could take advantage of the opportunities that a large city like Paris made profitable: the burgeoning artificial meadows and the redolent traffic in urban manure. And when transportation costs dropped and commercial networks were organized, farmers could specialize, grow new crops, and realize gains from trade. The specialization here was far from complete: it might be a seemingly insignificant vineyard carved from the hillside in the western Beaujolais. The trading outside Paris might seem equally modest: it might be the sale of products once consumed on the farm, such as the traffic in fodder. What limited trade and specialization, though, was not just the abysmal state of the roads and canals; it was the need to keep some land sown in grain, given the prohibitive costs that transportation heaped upon imported supplies. And it was the sheer difficulty of stitching together the networks of middlemen and traders. Given these dilemmas, had governments spent less on war and more on roads, the rural economy might well have prospered. But that was not the path of glory for the monarchies of the Old Regime.

CHAPTER SIX

Conclusion

LIKE A WILDFIRE driven by the wind, the French Revolution raced through the institutional underbrush of the Old Regime, destroying ancient social and political tinder, from fiscal privileges to the seigneurial system and the tithe. Soon the conflagration ignited revolutionary wars both inside France and beyond its borders, and the monarchy itself went up in a blaze of smoke.

But what effect did the Revolution have on economic growth, particularly within agriculture? That question, surprisingly, has not intrigued historians, despite all the historiographic furor over the French Revolution. In the past, when Marxist interpretations of the Revolution held sway, attention was riveted on the Revolution's origins. Its consequences (especially for economic growth) were largely ignored. What mattered was tracing how a bourgeois revolution had been touched off. One might be interested in how the bourgeoisie dismantled the seigneurial system, but whether their actions promoted economic growth did not deserve attention. Perhaps it seemed obvious that a bourgeois revolution would favor growth. Or perhaps it was embarrassing to confront the economic policies of revolutionary governments—policies difficult to reconcile with bourgeois virtues. And now that the historiography has turned from Marxism to political culture, interest in economic growth is at an all-time low.

Because the Revolution destroyed a number of burdensome institutions, from the tithe to the seigneurial system, one might reasonably argue that it fostered economic growth. Such a position would continue a line of argument that stretches back to the physiocrats and agricultural reformers of the Old Regime, who longed to free French agriculture from its shackles. On the other hand, one could maintain (as French historians did) that enterprising seigneurs were responsible for what little agricultural capitalism existed under the Old Regime. By driving them away, the Revolution retarded growth. Equally ominous was the Revolution's strengthening of the village community, supposedly one of the major obstacles to economic growth.[1]

Given what we know, such arguments seem doubtful. The weight of the seigneurial system was often light, the seigneurs were hardly the only source of innovation, and the village community was not the major obstacle to economic growth in agriculture. Yet it is still reasonable to ask how the Revolution's institutional changes affected agricultural productivity.

Several recent works suggest answers here. On the one hand, Jean-Laurent Rosenthal has demonstrated that the Revolution's legal and administrative reforms did clear the way for drainage and irrigation of farmland. Under the Old Regime, it would have paid to drain marshes or to irrigate arid soil, but the path was blocked by overlapping property rights and a judicial system that encouraged debilitating court suits. Once the legal and administrative reforms were securely in place, water projects proliferated.[2] Locally, the economic consequences often proved dramatic, but not all of the country could benefit from drainage or irrigation. Still, the overall effect on the French economy was appreciable. Rosenthal estimates that drainage alone boosted agricultural output by perhaps 2 to 4 percent during the years from 1815 to 1860. These were, to be sure, long-run changes. As Rosenthal points out, little was accomplished until the revolutionary turmoil was past and it was clear that the institutional changes would survive the Bourbon restoration.[3]

But the Revolution had other consequences for economic growth as well, consequences played out over the shorter period of time between the Revolution's beginning in 1789 and the Empire's end in 1815. In a recent survey, Gilles Postel-Vinay has argued that the Revolution and the Empire probably witnessed only a slight increase in agricultural output. The countryside did benefit from a redistribution of income, as wages rose, debts dissolved in the revolutionary inflation, and, at least in some regions, peasants profited from the sale of Church lands. Equaling or perhaps even outweighing the benefits, though, was the disruption of the circuits of commerce and credit. Agricultural trade was pummeled by the Reign of Terror, by price controls (the laws of the Maximum, thus named because they set maximum prices), and by government actions that diminished the commerce in specialty crops such as wine. In all likelihood, subsistence farming gained in importance. The flow of capital into agriculture was also interrupted during the Revolution. Landlords who furnished agricultural capital to tenants either lost their property or were scared away from lending by the prospect of repayment in a worthless currency, the *assignats*. Deprived of capital and of the trade that was a great source of productivity growth, agriculture languished.[4]

Tim Le Goff and Donald Sutherland are even more pessimistic. For them, the Revolution was "a lost generation for economic growth." Like Postel-Vinay, they stress the collapse of trade, brought on, they argue, by revolutionary politics—inflation and the Maximum, to be sure, but also military requisitions, the loss of exports, and the regulation of the grain trade.[5] All three authors note that the Revolution was a period of deurbanization, as if France could no longer feed itself.

Alas, it is impossible to pursue our own series of leases across the Revolution and Empire and check these conclusions. In most cases the properties we followed were confiscated and sold. Thereafter, they were often farmed by owner operators; their rental value is thus unknown. Furthermore, it is difficult to disentangle the effects on the rent of the abolition of the tithe and the change in the tax system. And the price controls of the Maximum make it impossible to calculate meaningful price statistics.

But we can at least sketch a range of possibilities for the course of agricultural productivity. Sutherland and Le Goff's review furnishes a number of rental figures. They also provide information on prices and wages, as does Postel-Vinay. Deriving TFP from their data would be pointless during the Maximum (1793-94), when markets ceased functioning. Yet it might be revealing to compare the last decade of the Old Regime with the years 1810–15—the end of the Empire and the beginning of the Bourbon restoration. Admittedly, the period 1810–15 was not without its problems, but the same could be said of the preceding decade and of the period 1815–20.[6]

The evidence, it is true, does not inspire much confidence. Nearly all of the leases come from properties in the north and west of France, but practically none from the south. The wages and price of wheat are national averages, while the other prices stem from particular locals. Combining such series on a national scale is even more problematic than under the Old Regime, for commerce was hobbled and prices gyrated wildly.[7] Worst of all is the dubious job of correcting the rent for the change in the tax system and the abolition of the tithe. Still, the calculation can at least suggest what was possible. I have therefore computed TFP indices for 1780–89 and 1810–15, using a range of different prices, rents, share weights, and corrections for taxes and the tithe (table 6.1). The table presents two extreme possibilities, one pessimistic and the other optimistic, depending on the shares and rents used and the assumptions about the effect of abolition of the tithe. Both cases point to declining TFP, and while the evidence or the choice of a period might well exaggerate the extent of the decline, it seems unlikely that the Revolution boosted productivity.

Evidence about physical inputs and outputs tells a story that is not so gloomy, but even by the standards of the Old Regime it is at best a tale of slow growth. The difficulty in working with physical quantities is getting reliable information about the surface under cultivation (in this era before the *cadastre*, or land registry) and about agricultural capital, from livestock and equipment to farm buildings and improvements to the soil. The amount of land under cultivation may have increased, but suppose that it remained the same—an assumption that will exaggerate any TFP growth. There is no way to tell about buildings and improvements to the soil, so let us assume that they were the same as well. As for livestock and equipment, although requisitions might have been severe locally, Le Goff and Sutherland argue that the number of cattle and sheep in the late Empire was probably similar to what it had been at the end of the Old Regime.[8] If the number of ani-

TABLE 6.1
Agricultural TFP in 1810–15 relative to 1780–89: Estimated Range from Rents and Prices

Index for	Pessimistic Estimate		Optimistic Estimate	
	Share	Index in 1810–15 (Index = 1 in 1780–89)	Share	Index in 1810–15 (Index = 1 in 1780–89)
Inputs				
Rent (corrected for the abolition of the tithe)	0.43	1.11	0.37	1.15
Wages	0.45	1.81	0.48	1.81
Rental price of capital	0.12	1.37	0.15	1.52
Outputs				
Grain	0.60	1.63	0.77	1.63
Other crops	0.20	2.18	0.02	2.18
Animal products	0.20	1.37	0.21	1.37
TFP		0.85		0.94

Sources: Le Goff and Sutherland, "The Revolution and the Rural Economy"; Postel-Vinay, "A la recherche de la révolution économique."

Note: Both calculations assume that shares are constant and that taxes paralleled land rents, as figures in Le Goff and Sutherland suggest. The pessimistic calculation assumes a 26 percent increase in rent between 1780–89 and 1810–15, of which 14 percent is due to the abolition of the tithe, leaving a true increase of 11 percent. The optimistic calculation assumes a 40 percent rent increase, of which 22 percent is due to the tithe. The effects of abolishing the tithe I derived by simulating what would happen with an 8 percent tithe assessed on 75 percent of output with a land share ranging from 33 to 50 percent. The rental price of capital is based on an interest rate (5 percent in both cases in 1780–89 and in the pessimistic case in 1810–15; 10 percent in the optimistic case in 1810–15), a depreciation rate (27 percent in the pessimistic case, 40 percent in the optimistic), and the price of mutton (index 1.37 in 1810–15), which I took to be a good proxy for the price of livestock. The grain index is taken from the price of wheat, the index of other crops is taken from the price of wine, and the index of animal products is derived from the price of mutton. All the figures here are subject to caution. Some of the prices are regional, while some are national averages. The rental figures represent a range derived from evidence in Le Goff and Sutherland. Since prices, wages, and rents were not available for all the years 1780–89 and 1810–15, the indexes are often based on a smaller number of years. Shares are rough estimates for the entire economy; the table assumes that a TFP calculation for the economy as a whole is valid.

mals—and agricultural capital in general—had not changed, the productivity of the late Empire would be reduced, for the late Empire's output would be produced with a relatively large stock of capital. I allow for that possibility, but also for a more optimistic one, at least as far as productivity is concerned: namely, that agriculture capital had declined by 10 percent (table 6.2).[9]

Again, the calculation rests upon premises and data that are far from perfect: that the agricultural technology takes a particular form, that output can be aggregated into one number, and that the estimates which form the basis of the data are at least informed guesses. With all the assumptions, the

TABLE 6.2

Agricultural TFP in 1810–15 relative to 1780–89: Estimated Range from Physical Inputs and Outputs

Index for	Pessimistic Estimate		Optimistic Estimate	
	Share	Index 1810–15 (Index = 1 in 1780–89)	Share	Index 1810–15 (Index = 1 in 1780–89)
Inputs				
Land	0.43	1.00	0.37	1.00
Labor	0.45	1.06	0.48	1.06
Agricultural capital	0.12	1.00	0.15	0.90
Outputs	1.00	1.06	1.00	1.06
TFP		1.04		1.05
Annual growth rate of TFP (percent per year)		0.12		0.17

Source: As in table 6.1

Note: As in table 6.1, the estimates are subject to considerable caution. The numbers are uncertain, and they do not all come from precisely the years 1780–89 and 1810–15. The land under cultivation may have actually increased, and the agricultural labor supply is assumed to be proportional to the rural population. Unfortunately, I had to use rural population figures of 1790 for 1780–89 and of 1806 for 1810–15. The supply of agricultural capital (here, livestock and equipment) is extremely difficult to estimate. On the one hand, Le Goff and Sutherland suggest that there was no decline in the number of cattle and sheep. On the other, Postel-Vinay cites the example of the Aisne, where the number of cattle may have dropped 40 percent due to requisitions and murrain in 1814–15. The situation in the Aisne in 1814–15 was probably worse than the rest of France over the years 1810–15, so I assumed that at worst agricultural capital dropped by 10 percent. As an alternative to this pessimistic assumption, I followed Le Goff and Sutherland and assumed that there was no drop in animal herds or in agricultural capital as a whole. As for agricultural output, the table assumes that it can be aggregated using the estimates of the volume of agricultural output made by Toutain, with corrections reported by Postel-Vinay for the years 1803–12 relative to 1781–90. Input and output shares are as in table 6.1. The calculation here rests on one assumption that is quite different from table 6.1—namely, that the agricultural production as a whole can be approximated by a Cobb-Douglass function. This is incompatible with the functional form that underlies table 6.1.

results are probably upwardly biased estimates of productivity growth. They indicate that some productivity growth might have occurred, but it was hardly rapid even by the standards of the Old Regime: between 0.12 and 0.17 percent per year. At best the Revolution continued the slow growth of the preceding centuries (table 4.9). And if we abandon the somewhat rosy premises of table 6.2 for the more realistic one of table 6.1, we confront a far grimmer scenario, in which TFP actually falls.

In all likelihood, then, the Revolution damaged agriculture, or at least condemned it to a generation of stasis. But a generation of stasis cost French farming dearly. Although much of French agriculture—in the west, for example—was in a sorry state in 1789, there were still many farms in northern France that could easily rival their counterparts across the English Channel. By 1850 that was no longer so. Yields on the rich arable of northern France had failed to keep pace.[10] Perhaps it was because French farms had to make up for twenty-five years of lost growth.

That the Revolution harmed farming should come as no surprise, given what we know about the effects of warfare on agricultural productivity. Warfare and troop movements nearly always jolted farming. They did so during the Revolution, just as they had during the Wars of Religion. Requisitions were hardly beneficial either. When we add how the Revolution cut off sources of agricultural capital and disrupted trade—the great source of productivity growth under the Old Regime—its deleterious effects on the economy are almost predictable. It is yet another example of how high politics shook the rural economy.

. . .

What then can we say about the rural economy as a whole and about its prospects for growth? In early modern France, peasants traded with one another in a local market that typically embraced a village and neighboring communities, or perhaps a town and surrounding hamlets. Some dealings undoubtedly extended over longer distances, but most were confined within the local market for the simple reason that the cost of transporting farm produce was high. Trading in the local market, it should be stressed, was not the self-sufficiency that many historians imagine.[11] It did not involve the peasants' tilling land that they owned and producing all of their own food. Although families certainly did grow some crops for their own consumption, total self-sufficiency was beyond the reach of most. Whether or not they strived for it—and there was ample reason not to—most families simply lacked the land necessary for producing their own food. They had to toil in the local labor market or rent in a highly competitive market for farmland. They served large-scale tenant farmers, leased land and the services of plow teams, and exchanged goods and services with fellow peasants. Their transactions did not constitute barter, for everything was evaluated in monetary terms—sales, purchases, debts, and credits. The local market in fact ran on credit, which compensated for a shortage of coins.

Engagement in the local market had important social and cultural implications, as a host of records make clear, from diaries and criminal court records to notarial acts and manuals for landlords. Within the local economy, the repeated economic dealings could forge personal relationships of reciprocity between master and servant, landlord and tenant, creditor and debtor. The problem for all of these relationships was that of moral hazard: each party could surreptitiously take advantage of the other. It was not just the master, the landlord, or the creditor who could do so. A servant could steal or loaf on the job. A tenant could skip maintenance or fall behind in his rent. A debtor could simply refuse to repay. Both sides in the transaction had to be wary of one another. An agricultural servant had to worry whether his master would reward his efforts with a raise. Or would his master mistreat him and withhold his due? For their part, masters had to devote considerable time to supervising hired hands. They also had to devise strategies for rewarding workers who proved diligent, such as the raises that the Cairon family utilized.

Similar problems affected dealings between landlords and tenants. To compensate for the greater risk of default by tenants leasing minuscule parcels, landlords demanded a higher rent. In contrast to what many historians argue, the higher rent did not usually reflect the land hunger of the small-scale tenants or the monopoly power of the large. On the other hand, if tenants hesitated to take on the risks of a fixed-rent lease, or if they could not furnish the livestock and equipment necessary to stock a farm, then both they and their landlords might prefer a sharecropping agreement. Besides reducing the tenant's risk, the share contract would require less supervision by the landlord, for unlike a wage contract it did give tenants some incentive to work. All of these matters were far from theoretical; they crop up repeatedly in leases, handbooks for landlords, and other contemporary records.

Clearly, the local economy could make or break a villager's reputation. If a tenant paid his rent and served his landlord well, he might be recommended to other landlords as a solvent and hardworking farmer. More likely still, he would find his lease renewed. Similarly, if a servant stole from his master, he probably had to flee, for who would hire a thief? Trustworthy servants and tenants might get loans, but a debtor who failed to repay a loan might be denied credit in the future. Such a debtor ran the risk of much worse: insults, court action, and even violence to ensure that the loan was repaid. But we should not assume that the exchanges in the local economy were a major source of village discord. Traditional communal institutions—communal grazing rights, for instance—were actually far more likely to provoke strife, while the economic transactions could just as easily forge personal relationships of reciprocity.

Which outcome villagers got—which equilibrium in the jargon of game theory—depended on the intricacies of village history. Whether villagers cooperated or sought instead to cheat one another reflected not just expectations about punishment and reward, but jealousies, family feuds, guesses about behavior, and implicit moral codes. Here, economics lapses into indeterminacy. To understand the outcome we must know all the details of local life—many of them forever lost—details that impassion social and cultural historians. The possible outcomes know no bound. A cheat might face sanctions that could range from the loss of future business with the individual he had wronged to the prospect of being shunned by the entire community. If his only punishment would come at the hands of the wronged party, we might expect severe sanctions, such as violence, or a pattern of long-term and exclusive relationships between the same two parties—what we would call clientage. On the other hand, if it was the whole community that retaliated, then we would presumably witness less violence, less clientage, and perhaps more concern with honor and reputation.

If we consider the problems of moral hazard that afflicted the local economy, it is clear that they worsened when trade stretched over longer distances. They might well grow insurmountable, even for the seemingly uncomplicated matter of selling a farmer's grain. The farmer might wish, for example, to consign his grain to a middleman, but if he did not know the middleman well, the simple trade would involve an extraordinary amount of trust. Would the farmer wait for payment from a middleman he did not know? Probably not. Yet if he and other farmers demanded payment in advance, then the middleman would have to mobilize large amounts of capital and take steps to ensure that the grain purchased in advance was actually delivered. The middleman would have to pay the farmer in scarce and cumbersome specie; presumably, the informal credit of the local economy would simply not work.

Repeated dealings between the farmer and the middleman might soon resolve all such difficulties, but imagine the obstacles to establishing an entire network of grain merchants and transporters, one big enough to take advantage of the economies of scale in the risks that middlemen faced. Such networks existed—around Paris in the eighteenth century, for example—and they cut the costs of transporting grain to market. But organizing one was not simple. To amass stocks, the network had to buy grain in advance and move large sums of specie out into the countryside. It needed agents to keep track of local market conditions: without them, the network risked acquiring grain where it was dear and shipping it where it was cheap. If farmers could not easily hire trustworthy servants, and if landlords fretted over the quality of their tenants, one can easily imagine the difficulty of finding reliable agents who might be entrusted with the perilous assignment of purchasing large quantities of grain. And to top it off, the government viewed activities and associations of the middlemen with the greatest suspicion.[12] Here, in short, was a major barrier to long-distance trade, and it was yet another reason (along with the high transportation costs) why much agriculture output never left the local economy.

The workings of the local economy bring to mind the long tradition in social thought of contrasting ancient and modern economies. The tradition is one that snakes through the sort of anthropology and sociology favored by historians and reaches back all the way to Max Weber. It consists in drawing a sharp line between ancient economies and modern ones. On one side of the line lie the ancient economies, where transactions are personal, mediated not by market prices but by custom. Here, it is argued, economic reasoning simply does not apply. On the other side stand the modern markets, replete with prices and impersonal exchange; they alone are the proper domain of economics and rational calculation. If asked where to place the local economy of the early modern countryside, most historians would probably put it with the ancient economies. Yet it does not really fit there. It had prices, and although transactions were personal, that resulted from the ubiquitous problem of moral hazard, which infected nearly every exchange in the local economy. The strategies villagers adopted to cope with moral hazard make eminent sense from the point of view of economics, and their local economy certainly seems amenable to economic analysis. Indeed, if early modern Europe is any indication, the contrast between ancient and modern economies is misleading and overdrawn.

Also misleading are the arguments commonly made about the village community. From Marx and Weber onward, historians and social scientists alike have regarded the rural community as an obstacle to agricultural capitalism and to improvements such as enclosures. Villagers, so the story goes, were devoted to communal property rights, which provided the poor among them with social insurance. They therefore defended communal property by attacking enclosures and other onslaughts of capitalist farming. But our examples tell a starkly different tale. Frequently it was the rich who monopolized the commons, not the poor. The poor often favored the dissolution of the commons, and in one instance in which the poor did fight for common grazing rights—in Varades—it was to protect their stake in what was clearly capitalist agriculture. Similarly, the real impediment to La Galaizière's enclosures in Lorraine was less the opposition of the village poor than strategic behavior by the wealthy—strategic behavior encouraged by the legal system of the Old Regime.

It thus seems wrong to blame the peasant community for stagnation in French agriculture. But was growth even a possibility in the early modern countryside? Here, the answer has to be yes. Economic growth was certainly feasible, despite what the consensus historians say, for farming in early modern France was far from sluggish and immobile. True, the performance of the rural economy as a whole was mediocre. On this point three methods of gauging agricultural growth come to surprising agreement: the tithe returns, Anthony Wrigley's demographic estimates, and our method utilizing rents and prices. Yet at the same time our method reveals far more variation and change than most historians assume. In the first place, it suggests that productivity growth was not peculiar to the late eighteenth century, as is so often supposed. In a number of places, in fact, growth erupted in the sixteenth and seventeenth centuries—in Normandy, near Paris, and in parts of the southeast. Nor did French farmers and landowners have anything to be ashamed of, for in a number of instances the productivity of their farms raced ahead at an extremely rapid pace by early modern standards—notably outside Paris, in the Beaujolais, and perhaps in the southwest. The problem was that productivity growth in France was far from uniform. It varied greatly from place to place and century to century, and in any region it might first soar, then screech to a halt, and finally crash to earth. It was battered by warfare and fiscal exactions, and if farmers in Normandy or outside Paris could rival their counterparts in England in terms of the absolute productivity of their farms, other parts of the kingdom (the west, for example) lagged far behind. The lesson is that it is folly to generalize about an entire country in early modern Europe. The task is to account for the regional and temporal patterns of productivity growth—in other words, to explain why it occurred when and where it did.

Our method uncovered several sources of productivity growth in the early modern agriculture. First came true technical change: a new crop such as maize or sainfoin, or a novel use for an implement, such as the scythe, which, though long employed to mow grass, could be turned to harvesting grain. There was also physical capital embedded in improvements to the land, such as drainage, the planting of orchards and vinestock, and the clearing away of weeds and brush from overgrown fields. Again, that does not exactly qualify as technical change, but our method counts it as increased TFP. And finally, there were gains from trade: converting arable to meadow in Normandy, planting vineyards in the Beaujolais, or producing fodder crops for the market in Paris.

The categories here do overlap somewhat. The planting of maize and sainfoin and the harvesting of grain with a scythe all entail skill and expertise—human capital, which, like the physical capital of improvements to the fields, is not counted directly. Planting the physical capital of vinestock was an attempt to specialize and hence to profit from comparative advantage. Raising fodder crops for Paris usually meant growing sainfoin to feed one's own herds. Still, the distinctions seem evident, and it is also clear that most of the productivity growth in the early modern countryside derived from capital in the soil and from gains from trade. It was not yet the era of the reaper, chemical fertilizer, or scientific agronomy. The capital and even more so the specialization for market were always limited by modern standards—transportation costs in France remained too high for farmers to specialize completely and purchase all that they consumed. But the specialization and the capital embedded in the soil did matter.

Given their importance, it is easy to understand why warfare ravaged the rural economy and caused productivity to plummet. Armies confiscated livestock and inventories of grain—in effect, a farmer's lifetime savings and working capital, which were not easily replaced. The soldiers drove tenants away, bringing tillage of the soil to a halt. Finding reliable replacements was difficult, and soon the fields were choked with brush, which destroyed in a few seasons the years of capital accumulated in clearing the land. Without steel plows, the work of clearing the land anew, as in the aftermath of the Hundred Year's War and the Wars of Religion, was arduous. Warfare disrupted trade as well, particularly the long-distance trade that depended on middlemen. Reknitting the commercial networks was no simple matter.

It is also easy to see why the fiscal system could disrupt the rural economy, at least before Colbert. Before his reforms, the fisc, like a marauding army, responded to tax delinquency by seizing the asset that was easiest to sell. In the countryside, that usually meant a farmer's livestock. Again, it was difficult to replace lost savings, and in the meantime fields sprouted brush. And fear of the fisc discouraged investment in livestock, a major component of agricultural capital, while internal tolls hobbled trade.

As elsewhere in early modern Europe, most of the taxes raised by the fisc paid for the escalating cost of war. Very little, unfortunately, went to pay for improvements in roads and canals, for transportation had to compete with the demands of the military. Colbert, for example, significantly increased spending for roads and waterways, but war with the Dutch used up the sums earmarked for transportation. Spending on roads did rise again in the eighteenth century, and the network of roadways improved, although waterways languished. Yet the spending was by and large dictated by politics or military needs, rather than the demands of commerce. The roads receiving greatest attention were those linking Paris to provincial capitals and the kingdom's borders. That was what interested the monarchy. Meanwhile, road networks within the provinces themselves were neglected, particularly in southern and western France, where productivity growth trailed behind the Paris Basin.[13] Lobbying for better transportation was often hopeless, because it meant organizing a host of scattered landowners who would benefit from improved roadways and canals. As for private improvements, they risked getting snagged in a thicket of legal troubles.

Factors commonly cited by historians left much less of a mark on agricultural productivity. Enclosures mattered enormously in some places—in La Galaizière's villages in Lorraine, for instance—but in the economy as a whole they counted for little. The same is probably true of drainage and irrigation. Farm size was more important, because large farms spared labor. But that, too, explained only a fraction of the productivity increase, and outside regions of severe fragmentation, there seemed to be no real limits to attaining the optimum farm size. The complaint that France lacked enough large enclosed farms—a complaint that has echoed back and forth from the eighteenth century to the present—thus seems misplaced. Finally, to the extent one can judge, peasant mentalities seemed no barrier at all.

The denizens of the countryside seized upon opportunities, and if one examines their use of resources, it appears quite efficient. Growth did not result from a sudden conversion to efficiency. Nor was it yet driven by patents and the diffusion of complex scientific knowledge that were beyond the peasants' ken.

The source of productivity growth was in fact much simpler. It was comparative advantage, and it depended on costs of transportation and opportunities for trade with the rest of the economy. Had the monarchy spent less on warfare and more on roads and canals, had the legal system not frustrated private efforts to improve transportation, then French agriculture might well have benefited. Precisely how much is impossible to say—and hence the lingering uncertainty here—for in the rare instances when the government did invest in better transportation, we lack the data needed to measure the impact on agriculture. But better transportation was not simply building roads and digging canals; it was also organizing networks of middlemen, from merchants to specialized transporters. In early modern Europe, the organizational problems may have loomed larger than the lack of money for social overhead capital.[14] Organization, after all, was the key to the grain trade about Paris and the traffic in wine from the Beaujolais. The networks of middlemen required physical security—roving armies kept frightened merchants at home—and the networks seemed to flourish most vigorously in the service of large cities such as Paris.

Opportunities for trade thrived around large cities as well, with Paris providing a splendid example. Demand from Paris made it profitable to plant artificial meadows over a wide area. Planting the artificial meadows released straw and fodder for sale within Paris, and when he was in Paris a farmer could purchase manure produced by the city's burgeoning population of animals. Elsewhere, such a traffic in fodder and manure would not work. Soil conditions were not appropriate, and outside smaller cities the demand was not strong enough (and prices not high enough) to push the artificial meadows past the threshold of profitability.

Not that the trade in fodder and manure was the only way to profit from urban demand. Outside Paris, the traffic in fodder and manure declined in the nineteenth century, and there were in any case many other ways to profit from the urban market. Peasants could plant vineyards and gardens, although such labor-intensive crops were often limited to minuscule plots hugging the city walls. They could specialize in producing high-quality wheat. Or, if they were far removed from the city, as in the Auge and other parts of the west, they could convert to raising livestock. The establishment of rural industry was yet another way to profit from exchange with a city, though the benefits may have accrued to textile manufacturing rather than to agriculture. Textile work was traded during the winter lull when the countryside had a comparative advantage in furnishing labor, without obliging the cottage workers to leave their homes, where they would be needed for fieldwork in the spring and the summer. Importing urban harvest workers did much the same, only in reverse.[15]

Agricultural productivity thus turned upon what happened outside of agriculture. It hinged on prices, on warfare and taxes, on urbanization and transportation, and on the legal freedom to organize trade. Despite what the consensus teaches, growth was affected only moderately by farm size, and it showed few signs of being held in check by the lack of enclosures or hostile peasant communities. Here, one might argue that the informal institutions of the peasants' local economy were themselves an obstacle to trade and thus a barrier to further productivity growth. But that would be to confuse cause and effect. The reciprocity and repeated dealings of the local economy were merely a means of coping with moral hazard. They were an effect, not a cause. The same problem of moral hazard impeded the creation of long-distance trade networks; along with high transportation costs, it was one reason why specialization was always modest in the early modern countryside. Most trade was therefore confined to the local economy, but the customs of that economy did not lead to economic stagnation. The causes must be sought outside the rural economy, in politics and in whatever it was that made the larger economy stagnate or thrive. We cannot blame the peasants or their customs.

There is a curious lesson for history and the social sciences here. The customs of traditional societies are certainly amenable to economic analysis. Economics can suggest, for instance, why sharecropping developed in one place and fixed-rent leases in another, why small-scale tenants paid higher rent, or why the transactions in traditional economies were imbued with reciprocity. But it cannot dictate everything within traditional economies. It often cannot tell us whether two parties in a transaction will cooperate or cheat, for typically both will be feasible outcomes. Nor can it predict how cheaters will be punished: via dishonor, shunning, the loss of a single patron, or even violence. The prediction is indeterminate, for the outcome depends on what we might call the indigenous culture—the local conditions that make the outcome sensible.[16]

Culture thus matters for the shape of local customs and institutions. But so do economic and political forces outside the local economy. Sharecropping and fixed-rent tenancy, for instance, would not have proliferated in early modern France had not the tax system encouraged absentee ownership of farmland. And it was these outside forces, not the peculiarities of local customs, that ultimately explained growth.

The Methods and Sources Used with the Notre Dame Sample

1. TREATMENT OF LEASES

Early modern leases bristle with complications, making even the payment of rent an intricate matter. Consider, for example, the lease that the Cathedral of Notre Dame and its tenant, Pierre Landry, agreed to in 1781. Landry was to continue operating Notre Dame's 95-hectare farm in Mesnil-Amelot for another nine years and to pay an annual rent of 1,200 *livres* in cash plus 216 Paris *setiers* (roughly 1,000 bushels) of wheat. The wheat had to be cleaned, ready for market, and delivered to the cathedral in Paris. Alternatively, Notre Dame could demand cash in place of the wheat. In that event, the wheat was to be evaluated at 5 *sous* per setier below the Paris price for the best quality wheat on the Feast of Saint-Martin (November 11), the date when the grain was to be delivered; the 5 sous per setier amounted to about a 1 percent discount below the maximum Saint-Martin price. In addition to the wheat, Landry was to deliver 200 *bottes* of straw to the cathedral in Paris or to pay cash in place of straw, with the straw evaluated via the Paris market price on the date of delivery. Landry had a number of other obligations as well—tending to upkeep of the farm, for example—and at the beginning of the new lease he was to pay a one-time entry fine amounting to 10 percent of the first year's rent.[1]

There are further intricacies in Landry's lease, but these details suffice to sketch the complexities of the rent payments involved. As with Landry, Notre Dame's other tenants might owe the cathedral annual rent in cash, in-kind payments, *pots-de-vin* (entry fines, almost always equal to a one-time payment of 10 percent of the first year's rent), or *charges* (obligations to make cash or in-kind payments for Notre Dame—to a local priest, for example). I spread the pots-de-vin evenly over the life of the lease (without discounting) and converted the in-kind payments into cash. If the in-kind payments entailed delivering grain to Paris (the usual case), they were evaluated using the average Paris price on the Feasts of Saint-Martin over the course of the outgoing lease (i.e., the current Feast of Saint-Martin and the eight previous ones). I chose prices on the Feast of Saint-Martin because contemporaries used them to evaluate in-kind payments, and because grain was typically due then. For wheat and rye, minimum Saint-

Martin prices were used, since Notre Dame expected the grain to fetch a price slightly less than the best quality wheat and rye. For the oats and barley, only maximum prices were available, but most in-kind payments involved wheat.

Before 1520 and after 1698, the Saint-Martin wheat prices in Paris ceased being available, so I used a proxy constructed by first regressing the Saint-Martin wheat prices on the annual Paris wheat price for the years 1520–1698. The regression was performed without an intercept term, and for the years before 1520 and after 1698, when the annual Paris price existed but the Saint-Martin price did not, I simply multiplied the annual Paris price by the regression coefficient to get the proxy. Saint-Martin prices were also lacking for the other grains before 1520 and after 1698, which necessitated similar proxies. For rye, I regressed Paris Saint-Martin rye prices on the annual Paris wheat price without an intercept term in the regression; I then used the regression coefficient to create a rye proxy for the years before 1520 and after 1698. For barley and oats, I simply resorted to twenty-five-year-average prices when the Saint-Martin prices were unavailable.

Grain delivered outside of Paris and other in-kind payments—usually very small—were evaluated using cash equivalents found in late-eighteenth-century leases. Ideally, one would prefer to evaluate them by multiplying the quantities due by the appropriate local market prices, but the local price series—say the price of wine in a small market town—might be lacking for a number of years. What I did, therefore, was to project the late-eighteenth-century cash equivalents back into the past, using long-term trends in Paris prices. I relied upon twenty-five-year-average prices of the items concerned. A quantity of wine delivered to a village priest and worth 10 *livres* in 1750–74, for example, I assumed to be worth $10h$ in 1650–74, where h was the ratio of the 1650–75 Paris price for wine to the 1750–74 Paris price. If the Paris price and the local market price diverged, this method would involve some error, but the error would in any event be minuscule, for most in-kind payments involved wheat delivered to Paris.

I made one change in the procedure for evaluating in-kind payments when experimenting with alternative prices in the agricultural price-cost index. When I averaged the prices and the wages in the index over the new lease (in other words, over the current year and eight years into the future), I evaluated all in-kind payments over the life of the new lease, too, instead of over the previous lease. I modified the procedure in an analogous way when I experimented with other prices and wages in the price-cost index.

One might wonder, of course, whether the results were sensitive to the way I evaluated the in-kind payments, but this seems not to have been the case. Regressions with those leases in which all the payments were in cash differed little from regressions that included the in-kind leases, except for a higher R^2. The reason for the higher R^2 with the cash-only leases was that the value of grain payments was volatile and made the dependent variable in the regressions vary randomly.

One occasional complication with early modern French leases was the practice of using *contre-lettres*: private letters attached to the leases that revised lease terms. Like other landlords, Notre Dame employed contre-lettres, but only for minor matters, and unlike many landlords, Notre Dame never used them to disguise the true rent. In the hands of other landlords, contre-lettres often served to reduce the tax assessments of large-scale tenants, whose tax assessments were based on the artificially low rent in their leases, not the actual rent in the contre-lettres. Notre Dame, though, never resorted to such practices. The reason, apparently, was that operating a large farm for Notre Dame typically involved paying sizable *charges*—typically to the local parish priest. Since these charges did not figure in the tax assessments either, the large-scale tenants of Notre Dame enjoyed an automatic tax reduction equivalent to that gained by other landlords via contre-lettres.

In addition to farmland, the Notre Dame leases might also involve rights to collect the tithe or seigneurial dues on property other than the land that was to be cultivated. Since these rights did not pertain to the operation of the farm, I subtracted their value from the lease. I determined their value from cash equivalents given in the late eighteenth century, suitably adjusted for changing prices. For none of the properties were such tithe rights or seigneurial dues large. If they or the property area changed by a significant amount (for example, more than a 14 percent change in the property area), I assumed that I was dealing with a different property and began a new time series.

2. Distance as a Proxy for the Cost of Transportation to Paris

The regressions use the logarithm of the distance to Paris as a proxy for the logarithm of the cost of transporting crops to Paris. Ideally, one would prefer the actual cost of shipping by the cheapest means available—overland for properties close to Paris, and by river for more distant properties, where the economies of river transport overtook the added costs of shipping crops to a river port and then loading them on boats. For our properties, though, evidence from the seventeenth and eighteenth centuries suggests that the shipping costs were highly correlated with simple distance from Paris.[2] Indeed, if one figures the cost of shipping to Paris via the cheapest means for the properties in our sample, then the logarithm of the cost is almost perfectly correlated with the logarithm of distance from Paris ($r = 0.99$), and the correlation does not seem sensitive to errors in the shipping cost figures. Using distance from Paris rather than shipping costs therefore seems justifiable.

3. QUALITY ADJUSTMENTS AND RENT AVERAGES

The quality adjustment that I employed is discussed in the text; it had a minor effect on the rent (figure A-1). The same held for other quality adjustments that I tried, all based on regressions with ln(rent). These other adjustments included running regressions with a dummy variable for each property; using locational and land-quality characteristics only, but no time-dependent variables; and replacing the time trend with an agricultural price-cost ratio. All gave nearly identical results.

The area-weighted average over all leases in force assumes that each lease lasted nine years or until renewed and that rents remained constant in the interim. Table 4.2, column three, calculates such an average, relying on the same regression for the quality adjustment but weighting each lease by the property area. The overall trend with this average over the leases in force is similar to that obtained with the average over the newly signed leases, but there are some differences (figure A.1). When the fighting during the Wars of Religion ravaged the Paris Basin in the 1590s, for example, ln(rent) fell for the leases signed in the decade (table 4.2, column four). If we average over all leases in force, though, the logarithm, buoyed up by leases signed in the previous decade, actually increases. The increase, however, is illusory, since many of the older leases were in fact no longer in force: tenants had fled before the warring armies, farms lay in ruin, and no one was actually paying rent.[3] Although the difference between the two methods is generally small, the average over the sample leases—the ones signed during the decade—seems a bit closer to reality.

The same holds in the eighteenth century, when rents were increasing. The average over all the leases in force may do a better job of representing the income landlords received, but it lags slightly behind the true rental value of the land. The average over the leases signed in a decade—the sample leases—does not. Between the 1730s and the 1780s, for instance, nominal rents adjusted for quality rise only 73 percent if we average over all leases in force (table 4.2, column three). If we average over the sample leases—those signed during the two decades—the increase is much larger: 105 percent (table 4.2, column two). The jump of 105 percent lies in the very center of the range of figures that other historians have unearthed for

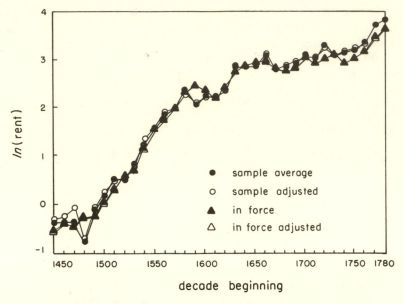

Figure A.1 Alternative Averages of Ln(Rent): Notre Dame Sample. The decennial averages were calculated with and without a quality adjustment for all leases in the sample that were signed during each decade. The calculation was then repeated for all the leases in force during each decade.

the Paris Basin: a gain of 79 to 120 percent between the 1730s and the 1780s. The close fit with other research argues in favor of using the average over the sample leases, particularly since we are interested not in the landlord's income but in true rental value.[4]

4. THE COMPARISON WITH THE VEYRASSAT-HERREN AND LE ROY LADURIE RENT SERIES

Veyrassat-Herren and Le Roy Ladurie published five-year averages of an index of deflated rent. To deflate, they divided nominal rents by a thirteen-year moving average wheat price, centered on year five of each lease. To reverse their steps, I multiplied their figures by the average wheat price over each five-year period of a thirteen-year moving average centered five years in the future. I also assumed that they had used their raw wheat price series as it was originally published, without corrections for typographical errors or for the changing size of the setier. Other ways of comparing their rent series and my own, such as subjecting my series to their deflation procedure, led to similar results.

5. FORMULAS FOR TFP AND TECHNICAL ASSUMPTIONS

Assume the farmer produces outputs $y_1, \ldots, y_m$ using factors of production $x_1, \ldots, x_n$, where x_1 is land. If the outputs can be sold at prices $p_1, \ldots, p_m$ and the factors of production bought at prices $w_1, \ldots, w_n$, then the farmer's profit is

$$\Pi = \sum_{i=1}^{m} p_i y_i - \sum_{j=1}^{n} w_j x_j \tag{1}$$

Although some of the farmer's transactions may have taken place outside the market, we assume that he was at least partially involved in the product and factor markets, so that the prices in equation (1) are market prices.

If the land and rental market is competitive with free entry, and if rents are revised frequently, then the farmer's profits will be driven down to zero: the profits will all go to the landlord. Therefore,

$$\Pi = \sum_{i=1}^{m} p_i y_i - \sum_{j=1}^{n} w_j x_j = 0 \tag{2}$$

Differentiating the left-hand side of equation (2) with respect to time and regrouping all the terms, we obtain

$$\sum_{i=1}^{m} p_i \frac{dy_i}{dt} - \sum_{j=1}^{n} w_j \frac{dx_j}{dt} = \sum_{j=1}^{n} \frac{dw_j}{dt} x_j - \sum_{i=1}^{m} \frac{dp_i}{dt} y_i \tag{3}$$

Dividing through by total revenue or cost R, where

$$R = \sum_{i=1}^{m} p_i y_i = \sum_{j=1}^{n} w_j x_j \tag{4}$$

yields

$$\sum_{i=1}^{m} u_i \dot{y}_i - \sum_{j=1}^{n} v_j \dot{x}_j = \sum_{j=1}^{n} v_j \dot{w}_j - \sum_{i=1}^{m} u_i \dot{p}_i \tag{5}$$

where the $u_i = p_i y_i / R$ are output shares in total revenue, the $v_j = w_j x_j / R$ are factor shares in total cost, and the dots refer to rates of growth (i.e., time derivatives of the logarithm). The expression on the left of equation (5) is the growth rate of TFP, the rate at which outputs are growing less the rate at which inputs are increasing, suitably weighted by output and factor shares. Equation (5) simply allows us to calculate the growth rate of TFP using prices instead of quantities, and it is the basis for the calculations of the growth rate of TFP in figure A.3 and table 4.4 and table A.2 (see later).

So far, we have only assumed that markets exist and that one of the markets, the land rental market, is competitive and open to entry. This assumption allows us to set the farmer's profits equal to zero and makes the tenant's compensation no more than he would earn in the labor market. Although such a treatment of the farmer's profits is obviously open to question—a subject to which we shall return below—it is common in the agricultural productivity literature.[5]

If product and factor shares are constant, then by integrating the right-hand side of equation (5) with respect to time we have that

$$TFP = \frac{w_1^{v_1} \cdots w_n^{v_n}}{p_1^{u_1} \cdots p_m^{u_m}} = (r+t)^s \frac{C}{P} \tag{6}$$

Here r is per-hectare rent, t is per-hectare taxes, $s = v_1$ is the factor share of land, and we have made the reasonable assumption that the burden of taxation falls on land so that $w_1 = r + t$. The variables C and P are indexes of agricultural costs and prices, given by

$$C = w_2^{v_2} \cdots w_n^{v_n} \quad P = p_1^{u_1} \cdots p_m^{u_m} \tag{7}$$

As a result,

$$\ln(TFP) = s \ln(r+t) - \ln\left(\frac{P}{C}\right) \tag{8}$$

Equation (8) serves as the basis for calculating ln(TFP) in all the dealings with the Notre Dame sample and throughout Chapter 4.

So far we have not invoked cost minimization or profit maximization, although without some optimizing behavior, our measure of TFP is simply a definition, with no necessary connection to the agricultural technology. We do have to assume the existence of a large number of risk-neutral tenants for the tenant farmer's profits to be driven down to zero as in equation (2), and risk neutrality is not far from profit maximization. Profit maximization is in any case hardly an unreasonable assumption for the large-scale tenants who operated farms in the Paris Basin: they owned considerable capital and had chosen to pay a fixed rent rather than to work for a wage.[6]

If we do assume profit maximization, and if (as seems to have been the case) all the product and factor markets are competitive—not just the rental market—then we can demonstrate that the growth rate of TFP is in fact the rate of technical change. Let us suppose that our farmer takes all the prices w_j and p_i as given and that the inputs and outputs are linked via a transformation function F with $F(x_1, \ldots, x_n, y_1, \ldots, y_m, t) = 0.$[7] Here F depends on time t because of technical change. If the technology is well behaved, we can use the implicit function theorem to solve for one output (say y_1) in terms of $x_1, \ldots, x_n, y_2, \ldots, y_m, t$, so that at least locally

$$y_1 = f(x_1, \ldots, x_n, y_2, \ldots, y_m, t) \tag{9}$$

Differentiating equation (9) with respect to time, we have

$$\frac{dy_1}{dt} = \frac{\partial f}{\partial x_1}\frac{dx_1}{dt} + \cdots + \frac{\partial f}{\partial x_n}\frac{dx_n}{dt} + \frac{\partial f}{\partial y_2}\frac{dy_2}{dt} + \cdots + \frac{\partial f}{\partial y_m}\frac{dy_m}{dt} + \frac{\partial f}{\partial t} \tag{10}$$

To avoid problems in the case of constant returns to scale, let us suppose as well that in the short run the farmer takes the supply of land x_1 as a fixed input—say over the course of a lease—and that he maximizes short-run profits.[8] Short-run profit maximization then implies that

$$p_1\frac{\partial f}{\partial x_j} = w_j \quad j = 2, \ldots, n \tag{11}$$

and

$$p_1\frac{\partial f}{\partial y_i} = -p_i \quad i = 2, \ldots, m \tag{12}$$

We can also characterize the partial derivative of f with respect to land x_1. Over the long run x_1 may vary, but the competitive rental market ensures that the landlord will absorb any profits from renting additional land. A simple application of the envelope theorem then yields

$$p_1\frac{\partial f}{\partial x_1} = w_1 \tag{13}$$

If we use equation (13) and the first-order conditions for profit maximization to express the partial derivatives of f in terms of prices, then equation (10) becomes

$$\frac{dy_1}{dt} = \frac{w_1}{p_1}\frac{dx_1}{dt} + \cdots + \frac{w_n}{p_1}\frac{dx_n}{dt} - \frac{p_2}{p_1}\frac{dy_2}{dt} - \cdots - \frac{p_m}{p_1}\frac{dy_m}{dt} + \frac{\partial f}{\partial t} \tag{14}$$

Multiplying both sides by p_1/R, where R is total revenue, yields

$$\sum_{i=1}^{m} u_i \dot{y}_i - \sum_{j=1}^{n} v_j \dot{x}_j = u_1 \dot{f} \tag{15}$$

where

$$\dot{f} = \frac{\partial}{\partial t} \ln(f) \tag{16}$$

The expression on the left of equation (15) is the growth rate of TFP; the expression on the right is the rate of technical change, the rate (in percentage terms) at which the production function f is shifting, adjusted for the relative importance of the output y_1. With only one output, for example, u_1 = 1 and the growth rate of TFP equals the partial derivative of $\ln(f)$ with respect to time. Note that this result does not depend on factor and product shares being constant.

In the context of profit maximization, the assumption of constant product and factor shares amounts to a choice of the form of the profit function and the path of technical change. The particular form implied by the constant shares assumption is only a local first-order approximation to an arbitrary profit function. Obviously, functional forms capable of providing a local second-order approximation (so-called flexible functional forms, such as a translog or a generalized Leontief) would be preferable, but the data needed to estimate such profit functions and thereby determine TFP are unfortunately unavailable, for the estimation requires information on both prices and quantities. As is shown in Appendix A, part 11, though, the loss of accuracy is minimal, at least in the one instance where we have the information to check it.[9]

6. Product and Factor Shares and the Rental Price of Agricultural Capital

The product and factor shares used to calculate TFP were taken from accounts of the farm of Bernonville, part of the village now known as Aisonville-et-Bernoville near Guise in the department of the Aisne. The Bernonville accounts for the year 1765 were analyzed (along with those of a number of other farms) in Charles Rebeyrol, *De la grande et de la petite culture*, pp. 35–44. Rebeyrol relied upon evidence published in 1767 in the *Éphémerides du citoyen*, a journal that, though polemical, was known for publishing reliable information concerning matters such as farm budgets.[10]

Supplemental information and evidence concerning farms elsewhere in the Paris Basin were gleaned from Tessier, *Agriculture*; M. Jouvencel, *Modèle de bail à cheptel pour servir d'instruction aux propriétaires ou capitalistes qui voudront établir des troupeaux de bêtes à laine dans les fermes des environs de Paris* (Versailles, 1810) [Jean-Henri] Hassenfratz, "Mémoire sur la comparaison des produits de la culture du Bourbonnais," pp. 105–22; Jacquart, *Crise rurale*, pp. 289–408; Emile Mireaux, *Une province française au temps du grand roi*, pp. 97–164, 322–41; Meuvret, *Subsistances*, vol. 1; and Moriceau and Postel-Vinay, *Ferme, entreprise, famille*. All of these sources are the work either of eighteenth-century experts or of modern authorities and they all draw upon evidence from actual early modern farms.

The Bernonville factor shares were: land, 0.267; labor, including in-kind compensation and labor provided by the tenant farmer, 0.361; wheat seed, 0.058; rye seed, 0.009; barley seed, 0.007; oat seed and feed, 0.109; bean and pea seed, 0.013; linseed, 0.004; horses, 0.044; cattle, 0.015; sheep, 0.052; pigs, 0.011; poultry, 0.013; and equipment, 0.035. Product revenue shares were: wheat output, 0.456; rye output, 0.080; barley output, 0.036; oats output, 0.101; bean and pea output, 0.073; flax output, 0.051; dairy output, 0.035; wool, 0.042; eggs, 0.015; beef, 0.012; mutton, 0.076; pork, 0.015; horses, 0.007.

Here and throughout the book, the shares for livestock and equipment were calculated using rental prices, which were set equal to the sales price multiplied by depreciation plus interest. The depreciation rates for the Bernonville farm were derived from evidence concerning the useful life of animals and from costs for equipment replacement and upkeep; they were: horses, 0.111; cows, 0.133; sheep, 0.25; pigs and poultry, 1; equipment, 0.143. The interest rates were the going rate on rentes.[11] A comparison of land rental rates and land sales prices suggests that the rentes did reflect the going rate of interest in the countryside; so do rental contracts for milk cows. In the Brie in the 1660s, for example, rentes paid 5 percent and cows were leased out at 17 percent of their value, to judge from the median of the rental contracts in AN S 471. Our depreciation rate for dairy cattle, from Tessier, s.v. "Bêtes à cornes," is 13 percent. The price of cattle was appreciating at about 1 percent annually, so we get an implied interest rate of $17 - 13 + 1 = 5$ percent, which is precisely the rente rate. Note that the rental cost of dairy cattle we would calculate for our cost index C (interest plus depreciation, or 18 percent of the price of a cow) was very close to the true rental cost of capital (17 percent of the price of a cow).

Although one might have doubts about the robustness of the depreciation rates here, very similar rates seem to have applied to most early modern herds. Wilhelm Abel, for example, provides evidence for medieval and early modern Germany that implies a depreciation rate for dairy cattle of 13 or 14 percent.[12] Since the depreciation rates for livestock and equipment exceeded the interest rate by a large margin after 1600, the rental costs of capital we calculated were relatively insensitive to variations in the interest rate.[13]

Seed and feed prices equalled prices of the respective grains multiplied by 1 plus the interest rate, because they had been stored for a year. Only net inputs and net outputs were considered, although we did assume the purchase of seed and oat feed. Products consumed on the farm in the form of in-kind wages were evaluated at market prices.

To be sure, some of the product and factor shares from Bernonville might seem questionable. The shares for wheat output and wheat seed imply a high seed-yield ratio, and the seed-yield ratio was indeed high in Bernonville—better than 8 to 1. However, such seed-yield ratios were far from unusual near Bernonville, where the soil was well suited for cereals. A careful investigation undertaken in the *généralité* of Soissons in 1716 revealed seed-yield ratios reaching 10 or 12 to 1 in the vicinity of Bernonville (more precisely, in the *subdélégation* of Guise), and according to the same document, seed-yield ratios of 8 or more were not uncommon throughout the whole généralité. Such a seed-yield ratio, it should be stressed, did not necessarily imply a high wheat yield per hectare, because seeding rates varied greatly. Even the high seed-yield ratios of 10 or 12 to 1 near Bernonville meant yields of only 13 to 15.6 hectoliters per hectare, well below the maximums observed in the Paris Basin in the seventeenth and eighteenth centuries.[14]

One might also worry slightly about oat production on the Bernonville farm. With the product shares of oats and the factor share of oat seed and feed nearly equal, the farm was essentially self-sufficient in oats; it consumed too much to be a net exporter. Obviously, other farms in the Paris area exported oats and had higher oat product shares. At Bernonville, though, the stiff soils required a somewhat larger number of plow horses, and the horses consumed oats that would otherwise have been exported. Fortunately, variations in the oat product share had little effect on the index of TFP, because the price of oats was highly correlated with other output prices.[15] The oat shares, in short, are no cause for worry.

In general, the technology of the Bernonville farm resembled that found elsewhere in the Paris Basin, not just in the eighteenth century but in the seventeenth and sixteenth centuries as well. If we examine farms in the Beauce in 1787, on the plains north of Paris in the 1740s, in the Brie in the early eighteenth century, and in the Hurepoix south of Paris in the period 1550–1670, we find similar outputs and similar factors of production.[16] Typically, between one quarter and slightly over a third of the arable land was devoted to winter grain; in Bernonville, the figure was 24 percent. The acreage devoted to spring grain on the other farms was about the same, though sometimes a bit higher; in Bernonville, it was 29 percent. Although the amount of artificial meadow on the Bernonville farm (15 percent of the arable) was a bit higher than on the other farms, it was hardly unusual for the Paris Basin, and the amount of fallow (30 percent) was perfectly normal.[17]

Labor use on the Bernonville farm was typical as well. If we consider, for example, the number of plowmen employed on farms in the Paris Basin, it turns out to have varied greatly, but the number in Bernonville was precisely in the middle of the range. On local farms, the number of plowmen might range from one for every 30 hectares down to only one for every 60 hectares, if we assume that all plows listed in death inventories were used. The number also seemed to diminish over time. On the plains north of Paris, for example, it went from one plow for every 30 hectares circa 1650 to one for every 45 hectares by 1790. Using one plow for every 30 hectares was the average for death inventories in the Hurepoix in the period 1550–1670, but in some of the inventories from the same period the number was as low as one for every 60 hectares.[18] In any event, in Bernonville the number of plowmen was precisely in the middle of this wide range: one for every 43 hectares.[19]

Harvest and temporary labor was also typical on the Bernonville farm. Harvest labor for grain crops typically cost 8 to 12 percent of the crop's harvest value in the seventeenth century, and if we add other related temporary labor, the fraction would rise to about 16 percent, whether we look at evidence from the sixteenth, seventeenth, or eighteenth centuries. On the Bernonville farm, the cost of harvest and related temporary labor was 18 percent of the grain harvest, very close to the 16 percent figure.

Finally, the amount of agricultural capital on the Bernonville farm resembled what one found elsewhere in the Paris Basin. The farm had 12 horses per 100 hectares, versus 8 to 9 on the plains north of Paris in the 1740s, and a median of roughly 8 in Hurepoix death inventories from large farms in the years 1550–1670. Because of the stiff soils, the Bernonville value is a bit high, but not outrageously so. The farm had 14 cows per 100 hectares, versus 10 in the Beauce in 1787, 12 on the plains north of Paris in the 1740s, 14 in the Brie in the 1730s, and a range of 6 to 15 in the Hurepoix large-farm inventories from the period 1550–1670. The number of sheep was equally close to the norm: 235 per 100 hectares in Bernonville, 152 in the Beauce, 192 on the plains north of Paris, 218 in the Brie, and a median of 254 in the Hurepoix inventories.[20]

There was perhaps a slight increase in the number of sheep per hectare, but it was neither considerable nor inconsistent with constant factor shares.[21] Since the number of animals did not vary greatly over time or from farm to farm, it is reasonable to assume that animal outputs (chiefly wool and mutton) did not vary much either. Breeding practices did not change drastically, despite much discussion in the late eighteenth century, and there was in any case little reason for farmers in the Paris Basin to shift drastically into stock raising.[22] The price of wool, mutton, and dairy products moved in parallel with that of wheat between 1520 and 1789, and transportation costs always favored grain production in the Paris Basin.

In addition to the farm accounts and death inventories, one can find evidence in favor of the Bernonville factor and product shares by examining sharecropping contracts. Sharecropping contracts were rare in the Paris Basin, but some did exist in parts of the Brie, where they involved a complicated division of outputs and inputs between tenant and landlord. Terms of the sharecropping contracts varied, but examples from the seventeenth and early eighteenth centuries imply that the product and factor shares must have satisfied several restrictions. For example, in one type of contract the landlord furnished nothing beyond the land and received one-third of the grain output and one-third of the hay. The land share must therefore have been less than one-third but greater than one-third times the grain product share. For Bernonville, the land share (0.267) satisfied both inequalities: it was less than one-third and greater than one-third of the grain product share (0.224). Other contracts imply that the land share plus half the expenditure on seed, feed, and harvest labor should be approximately one-half. For Bernonville, the numbers add up to 0.53, very close to one-half indeed.[23]

One final piece of evidence in favor of our constant shares assumption comes from demographic records. If the land and labor factor shares are constant, then the ratio of rent to wages will be proportional to the ratio of labor to land, which we can reasonably approximate by the rural population, provided that the labor force participation rate and the amount of capital invested in land do not change drastically. We can therefore detect drastic shifts in the factor shares of labor and land (provided they do not both change in a way that keeps their ratio constant) by plotting the ratio of rent to wages alongside a graph of rural population trends. If the land and labor factor shares changed, the graph of the rent-to-wage ratio would presumably diverge from the population curve.

We do not know the rural population precisely, but we might approximate it by rural baptisms. If we do so, we see that the curve of baptisms and the graph of the rent-wage ratio move together (figure A.2). The baptisms here come from a region that is much larger than that of our farms, and the graph covers only the period 1671–1720.[24] Still, despite all the approximations and assumptions, the agreement is impressive. And if we graph the rent-wage ratio over the period 1450 to 1789, it parallels what we know about the trend of the population, at least until the last decades of the eighteenth century.

We also calculated TFP using alternative shares from the Chartier farm north of Paris, whose accounts were analyzed by Jean-Marc Moriceau and Gilles Postel-Vinay.[25] The factor shares from the Chartier farm are as follows: labor, including compensation for the *fermier*, 0.476; rental cost of livestock, 0.132; equipment rental, 0.022; land, 0.370. Their product shares

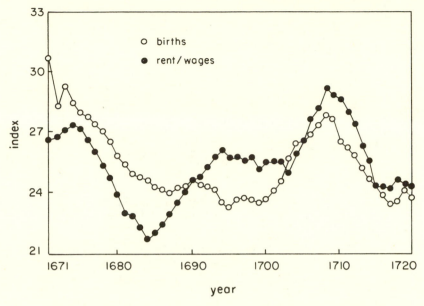

Figure A.2 Indices of Rural Births and of the Rent/Wage Ratio. Both indices are normalized to have the same mean and are measured using moving averages over the preceding nine years.

are: wheat output, 0.473; oats and straw, 0.299; other crops, 0.021; animal products, 0.206. Moriceau and Postel-Vinay's accounts give grain output net of seed, and hence I treated seed as an intermediate product, not as an input. I also refigured their cost of capital goods to reflect the rental cost, using interest and depreciation rates. The depreciation rates were the same as for Bernonville, except for equipment (0.244), which, as in the case of Bernonville, was derived from actual maintenance costs.

Although these alternative shares may at first glance seem very different from the Bernonville figures, most of the difference results from aggregating inputs and outputs and from treating seed as an intermediate product.[26] Had we followed the same procedure with the Bernonville accounts, the Bernonville shares would have been very close to the alternative shares from the Chartier farm. The Bernonville labor factor share, for example, would become 0.452, and the animal product share would be 0.254, both close to the alternative shares. Apart from the aggregation and the treatment of seed, the differences between the two sets of shares is therefore small, and the aggregation and treatment of seed turn out to have very little effect on the calculation of TFP. Aggregation merely lumps together correlated prices in the indices C and P, and treating seed as an intermediate

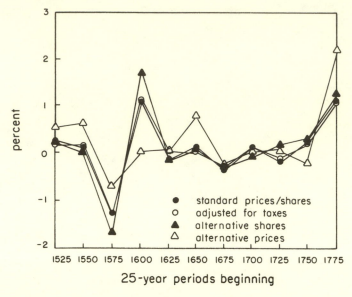

Figure A.3 Alternative Growth Rates of TFP for the Notre Dame
Sample: Tax Adjustment and Alternative Prices and Shares

good merely divides both C and P by very nearly the same number. In both
instances the ratio P/C, which is what we need to calculate TFP, remains
nearly unchanged.

As noted in the text, the effect of the alternative shares on the path TFP
took was not large. The alternative shares had an even smaller effect on the
growth rate of TFP (figure A.3), and they left the regressions with TFP and
with its growth rate largely unchanged (tables A.1 and A.2).

7. WAGES IN PARIS AND THE SURROUNDING COUNTRYSIDE

The evidence for the mobility of labor near Paris covers the period from the
fifteenth century through the eighteenth century, and in their study of the
Chartier family, Jean-Marc Moriceau and Gilles Postel-Vinay even suggest
that farm labor in the Paris Basin was more mobile in the eighteenth century than in the nineteenth.[27] Such high mobility supports the view that
wages in Paris and in the surrounding countryside (at least for the circum-
scribed area of our sample) tended to be equal. It argues in favor of using
the homogeneous series of daily wages for unskilled laborers in Paris as the
rural price of labor.

Still, one might prefer direct evidence for wage equality. Micheline
Baulant's work, which was cited in the text, supports wage equality for the
sixteenth century, but there remains the seventeenth and the eighteenth

TABLE A.1
TFP Regressions with Alternative Prices and Shares

Independent Variables	Regression Numbers	
	1	2
	Dependent Variables	
	Ln(TFP) Alternative Shares	Ln(TFP) Alternative Prices
Constant	0.48	–0.79
	(1.87)	(–4.01)
Dummy: years 1775 and after	0.10	0.084
	(2.33)	(1.54)
Dummy: war years, 1589–97	–0.42	–0.24
	(–8.68)	(–6.47)
Percentage of meadow	0.21	0.14
	(3.17)	(2.69)
Percentage of vineyard	0.012	–0.058
	(0.09)	(–0.50)
Dummy: good soil	–0.0016	0.000057
	(–0.08)	(–0.004)
Ln(distance to Paris in kilometers)	–0.093	–0.078
	(–6.02)	(–6.45)
Dummy: tenant holdover from previous lease	0.025	0.013
	(1.38)	(0.91)
Time (units of 100 years)	0.064	0.11
	(4.20)	(9.36)
Ln(area in hectares)	–0.033	–0.019
	(–3.69)	(–2.67)
Observations	638	620
R^2	0.30	0.34
Standard error	0.23	0.17
Mean of dependent variable	1.11	0.67

Source: As in table 4.3.
Note: In regression 1, TFP is calculated using alternative shares described in text. In regression 2, it is calculated using prices and wages for the expected term of the new lease (the year the lease was signed and the next eight years), and in-kind rent payments were evaluated using the same prices. See Appendix A, parts 6 and 9, for details. T statistics are in parentheses.

centuries—particularly the latter.[28] Unfortunately, data are lacking for this period, even in the archives. One reason is that the typical sources for rural wage data in the Paris Basin—hospitals and ecclesiastical institutions—run dry after the sixteenth century. Detailed accounts disappear, perhaps because the hospitals and monasteries relied more heavily on agents such as *fermiers* (tenant farmers) and *receveurs* (stewards).[29] When added to the

TABLE A.2
TFP Growth Rate Regressions with Alternative Prices and Shares

Independent Variables	Regression Numbers	
	1	*2*
	Dependent Variables	
	Growth Rate, TFP Alternative Shares (Percent per Year)	Growth Rate, TFP Alternative Prices (Percent per Year)
Constant	0.72	0.12
	(1.53)	(0.32)
Growth rate of taxes relative to rents	−2.25	−9.49
	(−0.82)	(−4.38)
Growth rate of Paris population	0.32	0.21
	(6.25)	(5.08)
Dummy: years 1775 and after	1.15	2.05
	(2.89)	(3.95)
Dummy: war years, 1589–97	−3.28	0.18
	(−5.90)	(0.40)
Dummy: building repairs	−0.46	−0.38
	(−0.95)	(−1.00)
Dummy: tenant holdover from previous lease	−0.13	−0.20
	(−0.71)	(−1.41)
Ln(distance to Paris in kilometers)	−0.13	−0.027
	(−0.93)	(−0.24)
Ln(area in hectares)	−0.023	0.036
	(−0.32)	(0.60)
Observations	648	630
R^2	0.21	0.08
Standard error	2.24	1.76
Mean of dependent variable	0.19	0.13

Source: As in table 4.4.

Note: Growth rates equal the rate of change of logarithms calculated from lease to lease, and, as in table 4.4, the TFP growth rates are not adjusted for taxes. TFP was calculated for alternative prices and shares, as in table A.1; see Appendix A, parts 6 and 9, for details. *T* statistics are in parentheses.

difficulty of dealing with in-kind payments and the enormous variations due to differences in strength and skill, it becomes difficult to find usable sources for rural wages.

Yet there is some evidence for the continuing equality of rural and urban wages. South of Paris, in Brétigny-sur-Orge, for example, a *charretier* (plowman and carter) earned 92 livres in 1614, plus in-kind compensation, which we might reasonably suppose was the equivalent of 3 Paris setiers of wheat. If we average the price of wheat over the period 1610–18, his total compensation amounted to 123 livres. In the same year, an unskilled Parisian day laborer, if he worked two hundred days (the typical number of days of work in a year for a day laborer), would earn 120 livres, nearly exactly the same amount. In 1622 in the same village, another charretier and his wife earned 72 livres and 9 Paris setiers of grain working for the seigneur, which works out to 186 livres at Paris prices. If the charretier had worked two hundred days in Paris and his wife had done the same for half the male wage (a typical value for female labor), they would have earned nearly the same amount—195 livres.

In 1714–15, unskilled building workers earned 15 to 25 sous a day in Brétigny; at the time, the modal wage for the unskilled in Paris was 20 sous a day. And in the last years of the Old Regime in Brétigny, the unskilled earned between 12 to 20 sous a day in winter and between 25 to 30 sous a day in summer. In Paris in the 1770s and 1780s, the mode of February wages ranged between 18 and 24 sous in February and between 22 and 28 sous in July. The winter wage in Brétigny was lower and the summer wage higher, but the annual earnings were about the same.[30] Nor was Brétigny exceptional. In the village of Seraincourt, 40 kilometers northwest of Paris, rural and urban earnings also seemed to be the same in the 1720s and the 1760s.[31]

One can certainly find examples of wage gaps between city and countryside, but the gap is usually much smaller than the enormous disparity of wages within the city itself or within any village. In 1754–55, for example, the average Paris wage (actually the average of monthly modal wages) was 21 sous per day for an unskilled day laborer. Out in the countryside, the Abbey of Maubuisson in Saint-Ouen, near Pontoise, was hiring workers to fish and to clean the fish pond for an average of 22 sous per day. The gap between the two is small and is dwarfed by the range of wages in Paris, where monthly modal wages in 1754–55 varied between 18 and 24 sous a day. Some evidence exists that wages were somewhat lower in the countryside, but none of it is conclusive for the Old Regime.[32] Nor can one demonstrate conclusively that rural wages were rising or falling relative to wages in Paris.[33] Given the overwhelming evidence for labor mobility in the vicinity of Paris, it seems reasonable to assume that wages in the city and in its hinterlands moved together.

8. Grain Prices and In-Kind Payments

Much grain seems to have escaped the market, reaching consumers in the form of payments in kind or self-production. One might therefore assume that the price of grain on the farm would bear no relationship to the market prices that enter into the agricultural price index P. For the Paris Basin, though, such a view seems untenable: near Paris it is simply absurd to maintain that the payments of grain in kind amounted to a second market, in which the price of grain bore no relation to that in the open market. The canons of the Cathedral of Notre Dame in Paris, for example, received numerous payments in kind, but they evaluated the grain at the price current in the relevant market—in Paris, if the grain was delivered there; in a local market, if they took possession in the countryside. And when it came time to sell grain from their stores, the canons watched the market to see what their grain would fetch.[34] The payments in kind, therefore, do not seem to have constituted a separate and unrelated market, all the more so since rights to the grain due in kind (tithe payments, for example) were often purchased for cash. The same logic casts doubt on the assumption that the price of grain on the farm was unrelated to the market price. Most peasants had to buy grain to meet their needs, and among the tenants who ran the farms in our sample there were many large-scale farmers who frequently sold on the market.

9. SETTING THE RENT, PRICES IN THE INDEXES P AND C, AND ALTERNATIVE PRICE AVERAGES

In renting out its properties, the Cathedral of Notre Dame did not simply follow local surveyor's indications about what land was worth; rather, it sought to make a profit. It wanted to lease properties under the best possible conditions (subject to what the local market would bear), and it made decisions about property management on the basis of profits. A decision to enlarge a barn in 1757 on the cathedral's property in Viersy, for example, hinged on whether the increased rent would yield an investment return greater than that available from *rentes* (perpetual annuities). The cathedral did fear that charging exorbitant rents might bankrupt tenants, but such fears were hardly inconsistent with profit maximization. After all, a bankrupt tenant would sap profits in the long run.[35]

When deciding if the rent on a farm should be increased, Notre Dame estimated the tenant's revenues and costs. If the revenues exceeded the costs, the cathedral raised the rent, taking care again that the tenant not be pressed into bankruptcy. During the whole process, the point of reference was the previous lease. Whether Notre Dame was implicitly using current prices or prices averaged over the recent past to calculate profits is not clear, but the calculations never involved guesses about future prices.[36]

Other landlords seemed to do the same. When the knowledgeable agronomist Abbé Tessier wrote on leases in the *Encyclopédie méthodique*, his concerns were nearly identical to those of Notre Dame. He aimed to increase profits, although his own practical experience as a property manager made him realize, as did Notre Dame, that pressing a tenant too hard would backfire in the long run.

When it came to estimating the rent that a property would yield, Tessier urged his readers to follow the analysis of a memoir published in 1789 by Varenne de Fenille, a correspondent of the Société d'Agriculture de Paris. "I have never found anything that shed more light on evaluating the rent that agricultural land could yield," said Tessier, and he quoted the memoir in its entirety.[37]

Varenne de Fenille shared Tessier's concerns about tenant bankruptcy, but what was most noticeable about Varenne de Fenille's memoir were the grain prices that he used in analyzing rental value. He performed his calculations using two different grain prices. One was a low price, apparently below the prevailing market price. He used this low price out of a concern that undue pressure not be placed on the tenant farmer; it was in no sense a forecast of the price in the future. The other price he used was a high price equal to the average price over the previous ten years. This ten-year average, he believed, would better reflect the true price that grain would actually fetch, and we can surmise that it would presumably yield a rent figure closer to what a profit-maximizing landlord would charge. Varenne de Fenille's calculation of rent thus seems to have been based on prices averaged over the recent past, and it would seem reasonable that our indexes P and C do the same.[38]

Following Varenne de Fenille and in the spirit of Notre Dame's own practices, I therefore averaged all prices in the indexes P and C over the current year and the previous eight years—in other words, over the outgoing lease.[39] To check how sensitive my results were to this choice of prices, I also computed TFP with prices averaged over the new lease (in other words, over the current year and the next eight years); but as noted in the text, the effect on the TFP trend was small. Using prices over the new lease also led to roughly similar patterns for the growth rate of TFP (figure A.3) and very similar regression coefficients (tables A.1 and A.2). Other price averages (such as a three-year moving average centered on the current year) had an equally small effect on our results.

10. Entrepreneurial Profits

While there were certainly farms where the tenants made fortunes, entrepreneurial profits—defined here to be what the tenant earned over what he would have made on the labor market—were probably low on average. In 1784, for example, Boullanger, a government civil engineer, provided a detailed analysis of the profits from Paris Basin farming for an article on taxes in the *Encyclopédie méthodique*.[40] The analysis rested on calculations he had made while levying taxes in order to pay for road building in the Champagne and the Soissonais in the 1750s. It derived from the costs and profits of local farms and was done with extraordinary care. After carefully deriving the profits from a farm of a fixed area, Boullanger compared them with rent and taxes. Before rent and taxes were paid, the profits amounted to 6,986 livres; the rent and taxes to be paid out of these profits came to 6,232 livres. The remainder, 753 livres, or 12.1 percent of the rent plus taxes, was the tenant's net profit after rent and taxes. According to Boullanger, such a figure was typical, for in general the tenant's profits were about one-eighth of the sum spent on rent plus taxes.[41]

If we take one-eighth of rent plus taxes as the average for the tenant's entrepreneurial profits, and if we assume that rent and taxes paid for land, then with the Bernonville land share (0.267), the factor share for the tenant's entrepreneurial input would be only 0.267/8, or 0.033 of total cost. This is small, but other contemporary authorities would put it even lower: Lavoisier even claimed that entrepreneurial profits were zero on average.[42]

With a share of only 0.033 of total cost, entrepreneurial profits would have very little effect on our calculation of TFP. Moreover, they would disturb our calculations only if they diverged significantly from the trend of wages. The reason is that we treated compensation for the entrepreneur (i.e, the tenant farmer) as part of the labor input; in other words, we assumed that the tenant would earn no more than he would in the labor market. Even if his earnings did exceed his income as a laborer, our calculation of TFP would involve no error, provided that the trend of entrepreneurial earnings paralleled the trend of wages (i.e., provided that their ratio remained constant). As long as the two moved together, we could simply view his higher wage as compensation for his skill, with a fixed conversion factor between his skilled wage and that of an unskilled laborer. His compensation could then simply be aggregated together with that of the rest of labor in calculating TFP. In mathematical terms, if w_2 is the cost of the tenant's entrepreneurial input, w_3 is the wage of unskilled labor, and $k > 1$ is a constant such that $w_2 = kw_3$, then

$$TFP = \frac{w_1^{v_1} w_2^{v_2} w_3^{v_3} \cdots w_n^{v_n}}{p_1^{u_1} \cdots p_m^{u_m}} = k^{v_2} \frac{w_1^{v_1} w_3^{v_2+v_3} \cdots w_n^{v_n}}{p_1^{u_1} \cdots p_m^{u_m}} \tag{17}$$

and aggregating the entrepreneurial input with the rest of labor only multiplies the TFP index by a constant.

There were, of course, times when wages and entrepreneurial earnings undoubtedly diverged. After many tenants went bankrupt in the late seventeenth century and the first decades of the eighteenth century, those who survived may have earned high returns relative to unskilled wages. But by 1750, Notre Dame had discovered the higher profits and raised the rent, and entrepreneurial earnings by tenants probably returned to a level in harmony with wages.[43] In any event, the effect on our TFP index is probably small. Suppose, for example, that the ratio of the tenant's skilled entrepreneurial wages—w_2 in equation (17)—to unskilled wages (w_3) varied from 1.67 to 2.5. This was the maximum range of the ratio of skilled to unskilled wages in the Paris building trades over three centuries; normally the ratio was close to 2.[44] Our TFP index would then err by at most 0.7 percent, very little indeed and not enough to change our story.

We can also take comfort from our TFP regressions. Presumably, the farmers who made large profits would be those who repeated as tenants. Their large profits would keep them on the same farm, depress the rent, and produce lower measurements of TFP and less measured TFP growth. But if we examine the coefficients of the variables for tenant holdovers in tables 4.3 and 4.4, we see that nothing of the sort occurred. If anything, repeat tenants increased the level of TFP and depressed TFP growth by only a minimal amount.

Even though entrepreneurial profits seem small on average, one might still worry that in the short run they could vary enough to disturb our TFP calculations and TFP regressions. Given inelastic agricultural demand and given rents, wages, and capital prices that varied relatively little in the short term (say, during a harvest year or over the course of a nine-year lease), the short-term entrepreneurial profits e would, as we argued in the text, be an increasing function of the rate of increase I of agricultural prices. Let $T = r^s C/P$ be TFP as we measure it, where r is rent and taxes, s is the land share, C is the cost index of nonland inputs, and P is the agricultural price index. Let $W = (r + e)^s C/P$ be the true TFP, calculated with entrepreneurial profits. Then

$$
\begin{aligned}
\ln(W) &= s \ln(r + e) + \ln \frac{C}{P} \\
&= s \ln(r(1 + \frac{e}{r})) + \ln \frac{C}{P} \\
&= \ln(T) + s \ln(1 + \frac{e}{r})
\end{aligned}
\tag{18}
$$

Since e is small relative to r, the last expression is very nearly

$$
\ln(T) + \frac{se}{r}
\tag{19}
$$

Since e is an increasing function of I, it seems reasonable to suppose that e/r—entrepreneurial profits as a fraction of rent—is itself a function of I, which we can approximate by a simple linear function $a + b I$. Since e is zero on average, a must be zero too, and because e/r is an increasing function of I, b is greater than or equal to zero. Hence $\ln(W) = \ln(T) + sbI$. The error involved in ignoring the short-term entrepreneurial profits is thus sbI, and if sb is zero, the error will be zero, meaning that we can ignore the short-term profits. We can actually determine sb by regressing $\ln(T)$ on I and on any additional variables $z_1, \ldots, z_n$ which affect $\ln(W)$. If

$$\ln(W) = e_1 z_1 + \ldots + e_n z_n + u \tag{20}$$

is the true relationship (here, u is the error term and the e_i are coefficients), then our $\ln(T)$ will be

$$\ln(T) = -sbI + e_1 z_1 + \ldots + e_n z_n + u \tag{21}$$

By including I in the regressions with $\ln(T)$, we can thus check for the effect of entrepreneurial profits. If the regression coefficient of I is negative, significant, and large in absolute value, then entrepreneurial profits matter. Fortunately, that is never the case, even if we vary the way we measure I. Furthermore, the coefficient of I implies only a tiny correction to TFP, and adding I to the regression does not usually disturb the other regression coefficients. In short, the regression suggests that we can ignore entrepreneurial profits in our calculations and in our regressions. We have therefore omitted I from the regressions and not used sbI to correct T.

11. A Comparison of Our Productivity Index and the Törnqvist-Translog Index

Part 6 of this appendix described the factor and product shares from the Chartier farm. The factor and product shares come from the farm's accounts for the 1740s, but accounts for the farm also exist for the 1780s.[45] Taken together, the two sets of accounts let us calculate how TFP on the farm changed between the 1740s and 1780s, and since the information in the accounts allows us to calculate TFP with considerable precision, we can use the results to check the accuracy of the TFP index used throughout the text of the book.

The way to measure TFP precisely is to use the modern theory of index numbers, which permits calculating TFP without estimating production, cost, or profit functions. Let us suppose that we want to compare the productivity of two farms, both of which produce multiple outputs. The two farms can exist at different times, and we can even compare the same farm at different moments. Because of productivity differences, the two farms will have different production functions, but we assume that the two distinct production functions at least share a common functional form, in a sense to be made precise below.

In this situation, if the two farms exhibit constant returns to scale, if all product and factor markets are competitive, and if the two farmers optimize (in the sense that they minimize costs conditional on output levels and maximize revenues conditional on input levels), then we can compare the productivity of the two farms by using an appropriate index of inputs, outputs, and prices. The choice of a particular index amounts to a choice of the functional form common to the two production functions; the ideal index would correspond to a functional form such as the translog that can provide a second-order approximation to an arbitrary production function. Such an index is called superlative.[46]

In particular, suppose that we are comparing the productivity of the Chartier farm in the 1780s with its productivity in the 1740s. Let the production functions for our farms (or strictly speaking, the transformation function, since the farms produce multiple outputs) have the translog form with identical second-order coefficients for both farms. The first-order coefficients may be completely different. Under these assumptions, the so-called Törnqvist index provides a measure of the TFP of our farms, and the ratio of TFP on the farm in the 1780s to TFP in the 1740s is

$$
\frac{TFP_{1780}}{TFP_{1740}} = \frac{(\frac{y_1'}{y_1})^{\frac{u_1+u_1'}{2}} \cdots (\frac{y_4'}{y_4})^{\frac{u_4+u_4'}{2}}}{(\frac{x_1'}{x_1})^{\frac{v_1+v_1'}{2}} \cdots (\frac{x_4'}{x_4})^{\frac{v_4+v_4'}{2}}} \tag{22}
$$

Here, $y_1, \ldots, y_4$ are the four farm outputs (wheat, oats and straw, other crops, and animal products) in the 1740s; the u_i, the corresponding output shares; the x_i, the four inputs (labor and the tenant's entrepreneurial input, livestock rental, equipment rental, and land) in the 1740s; the v_i, the corresponding factor shares; and the variables with primes are the same quantities in the 1780s.

We can calculate the expression on the right of equation (22) using the evidence from the farm accounts. The accounts give the revenue produced by each output and the cost of each input in the 1740s and 1780s; I divided the revenues and the costs by the appropriate prices to get the quantities.[47] The prices I used included the local price of wheat (rather than the Paris price) for wheat output; the Pontoise price of oats for oats and straw; the interpolated Paris price of beans for other crops; the interpolated price of meat for animal products; the local wage (rather than the Paris wage) for labor; the rental price of horses for livestock; and the rental price of equipment. All rental prices equaled the sales price multiplied by interest plus depreciation, with the depreciation rates given in Appendix A, part 6. For land, instead of dividing costs by a price, I used the ratio of the actual physical quantities of land employed.[48]

If we perform the calculation, we find that TFP increased 9.79 percent on the farm between the 1740s and the 1780s. The 9.79 percent figure is very close to the 9.03 percent that our own TFP index yields when applied to the Chartier farm, even though our index employs Paris prices, and factor and product shares from the very different property in Bernonville. The accuracy here is obviously a strong vote of confidence for our method.

It should also be noted that little of the small gap between the two figures derives from our assumption of constant shares. Most of it stems from differences between Bernonville and the Chartier farms and from the fact that our method relies on Paris prices.[49] With constant shares mattering little, at least in this instance, the sort of sophisticated flexible functional forms discussed at the end of Appendix A, part 5, would seem to have very little to offer us.

12. AVERAGING TFP

Suppose that we want to average ln(TFP) for each twenty-five-year period in order to chart productivity trends. From equation (8) we know that

$$\ln(TFP) = s\ln(r+t) - \ln\left(\frac{P}{C}\right) \tag{8}$$

One obvious way to proceed would be to average the expression on the right-hand side of equation (8) lease by lease for all leases in a given twenty-five-year period. Alternatively, we could average $s\ln(r+t)$ over all leases in the period and then subtract $\ln(P/C)$ averaged over each of the years in the same period.[50] The two procedures will not necessarily give the same answer, for in the one case we are averaging $\ln(P/C)$ over all the leases drawn up in the period, weighting each lease equally, and in the other case we are averaging it over all the years in the period, weighting each year evenly. If all the leases were clustered toward one end of the period, for example, the procedures might yield very different values of TFP.

In practice however, the two procedures yield results that are practically indistinguishable (figure A.4). The same is true if we average ln(TFP) by decade. Since there is practically no difference between the two methods, we will compute our average of ln(TFP) lease by lease. Working lease by lease fits our regressions, and it has the indisputable advantage of allowing direct comparison with the TFP growth rate figures, which must be calculated lease by lease and which are the only device we have to estimate the effect of taxes.

In figure A.4, I adjusted the rent for variations in land quality, but I did not correct either average for the omission of taxes. In other words, both curves assume taxes are zero and simply average $s\ln(r) - \ln(P/C)$ for each twenty-five-year period. Since the tax correction merely involves adding the same term to both averages, it would have an identical effect on each of them and would do nothing to drive them apart.

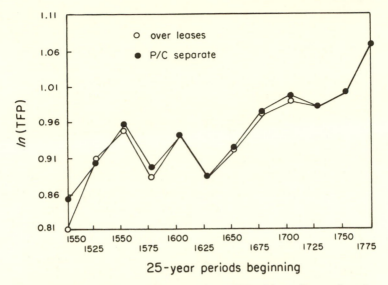

Figure A.4 Alternative Averages of Ln(TFP): Notre Dame Sample. One averages TFP over all the leases in each twenty-five-year period. The other calculates *P/C* separately and then combines it with the average rent during the twenty-five-year period. Neither average is adjusted for taxes.

13. TREATMENT OF TAXES

Unfortunately, we do not know precisely what the taxes on an individual farm were, and as a result we first calculate TFP and its growth rate with rent r alone, ignoring taxes t in formulas such as equation (8). In other words, we begin by using $T = r^s C/P$ as a substitute for TFP $= (r + t)^s C/P$. We then add an adjustment for the omission of taxes. To derive the adjustment, let

$$\frac{r}{r+t} = g \tag{23}$$

where g is the fraction of gross rent w_1 that goes to the landlord rather than to the fisc. Note that the tax rate as a percent of gross rent is simply $1 - g$. Since $r + t = r/g$, we have that ln(TFP) is simply

$$s \ln(r + t) - \ln(\frac{P}{C}) = s \ln(\frac{r}{g}) - \ln(\frac{P}{C}) = \ln(T) - s \ln(g) \tag{24}$$

Similarly, the rate of growth of TFP is

$$\dot{T} - s\dot{g} \tag{25}$$

All we need to know is g or its rate of growth, and we can easily correct for the error involved in using T as a substitute for TFP.

We do not know g precisely, and it probably varied from property to property. But one reasonable assumption is that for the i-th property,

$$\ln(g) = b \ln(\frac{t_a}{r_a}) + c_i \tag{26}$$

where b is a negative constant that is the same for all properties, t_a is the average per-capita tax assessment, r_a is the average per-hectare rent in the region, and c_i is a constant that varies from property to property. All that equation (26) says is that taxes were apportioned with an eye toward average rent and average population levels and that while tax rates varied from property to property, they also rose and fell with average tax assessments and average rent levels.

Note that

$$\dot{g} = b\frac{d}{dt} \ln(\frac{t_a}{r_a}) \tag{27}$$

Suppose we have a linear relationship involving the growth rate of TFP and various explanatory variables $z_1, \ldots, z_k$:

$$\frac{d}{dt} \ln(TFP) = d_1 z_1 + \ldots + d_k z_k + u \tag{28}$$

where u is the error term. Then from expression (25) and equation (27), we have that

$$\dot{T} = sb\frac{d}{dt} \ln(\frac{t_a}{r_a}) + d_1 z_1 + \ldots + d_k z_k + u \tag{29}$$

According to equation (29), all we need do is regress the growth rate of T, which we can observe since T is simply r^sC/P, on the variables z_j, and on

$$\frac{d}{dt} \ln(\frac{t_a}{r_a}) \tag{30}$$

which we can also measure. We will then recover the coefficients in the true relationship between the growth rate of TFP and the variables z_j, and the coefficient of expression (30) will be sb, which we can use to correct the growth rate of T for the omission of taxes via

$$\frac{d}{dt} \ln(TFP) = \dot{T} - s\dot{g} = \dot{T} - sb\frac{d}{dt} \ln(\frac{t_a}{r_a}) \tag{31}$$

In the regressions in tables 4.4 and A.2, the rate of growth of taxes relative to rents is expression (30), calculated from a national average per-capita tax rate by decade and average decennial nominal rents. The coefficient of expression (30) then allows us to correct the observed growth rate of TFP for the omission of taxes via equation (31). The correction turned out to be minimal: taxes certainly rose, but not by enough relative to nominal rents (figure A.3).[51] The growth rate of TFP is thus almost exactly the growth rate of T. Note, too, that using the growth rate of T in place of the growth rate of TFP in tables 4.4 and A.2 will not change the resulting regression coefficients. Again, the inclusion of the growth rate of taxes relative to rents among the explanatory variables will make the other coefficients precisely what they would be if the dependent variable were the true growth rate of TFP.

Multicollinearity rules out adding the analogous term to the regressions in tables 4.3 and A.1 in order to correct the levels of TFP for the omission of taxes. We can, however, derive a correction for $\ln(TFP)$ from the growth rates. From equations (24) and (26),

$$\ln(TFP) = \ln(T) - s\ln(g) = \ln(T) - sb\ln\left(\frac{t_a}{r_a}\right) - sc_i \tag{32}$$

We know T, t_a, and r_a, and the regression with the growth rate of T yields sb. The only other terms are the sc_i, which vary from property to property but not over time. Since they are constants, they do not affect the trend of TFP. If, for instance, we average $\ln(TFP)$ by twenty-five-year periods, the sc_i terms merely add the same constant to the average for each period, and we can ignore them as far as the trend is concerned.[52] In other words, we need only subtract $sb\ln(t_a/r_a)$ from $\ln(T)$ to adjust the level of $\ln(TFP)$ for the omission of taxes. That is what has been done in figure 4.2 and throughout Chapter 4 when we calculated relative levels of TFP.

It is still true that the sc_i terms could affect our regression coefficients in the $\ln(TFP)$ regressions of tables 4.3 and A.1. If the true relationship between $\ln(TFP)$ and the explanatory variables $z_1, \ldots, z_k$ is

$$\ln(TFP) = e_1z_1 + \ldots + e_kz_k + u \tag{33}$$

then for the i-th property

$$\ln(T) - sb\ln\left(\frac{t_a}{r_a}\right) = sc_i + e_1z_1 + \ldots + e_kz_k + u \tag{34}$$

We could determine the sc_i by adding a dummy variable for each property to the regressions of $\ln(T) - sb\ln(t_a/r_a)$ on the z_j, but with thirty-nine properties, multicollinearity rules out such a course of action. Unfortunately, ignoring the sc_i amounts to omitting variables in the regression, which might well bias our coefficients e_j. On the other hand, it seems reasonable to assume that the sc_i are uncorrelated with the other explanatory variables z_j. After all, the sc_i reflect idiosyncracies of the tax system peculiar to each property.[53] If so, then the regression of $\ln(T) - sb\ln(t_a/r_a)$ on the z_j will produce the true regression coefficients e_j, and we can correct $\ln(TFP)$ for taxes in the regressions merely by subtracting $sb\ln(t_a/r_a)$. That is what I have done in tables 4.3 and A.1.[54]

It is worth noting one other implication of equations (24) and (26). If we look at the change in $\ln(TFP)$ between two fixed periods for several properties, as we did for figure 5.1, then for any property it will equal the change in $\ln(T)$ minus the change in $s\ln(g)$, which from equation (26) will be the same for all the properties since the sc_i terms will drop out. The tax correction will merely add the same constant to the TFP growth rate for each property, and as long as we are only interested in the relative productivity growth of the properties, we can simply ignore the tax correction. Figure 5.1 therefore involves no adjustment for taxes.

14. SOURCES

The prices and wages that enter into the indexes P and C were taken from printed sources. Published price series for the Paris region are excellent for most commodities. They betray a care and a concern for detail that are all too often lacking in collections of rental figures, where details surrounding in-kind payments, variations in land quality, and other complexities are often passed over in silence. The published series merit our confidence, and as for the commodities that are exceptions to this rule—chiefly meat and livestock—they are ones for which further research will likely be of little avail. To be sure, a high-quality series of wages from the Paris countryside would certainly be desirable. But as explained in Appendix A, part 7, suitable collections of rural wages are hard to find for the region, even in the archives.

The grain prices in the index P were prices in Paris on the Feast of Saint-Martin (November 11). As I explained in part 1, I selected the Saint-Martin prices because grain payments were due then. Choosing the Feast of Saint-Martin also provided a way of dealing with seasonality. The Saint-Martin prices were taken from Baulant and Meuvret, *Prix des céréales*, 2:142–51. For wheat and rye, I used minimum prices on the Feast of Saint-Martin, as was the case with the in-kind payments; for barley and oats, only maximum prices were available.

Since the Saint-Martin prices ceased being available after 1698, I resorted to proxies. For wheat, I relied upon the proxy that I used for in-kind payments. As described in part 1, it was constructed by first regressing the Saint-Martin wheat price on the annual Paris price without an intercept term. After 1698, when the annual Paris price existed but the Saint-Martin one did not, I multiplied the annual price by the regression coefficient to get the proxy. The annual Paris price came from Baulant, "Le prix des grains."

For rye, barley, and oats, I constructed similar proxies for the years after 1698 by regressing the Paris Saint-Martin price on the Pontoise Saint-Martin price without an intercept. The regressions were limited to the years 1661–98, because the size of the Pontoise setier was in doubt before 1661. The Pontoise prices came from Dupâquier, *Mercuriales*.[55] In constructing the Paris grain price series, I corrected the published Paris price for two typographical errors, and I also adjusted the price of all grains for an 8 percent increase in the size of the Paris setier between 1573 and 1586.[56]

Since the evidence was fragmentary, the prices of beef, mutton, and pork in the index P were interpolated from twenty-five-year averages.[57] The averages were spliced together from prices in Georges d'Avenel, *Histoire économique de la propriété, des salaires, des denrées, et de tous les prix en général depuis l'an 1200 jusqu'en l'an 1800*, 4:132–79, 586; Labrousse, *Esquisse*, 1:301–3 (his raw prices rather than his index); Mohamed El Kordi, *Bayeux aux XVIIe et XVIIIe siècles*, pp. 303–5; and Perrot, *Genèse d'une ville moderne*, 2:1032–34. Admittedly, the old collection by d'Avenel is far from perfect, and the other sources are not necessarily Parisian. Yet the criticisms of d'Avenel are often exaggerated, and most of the non-Parisian prices were taken from nearby provinces such as Normandy, where long-distance trade in livestock would have brought local prices in line with those prevailing in Paris.[58]

For the remaining outputs (beans and peas, flax, dairy products, wool, eggs, and horses), I also interpolated from twenty-five-year averages. The sources for beans and peas included Mantellier, *Mémoire sur la valeur*, pp. 89–98, 381; Baulant, "Prix et salaires"; and Hauser, *Recherches et documents*, pp. 127–29. For flax, I relied upon prices of *fil de lin* in Mantellier, *Mémoire sur la valeur*, pp. 276–77; Baulant, "Prix et salaires"; and d'Avenel, *Histoire économique*, 5:527–30. For dairy products, I used butter prices gleaned from Hauser, *Recherches et documents*, pp. 136–38; Baulant, "Prix et salaires"; and El Kordi, *Bayeux*, pp. 305–6. The sources for eggs were Baulant, "Prix et salaires"; El Kordi, *Bayeux*, p. 228; Hauser, *Recherches et documents*, pp. 140–41; Bottin, *Seigneurs et paysans (1540–1650)*, annex B; and Léopold Nottin, *Recherches sur les variations des prix dans le Gâtinais*, p. 136. For horses, d'Avenel, *Histoire économique*, 6:455–86; Bertrandy-Lacabane, *Brétigny-sur-Orge*, p. 331; and Mantellier, *Mémoire sur la valeur*, pp. 319–23. While some of these prices come from areas other than Paris, the differences turn out to be small, for once again the prices were taken from nearby areas such as Normandy and the transport costs for the commodities in question were generally low. The effect on the index would be smaller still since the product shares for these commodities were all small.

Sources for the prices in the cost index C were as follows. As is discussed in the text and in part 7, wages were the modal wages for unskilled Paris day laborers. The sources were Baulant, "Le salaire des ouvriers," and Durand, "Recherches sur les salaires." As explained in part 6, the price of seed and feed equaled output prices times one plus the interest rate, and prices of capital goods were rental prices, derived from the sales price via the interest rate and a depreciation rate. Sources for the interest and depreciation rates are given in part 6. The rental prices of horses, cattle, sheep, pigs, and poultry were interpolated from twenty-five-year averages.

The sales price of equipment was assumed to be proportional to wages, and the sales price of horses was the same as the output price given above. The sales prices of cattle, sheep, pigs, and poultry were spliced together from twenty-five-year averages. The sources for cattle were Bertrandy-Lacabane, *Brétigny-sur-Orge*, p. 333; d'Avenel, *Histoire économique*, 4:75–94; and Baulant, "Prix et salaires." For sheep, Hauser, *Recherches et documents*, pp. 191–92; d'Avenel, *Histoire économique*, 4:100–115; and Baulant, "Prix et salaires." For pigs and poultry, d'Avenel, *Histoire économique*, 4:115–30, 585, 591. Again, low transportation costs and small factor weights justified using some prices outside Paris.

Most of the explanatory variables in the regressions were derived using prices and information in the leases and associated property descriptions. The sources for the others are as follows. The index of per-capita taxation (t_a) for the years after 1560 was calculated using decennial averages based on population figures and central treasury receipts from table 1 of Hoffman, "Early Modern France." For the period before 1560, I spliced the series of central treasury receipts to *taille* levels given in J. J. Clamageran, *Histoire de l'impôt en France*, 3 vols. (Paris, 1867–76), and used population figures in Dupâquier, ed., *Histoire de la population française*, 1:513–24, 2:51–68, interpolated and adjusted for changes in frontiers. A local tax series would have been preferable to the central treasury receipts, but a usable series does not exist.

Soil quality was derived from information in Jacques Dupuis, *Carte pédologique de la France* (Paris, 1967). For the population of Paris, I relied upon a variety of sources, including Jean-Noël Biraben and Alain Blum, "Population Trends in France, 1500–1800: Comparison with Other Countries" (unpublished manuscript); Lachiver, "L'approvisionnement de Paris en viande au XVIIIe siècle," pp. 345–54; Dupâquier, ed., *Histoire de la population française*; E. Charlot and J. Dupâquier, "Mouvement annuel de la population de Paris de 1670 à 1821," *Annales de démographie histo-*

rique (1967), pp. 511–19; and a data base put together by Philip Benedict. The destruction of records makes estimating the population of Paris difficult, but Benedict has assembled what seem to be the most reliable estimates. In "Was the Eighteenth Century an Era of Urbanization in France," he faults the accuracy of the Paris population figures in Dupâquier's *Histoire de la population française*, and I have therefore given preference to his numbers and to those in the articles by Biraben, Charlot, and Lachiver.

Measuring TFP with Other Samples of Leases

1. CALCULATING TFP WHEN SHARES CHANGE AND COMPARING PRODUCTIVITY LEVELS

In terms of prices and rent, the rate of growth of TFP is

$$\sum_{j=1}^{n} v_j \dot{w}_j - \sum_{i=1}^{m} u_i \dot{p}_i \tag{1}$$

Here the p_i's and u_i's are the output prices and output shares in total revenue; the w_j's and v_j's, the factor prices and factor shares in total cost; and dots refer to growth rates. If the output and factor shares are constant, it is easy to integrate expression (1) with respect to time to get an index for TFP, but if the shares vary, things become more difficult. The problem—though the mathematical concept here is not one that economists typically use—is that expression (1) is really a differential form. Unless its exterior derivative is zero—highly unlikely if the shares vary—the integral will depend on the path that prices and wages take as they vary through time.

We can resolve this problem if we are willing to make a number of assumptions. Let us assume (as we did in Appendix A, part 5) that in the short run farmers maximize profits holding land fixed, and that in the long run landlords absorb untaxed profits as rent. Let us suppose, too, that we can approximate the short-term profit function by a translog functional form, which changes over time in a particularly simple way—essentially via multiplication by a function of time alone. Under these assumptions— which amount to choosing a particularly simple path of technical change and a particular form for the profit function—then the ratio of the TFP index at time t_2 to its value at time t_1 will be:

$$\frac{(\frac{w_1}{\tilde{w}_1})^{v_1} \ldots (\frac{w_n}{\tilde{w}_n})^{v_n}}{(\frac{p_1}{\tilde{p}_1})^{u_1} \ldots (\frac{p_m}{\tilde{p}_m})^{u_m}} \tag{2}$$

Here w_1 is rent plus taxes; the other w's are prices of the factors of production; the prices without the tilde refer to t_2 and the prices with the tilde refer to t_1; and the v's are the average of the factor shares at t_1 and t_2 and the u's are the average of the product shares at t_1 and t_2.[1] Intuitively, what we are doing is assuming that the change in the shares can be approximated by particularly simple functions.

The same technique applies if we are comparing two farms in different regions: all we assume is that the profit function on one farm (or equivalently, the production function) can be smoothly deformed via the same simple process of change to give us the profit function of the other farm. In that case, the ratio of TFP on one farm to TFP on the other farm is given by expression (2), with prices, wages, and rents on both farms measured in the same units. Note that the same formula applies even if the farms are in two different countries and the currencies are different, as long as we use the same physical units to measure prices, wages, and rents. The reason is that, whatever the appropriate exchange rate, it drops out of expression (2) because the average shares in both numerator and denominator sum to 1.

2. TFP Calculations, Tax Corrections, and Sources for the Properties Outside of the Paris Basin

Farms in the Orléanais and Near Amiens

The rental figures for the *terre et seigneurie* of Châtillon-sur-Loing in the Orléanais come from twenty-three leases for the property in Nottin, *Recherches sur les variations des prix*, p. 117. Admittedly, the property included seigneurial dues, and some of it perhaps shifted from arable to stock raising in the late eighteenth century, a change that would have modified the factor and product shares. Still, over most of the period of interest to us, the local crops and farming techniques resembled those closer to Paris, and I therefore used the Bernonville and Chartier shares to calculate the indices C and P.[2] I also used Paris prices and wages to calculate C and P, because the property was not too distant from the city.

For the thirty-four properties of the Hôtel-Dieu of Amiens, rent and evidence about the properties came from Deyon, *Contribution à l'étude des revenus fonciers en Picardie*, pp. 4, 65–67, 82. I used only the properties leased for cash rent, since Deyon's in-kind rents included payments that he did not evaluate. As explained in the text, the rent for each property was measured relative to the property's rent in 1750–59.[3]

Deyon's properties grew grain, much like farms nearer Paris. I therefore felt justified in calculating TFP with the Bernonville shares as my standard and the Chartier shares as my alternative. Given low transportation costs for livestock (on this, see Appendix A, part 14), I also felt it appropriate to use the Paris prices for meat and livestock capital. Because of gaps in local wage series, I was forced to employ Paris wages, but the fragmentary evidence suggests that the wages, though lower near Amiens, followed a similar trend, at least in the seventeenth century: Deyon, *Amiens, capitale provinciale*, pp. 516–19. For grain, I relied on wheat and oat prices from the nearby city of Montdidier in Victor de Beauville, *Histoire de la ville de Montdidier*, 2 vols. (Paris, 1857), 2:487–93. Leases on the farms near Amiens lasted nine years and were generally auctioned off, at least after the early seventeenth century.[4] I therefore computed my standard TFP index (using the Bernonville shares) by first averaging prices in the indexes P and C over the current year and the previous eight years of the outgoing lease, as with the Notre Dame sample; I then computed decennial averages of P and C to match the decennial rental figures. For the alternative shares index, I followed the same procedure but used the Chartier shares; and for the alternative prices TFP index, I employed the Bernonville shares and averaged P and C over the current year and the next eight years—in other words, over the new lease. Simple decennial averages of current prices led to similar results. Finally, the TFP estimates were subjected to the same tests for entrepreneurial profits as the Notre Dame sample and were corrected for taxation in precisely the same way. As with the Notre Dame sample, the tax correction involves a regression of the uncorrected rate of change of TFP on property characteristics and the rate of change of per-capita taxes relative to average rents, with the coefficient of the rate of change of per-capita taxes relative to rents yielding the tax correction (table B.1).[5]

Lorraine

For Lorraine, rental rates were taken from the twenty-five-year averages for farms (*gagnages*) in Guyot, "Essai sur l'aisance relative du paysan lorrain." Guyot says that he followed roughly fifty gagnages, except for the nineteenth century, but it is not clear that his rental series are for precisely the same properties, particularly in the sixteenth century. The discussion in Guyot's *Histoire d'un domaine rural en Lorraine*, pp. 32–35, suggests that the rental market in Lorraine was competitive: leases were renewed every nine years, and it was rare for the same person to repeat as tenant in Lorraine.[6]

Usable accounts were not available for local farms, but it seemed reasonable to adapt the figures from the Chartier farm for the shares and the depreciation rates of the gagnages, which were arable farms in the plain, not stock-raising farms in the mountainous Vosges. The agricultural technology on the gagnages was similar to that near Paris, but it was less productive.[7] In particular, grain yields were lower, ranging from perhaps 9.2 hectoliters per hectare to 17 hectoliters per hectare for wheat, versus over 19 hectoliters per hectare on the Chartier farm by 1700.[8] I therefore calculated new shares for the Chartier farm with the same inputs but with yields that were either 9.2 hectoliters per hectare (low yields), 13.5 hectoliters per hectare (medium yields), or 17 hectoliters per hectare (high yields).[9] The information about yields and about the agricultural technology in Lorraine was taken from Guy Cabourdin, *Terre et hommes en Lorraine 1550–1635*, 2 vols. (Nancy, 1977), 2:639–74; Guyot, *Histoire d'un domaine rural en*

TABLE B.1
TFP Growth Rate Regressions

Sample	Constant	Growth Rate of per Capita Taxes Relative to Rents (Percent per Year)	Ln(Property Area in Hectares)	Dummy: Tenant New and Unrelated to Previous Tenant	Dummy: Vineyard on Property	Ln(Distance to Market in Kilometers)	R^2	Number of Cases
				Regression Coefficients				
Near Amiens[a]	-0.18 (-0.41)	-0.19 (-5.44)	0.06 (1.06)	—	—	0.00 (0.01)	0.11	249
Ille-et-Villaine[a]	-0.28 (-1.77)	-0.18 (-2.44)	—	—	—	—	0.12	44
Near Angers: two properties[a]	-0.19 (-0.69)	-0.14 (-1.50)	—	—	—	—	0.05	46
Near Angers: eight farms of hospital[a]	0.08 (0.64)	-0.13 (-2.97)	—	—	—	—	0.16	48
Near Le Mans: ten farms of Hôtel-Dieu[a]	-0.33 (-1.61)	-0.05 (-0.48)	—	—	—	—	0.005	50
Gâtine Poitevine[a]	0.09 (0.23)	-0.32 (-2.21)	—	—	—	—	0.140	33
Near Nantes[a]	-0.20 (-0.24)	-0.04 (-0.30)	0.06 (0.22)	0.15 (0.14)	—	—	0.004	38
Near Nantes	-0.16 (-0.26)	-0.04 (-0.32)	—	—	0.17 (0.24)	—	0.004	39

Source: Prices and samples of leases are described in Appendix B, part 2.

Note: The dependent variable in each regression is the growth rate of TFP in percentage per year. It is calculated from lease to lease using the standard shares and prices averaged over the current year and the previous eight. There is no correction for taxes, but the coefficients will not be affected, because, as is explained in Appendix A, part 13, the growth rate of taxes relative to rents figures among the explanatory variables. T statistics are in parentheses.

[a] Used for tax correction.

Lorraine; Morineau, *Les faux-semblants*, pp. 39–47, 163–231; and the 1840 agricultural census (*SA 1840*).

The low- and medium-yield shares represent the likely range of what was possible for farms in Lorraine, with the high-yield shares being highly unlikely. Perhaps the lower yields prevailed in the sixteenth century and the medium yields in the eighteenth century. In any event, factor and product shares do not seem to have shifted drastically. In the first place, crops did not change, and land was not converted from arable to pasture—a sign that outputs stayed about the same. Furthermore, a graph of the rent-wage ratio moves in parallel with the regional population over the course of the sixteenth, seventeenth, and eighteenth centuries. The parallel movement, we know, is evidence that the crucial land and labor factor shares remained constant.

For prices and wages I also relied upon Guyot's twenty-five-year averages. The prices I needed were those of wheat, oats (for oats and straw), peas (for other vegetable output), *viande de boeuf* (beef, for animal output), horses (for livestock), the interest rate on *rentes* (for capital rental rates), the wages of an unfed *manoeuvre* (unskilled laborer, for wages and for the price of equipment), and the rental rate on some fifty farms (*gagnages*) that Guyot followed.[10] Some data were missing and had to be interpolated. For wages, missing data were filled in using trends in the wages for *porteurs* (carriers) and *vignerons* (vinedressers): their wages tended to move with those of *manoeuvres* when all were available. For horses, missing data were completed using the price of oxen; for peas, data were interpolated linearly. As with the Notre Dame farms, the costs of capital (livestock and equipment) were rental costs derived from the interest rate, the price of the capital good, and a depreciation rate.

Normandy (Bretteville-l'Orgueilleuse, Cheux, Rots, Pays de Caux, Auge)

The leases for Bretteville-l'Orgueilleuse came from manuscript sources at the AD Calvados: notarial documents, the records of the Abbey of Saint-Etienne of Caen, and the papers of the Cairon family, including its diaries and account books.[11] In a number of instances, the leases did not reveal the area of the property to be rented, and the areas had to be identified by locating the properties in the magnificent *terriers* (land-holding books) and land surveys that exist for Bretteville and surrounding towns.[12] Rents for the nearby towns of Cheux and Rots were taken from J. M. Pavard, "Le mouvement de la rente foncière dans la plaine de Caen d'après trois échantillons de la fin du XVIe siècle à la Révolution: Bilan provisoire," in Goy and Le Roy Ladurie, eds., *Prestations paysannes*, 2:693–97. In contrast to some parts of Normandy, there was no problem with contre-lettres that secretly revised rents, and to judge from the Cairon papers, landlords had no difficulty getting rid of tenants.[13] Furthermore, a test for entrepreneurial profits with the leases from Bretteville, Cheux, and Rots turned up nothing of significance.

I could not correct for taxes in Bretteville in the same way that I did in the Paris Basin, because I was not following the same properties through time. But I was able to collect figures for the *taille* and related taxes in Bretteville during the years 1691–1789 from AD Calvados 2 C 1174. I assumed that the taxes were paid by both nonprivileged owners and the tenants of privileged owners and that the fiscal burden was therefore spread evenly over all the farmland in Bretteville.[14] I then simply added the per-hectare tax burden to the rent, and I assumed that the tax burdens in Cheux and Rots were the same. For taxes before 1691, I spliced tax totals in Bretteville to the national per-capita series used for the Paris Basin.

Unlike farming in parts of Normandy that were converted to pasture, farming in Bretteville kept its focus on grain; the same was true for the nearby villages of Cheux and Rots. We can see as much from the early-nineteenth-century *cadastre* (register of the survey of lands) for the three villages, but local terriers and their accompanying maps tell the same story in the middle of the seventeenth century and—at least for Bretteville—at the end of the fifteenth century. So do the leases themselves and the inten-dant's descriptions of local agriculture in the eighteenth century.[15] The local farms thus resembled those near Paris, and although local account books do not permit a direct calculation of input and output shares, they make it clear that the shares were close to those we used for the Paris Basin. Local grain yields were comparable to those near Paris; so was the use of labor and capital. Near Paris, for example, a farm might have one plowman for every 30 to 60 hectares; the Chartier farm had one plowman per 33 hectares circa 1700 and one per 45 hectares a century later. In Bretteville, it was one plowman per 38 to 46 hectares circa 1700. In the Paris Basin, a farm might make do with seven to twelve horses per 100 hectares, depend-ing on the soil and the century; in Bretteville, it had ten per 100 hectares in the late seventeenth century and perhaps twelve circa 1500. The number of horses and plowmen per hectare thus declined over time, as on the Chartier farm, but not by enough to radically change the shares. And to judge from the focus on grain farming, the output mix did not change either. It there-fore seemed reasonable to assume that the input and output shares in Bretteville (and Cheux and Rots as well) were roughly constant and similar to those common around Paris. For the sake of simplicity, I relied upon the Chartier shares, which required fewer prices. The Bernonville shares gave similar results, although to use them I had to consolidate certain inputs and outputs when prices were unavailable.[16]

To calculate the indexes C and P for Bretteville, Cheux, and Rots, I needed the prices of wheat, oats, peas (for miscellaneous vegetable output), meat (for animal products), labor, the rental cost of equipment, and the rental cost of livestock. Unfortunately, getting the requisite prices was an arduous task, even with archival sources at my disposal. The price of wheat was taken from annual prices in Caen, which lay less than 10 kilometers from Bretteville, Cheux, and Rots. The sources were Perrot, *Genèse d'une ville moderne*, Annexe 29 (for 1727–92), and AD Calvados F 1697 (for 1568–1727). The latter source, though, gave no prices for a number of years; to fill the resulting gaps, I was forced to regress the available series of annual wheat prices in Caen on annual wheat prices in Bayeux, which was less than 18 kilometers from Bretteville, Rots, and Cheux. The regressions were performed without a constant, and they allowed me to fill most of the gaps with a multiple of the price of wheat in Bayeux. The Bayeux prices came from El Kordi, *Bayeux*, pp. 282–89. When evidence from Bayeux ran dry, I relied on a similar regression, this time on the price in more distant Coutances, from Hauser, *Recherches et documents*, pp. 171–73.[17] A few more gaps still remained, however, as did the larger problem of wheat prices before 1568. For the period before 1568, I took as my base the harvest-year prices in Montivilliers, near Le Havre, for the period 1525–61. To link the Montivilliers series with the prices from after 1568, I regressed the post-1568 series on prices in Rouen, which allowed me to reach back to 1563. The Rouen and Montivilliers prices came from Bottin, *Seigneurs et paysans*. I then used similar regressions on the Paris prices to close the short gap between 1563 and 1561 and to extend the resulting series back before 1525. The errors involved in using the Paris series for the years before 1525 are minor: only two of the leases I use date from before 1525, and removing them would not change the results I observe.

The price of oats was also problematic: the data in AD Calvados F 1697 were full of holes. I therefore began with the price of oats in Bayeux, from El Kordi, *Bayeux*, pp. 291–93, for the years 1709–93, which I spliced to the price of oats in Coutances for the years 1676–1778, from Hauser, *Recherches et documents*, pp. 181–83, via regressions without a constant. For the earlier period, I had the price in Montivilliers for the years 1525–61, from Bottin, *Seigneurs et paysans*, Annexe B, but AD Calvados F 1697 was too fragmentary to span the gap between 1561 and 1676. I therefore regressed my 1676–1778 series of annual oats prices on my series of annual wheat prices without a constant to create a proxy oats series that could be spliced to the Montivilliers series and pushed back before 1525. The resulting set of annual prices for oats agreed well with the fragmentary evidence in AD Calvados F 1697 and in Aubert, "Notes extraites de trois livres de raisons de 1473 à 1550."

The prices of peas and meat (beef) were interpolated from twenty-five-year averages as for the Paris Basin. The price of peas came from Perrot,

Genèse d'une ville moderne, Annexe 30, but his evidence covered only 1727–91. Because manuscript sources such as AD Calvados F 1697 provided little or no information about the price of peas or beans, I was forced to use sources from distant markets for earlier periods, including d'Avenel, *Histoire économique de la propriété* (prices from various parts of northern France), 4:421–42, 594; Mantellier, *Mémoire*, pp. 89–98, 381 (prices in Orléans). The effect of the distant prices on the index should be minimal because the share weight of peas is very small. As for meat (beef) the twenty-five-year averages came from Perrot, *Genèse d'une ville moderne*, Annexe 30 (prices in Caen, 1751–89); El Kordi, *Bayeux*, pp. 303–5 (prices in Bayeux, 1672–1782); and, for the earlier periods, d'Avenel, *Histoire économique de la propriété*, 4:132–79, 586. Given the low cost of transporting livestock, the effect of using the evidence from more distant markets in d'Avenel should be small.

The cost of capital was, as always, a rental price calculated from a depreciation rate, an interest rate, and the sales price of the capital goods. The depreciation rates were taken from the Chartier farm, and the interest rates were twenty-five-year averages taken from the rate on rentes in notarial records and the Cairon family papers: AD Calvados 7 E 174–75, F 1697, F 1653–67. The sales price of horses came from d'Avenel, *Histoire économique de la propriété*, 6:455–866; again, low transportation costs justified using prices from a wide area. The sales price of equipment was assumed to be proportional to wages.

A suitable wage series was difficult to assemble. I began with wages for unfed, semiskilled carpenters from Rosenthal, *The Fruits of Revolution*, p. 183. Rosenthal's wages cover the period from 1702 into the nineteenth century. They come from the records of the Abbey of Troarn, which was just on the other side of Caen and no more than 25 kilometers from Bretteville, Cheux, and Rots. The problem was finding wages for earlier periods—in particular, for the sixteenth century. I had some fragmentary evidence in the Cairon account books and local ecclesiastical records, and from a published series for Bayeux from El Kordi, *Bayeux*, p. 256. But the manuscript evidence was not enough to build a good series back to the beginning of the sixteenth century, and the El Kordi evidence began only in 1673.

There was, though, considerable evidence for wages in the vicinity of Rouen: wages for Rouen itself, which reached back to the fifteenth century, and eighteenth-century wages for Saint-Pierre-du-Bosguérard, which was 20 kilometers outside Rouen. The series for Rouen and Saint-Pierre-du-Bosguérard were taken from Guy Bois, *Crise du féodalisme* (Paris, 1981), pp. 390–92 (summer wages for unskilled building workers in Rouen, 1450–1572); Bottin, *Seigneurs et paysans*, pp. 154–55 and graph 48 (unskilled building workers in Rouen, 1520–1622); and Hauser, *Recherches et documents*, pp. 193–94 (harvest workers in Saint-Pierre-du-Bosguérard, 1720–83). I therefore decided to build up a series for the area near Rouen, using the Rouen and Saint-Pierre-du-Bosguérard wages, and then link the Rouen area wages to the Troarn series.[18] Admittedly, Rouen and Saint-Pierre-du-Bosguérard lay slightly over 100 kilometers from Bretteville, Cheux, and Rots, but I felt I could use the Rouen wage series because workers had long migrated from the area around Caen and Bretteville into the area of Rouen.[19] Wages near Caen and Bretteville were generally a bit lower than near Rouen, and the Troarn wages were for semiskilled workers. To take these differences into account, I regressed the eighteenth-century Troarn series on the Rouen series without a constant and used the regression coefficient to splice the Rouen series to the Troarn wages. There remained, though, a rather large hole in the middle of the seventeenth century, which I filled via a similar regression on Paris wages. Paris was of course even further away, but the Rouen wages seemed closely related to the Paris wage. Furthermore, the mobility of labor and the stickiness of nominal wages would keep the resulting errors small.

Leases in Bretteville, Cheux, and Rots tended to last nine years, so once I had assembled the prices and wages, I averaged them over the outgoing lease—in other words, the current year and the previous eight years—to calculate *C* and *P*. Averaging over the new lease did not change matters greatly. Obviously, the prices in *C* and *P* are far from perfect, particularly as one moves back into the sixteenth century and relies more and more on prices from more distant markets. Unfortunately, there were really no alternative wages or grain prices that I could test—evidence from the sixteenth century was simply too fragmentary. I did attempt to use alternative prices for livestock, animal products, and miscellaneous vegetable output: sheep instead of horses, butter instead of meat, and cider instead of peas. The indexes *C* and *P* were hardly changed.

For the *Pays de Caux*, I took rents from Guy Lemarchand, *La fin du féodalisme dans le pays de Caux* (Paris, 1989), pp. 565: an annual rent index for sixteen farms.[20] From the descriptions in Lemarchand, pp. 66–67, 148–49, 288–94, the local rental market seemed competitive, and agriculture resembled that around Paris—the amount of livestock and equipment was similar, as were the grain yields. I therefore adopted the shares from the Chartier farm, using the price of wheat, oats (for oats, fodder, and other vegetable products, which were all lumped together), *veaux de rivière* (for animal output), sheep (for livestock), and the wages of an unfed rural *manoeuvre* (for labor and for the sales price of equipment). The rental price of equipment was calculated using Parisian interest rates and the Chartier depreciation rates. I averaged prices over the current year and the previous eight years; averaging them over the current year and the next eight led to similar results.

For the Auge, I had no accounts and no precise way of calculating the one factor share I needed—the land share both before and after conversion to pasture. However, the factor share of land would have undoubtedly increased when the land was converted from arable to pasture, because grain farming was labor intensive, and the share after conversion ought to have resembled the factor share on other farms where livestock raising was the focus of activity. For farms in the Gâtine Poitevine and the Bas Maine, where livestock was also important, surviving accounts suggest a land share of perhaps .44 to .51.[21] Before the conversion the land share must have resembled that on arable farms, such as in Bretteville; a land share of .37 to .45 (net of seed) would be a reasonable range.[22] The average of the land shares before and after conversion would be between .41 and .48, where the larger number would yield a bigger estimate for the TFP increase.

The only other figure needed to calculate the TFP increase for the Auge is the ratio of the rental price of pasture to the rental price of arable at any one time—preferably at a time when pasture conversion is taking place. In the middle of the nineteenth century, the conversion was still under way, and the ratio of the rental price of pasture to the rental price of arable can be calculated from the 1852 agricultural census. The areas affected lay in the arrondissements of Lisieux and Pont-l'Evêque, where, according to the 1852 census, the ratio was 2.46 for the land of the *deuxième classe* in the arrondissement of Lisieux, and 1.63 in the arrondissement of Pont-l'Evêque. The 1852 census is perhaps a bit late for the process we are describing, but tax roles from the Old Regime suggest a similar ratio: 2.42 for the *élection* of Pont-l'Evêque in the middle of the eighteenth century for land of average quality or perhaps as much as 3.00 for the best property.[23]

If we take the highest ratio (3.00) and the largest average share (.48) and assume that 70 percent of the farmland (which we take to be arable, meadow, and pasture) was arable in 1600 and only 35 percent was in 1830, then the TFP increase works out to be only 0.08 percent per year. With the same share and the 2.42 ratio, it is only 0.06 percent per year.[24] Both numbers are upper bounds: they ignore the costs of conversion and they also gloss over the fact that some of the conversion may have simply been an adjustment to changing relative prices, with no increased productivity.

Admittedly, there is perhaps a problem of self-selection here, a problem that may bring our upper-bound estimates of the TFP increase closer to reality. The reason is that the arable which was in fact converted to pasture was presumably the land where the gains from conversion were highest. If the costs of conversion were uniform, then the gains would be highest where the ratio of the postconversion rental price to the preconversion price was largest. It is thus conceivable that the ratio of the rental price of existing pasture to existing arable would actually understate the true gains from conversion, because it would leave out all the land that was already converted, land for which the ratio must have been even higher. Obviously, we can ensure that this problem is not too large by preferring the highest reasonable figures for the ratio of rent on existing pasture to rent on existing arable—say the 3.00 ratio observed for the best land in the middle of the eighteenth century.

The West

Rents for the west of France come from the following sources: AD Loire Atlantique, H 275 (fifty-four leases from three nearby farms, all located roughly 20 kilometers east of Nantes: the métairie of La Chapelle-aux-Moines, the bordage of La Robinière, and the métairie of Coudray); L. Michel, "Quelques données sur le mouvement de la rente foncière" (fifty leases from the farms of Chavais and L'Epinay near Angers); Daniel Zolla, "Les variations du revenu et du prix des terres en France au XVIIe et au XVIIIe siècles," *Sciences politiques* 8 (1893): 299–326, 439–61; 9 (1894): 194–216, 417–32 (eighty-eight decennial rent observations from eight farms near Angers and sixty decennial rent observations from ten farms near Le Mans); Peret, *Seigneurs et seigneuries en Gâtine poitevine*, pp. 152, 185–87, 206 (thirty-six leases from the three métairies of Vignauderie, Grolière, and La Creuse in the Gâtine Poitevine, including pots-de-vin); and Meyer, *La noblesse bretonne*, 2:702–3 (fifty-six leases from twelve farms in the Ille-et-Vilaine in eastern Brittany).[25] Additional information about the farms from Nantes came from AD Loire Atlantique, H 274, and Malestroit and Laure, *Histoire de Vallet*, pp. 101–27.

The western rental markets seemed competitive. On the farms studied by L. Michel, tenants did repeat, but there was little evidence of anything like *mauvais gré*; nor was there any sign of it in eastern Brittany. On the three métairies in the Gâtine Poitevine, only one farmer repeated as a tenant. Near Nantes, tenants and their families did persist, but their persistence did not reduce rent increases, as one would expect in the face of tenant market power. Throughout the west, leases were renewed every nine years or less, and regressions failed to turn up any consistent signs of disturbing entrepreneurial profits.[26]

Calculating TFP from shares and prices therefore seemed reasonable for the western samples. I calculated it much as I did with the Amiens sample: going lease by lease, following the same farms through time, and measuring rents relative to a common base period for each sample so as to adjust for property differences. I corrected for taxes via the same method used with the Notre Dame leases; the necessary regressions are shown in table B.1.

I computed factor and product shares for the west from evidence concerning farming in the Gâtine Poitevine and from accounts from a farm near Laval. The source for the Gâtine was Merle, *La métairie*—in particular, his accounts for the métairie of Sunay for the years 1730–50, on pp. 155–60, and also his description of grain yields, farm capital, and sharecropping contracts.[27] In calculating the shares, I netted out seed and feed, aggregated outputs into two categories and inputs into four, and calculated rental rates of capital via an interest rate and a depreciation rate. The output shares were as follows: grain and vegetable output, most of which was rye, 0.489; animal products, chiefly from the sale of livestock, 0.511. As expected in a region where raising livestock was important, a much greater share of the revenue derived from animal products than in, say, the Paris Basin. As for the factor cost shares, they were: labor, including the tenant's input, 0.359; livestock rental, 0.135; equipment rental, 0.064; land, 0.442. The depreciation rates for capital were 0.032 for livestock and 0.200 for equipment.

The shares for the farm near Laval came from the accounts and the description of the métairie of La Chopinnière in the village of Bonchamps-lès-Laval in Morineau, *Les faux-semblants*, pp. 233–71, for the years 1747–55. Rather than using Morineau's totals, I aggregated certain inputs and outputs where necessary and recomputed the revenues and costs so as to take into account expenses such as interest and depreciation. The resulting factor shares were as follows: labor, 0.522; livestock rental, 0.079; equipment rental, 0.045; land, 0.355. To compute the livestock and equipment rental costs, I borrowed the depreciation rates from the Gâtine farm. The product shares were: grain (chiefly rye) and other vegetable output, net of seed and feed, 0.584; animal products, chiefly the sale of animals themselves, 0.416. Though lower than in the Gâtine, the share of revenue from animal products was still much higher than in the Paris Basin.

In computing the factor shares for the farm in Laval, I attributed the profit made by the landlord's *fermier-général* (steward)—the farm was leased to a *fermier-général* and then sublet to a sharecropper—to the labor input. My reason for doing so was that the fermier-général absorbed some of the risks and performed some of the tasks normally taken on by a fixed-rent farmer: for example, he furnished much of the farm capital. Had I treated the fermier-général's profits differently—attributing them to land, for instance, on the grounds that the fermier-général was really like a landlord—the shares would have been very close to those in the Gâtine. But it seemed best to exaggerate the difference between the Gâtine shares and the Laval shares so as to test the robustness of the results.

I also estimated shares for the métairie of La Chapelle-aux-Moines, east of Nantes, a part of which was vineyard. To estimate the shares, I assumed that except for the vineyard the métairie operated like the métairie of Sunay in the Gâtine, which had very nearly the same amount of arable. I then added the costs and revenues of operating the vineyard in La Chapelle-aux-Moines, using information on local practices in Young, *Voyages en France*, 3:692. The product revenue shares were as follows: grain, 0.283; wine, 0.420; animal products, 0.297. The factor shares were: labor, 0.456; equipment rental, 0.037; livestock rental, 0.174; land, 0.333. The depreciation rates came from the Gâtine farm. The process of calculating these shares of course involved a number of assumptions, and when faced with alternatives, I consistently chose numbers that would magnify the revenue share of wine and thus exaggerate the impact of adding the vineyard. The true shares for the métairie may thus actually be much closer to those of the Gâtine farm.[28]

While the shares may have varied somewhat from farm to farm, the evidence suggests that they did not vary greatly over time. The evidence here is not as overwhelming as for the Paris Basin, but it still seems convincing. In the first place, livestock raising had long been important in the west, and the late medieval métairies (according to evidence from Anjou) resembled those found in the Gâtine in the eighteenth century: they were of a similar size, produced similar yields, raised similar crops with the same crop rotations, and had nearly the same amount of livestock per hectare. The implication is that the use of labor, land, and livestock and the output of grain and animal outputs must have been roughly the same. One might worry about the Gâtine, where small peasant farms were consolidated to form larger métairies during the sixteenth and seventeenth centuries, but most of this occurs before our TFP series begin. Moreover, even in the Gâtine, farming practices remain much the same on the métairies themselves, which tend to dominate western agriculture in the period of concern to us.[29] Finally, if the major factor shares—those of land and labor—did shift, we could uncover evidence of the shift by doing what we did with the Paris leases: comparing demographic records with the ratio of rent to wages. But there is really no deviation between the population of the rural west and the rent-wage ratio for the farms near Anjou and Nantes.[30]

The prices for the west were far from perfect. Since rye was the predominant grain crop and since Angers was roughly in the middle of the western properties, I used the price of rye in Angers for grain and other vegetable output. My source was Hauser, *Recherches et documents*, pp. 248–51, 263–67 (annual price of rye, 1580–1789). Hauser's prices for Angers were taken from notes made by *feudistes* (specialists in feudal law), which might be a cause for worry, but he presents some fairly strong evidence in their behalf. One bit of evidence in favor of the Angers grain prices is the fact that they moved in parallel with prices in Rennes. If one graphs the annual price of wheat in Angers (from Hauser, pp. 258–62, for the years 1580–1789) against the annual price of wheat in Rennes (also from Hauser, pp. 291–94, for the years 1615–1786), they have the same peaks and valleys and are highly correlated ($r = 0.87$). More important, there is no sign that the ratio of wheat prices in the two cities was moving up or down. This is immediately apparent from a look at the ratio of the Angers wheat price to the Rennes wheat price, and it also is confirmed by a regression of the logarithm of the ratio on a constant and the year. The parallel movement of the wheat prices in Angers and Rennes explains why refiguring TFP with Rennes prices does little to disturb the trend, and it justifies our use of a single set of prices throughout the west.[31]

The wine price used to compute TFP for the métairie with a vineyard (La Chapelle-aux-Moines) was also from Angers; it was taken from Hauser, *Recherches et documents*, pp. 281–83 (annual price of wine, 1695–1789). For the price of animal products, I began with the prices in Zolla, "Les variations du revenu et du prix des terres en France," *Sciences politiques* 8 (1893): 460, and 9 (1894): 212–14, for butter in Angers (by decade or five-year period from 1650–59 to 1785–89) and meat in Le Mans (by decade or five-year period, from 1690–99 to 1785–89). The real problem was extending these prices back into the seventeenth century. Graphs of price ratios suggested that the price of meat in Le Mans tended to move in parallel with that of butter in Angers and that of fattened pigs in Château-Gontier, which lay north of Angers. The price of pigs came from Hauser, *Recherches et documents*, pp. 218–19 (fattened pigs, price per head, 1616–1792, with numerous gaps, particularly before 1733). The meat and butter prices were the obvious ones to use to create an animal output price series for the west, because cattle were so important in western agriculture, but the parallel in prices and the fact that pork was a substitute for beef suggested that it would be reasonable to use the price of fattened pigs, too. I therefore began by setting my animal output price series equal to the price of meat in Le Mans. I assumed that the animal output prices were constant over each five-year period (or, when Zolla gave only decennial prices, over each decade). I then regressed the price of meat in Le Mans on the price of fattened pigs in Château-Gontier without a constant and used the regression coefficient to extend my animal output price back a bit into the seventeenth century: the regression gained an additional fourteen years scattered between 1616 and 1698. I next used the same technique, this time regressing on the price of butter in Angers, which pushed the animal output price series back to 1650 without a gap and gave me at least some data for the years 1616–49.

Facing the same problems with the sales price of livestock, I went through a similar exercise. I began with the price of *boeufs* (oxen) in Angers in Zolla, "Les variations du revenu," *Sciences politiques* 8 (1893): 460–61 and 9 (1894): 212–13 (price per head, by decade or five-year period, 1665–69 to 1785–89). Boeufs were the major draft animals in the west and an important part of livestock herds. I therefore set the sales price of livestock equal to the price of boeufs, assuming that prices were constant over each five-year period or decade. To push the livestock sales prices back before 1665, I regressed the price of boeufs on the price of cows in Château-Gontier, from Hauser, "*Recherches et documents*," p. 221 (price per head, 1645–1791, with numerous gaps). The regression was done without a constant, but it gave me only three additional years and left me with a large gap with no prices between 1646 and 1664, which I filled via linear interpolation. The rental price of livestock I then calculated by multiplying my sales price times the Paris interest rates and the depreciation rate from the share calculations. Needless to say, the livestock prices before 1665 and the meat prices before 1690 leave much to be desired, but whatever errors they cause only affect a few of the TFP series, and then only in the earliest years. Furthermore, it would be nearly impossible for the errors to be large enough to change the overall shape of the TFP graphs.

Wages were also problematic: the difficulty was constructing a homogenous series that would reach from the seventeenth century up to 1789.[32] I began with the daily wage of a *journalier nourri* (fed day laborer) in Château-Gontier, since it seemed roughly in the middle of our properties; it came from Hauser, *Recherches et documents*, pp. 244–45 (1613–1791, with numerous gaps). The gaps in this cash wage I filled by linear interpolation, a process that seemed justified, given the stickiness of cash wages. I then added the value of the food the *journalier* received. I assumed that if he worked two hundred days per year, the food he would receive would amount to three Paris *setiers* of rye. Evaluating the rye at Angers prices yielded a cash equivalent for the wage and food that was very close to the daily wages of unfed laborers in Brittany.[33] It was lower than both the isolated figures for manoeuvres in AM Nantes DD 185 and the brief series of wages in Léon Vignols, "Salaires des ouvriers et prix des matériaux employés aux travaux publics, à Saint-Malo de 1737 à 1744 et 1755 à 1762," *Annales de Bretagne* 39 (1930–31): 351–69; but it led to similar estimates of the rate of wage increase between the two periods Vignols studied, 1737–44 and 1755–62. Reasonable variations in the size of the food ration led to similar results for my wage series. Finally, my wage series also served as the sales price of equipment; the rental price was computed using the Paris interest rate and the depreciation rate from the share calculations.

In the west, as elsewhere, the prices and wages in the indexes *C* and *P* are averaged over the outgoing lease—typically the current year and the previous eight. For the sake of caution, I also tried the alternative of averaging prices over the new lease. That made no difference except in the case of the properties near Nantes and in the Ille-et-Vilaine (figures B.1 and B.2), but even in these two graphs the trend of TFP with the alternative prices never stands out from the rest of the west by rising rapidly. Figures B.1 and B.2

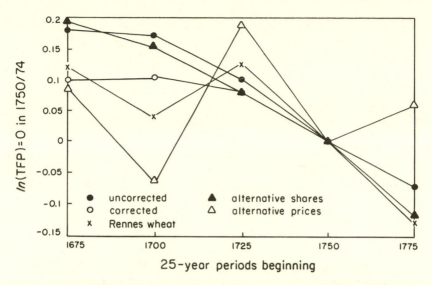

Figure B.1 Ln(TFP) in the Ille-et-Vilaine: Twelve Farms. Ln(TFP) has been corrected for taxes and calculated with alternative shares and price averages. It has also been calculated using the price of Rennes wheat in place of Angers rye. The size of the tax correction is shown for the standard shares and prices only. All the other lines include similar tax corrections.

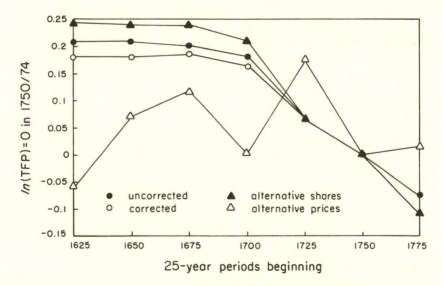

Figure B.2 Ln(TFP) near Nantes: Three Farms in Vallet. Ln(TFP) has been corrected for taxes and calculated with alternative prices and shares. The size of the tax correction is shown for the standard prices and shares only; the alternate price and share lines include similar tax corrections.

also display typical tax corrections (done as with the Notre Dame sample), and they show TFP calculated from the alternative shares—the shares from the farm near Laval rather than from Gâtine. Note that alternative shares and the tax correction change TFP very little.

For the farms in the Ille-et-Villaine, I have also calculated TFP using grain prices from Rennes rather than Angers, which provided the grain prices for all of the western TFP calculations. Rennes lay in the middle of the Ille-et-Vilaine and was much closer to properties there. If price differences in the west or varying transport costs affected TFP, it should be evident here, but the graph with the Rennes wheat differs little from the others (figure B.1). It suggests that price differences were small and that our results do not depend on the use of prices from Angers.[34]

The Southeast: Bouches-du-Rhône and Vaucluse

Leases and sales prices from the Bouches-du-Rhône and the Vaucluse came from a variety of sources, including Baehrel, *Une croissance*, 1:134 (eleven leases on two parcels of land near Marseille, 1697–1783); AD Vaucluse, 1 G 530, 611, 612 (eleven leases for the Grange de la Sacristie, a farm near Avignon, 1616–1789); and Rosenthal, *The Fruits of Revolution*, p. 187 (sales price of unirrigated land from notarial records in Cavaillon, every five years from 1700 to 1790). Rosenthal's land sales prices were converted to rental rates by multiplying by the local interest rate on those *rentes* in which farmers were borrowers.[35]

For the land prices in the village of Grillon in the northern Vaucluse, I relied on a sample of land sales contracts transcribed by the notaries who practiced in Grillon. Now classified with the records of two notarial *études* from the nearby town of Valréas, the contracts can be found at AD Vaucluse in the following registers: 3 E, Etude Evesque in Valréas, *registres* 33, 36, 38, 43, 46, 55, 56; 3 E, Etude Petit in Valréas, *registres* 14 and 23. They are spread over the years 1558–1745, but the lack of prices made TFP calculations impossible before 1580.[36] The land prices were converted to rental rates via multiplication by the median interest rate on rentes in the same notarial registers. The imputed rental rates were in turn corrected for variations in land quality by regressing their logarithm on property characteristics and then following a procedure like that used for the Paris rental index.[37] In the southeast, the land rental market seemed competitive, for leases were short—often six years or less—and tenants were easily dislodged. Customs such as mauvais gré were simply unknown. And when tenants did remain on a farm, they did not hold down the rent.[38] Given the competitive rental market and the ready availability of credit for loans secured by agricultural property, it seemed reasonable to assume that the land sale market was competitive, too.

Product and factor shares were derived from two distinct sources. The first source was a questionnaire in AD Vaucluse, 6 M 378, for the agricultural census of 1852; it gave information on costs and revenues for the canton of Valréas, which included the village of Grillon. In deriving the shares, I assumed that farms used three factors of production: land, labor, and capital, which was chiefly livestock. The factor shares were: land, 0.49; labor, including compensation to the farmer, 0.37; rental cost of capital, 0.14; the depreciation rate of capital was 0.34. The farms in turn produced three goods: grain (chiefly wheat), other vegetable crops (chiefly wine), and animal products, of which mutton and wool were the most important. The product revenue shares were: grain, net of seed, 0.43; other vegetable crops, 0.46; animal products, 0.11.

A second set of shares was derived from Le Roy Ladurie, *Les paysans de Languedoc*, 1:297–301 and 2:757–58, and assumed the same products and factors of production. The evidence included actual revenues from eighteenth-century farms and from hypothetical farm accounts that Le Roy Ladurie constructed for a sixteenth-century farm. The product shares were: grain, net of seed, 0.60; other vegetable products, 0.20; animal products, 0.20. Factor shares were: land, 0.43; labor, 0.45; rental cost of capital, 0.12. Capital had a depreciation rate of 0.27.

Le Roy Ladurie's shares served as my standard, and I used the shares derived from the questionnaire as the alternative. To be sure, Le Roy Ladurie's book concerns Languedoc, but most of his evidence comes from the southeast of the province, which was not far from the Bouches-du-Rhône and the Vaucluse. Crops and agricultural techniques there resembled those used in the Bouches-du-Rhône and the Vaucluse, and the factor shares turned out to be close to those derived from the 1852 questionnaire.[39] The output shares were a bit different, but the discrepancy was too small to affect the TFP calculations.

There is some evidence that these shares varied over time, but not by enough to affect our calculations. In the community of Grignan, near our village of Grillon, the amount of land in pasture increased somewhat in the sixteenth century, as peasants planted new fodder crops; and the composition of livestock herds shifted, too. Elsewhere in the region vineyards spread, particularly in the late eighteenth century. But none of these changes was drastic. In Grignan, pasture went from roughly 5 to 10 percent of the farmland, and the change in livestock herds was slight. Similarly, the planting of vineyards in the eighteenth century did not change the face of agriculture drastically.[40]

Unfortunately, population figures for the regions, including the Bouches-du-Rhône and the Vaucluse, were too fragmentary to check the constancy of the land-labor share ratio against population trends, but we can look for information about agricultural practices in sharecropping contracts, which contain a wealth of information about crops and procedures and suggest limits for the likely product and factor shares. Whether we look at contracts from Grillon or nearby regions, the sharecropping contracts suggest that the shares did not vary greatly between the sixteenth and the eighteenth centuries. Overall, crops and agricultural techniques remained much the same, and even if the shares did vary somewhat, the variation would have in all likelihood been too small to affect the TFP.[41]

Product prices for the southeast were local prices taken from the following sources: the price of wheat in Aix-en-Provence, 1570–1789, from Baehrel, *Une croissance*, 1:535–36; the price of new wine in Aix, 1570–1681, and in Draguignan, 1616–1790, from Baehrel, *Une croissance*, 1:560, 563; and the price of mutton in Auriol, 1601–1788, from Baehrel, *Une croissance*, 1:594–96. The wheat price was used for grain output since it was the major grain crop, and for similar reasons wine was used as the price of other vegetable crops. Gaps in the price of mutton were filled via a regression (without a constant) of mutton prices on the price of ewes in Arles, 1594–1789, also taken from Baehrel, *Une croissance*, 1:580. For the years 1580–93, when no meat prices were available, I assumed that the price of meat was constant and equal to its value in 1594–1602.

Factor prices were also local. The price of capital was a rental price calculated from the depreciation rate, an interest rate, and the price of ewes in Arles. Gaps in the price of ewes were filled via a regression on mutton prices without a constant or via interpolation. As with mutton, I assumed that the price of ewes was constant in 1580–93 and equal to its value in 1594–1602. The interest rate came from rentes and mortgages in the Grillon notarial registers and, for the eighteenth century, from similar interest rates collected by Jean-Laurent Rosenthal from notarial registers in Cavaillon. Wages also came from the Cavaillon region, from a sample collected for every fifth year from 1600 into the nineteenth century by Jean-Laurent Rosenthal; the wages were for unskilled laborers without food. For the years 1580–99, I assumed that the nominal wage remained constant and equal to its value in 1600–1605.

Albigeois

The land sales figures, factor shares, and prices for the Albigeois were all taken from Pierre Rascol, *Les paysans de l'Albigeois à la fin de l'ancien régime* (Aurillac, 1961), a source that is far from perfect.[42] The land sales figures, which came from pp. 264–71, covered the years 1701–89. I was forced to use the sales prices because of the prevalence of sharecropping in the Albigeois, as elsewhere in the southwest; they were converted to rental rates by multiplying the sales price times the interest rate on rentes.[43] To correct for variations in property quality, I regressed the logarithm of the imputed rental rate for each property on a dummy variable for each of the property locations and then followed the same procedure used to adjust the Notre Dame rents for variations in the sample. Unfortunately, although leases tended to be short, there was no way to ensure that the rental market or the land sales market was competitive.

The shares were calculated from evidence about crops, costs, and share-cropping contracts in Rascol, *Les paysans de l'Albigeois*, pp. 30, 45–60, 226–27, 263. I assumed that farms produced two outputs—animal products and grain-vegetable crops—and that they used land, labor, and capital. The output shares were as follows: animal products, 0.54; grain and vegetable crops, 0.46. The factor shares were: land, 0.46; labor, 0.46; and capital, 0.08. The depreciation rate of capital was assumed to be the same as for the Le Roy Ladurie shares discussed above. I cannot be certain about the accuracy or the constancy of these shares, but they do fit the evidence from sharecropping contracts.

Given the meager price information, I assumed that prices and wages were constant during each of three periods: 1701–30, 1731–60, 1761–89. For vegetable products and grain, I used the price of wheat, the major crop in statistics collected in the year IX; for animal products, I used the price of *viande de boeuf* (beef), again because cattle predominated in the year IX statistics. The prices came from Rascol, *Les paysans de l'Albigeois*, pp. 272, 294. For labor, I used the wage of a rural *brassier* (a cottager who also worked for a wage), from Rascol, *Les paysans de l'Albigeois*, p. 293. The price of capital was assumed to be the rental price of oxen, the major form of agricultural capital. I calculated it from the interest rate, the depreciation rate, and the sales price of oxen, which I took from Rascol, *Les paysans de l'Albigeois*, p. 275.

Southeastern Languedoc

The leases for the six properties in southeastern Languedoc came from Le Roy Ladurie, *Les paysans de Languedoc*, 2:860–64; information on the properties was gleaned from the same book (1:281–89, 586–92).[44] The leases covered the years 1526–1750, but the lack of price series made it impossible to measure TFP before the 1580s. The rental market from which the leases were drawn seemed competitive. The leases were short— as brief as two years in some cases—and customs such as mauvais gré were unknown. Regressions to test for entrepreneurial profits revealed nothing.

Because leases in the region varied greatly in duration (from as short as two years to as long as eight), it seemed reasonable to average prices in several ways: not only over the current year and the next eight years, or the current year and the previous eight, as with the other samples, but also over the current year, the previous four years, and the next four years. Fortunately, the different price averages all yielded similar TFP trends.

The standard shares for southeastern Languedoc (derived from Le Roy Ladurie, *Les paysans de Languedoc*, 1:297–301 and 2:757–58) are described above in the section on the Bouches-du-Rhône and the Vaucluse. The same source also furnished an alternative set of shares, which assume different costs for capital, labor, and the compensation due the farmer. The alternative product revenue shares were the same, but the alternative factor shares were: labor, including compensation to the farmer, 0.29; land, 0.43; rental cost of capital, 0.29. The rental cost of capital was based on a depreciation rate of capital of 0.27.

It is possible that the factor and product shares varied over the centuries. The terms of sharecropping contracts show some variation, and Le Roy Ladurie argues that laborers, farmers, and landowners did better at some times than at others. Crops changed somewhat, too: vineyards, for example, expanded in the early seventeenth century and again after 1700.[45] But the crop changes would probably not disturb our aggregate output categories, and in any case the major crops remained much the same. As for factor shares, the rent-wage ratio parallels population trends, suggesting that the major factor shares, those of land and labor, did not shift relative to one another.[46] Even if they had, the effect on TFP would be minimal, for varying the factor costs, as we did with our alternative shares, hardly altered the trend of TFP.

With both sets of shares the following product prices were used: for grain output, the price of wheat in Béziers (1587–1759), from Le Roy Ladurie, *Les Paysans de Languedoc*, 2:821–22; for other crops, the price of wine in Béziers (1588–1789), from Le Roy Ladurie, *Les Paysans de Languedoc*, 2:823–25; for animal output, the price of mutton in Narbonne (1533–1790), from the same source, 2:826–28, with gaps filled by linear interpolation. The major form of capital was sheep, and because a reliable sheep price series was lacking, I used the price of mutton as a proxy. The capital rental price was computed by multiplying the price of mutton by the depreciation rate and the interest rate on rentes.[47]

The wage series was spliced together from several sources. I began with two series of wages for a *manoeuvre maçon* (hod carrier) in Montpellier (1580–1600) and Béziers (1603–1714), which were close enough to simply link together. Both these series had numerous gaps, though, so I used a regression without a constant on the wages of a *maître plâtrier* (master plasterer) in Béziers (1605–1729) to fill in the gaps and extend the series further into the eighteenth century. These wage series were derived from tables or graphs in Le Roy Ladurie, *Les Paysans de Languedoc*, 2:1011, 1018–19. Gaps still remained, and I needed wages for the years 1730–50. Wage series from near Montpellier suggested, though, that nominal wages for unskilled workers such as *manoeuvres* were essentially constant in the years 1715–50.[48] I therefore set my wage in the years 1730–50 equal to its mean value in 1715–29. The process of averaging prices (either over the current year and the previous eight years; the current year and the next four years; or the current year, the previous four, and the next four) then filled the remaining gaps.

The wages series are far from perfect, but it is unlikely that the problems explain the downturn in the TFP. The stickiness of nominal wages in the Old Regime would seem to justify filling in the gaps via a process of averaging, and in any case all the different price averages lead to nearly identical estimates of TFP. Wage stickiness and the evidence for nearly constant nominal wages in the years 1715–50 also excuse setting the wage after 1729 equal to its mean value in the years 1715–29. And even if this does introduce some error, it cannot explain the decline of TFP, which was well under way by the 1690s.[49]

Salers

To estimate TFP growth for the regions about Salers, I assumed a translog production function, just as I did when calculating TFP using physical inputs and outputs for the Chartier farm. The estimate involved a Törnqvist index of the inputs used and the outputs produced; I had to compute its value in 1705–20 relative to its value in 1775–89. To do so, I needed the ratio of the amount of each output produced in 1775–89 to the amount of the same output produced in 1705–20, as well as the analogous ratios for each input. I also needed the average of the factor and product shares for the two periods.[50]

To simplify the calculation, I made a number of assumptions, all of which tended to exaggerate the rate of TFP growth and make my estimate an upper bound. In the first place I supposed that the increased cheese production entailed using no more labor and land and that it was not the result of bigger or longer-lived cattle, which would amount to an increase in the capital input. All of these assumptions were unrealistically optimistic, because the cheese production obviously did involve slightly more labor, and it may well have resulted from lower cattle mortality and better feed.[51] I made the reasonable assumption that the output of crops did not increase and I supposed—again a likely exaggeration—that all the other animal outputs increased at the same pace as cheese production, namely 31 percent between 1705–20 and 1775–89.

Under these assumptions, the input ratios are all 1, as are all the output ratios for crops. The TFP increase between 1705–20 and 1775–89 then boils down to 1.31^u, where u is the combined product share for all animal products, including cheese, and the 1.31 is the ratio of animal output in

1775–89 to output in 1705–20. One source for the share u is the 1840 agricultural census, because the average share throughout the eighteenth century would probably not differ much from what it was in 1840. Admittedly, the 1840 agricultural census is far from reliable, but if we simply ignore the difficulties of estimating crop revenues in an era before cadastres were complete and the even greater uncertainty surrounding animal revenues, we can use what the census says for the department that included Salers, the Cantal. There, some 31 percent of the revenue from crops and animals in Cantal supposedly came from animals.[52] Unfortunately, some of this revenue would probably include intermediate products such as manure and service as draft animals. The true share is thus probably smaller. But to exaggerate the TFP increase—to make the estimate an upper bound—I used the 0.31 figure and an even larger share of 0.5. The TFP increase then works out to be between roughly 9 and 15 percent, or 0.1 to 0.2 percent per year. Again, these are all upper bounds; the true rate of TFP growth was probably much lower.

Beaujolais

Calculating the TFP increase in the western Beaujolais involves the same formula used for the Auge: $(r_{after}/r_{before})^s$, where r_{after} is the average rent after conversion to vineyard, r_{before} the rent before, and s the average of the factor shares of land before and after conversion. The land shares before and after conversion I took from the accounts of a local farm with no vines and from the one where wine was by far the dominant crop.[53] The land share for the farm without vines was 0.58; where viticulture dominated, it was 0.53. Likely variations in these land shares did not disturb the results.

As for the competitiveness of the local rental market, Georges Durand argues that tenant farmers in the region did retain some profits but only enough to prevent bankruptcy in bad years.[54] It seems reasonable therefore to assume that the rental market was competitive. Of course, if it was not competitive and tenants did capture some of the gains from planting vineyard, then TFP growth would be even higher.

The ratio of the rental rate of vineyard to the rental rate of arable I took to be 2.7, based on late-eighteenth-century evidence in Durand, *Vin, vigne, vignerons*, pp. 225–26. In *Le patrimoine foncier de l'Hôtel-Dieu*, pp. 93–99, Durand suggests an even higher ratio of 5.0, but I took the lower 2.7 number to bias my TFP estimate downward. What we actually need, though, is the average land rent before and after conversion, where we take into account the fraction of land in arable and the portion in vineyard. Based on evidence in Gruter, *Naissance d'un grand vignoble*, pp. 66–67, and the fraction of the arrondissement of Villefranche that was listed as being in vineyard in 1840, I assumed that before the conversion between 0 and 10 percent of the farmland was in vineyard, and that afterward 28 percent was.[55] The only other ingredient I needed was the time it took to convert the land to vineyard; this allowed me to compute the rate of annual TFP growth. From Dion, *Histoire de la vigne*, pp. 576–93, I assumed that the process of conversion in the western Beaujolais lasted fifty years.

German North Sea Coast

The rental rates and evidence about agriculture on the German North Sea coast came from Wilhelm Abel, *Agrarkrisen und Agrarkonjunktur: Eine Geschichte der Land- und Ernährungswirtschaft Mitteleuropas seit dem hohen Mittelalter*, 3rd ed. (Hamburg, 1978), pp. 132–36, 213–14. The sixteenth-century rental rates came from the region of Eiderstedt in Schleswig-Holstein; the eighteenth-century ones from the community of St. Annen in the same region. Further information on local agriculture came from Wilhelm Abel, *Geschichte der deutschen Landwirtschaft*; Volkmar von Arnim, *Krisen und Konjunkturen der Landwirtschaft in Schleswig-Holstein vom 16. bis zum 18. Jahrhundert* (Neumünster, 1957); and especially Wiese and Bölts, *Rinderhandel*.

Product and factor shares were derived from descriptions of the output, labor, capital, and land rental costs on stock-raising farms on or near the German North Sea coast. The information was assembled from Wiese and Bölts, *Rinderhandel*, pp. 152, 170–72, 180–96, 201–7, 216, 226, 236–37. The calculations assumed a 20-hectare peasant farm with two adult male workers and one adult female worker, who raise twenty-five dairy cattle and grow enough rye to feed themselves. I supposed that the adults earned a wage equal those paid male and female servants on local farms and that the cost of capital was the rental price of the livestock herd, with depreciation of 20 percent and interest at 7 percent. The shares were as follows: capital, which was chiefly cattle rental, 0.11; labor, which was low for the stock-raising farms, 0.12; land, which was correspondingly high, 0.77. Output revenue shares were: rye, 0.15; animal products, which were chiefly butter and cheese, 0.85. I also tried an alternative set of shares, which were based on different assumptions. The factor shares were: capital, 0.11; labor, 0.21; land, 0.68. There were three output shares: rye, 0.08; butter, 0.76; veal, 0.16. Changing the shares hardly affected the TFP growth rates: for the sixteenth century the growth rates ranged between 0.8 and 1.0 percent when the shares were varied.

For the sixteenth century, the TFP increase was calculated by comparing rents, prices, and wages between the two periods: 1526–50 and 1576–1600. The prices and wages came from the following sources: Abel, *Geschichte der deutschen Landwirtschaft*, p. 193 (wages and the price of butter in Hamburg, both read from a graph); idem, *Agrarkrisen*, pp. 132–36, 308–9 (the interest rate in the sixteenth century, which was deduced from the ratio of land rental and land sales prices in Eiderstedt, and the price of rye in Schleswig-Holstein); Wiese and Bölts, *Rinderhandel*, pp. 79–91 (price of oxen in Hamburg, Cologne, Stade, and Lübeck).[56]

The TFP calculations for the eighteenth century were calculated using rents, prices, and wages in 1750–59 and 1800–1809. In some ways the calculations for the eighteenth century are subject to more uncertainty than for the sixteenth. In the first place, rents jumped enormously in the 1800s, but it is not clear whether the increase represented a productivity increase or the distortions caused by war. Had we computed TFP for 1790–99 instead of 1800–1809, TFP would have actually declined. There is also a degree of uncertainty about the earlier period: we lack the wages needed to calculate TFP for the 1740s or before.

The prices and wages for the eighteenth century came from the following sources: Abel, *Agrarkrisen*, pp. 308, 339 (rye prices in Hamburg and Schleswig-Holstein and interest rates); Wiese and Bölts, *Rinderhandel*, pp. 82, 85, 226 (the price of oxen in Lübeck and the amount of butter that could be purchased in the north coast region with 100 kilograms of rye, from which I deduced butter prices for 1731–99); E. Waschinski, *Währung, Preisentwicklung und Kaufkraft des Geldes in Schleswig-Holstein von 1226–1864*, (Neumünster, 1959), pp. 90, 206, 210 (butter prices in 1791–1809); and Hans-Jürgen Gerhard, ed., *Löhne im vor- und frühindustriellen Deutschland* (Göttingen, 1984), pp. 89–106 (wages in Bremen, the closest city for which continuous wage series were available, for 1750–1810).

Needless to say, the calculations for Germany involve greater uncertainty than for France. There was no way to determine whether the land market was competitive and no way to correct for taxes. Fortunately, the region was one where one form of taxation—seigneurial dues—was light. Furthermore, although the product and factor shares may have varied, particularly in the sixteenth century, the results seem relatively insensitive to the precise shares used.

Comparison of the Paris Basin and England

The rents collected in England by Arthur Young in 1768–71 provided an ideal basis for comparing the TFP of the Paris Basin with the TFP of an English county, and it seemed most appropriate to make the comparison with one of the Home Counties of Bedfordshire, Essex, Buckinghamshire, or Hertfordshire, because they were relatively close to London. Bedfordshire was simply too far away from London to compare with the farms in the Notre Dame sample, which lay relatively close to Paris; moreover, Young's rents are not available for Bedfordshire. Essex had too much livestock fattening for a comparison with the arable farms of the Paris Basin, as did south Buckinghamshire, the part of Buckinghamshire for which Young's rents are available. That left Hertfordshire, but it seemed an ideal target for comparison. The distance between it and London was only slightly more than that between the average farm in the Notre Dame sample and the city of Paris. Its soil resembled that of the Paris Basin, and although it had a fair amount of grassland, arable farming was also important, particularly at the end of the eighteenth century. Finally, Hertfordshire was no straw man. Agriculture in the county was advanced, and crop rotations were quite complex.[57]

In the comparison, I used the Chartier shares for the Paris Basin and experimented with three sets of shares for Hertfordshire: the Chartier shares themselves, which would be appropriate if arable farming in Hertfordshire was important; a second set of shares derived from the 1824 and 1826 balance sheets of a 600-acre farm in western Norfolk, which allowed for more animal output; and a third set of shares that derived from an eighteenth-century rule of thumb about the cost of land, labor, and agricultural capital. All three sets of shares were calculated net of seed, and all three involved the same three outputs and the same four inputs. The three outputs and their respective shares from the Norfolk accounts were: wheat, 0.29; oats, barley, and straw, 0.17; other crops, 0.16; and animal products 0.38. The factors of production and the Norfolk factor shares were: land (rent, tithe, and taxes), 0.37; livestock, 0.12; equipment, 0.04; and labor, 0.48. The rule-of-thumb output shares were the same as the Chartier output shares, but the rule-of-thumb factor shares of land, labor, and livestock were each one-third, while the equipment share was zero.[58]

Difficulties assembling comparable prices limited me to making the Hertfordshire comparison with the Paris Basin in the 1760s and the 1780s—in other words, shortly before and shortly after the Hertfordshire rents were collected and shortly before and shortly after TFP in the Basin began to increase rapidly. For the Paris Basin, I simply averaged all my prices over the 1760s or the 1780s; I did not use nine-year moving price averages. The output prices I used were the price of wheat in Pontoise, because it was roughly the same distance from Paris as the average farm in the Notre Dame sample and its wheat price thus served as a local price; the price of oats in Pontoise (for oats, barley, and straw); the price of peas in Paris (for other crops); and the price of mutton, which I took from Labrousse's national average but which should not differ greatly from the Paris area price given the mobility of livestock. The price of livestock was a rental price, based on the interest rate, a depreciation rate, and a sales price. I experimented with two different sales prices for livestock: the price of horses outside Paris, and the price of mutton again, which had the advantage of avoiding the problems of different breeds. As for equipment, its price was also a rental price, with the sales price being the wage rate.[59]

Prices for Hertfordshire were for identical items, with all prices converted to common units, although the currencies were different. Unfortunately, contemporary grain prices were not available for markets in Hertfordshire itself, so I used wheat, oat, and pea prices from Reading, which was roughly the same distance outside London as most of Hertfordshire. Mutton prices were from London, and horse prices were from Norfolk—a bit distant, and therefore all the more reason to try another sales price for livestock.[60]

As for wages, I restricted myself to wages for identical tasks and at identical times of the year in both countries. In the Paris Basin in the 1760s, I used winter wages for an unskilled rural laborer, with food; the comparison was with the median winter wage in Hertfordshire for a rural labor with board in the years 1768–71. For the Basin in the 1780s, I relied upon nonharvest wages without food, which I compared with analogous wages for Hertfordshire in 1789–90. The results were not sensitive to the choice of a wage. Indeed, using the winter wage from Hertfordshire with board and the Paris area wage from the 1780s without food led to similar results.[61] Again, the wage series also served as a sales price for equipment.

The last difficulty was taxes. For France, I used the tax rates (calculated both with and without the tithe, since Notre Dame's properties were often tithe exempt) calculated from the Bernonville accounts. For England, I experimented with various tax rates. The Norfolk accounts suggested that taxes were perhaps 32 percent of the rent, but this figure, which was based on evidence from 1824–26, seemed high for the eighteenth century, particularly for tenants, whose landlords often paid the land tax. For them a lower tax rate of perhaps 14 percent was conceivable. I also used the total tax and tithe rate of 4.2 shillings per acre that Robert Allen derived from Arthur Young's observations.[62] Clearly, the higher English tax rates would tend to sway the calculations in England's favor by boosting total rent and hence our index of TFP. In reality, however, the lower tax rate of 14 percent might have been closer to the truth.

I also experimented with the rents. I used the higher rents that Young collected in south Buckinghamshire, tried Allen's figures for the profits retained by tenants, and multiplied the Hertfordshire rents by 2.5. In all these experiments the rest of the prices were the same ones that I used with the original Hertfordshire rents.

3. CONTROLLING FOR PROPERTY DIFFERENCES BY MEASURING RENTS RELATIVE TO A COMMON BASE PERIOD

Typically, we have calculated TFP as r^sP/C, where r is rent, P is the output price index, and C is the price index of the factors of production. The calculation ignores taxes, but we correct for the error via difference regressions as explained in Appendix A, part 13. What interests us primarily is the time trend of rents and of TFP. We are less interested in the spatial variations in

TFP due to the idiosyncracies of each individual property—the soil fertility, for example. With the Notre Dame sample, we corrected for such idiosyncracies via rent regressions, which gave us a standardized rent as properties jumped in and out of the sample (see Appendix A, part 3, for details). We knew enough about each of the Notre Dame properties to use such regressions.

With the other samples, though, such a technique is often impossible, because we know far less about the individual properties. But we can correct for the idiosyncracies via a simple technique commonly used with panel studies. The technique works whenever we follow the same properties throughout time, as with the sample of properties near Amiens and with many of our other samples (table 4.5). The technique simply involves measuring rents relative to a common base period for each property. Suppose that at time t, the rent of the i-th property in a sample, $r(i,t)$, can be decomposed in a simple way as:

$$r(i, t) = f(i)\, h(t) \tag{3}$$

where f is the portion of the rent that is idiosyncratic to the property and h is the time trend in the rent, the part that interests us most. Suppose that in calculating $\ln(\text{TFP})$ for all the properties in the sample we measure rents relative to a common base period when $t = 0$. Then for the i-th property $\ln(\text{TFP})$ will be:

$$s\ln(r(i, t) / r(i, 0)) - \ln(P/C) = s\ln h(t) - s\ln h(0) - \ln(P/C) \tag{4}$$

The idiosyncratic effects $f(i)$ will thus drop out for each property, leaving us with the time trend $s\ln(h(t))$ of the rents plus a constant, $s\ln(h(0))$, which is the same for all properties. Since it is this time trend that interests us, we have calculated TFP with rents measured relative to a common base period for every sample where we followed the same properties through time.

The Economics of Urban Fertilizer

ASSUME THAT an Old Regime farmer produces wheat. He fertilizes his field with manure, which can come either from his own livestock or from animals in a nearby city. Presumably he chooses a combination of manure from his own animals and from urban sources that will minimize his costs. Of course, he cannot dispense with his own livestock completely, for he needs them for other tasks besides fertilizing the fields—for plowing, for example. The urban manure is thus not a perfect substitute for livestock, and there will in fact be some minimal level of livestock needed to make wheat production possible.

Figure C.1 uses simple production economics to develop these ideas. The curve in the figure—part of an isoquant—shows the combinations of livestock and urban manure that the farmer can use to produce one ton of wheat; for the sake of simplicity, we hold the other inputs constant. The isoquant is curved because livestock and urban manure are not perfect substitutes, and because farms had to keep a certain minimal quantity of livestock on hand. Note that the isoquant touches the y axis: it is possible to produce one ton of wheat using no urban manure at all.[1]

If the farmer minimizes costs, and if urban manure is expensive, he will indeed produce wheat without urban manure. He will end up at point A, because that is the cheapest point on the isoquant. Such a situation might occur, for instance, if the amount spent on livestock at A would only purchase the amount of urban manure represented by the point B. The slope of the constant cost line AB would give us the relative price of livestock and urban manure, and since urban manure is expensive, a cost-minimizing farmer would use none of it.

Should urban manure decline a bit in price, so that the money spent on livestock at A would purchase an amount B' of urban manure, the farmer would still use none of it. Again, given the relative costs, A would still be the cheapest way to produce the wheat. In other words, a small reduction in the cost of urban manure would not induce the farmer to use it. He would do so only if the cost of urban manure declined substantially—so that, for example, A and C would be on the same cost line. In that case, the farmer could cut his costs dramatically (and presumably increase his profits) by buying some urban manure and producing his wheat at the point C'.

This figure helps explain the relationship between urbanization and productivity increases that we observed around Paris but not in the vicinity of

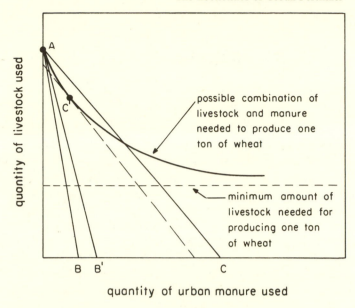

Figure C.1 The Trade-off between Farm Livestock and Urban Manure in the Paris Basin. The figure shows hypothetical costs and quantities used to grow one ton of wheat.

other cities. Paris had better roads than other cities, so that it was cheaper to bring farm produce into Paris by cart and to return home with a load of manure. Hence the farm-gate price of urban manure—the price that the farmer faces and that is relevant to the cost lines in figure C.1—would be lower, too. Furthermore, there were far more horses in Paris than in other cities, because Paris was so much wealthier and larger. Hence, the supply of urban manure (particularly horse manure) was larger in Paris, which would make urban manure relatively cheap around Paris. The net result would be that around Paris, farmers would be much more likely to be facing cost lines like *AC* rather than *AB*. They would use urban manure, and their lower costs would show up as higher productivity. Furthermore, each increase in the city's population would add to the supply of horses and other animals, making urban manure cheaper still; that, in turn, would foster additional increases in productivity. Hence, the relationship we observed between population increases and TFP around Paris. In other cities, by contrast, increases in the urban population might drive down the price of urban manure, but farmers would not yet be at the threshold where it paid to use urban manure: the lower price of urban manure would only shift the cost line from *AB* to *AB'*. Near other cities, therefore, we would not find the same relationship that holds around Paris.

Hedonic Wage Regressions

IN THE model of employment used in Chapter 3, part 1 (Rural Labor Markets), wages are initially low and then rise over time for employees who work hard and remain with an employer.[1] Hired at low wages, employees who survive and exert themselves earn raises until their pay equals their marginal product, creating a hierarchy of wages and a nondecreasing wage-tenure profile. The promise of a raise is in fact their incentive; it is what solves the employer's problems of moral hazard and adverse selection. When this model is applied to the farms of early modern France, it implies that servants' wages should be low when they were first hired and higher for those who remained. If rural wages actually behaved this way in early modern France, it would support our argument about the strategies that farmers adopted to supervise servants.

One might doubt, of course, that such a model would suit the countryside of an early modern country. One might worry, as development economists once did, that rural wages in early modern agriculture were rigid and institutionally set, and that decisions about wages in the countryside were completely isolated from economic processes. Such a view of rural labor markets, though, is in its death throes in development economics, and there is little reason to resuscitate it for the sake of economic history. As we know, nineteenth-century evidence demonstrates that rural wages tracked urban wages quite closely—a fact that is hard to reconcile with isolation from economic processes. Even under the Old Regime the gaps between rural and urban wages were small. And although nominal wages certainly were sticky, they did vary greatly among individuals and over the course of the year, just as in developing countries.[2]

The problem is removing the wage variations among individuals and over the course of the year. We must filter out these extraneous factors to demonstrate that wages were initially low and then rose, as the model suggests. The obvious way to do so is with hedonic wage regressions. The regressions assume that each servant's wage is a function of the seasonal variation in wages, the servant's personal characteristics, and the length of the time he had worked for his current master. The seasonal variation would entail higher wages in the summer, because of the longer days and the demand for harvest labor, and perhaps lower wages in the winter. The personal characteristics would include gender, skill, and strength. As for the length of time spent with the master, we adopt a simple interpretation of the model: wages would be lower when a servant was first hired and higher if he were rehired. Wages would also presumably be lower if the servant did not begin work at a time of local hiring fairs, for in that case his master might reasonably suppose that he had been fired at his previous post. Only if the master had difficulty hiring between fairs would we expect such a servant to get the same wage. Finally, we might expect wages to vary with distance. A master might know a servant from his own village well enough to offer him a high wage at the onset of employment; the same would be true if he dealt repeatedly with the servant's family. If so, then a servant hired locally would not have to wait for a raise, and his wages would not rise if he remained in service.

Let us suppose that the wage of servant i in period t is $w(i, t)$. Here t refers to the servant's own tenure: it is 0 when he is first hired, 1 the first time he is rehired, 2 the next time, and so on.[3] One complication is that we know only the cash wage $c(i, t)$, agreed upon when the servant was hired.[4] But servants typically received room and board as well, or at least a portion of it. There are several ways to contend with such perquisites. One is to assume that the room and board have a constant value, $k(i)$, which might depend on the servant. If so, then

$$w(i, t) = c(i, t) + k(i) \tag{1}$$

Alternatively, the total wage might be a constant multiple, $m(i)$, of the cash wage, $c(i, t)$, with the multiple again depending on the servant

$$w(i, t) = m(i)c(i, t) \tag{2}$$

One can make a case for either equation (1) or (2). The first would apply, for instance, if servants all received essentially the same fare, provided that prices do not change greatly. The second is what ratios of fed and unfed wages from the Old Regime imply. One other difference between the two different assumptions is that the first implies that we should regress wages on personal characteristics; the second, that we should regress the logarithm of wages. We shall adopt the second assumption, because using the logarithm of wages is customary in hedonic wage regressions. But the table will include the alternative regressions with the actual wages themselves. Both assumptions lead to similar results.

As I explain in Chapter 3, the data for the regressions came from two journals kept by the Cairon family. The first covered hiring on the family farm from 1473 to 1485; the second, from 1691 to 1705. Both journals give servants' names, their place of origin, their cash wage, and the date when they were hired. In the earlier journal, servants were hired for a year or a portion of a year; in the later one, they were all taken on for an entire year, though some did not finish. The later journal also distinguishes the post they were expected to fill—for example, that of a *petit valet* or a *valet de harnois*. Similar information is lacking in the earlier journal.

If wages rise with tenure, the same will be true of the logarithm of wages. The relevant regression will have the form

$$\ln(w(i,\ t)) = \ln(m(i)) + \ln(c(i,\ t)) = a + bx(i) + cy(i,\ t,\ s) + u \qquad (3)$$

Here a is a constant; u is an error term; b and c are matrices of coefficients; x is a vector of unvarying personal characteristics of servant i; and y is a vector of independent variables depending on i, on t, and on s, the season when the servant is hired. The simplest test is to verify whether the logarithm of wages is actually higher after initial employment; in that case, the variables, y, must include a dummy variable that is 0 when the servant is initially hired and 1 afterward.

One problem is that we do not know some of the characteristics, $x(i)$, even though they were obvious to the master when the servant was first hired: the servant's age, size, and, in the earlier journal, the post that the servant was to fill. We also do not know the room and board multiple, $m(i)$. One obvious tactic here is to subtract the initial wage from the left-hand side of equation (3) and the initial value of the right-hand-side variables from the right-hand side of the equation.[5] We end up with the following regression:

$$\ln(c(i,\ t)) - \ln(c(i,\ 0)) = c(y(i,\ t,\ s) - y(i,\ 0,\ s)) + v \qquad (4)$$

where v is the new error term, and $t = 0$ refers to values when the servant is first hired. It is worth noting that although the dependent and independent variables are now measured as differences from their initial values, the coefficients still have the same interpretation.

For both sets of wages, y will include the dummy variable, called y_1, which is 0 when the servant is first hired and 1 if he is rehired. Its coefficient will give the average raise that servants receive after their initial period of employment. The average will admittedly mix together the raises that servants get when first rehired and subsequent raises received thereafter. Whether this average raise is lower for employees hired locally is also of interest. Finding out means adding to y an interaction term between the dummy variable y_1 and the distance to the servant's home. In addition, there is the issue of seasonality, at least for wages from the first journal. In the second journal, servants were always supposed to work an entire year, so that seasonality was not an issue, but in the first journal they were hired in the early summer (at the Feast of Mary Magdalene) or in early November (on All Saints' Day or the Feast of Saint-Martin). They might work for the entire year, for the summer and early fall (from the Feast of Mary Magdalene to early November), or for the winter and spring. Daily or monthly wages in the summer and early fall were presumably higher than in the winter and spring because of long days and the press of the harvest. If we take the monthly wages of a servant hired for the entire year as our base, then a second dummy variable y_2, which is 1 for servants hired over the summer and early fall, will measure the summer wage premium relative to year-round work.[6] A third dummy variable, y_3, for winter-spring work, will test for the lower wages in the winter and spring. Finally, we include a fourth dummy variable, y_4, for servants hired at times other than All Saints' Day and the Feasts of Saint-Martin and Mary Magdalene. They presumably were not hired at local fairs. It would have been reasonable to suppose that they had been fired by their previous employer, because they had not lasted the entire year. Unless it was difficult to hire between fairs, their wages would be lower, as they had to rebuild their reputations.

Table D.1 shows the regressions with the logarithm of wages. Again, I have subtracted from the left-hand side the values of the dependent variables when the servant is initially hired, and I have done the same with the explanatory variables on the right. All the variables therefore measure differences from their values when the servant was initially hired. The table does show the actual wages servants earned, with all wages converted to sous per month for the first journal and livres per year for the second.

Nearly all the coefficients have the expected signs, and the t statistics suggest that chance results are not a problem. According to the coefficients of the dummy variables for seasonality, servants taken on for the summer of 1473–85 earned 2.37 times the monthly wage of servants hired for the entire year. Servants earned 22 percent less per month if they worked only in the winter and spring. If servants did not start at the times of what were presumably the local hiring fairs, their wages were 10 percent lower than the yearly average, just as the reasoning behind the model would lead us to expect.[7] Given the coefficients of y_1 and its interaction with the distance to a servant's home in 1473–85, it appears that rehiring implied a large raise, though the raise actually declined with distance. For the servant who came the average distance to the Cairon farm (11.34 kilometers), the average raise, including both an initial rehiring and any subsequent reemployment, turned out to be 31 percent.

The wages from the second journal also point to raises, but only for servants from afar: in contrast to the pattern in the first journal, raises actually increased with distance in 1691–1705. A local servant could expect no raise in these years, but one hired from the average distance (in this period only 3.51 kilometers) would see his pay increase 10 percent. Unfortunately, in 1691–1705, servants were only hired for the entire year, so that the second journal shed no light on seasonality.

The right-hand columns in the table repeat the same sort of regressions, this time with the wages themselves rather than their logarithms. The re-

TABLE D.1
Hedonic Wage Regressions: Cairon Farm Servants

Independent Variables	Dependent Variables			
	Ln(Wage)	Ln(Wage)	Wage	Wage
	Period			
	1473–85	1691–1705	1473–85	1691–1705
Dummy variable y_1: 0	0.361	−0.035	2.97	−0.732
when initially hired, 1	(12.41)	(−0.98)	(8.20)	(−1.11)
when rehired				
Interaction term : y_1 times	−0.00808	0.036	−0.061	0.680
distance to servant's	(−4.71)	(4.73)	(−2.85)	(4.87)
home in kilometers				
Dummy variable y_2: hired	0.863	—	7.16	—
for summers and early	(14.34)		(9.54)	
fall				
Dummy variable y_3: hired	−0.245	—	0.153	—
for winter and spring	(−3.91)		(0.20)	
Dummy variable y_4: not	−0.108	—	−1.02	—
hired at time of fairs	(−2.00)		(−1.50)	
Observations	144	50	144	50
R^2	0.91	0.35	0.74	0.36
Standard error	0.194	0.12	2.43	2.23

Mean Wage (All Servants) During Years		
	1473–1485	1691–1705
When initially hired	6.77	23.42
Overall	8.13	24.17
Units	sous/month	livres/year

Source: AD Calvados F 1652, F1697.
Note: As is explained in the text, both the dependent variables and the independent variables are measured as differences from their values when the servant is initially hired by the Cairon family. That is why there is no constant term in the regressions, nor any dummy variables for skills and gender. The actual mean wages of all servants (before taking the differences) are shown at the bottom of the table. The servants here include both men and women hired for various lengths of time over the years shown. Their wages, which are converted to the units shown, do not include the room and board that they received. T statistics are in parentheses.

gressions derive from similar calculations—this time starting from equation (1). Once again the variables are all measured as differences from their initial values. The results are by and large the same. In 1473–85, for example, the regression with wages rather than logarithms suggests that the average raise is 28 percent, instead of the 31 percent implied by the logarithmic regression. The results for 1691–1705 are equally close.

Notes

INTRODUCTION

1. Cf. Donald N. McCloskey, "1790–1860: A Survey," *The Economic History of Britain since 1700*, ed. Roderick Floud and D. N. McCloskey, 2d edition, vol. 1 (Cambridge, 1994), pp. 242–70. For a brief overview of the facts about contemporary growth and the relevant literature, see Gene M. Grossman and Elhanan Helpman, *Innovation and Growth in the Global Economy* (Cambridge, Mass., 1991), pp. 1–6. There are a number of correlates of growth, from human capital to government policies, which economists are busily weaving into new theories of growth. But the variation in growth rates cannot yet be explained.

2. For France, see Jean-Yves Grenier and Bernard Lepetit, "L'expérience historique: A propos de C. E. Labrousse," *AESC* 44 (1989): 1337–60. The case of early modern Germany is not all that different.

3. For a discussion of the literature involved here, see Chapter 1.

4. Patrick O'Brien and Caglar Keyder, *Economic Growth in Britain and France, 1780–1914: Two Paths to the Twentieth Century* (London, 1978).

5. Pierre Clément, ed., *Lettres, instructions et mémoires*, 8 vols. (Paris, 1861–82), 1:71, 73, 89, 120, 126, 168; Robert William Fogel, "New Sources and New Techniques for the Study of Secular Trends in Nutritional Status, Health, Mortality, and the Process of Aging," *Historical Methods* 26 (1993): 5–43.

6. C. Peter Timmer, "The Agricultural Transformation," pp. 288–92, and Moshe Syrquin, "Patterns of Structural Change," pp. 244–45, both in volume 1 of the *Handbook of Development Economics*, ed. Hollis Chenery and T. N. Srinivasan, 2 vols. (Amsterdam, 1988). John Nye's forthcoming work on the French wine trade will demonstrate the impact that agriculture could have on economic growth via comparative advantage; for initial results, see his "Changing French Trade Conditions, National Welfare, and the 1860 Anglo-French Treaty of Commerce," *Explorations in Economic History* 28 (1991): 460–77.

7. Cf. Emmanuel Le Roy Ladurie, *The French Peasantry 1450–1660*, trans. Alan Sheridan (Berkeley, 1987), pp. 401–19, which takes up ideas already present in his "De la crise ultime à la vraie croissance, 1660–1789," *HFR*, 2:576–92. For works by a younger generation of social historians that raise doubts about the *société immobile*, see Chapter 1.

8. For the new economic history of the French countryside, and relevant works on the rest of Europe, see Chapter 1.

9. See, for example, Marshall Sahlins, *Stone Age Economics* (Chicago, 1972), p. xiv, and Karl Polanyi, *The Great Transformation* (New York, 1944).

10. See, for example, Max Weber, *Gesamtausgabe*, ed. Horst Baier et al., series 1, vol. 19, *Die Wirtschaftsethik der Weltreligionen*, ed. Helwig Schmidt-Glintzer and Petra Kolonko (Tübingen, 1989), pp. 488–89.

11. For an excellent example, see Robert Bates, *Beyond the Miracle of the Market: The Political Economy of Agrarian Development in Kenya* (Cambridge,

1989). For more general remarks, see his "Contra Contractarianism: Some Reflections on the New Institutionalism," *Politics and Society* 16 (1988): 387–401; and John Ferejohn, "Rationality and Interpretation: Parliamentary Elections in Early Stuart England," in *The Economic Approach to Politics*, ed. Kristen Renwick Monroe (New York, 1991), pp. 279–305.

12. Arthur Mitzman, *The Iron Cage: An Historical Interpretation of Max Weber* (New York, 1970); Weber, *Die Wirtschaftsethik der Weltreligionen*, pp. 488–89, 512. Despite Weber's great erudition, one can also argue that he misunderstood the evolution of the West, and that he was mistaken about medieval Europe and about the nature of the Reformation. Cf. Alan Macfarlane, *The Origins of English Individualism* (Cambridge, 1978), p. 152, and my own *Church and Community in the Diocese of Lyon, 1500–1789* (New Haven, 1984), pp. 94, 169–70, 223–24.

13. David Kreps, *A Course in Microeconomic Theory* (Princeton, 1990), pp. 387–774; Joseph E. Stiglitz, "Economic Organization, Information, and Development," in *Handbook of Development Economics*, ed. Hollis Chenery and T. N. Srinivasan, 2 vols. (Amsterdam, 1988), 1:93–160; Lloyd G. Reynolds, "The Spread of Economic Growth to the Third World: 1850–1980," *Journal of Economic Literature* 21 (1983): 941–80; Avner Greif, "Contract Enforceability and Economic Institutions in Early Trade: The Maghribi Traders' Coalition," *American Economic Review* 83 (1993): 525–48; idem, "Reputation and Coalitions in Medieval Trade: Evidence on the Maghribi Traders," *JEH* 49 (1989): 857–81; idem, "Cultural Beliefs and the Organization of Society: A Historical and Theoretical Reflection on Collectivist and Individualist Societies," *Journal of Political Economy* 102 (1994): 912–50; Paul David, "Path-Dependence: Putting the Past into the Future of Economics," IMSSS Technical Report 533, August, 1988, Stanford University, Palo Alto, California; Philip T. Hoffman, Gilles Postel-Vinay, and Jean-Laurent Rosenthal, "Private Credit Markets in Paris, 1690–1840," *JEH* 52 (1992): 293–306; Douglass C. North, *Institutions, Institutional Change, and Economic Performance* (Cambridge, 1990); Richard A. Posner, *The Economics of Justice* (Cambridge, Mass., 1983), pp. 146–230; Robert Axelrod, *The Evolution of Cooperation* (New York, 1984); Bates, *Beyond the Miracle of the Market*. Robert Allen's *Enclosure and the Yeoman* (Oxford, 1992) is an excellent example of how economics need not lead to conservative conclusions: he argues that English enclosures were in effect class robbery.

14. Clifford Geertz, "The Bazaar Economy: Information and Search in Peasant Marketing," *American Economic Review* 68, no. 2 (May 1978): 28–32; Clifford Geertz, Hildred Geertz, and Lawrence Rosen, *Meaning and Order in Moroccan Society* (Cambridge, 1979), pp. 123–314.

15. One other criticism of economics is that it assumes the existence of modern, autonomous individuals. That it does analyze individual decision making is undeniable. But to suppose that individuals did not make any decisions in the past (or in the present, for that matter) strains credulity. In its most extreme form (as in certain writings of Michel Foucault) human action completely disappears, leaving us all prisoners of language with absolutely no realm for maneuver. Such a view of the human condition may appeal to some, but I simply cannot accept it. A more reasonable argument is that language and custom constrain our behavior, without

completely eliminating a role for human action. That is a position which can readily be reconciled with economics.

16. See, for example, René Baehrel, *Une croissance: La Basse-Provence rurale de la fin du XVIe siècle à 1789* (Paris, 1961; new edition, Paris, 1988), pp. 150, 163, where peasants may not calculate but they do respond to prices and seize upon what improves their lot; Jean Meuvret, *Le problème des subsistances à l'époque Louis XIV*, 3 vols. (Paris, 1977–88), vol. 1, pt. 1 (*Texte*), pp. 101–2, 121–64, pt. 2 (*Notes*), pp. 39–40, where peasants respond to prices and even innovate and where their techniques, far from being irrational, embody practical wisdom, given the obstacles they face; and finally, Jacques Mulliez, "Du blé, 'mal nécessaire.' Réflexions sur les progrès de l'agriculture de 1750–1850," *Revue d'histoire moderne et contemporaine* 26 (1979): 3–47, where seemingly irrational stock-raising techniques are shown to make eminent sense. Cf. Bruce M. S. Campbell, "Agricultural Progress in Medieval England: Some Evidence from Eastern Norfolk," *Economic History Review* ser. 2, no. 36 (1983): 26–46, where late medieval peasants respond to prices and wages; and Giovanni Levi, *Inheriting Power: The Story of an Exorcist*, trans. Lydia G. Cochrane (Chicago, 1988), pp. xiii–xviii, where peasant strategies are formed within a "framework of a full but limited system of rationality."

17. Liana Vardi, *The Land and the Loom: Peasants and Profit in Northern France* (Durham, 1993); Robert Forster, *The House of Saulx-Tavanes: Versailles and Burgundy, 1700–1830* (Baltimore, 1971); Jonathan Dewald, *Pont-St-Pierre, 1398–1789: Lordship, Community, and Capitalism in Early Modern France* (Berkeley, 1987); Jean-Marc Moriceau and Gilles Postel-Vinay, *Ferme, entreprise, famille: Grande exploitation et changements agricoles, XVIIe–XIXe siècles* (Paris, 1992).

CHAPTER ONE
PEASANTS, HISTORIANS, AND ECONOMIC GROWTH

1. Marc Bloch, *Les caractères originaux de l'histoire rurale française* (Oslo, 1931). The English translation by Janet Sondheimer, *French Rural History* (Berkeley, 1966), is still in print, and the most recent French edition dates to 1988. Pierre Goubert, *Beauvais et le Beauvaisis de 1600 à 1730*, 2 vols. (Paris, 1960), was condensed in 1977 and reprinted in its entirety in 1982. Emmanuel Le Roy Ladurie, *Les paysans de Languedoc*, 2 vols. (Paris, 1966), was translated into English in 1974; the most recent French reprint dates to 1985. Le Roy Ladurie's *Montaillou, village occitan de 1294 à 1324* (Paris, 1975), appeared in English in 1978 and in a revised French edition in 1982. It and the other works have been translated into other languages as well: Bloch's book, for example, appeared in Russian in 1957. The most notable example of the Italian literature I have in mind is Carlo Ginzburg, *Il formaggio e i vermi: Il cosmo di un mugnaio del '500* (Turin, 1976). Alan Macfarlane's *Origins of English Individualism* has certainly been important, but it cannot approach the influence of Bloch's and Ladurie's work.

2. Robert Darnton, *The Great Cat Massacre and Other Episodes in French Cultural History* (New York, 1984), pp. 9–72.

3. What follows is based chiefly upon Bloch, *French Rural History*; Le Roy

Ladurie, *Les paysans de Languedoc*; and the two syntheses, which include essays by Goubert, Le Roy Ladurie, and others: Georges Duby and Armand Wallon, eds., *Histoire de la France rurale*, 4 vols. (Paris, 1975–76), vol. 2; Fernand Braudel and Ernest Labrousse, eds., *Histoire économique et sociale de la France*, 4 vols. (Paris, 1970–82), vol. 1, pt. 2, and vol. 2. Le Roy Ladurie's contribution to the Braudel and Labrousse volume has been translated in English, and the translation contains an updated conclusion that has proved quite useful: *French Peasantry*, pp. 401–19. I have also drawn upon the perceptive comments of three historians who have themselves analyzed the social history: Daniel Hickey, "Innovation and Obstacles to Growth in the Agriculture of Early Modern France: The Example of Dauphiné," *French Historical Studies* 15, no. 2 (Fall 1987): 208–40; Vardi, *The Land and the Loom*, pp. 1–14; and James L. Goldsmith, "The Agrarian History of Preindustrial France. Where Do We Go from Here?" *Journal of European Economic History* 13 (1984): 175–199.

4. Bloch, *French Rural History*, pp. 126–49.

5. Bloch, *French Rural History*, pp. 145, 194–95.

6. Le Roy Ladurie, *French Peasantry*, pp. 409–10.

7. Pierre Goubert, "Les cadres de la vie rurale," *HESF*, 2:88–89.

8. Pierre Goubert, "Les paysans et la terre: Seigneurie, tenure, exploitation," *HESF*, 2:146–47. Cf. Bloch, *French Rural History*, p. 195. For Labrousse, see Grenier and Lepetit, "L'expérience historique."

9. Ernest Labrousse, "Aperçu de la répartition sociale de l'expansion agricole," *HESF*, 2:484–86.

10. Lefebvre, as quoted in Labrousse, "Aperçu de la répartition sociale," 2:485.

11. Le Roy Ladurie, *French Peasantry*, p. 401.

12. Emmanuel Le Roy Ladurie, "De la crise ultime à la vraie croissance, 1690–1789," *HFR*, 2:410–12.

13. Le Roy Ladurie, "De la crise ultime à la vraie croissance," pp. 568, 570–71, 581–82. For an alternative explanation of the rising number of tenant farmers in the sixteenth and seventeenth centuries, see Philip T. Hoffman, "Taxes and Agrarian Life in Early Modern France: Land Sales, 1550–1730," *JEH* 46 (1986): 37–55.

14. Goubert, "Les paysans et la terre," p. 150.

15. Le Roy Ladurie, *French Peasantry*, pp. 312–15, 406; idem, "De la crise ultime à la vraie croissance," p. 580.

16. Michel Morineau, "Y a-t-il eu une révolution agricole en France au XVIIIe siècle?" *Revue historique* 239 (April–June, 1968): 299–326; idem, "Cambrésis et Hainaut: Des frères ennemis?" in *Prestations paysannes: Dîmes, rente foncière et mouvement de la production agricole à l'époque préindustrielle,* ed. Joseph Goy and Emmanuel Le Roy Ladurie, 2 vols. (Paris, 1982), 2:625–43; idem, "La dîme et le zeste, XIVe–XXe siècles," ibid, 2:645–61; idem, *Les faux-semblants d'un démarrage économique: Agriculture et démographie en France au XVIIIe siècle* (Paris, 1971).

17. Steven Lawrence Kaplan, *Bread, Politics and Political Economy in the Reign of Louis XV*, 2 vols. (The Hague, 1976), pp. xvi–xix; Emmanuel Le Roy Ladurie and Joseph Goy, "Première esquisse d'une conjoncture du produit décimal et domanial: Fin du Moyen Age-XVIIIe siècle," in their jointly edited *Les fluctuations du produit de la dîme: Conjoncture décimale et domaniale de la fin du Moyen*

Age au XVIIIe siècle (Paris, 1972), pp. 334–74; Le Roy Ladurie, *French Peasantry*, pp. 7–20, 118–23, 231, 303–4, 402–19. The most influential work on the subsistence crises was undoubtedly Goubert's *Beauvais et le Beauvaisis*; for a review of the more recent historiography, see Guy Cabourdin, Jean-Noël Biraben, and Alain Blum, "Les crises démographiques," in *Histoire de la population française*, ed. Jacques Dupâquier, 4 vols. (Paris, 1988), pp. 175–219.

18. For this and the following paragraph, see Bloch, *French Rural History*, pp. 198–234; idem, "La lutte pour l'individualisme agraire dans la France du XVIIIe siècle," *Annales d'histoire économique et sociale* 2 (1930): 329–83, 511–56; Le Roy Ladurie, "De la crise ultime à la vraie croissance," pp. 568–75, 581–83; idem, *French Peasantry*, pp. 408–11. Cf. Hickey, "Innovation and Obstacles to Growth." In discussing enclosures and communal property rights, Le Roy Ladurie draws upon the fundamental work of Pierre Saint-Jacob, *Les paysans de la Bourgogne du nord au dernier siècle de l'ancien régime* (Dijon, 1960).

19. Bloch, *French Rural History*, pp. 223–28; cf. his "La lutte pour l'individualisme agraire." As Bloch points out, resistance to enclosure might in some cases come from nobles or administrators, and opposition to other changes in property rights—division of the commons, for instance—might be different still.

20. Robert Brenner, "Agrarian Class Structure and Economic Development in Pre-Industrial Europe," and "The Agrarian Roots of European Capitalism," in *The Brenner Debate: Agrarian Class Structure and Economic Development in Pre-Industrial Europe*, ed. T. H. Aston and C.H.E. Philpin (Cambridge, 1985). For the debate with Le Roy Ladurie and others, also see *The Brenner Debate*. There are spirited arguments over similar issues in American history as well.

21. Karl Marx, *Capital: A Critique of Political Economy*, ed. Ernest Untermann, revised edition, 3 vols. (Chicago, 1906–9), 1: 784–88, 795–800, 814–16; H. H. Gerth and C. Wright Mills, eds., *From Max Weber: Essays in Sociology* (Oxford, 1967), pp. 364–68; Macfarlane, *Origins of English Individualism*, pp. 37–52.

22. James C. Scott, *The Moral Economy of the Peasant: Rebellion and Subsistence in Southeast Asia* (New Haven, 1976), especially pp. viii, 23–25, 207–12.

23. E. P. Thompson, *Customs in Common* (New York, 1991), pp. 97–184; idem, "The Grid of Inheritance: A Comment," in *Family and Inheritance: Rural Society in Western Europe 1200–1800*, ed. Jack Goody et al. (Cambridge, 1976), pp. 328–60; idem, "The Moral Economy of the English Crowd in the Eighteenth Century," *Past and Present* 50 (1971): 76–136.

24. Scott, *The Moral Economy*, pp. 5–9, 32–34; George Dalton and Jasper Köcke, "The Work of the Polanyi Group: Past, Present, and Future," in *Economic Anthropology: Topics and Theories*, ed. Sutti Ortiz (New York, 1983), pp. 21–50; Lucette Valensi, "Anthropologie économique et histoire: L'oeuvre de Karl Polanyi," *AESC* 29 (December 1974): 1311–19. There are further parallels between the French historians and the work of sociologists such as Thodor Shanin and anthropologists such as Eric Wolf: see Vardi, *Land and the Loom*, pp. 6–8. One additional thinker who has influenced social scientists and historians alike is the Russian Chaionov. For his ideas about peasant labor markets, see Chapter 3.

25. Polanyi, *The Great Transformation*.

26. In addition to Chapter 4, see George Frêche, "Dîme et production agricole: Remarques méthodologiques à propos de la région toulousaine," in Goy and Le Roy

Ladurie, eds., *Fluctuations du produit de la dîme*, pp. 214–44; Michel Morineau, "Réflexions tardives et conclusions prospectives," in ibid., pp. 320–33; idem, "Cambrésis et Hainaut"; idem, "La dîme et le zeste"; idem, *Les faux-semblants*, pp. 21–22.

27. Jean-Noël Biraben, Didier Blanchet, and Alain Blum, "Le mouvement de la population," in Dupâquier, ed., *Histoire de la population française*, 2:145–74.

28. David R. Weir, "Life under Pressure: France and England, 1670–1870," *JEH* 44 (1984): 27–47.

29. Cabourdin, Biraben, and Blum, "Les crises démographiques"; David R. Weir, "Markets and Mortality in France, 1600–1789," in *Famine, Disease and the Social Order in Early Modern Society*, ed. John Walter and Roger Schofield (Cambridge, 1989), pp. 201–34; John Walter and Roger Schofield, "Famine, Disease and Crisis Mortality in Early Modern Society," ibid., pp. 1–73.

30. Bernard Garnier, "La mise en herbe dans le pays d'Auge aux XVIIe et XVIIIe siècles," *Annales de Normandie* 25 (1975): 157–80; idem, "Pays herbagers, pays céréaliers et pays 'ouverts' en Normandie (XVIe–début du XIXe siècle)," *Revue d'histoire économique et sociale* 53 (1975): 493–525; Mulliez, "Du blé, 'mal nécessaire'"; Goldsmith, "Agrarian History of Preindustrial France"; Hickey, "Innovation and Obstacles to Growth"; T.J.A. Le Goff and D.M.G. Sutherland, "The Revolution and the Rural Economy," in *Reshaping France: Town, Country, and Region during the French Revolution*, ed. Alan Forrest and Peter Jones (Manchester, 1991), pp. 52–85; Vardi, *The Land and the Loom*. One must add Jean-Marc Moriceau's *Les fermiers de l'Ile-de-France: XVe–XVIIIe siècle* (Paris, 1994) here; although it reached me after I had completed my own manuscript, his conclusions fit my own.

31. For French rural history alone, a list (far from exhaustive) of recent works of new economic history might include Jean-Pierre Bompard, Thierry Magnac, and Gilles Postel-Vinay, "Emploi, mobilité et chômage en France au XIXe siècle: Migrations saisonnières entre industrie et agriculture," *AESC* 45 (1990): 55–76; idem, "Migrations saisonnières de main-d'oeuvre: Le cas de la France en 1860," *Annales d'économie et de statistique* 19 (1990): 97–129; Jean-Michel Chevet, "Le Marquisat d'Ormesson, 1700–1840. Essai d'analyse économique," 2 vols., Thèse de 3e cycle, Ecole des Hautes Etudes en Sciences Sociales, Paris, 1983; George W. Grantham, "The Persistence of Open-Field Farming in Nineteenth-Century France," *JEH* 40 (September 1980): 515–31; idem, "The Diffusion of the New Husbandry in Northern France, 1815–1840," *JEH* 38 (June 1978): 311–37; idem, "Agricultural Supply during the Industrial Revolution: French Evidence and European Implications," *JEH* 49 (March 1989): 43–72; Philip T. Hoffman, "The Economic Theory of Sharecropping in Early Modern France," *JEH* 44 (1984): 309–19; idem, "Taxes and Agrarian Life"; idem, "Institutions and Agriculture in Old-Regime France," *Politics and Society* 16 (1988): 241–64; idem, "Land Rents and Agricultural Productivity: The Paris Basin, 1450–1789," *JEH* 51 (1991): 771–805; Jean-Marc Moriceau and Gilles Postel-Vinay, *Ferme, entreprise, famille*; Jean-Laurent Rosenthal, *The Fruits of Revolution: Property Rights, Litigation, and French Agriculture, 1700–1860* (Cambridge, 1992); Gilles Postel-Vinay, "A la recherche de la révolution économique dans les campagnes (1789–1815)," *Revue économique* 40 (1989): 1015–45; Gilles Postel-Vinay and Jean-Marc Robin, "Eating, Working,

and Saving in an Unstable World: Consumers in Nineteenth-Century France," *Economic History Review* 45 (1992): 494–553; David R. Weir, "Les crises économiques et les origines de la Révolution française," *AESC* 46 (1991): 917–47. To this list one must add Chevet's, Grantham's, and Weir's work in progress.

32. Cf. Jean-Marc Moriceau, "Au rendez-vous de la 'révolution agricole' dans la France du XVIIIe siècle: A propos des régions de grande culture," *AESC* 49 (1994): 27–63.

33. Works of new economic history on agriculture in the rest of Europe have provided rich examples here; they include Jan de Vries, *The Dutch Rural Economy in the Golden Age* (New Haven, 1974); Allen, *Enclosure and the Yeoman*; and the excellent essays collected by William N. Parker and Eric L. Jones, eds., *European Peasants and Their Markets: Essays in Agrarian Economic History* (Princeton, 1975); and by Bruce M. S. Campbell and Mark Overton, eds., *Land, Labour, Livestock: Historical Studies in European Agricultural Productivity* (Manchester, 1991).

CHAPTER TWO
COMMON RIGHTS AND THE VILLAGE COMMUNITY

1. Jean Meyer, *La noblesse bretonne au XVIIIe siècle*, 2 vols. (Paris, 1966), 1:533–90; Henri Sée, *Les classes rurales en Bretagne du XVIe siècle à la Révolution* (Paris, 1906), pp. 208–40; AD Loire-Atlantique, C 30–47.

2. What follows is taken from AD Loire-Atlantique, G 604, C 139, E 254; Henri Michel Gasnier, *Varades: Histoire d'une bourgade du Val de Loire* (Paris, 1985), pp. 93–100. Even in a parish like Varades, where habitations were dispersed in a town and a number of villages and hamlets, parishioners knew one another. They could identify each other and even guess the identity of other parishioners' animals. That, at least, is what one can deduce from a court case in a region with a similar pattern of habitation, the Massif Central. There it was considered possible that witnesses could identify the persons who seized a farmer's crop at night: they were asked if they could recognize the oxen hauling the crop or identify the animals' drivers—if necessary, by the sound of their voices. See AD Cantal, 7 B 189 (17 December 1663).

3. AD Loire-Atlantique, E 254, 12 December 1661.

4. AD Loire-Atlantique, B 10240-B 10242.

5. AD Loire-Atlantique, C 139, E 254, G 604. In 1734, herds of up to 420 sheep were grazing on the common pasture, a sign that richer peasants may have been grazing animals on the commons. In any case, sheep were still a rarity in probate inventories, for only three of twenty-nine inventories in the years 1728–47 mention sheep, whereas seventeen mention cattle. The inventories are from B 10248, B 10249, and 4 E, Etude XXXI, 54.

6. Meyer, *La noblesse bretonne*, 1:533–90; Sée, *Les classes rurales en Bretagne*, pp. 208–40. For agricultural productivity in Brittany, see Chapter 4. See also Alexandre-Henri Tessier et al., *Encyclopédie méthodique ou par ordre de matières: Agriculture*, 7 vols. (Paris, 1787–1821), s.v. "Bêtes à laine" and "Consommation de Paris"; and J.-M. Vallez, "Le commerce des bestiaux en Normandie: L'activité de la famille Mollet (1680–1730)," *Annales de Normandie* 38 (1988): 342–43.

7. Heide Wunder, *Die bäuerliche Gemeinde in Deutschland* (Göttingen, 1986), pp. 8–9, 141–42.

8. Ibid., pp. 8–9, 20–21, 26–27, 30, 48–51; Werner Rösener, *Bauern im Mittelalter* (Munich, 1986), pp. 57–61, 72, 130, 156–64; Jean Chapelot and Robert Fossier, *The Village and the House in the Middle Ages*, trans. Henry Cleere (Berkeley, 1985); Wilhelm Abel, *Geschichte der deutschen Landwirtschaft*, 3d ed. (Stuttgart, 1978), pp. 19–20, 73–83.

9. AD Moselle, B 5694 (justice de Vionville,1764–73). In a nine-month period of 1772–73, I counted 162 fines for breaking the rules of field use. For similar examples in the same region, see AD Moselle, B 5058 (justice de Gorze); B 5716 (justice de Waville); B 5691, 5692, 5695 (justice de Vionville); E dépot 257 (archives communales de Gorze). Open fields did not always lead to strife. In the village of La Grande-Paroisse southeast of Paris, for example, wandering animals caused relatively little trouble: AN Z2 4604 (registre de greffe, 1723–92). In the nineteenth century, strife over the boundaries of open-field parcels was routine; consolidating and rearranging parcels reduced the number of lawsuits considerably: A. Bretagne, *Nouvelle étude sur le cadastre et les abornements généraux* (Nancy, 1870), pp. 123–24.

10. Among the countless examples, see AD Yvelines, B, Bailliage de Brétigny, pièces de greffe, liasse 1 (19 August 1616), 101 (2 September 1750); AD Rhône, 4 B 5, justice d'Amplepuis (30 July 1743); AD Vaucluse, archives communales de Grillon, FF 7 (13 October 1457, 23 October 1544, 1730, 1784); AD Cantal, 7 B 112 (20 January, 1778; peasants from different hamlets of the same parish go to court over pasture rights in woods); 7 B 189 (29 March 1662, 30 December 1666, 16 September 1666: disputes over trespassing animals within the same village or hamlet and even within the same family); AD Hautes-Pyrénées, archives de la vallée de Barèges, DD39, pièces 6 & 10; Robert Muchembled, *L'invention de l'homme moderne: Sensibilités, moeurs et comportements collectifs sous l'ancien régime* (Paris, 1988), p. 30. For regulation of open fields, see AD Moselle, B 5694 (justice de Vionville, 8 August 1773); E dépot 257, Gorze, liasse 2 (1739); and the analogous English examples in Warren O. Ault, *Open Field Farming in Medieval England: A Study of Village By Laws* (London, 1972).

11. AD Yvelines B, bailliage de Brétigny, liasse 5 (cover dated 23 May 1619; actual date 1618): One evening, three drunken local youths threatened the tenant farmer Claude Pelletier and tried to take his horses. Then they attacked the house of a neighbor, Louis Tromballet, in an attempt to rape Tromballet's young wife. Tromballet cried, "Aux voleurs et au feu affin de faire plus tôt venir à luy les voisins mais il n'en survint aucunes." Actually, Pelletier had sneaked up and witnessed the scene, and another neighbor eventually arrived, too. Afterward, several neighbors filed criminal complaints, which suggest that their failure to intervene was due to fear rather than to any belief that Tromballet deserved chastisement for having married a woman ten years younger than he was. On other occasions in the same village, neighbors were perhaps more helpful. They were inside a widow's house, when it came under attack by village youth, probably to protect her and her daughter: 11 (14 April 1623). Still, village or neighborhood solidarity was fickle. Cf. AD Rhône, 4 B 5, justice d'Amplepuis (13 June 1743).

12. Noel du Fail, *Les propos rustiques: Texte original de 1547: Interpolations et*

variantes de 1548, 1549, 1573, ed. Arthur de la Borderie (Paris, 1878; reprint, Geneva, 1970), pp. 27–30, 85–89, 228–29: Despite du Fail's nostalgic view of village life, strife among neighbors seems a commonplace, and a moral lesson he gives for village youth suggests that gossip and jealously were regular features of their lives. Admittedly, the quarreling neighbors here were ancient enemies from different villages—villages whose mutual hostility might suggest community solidarity. Yet what is striking in du Fail is that strife between neighbors seems habitual. In Rétif de la Bretonne's idealized Burgundy, villagers nonetheless stole, cheated, schemed against one another, infringed on one another's property, and failed to cooperate: Nicolas-Edme Rétif de la Bretonne, *La vie de mon père*, ed. Gilbert Rouger (Paris, 1970), pp. 8–9, 12, 129, 134–35, 145.

13. Keith P. Luria, *Territories of Grace* (Berkeley, 1991); Allain Collomp, *La maison du père: Famille et village en Haute-Provence aux XVIIe et XVIIIe siècles* (Paris, 1983); Elisabeth Claverie and Pierre Lamaison, *L'impossible mariage: Violence et parenté en Gévaudan: XVIIe, XVIIIe, XIXe siècles* (Paris, 1982). Cf. Wunder, *Die bäuerliche Gemeinde*, pp. 19–21; David Warren Sabean, *Power in the Blood: Popular Culture and Village Discourse in Early Modern Germany* (Cambridge, 1984).

14. AD Loire-Atlantique, G 604 (disputes in 1571 reported in factum of 1651), B 10333 (16 May 1743); A. M. Poullain du Parc, *Journal des audiences et arrests du Parlement de Bretagne*, 5 vols. (Rennes, 1737–78), 2:256–59; E. P. Thompson, *Customs in Common* (New York, 1991), pp. 97–184; Hans Medick and David Warren Sabean, "Introduction," in *Interest and Emotion: Essays on the Study of Family and Kinship*, ed. Hans Medick and David Warren Sabean (Cambridge, 1984), pp. 1–8; Samuel Popkin, *The Rational Peasant: The Political Economy of Rural Society in Vietnam* (Berkeley, 1979). The sort of anthropology I have doubts about is exemplified by Clifford Geertz's *The Interpretation of Cultures* (New York, 1973); for a critique of it, see Vincent Crapanzano, "Hermes' Dilemma: The Making of Subversion in Ethnographic Description," in *Writing Culture: The Poetics and Politics of Ethnography*, ed. James Clifford and George E. Marcus (Berkeley, 1986), pp. 70–76. Here, it is interesting to consider the villagers' problem from a different perspective—that of game theory. Because villagers interacted with one another repeatedly, game theorists might expect that they could easily cooperate. The problem, though, was that collective action—say in defense of commons—was typically a brief affair. It was a one-shot game that lent itself to free riding.

15. Meuvret, *Subsistances*, vol. 2, pt. 1 (*Texte*), pp. 21–27, 40–45; vol. 2, pt. 2 (*Notes*), pp. 16–30, 61–63.

16. Anne Zink, "Pays et paysans gascons sous l'ancien régime," 9 vols. (Thèse d'état, University of Paris I, 1985), 3:912; Baehrel, *Une croissance*, pp. 192–200, 476–78. Elsewhere in Provence the best commons were off limits to the poor: Collomp, *La maison du père*, pp. 242–46.

17. AN S 281, S 292 (15 September 1782).

18. Kathryn Norberg, "Dividing up the Commons: Institutional Change in Rural France, 1789–1799," *Politics and Society* 16 (1988): 265–86. A number of her communities opposed division, but they apparently did so only because the commons were of too little value to be divided and farmed individually.

19. Abbé François Rozier, *Cours complet d'agriculture*, 10 vols. (Paris, 1781–1800), s.v. "Communes, communaux."

20. AD Meurthe-et-Moselle, C 320; Philip T. Hoffman, "Institutions and Agriculture"; André J. Bourde, *Agronomie et agronomes en France au XVIIIe siècle*, 3 vols. (Paris, 1967), 2:1156, 1183–89. As Bourde points out, the Parlement of Nancy would probably have accepted an edict authorizing villages to divide their own commons; what they would not accept was another part of the same edict, which abolished *parcours*, the right to graze on other villages' commons.

21. For the rent increase throughout France in the eighteenth century, see David Weir, "Les crises économiques." For use of *feudistes*, seigneurial reaction, and the villagers' use of the courts, see P. M. Jones, *The Peasantry in the French Revolution* (Cambridge, 1988), pp. 42–59; Robert Forster, *The House of Saulx-Tavanes*; Hilton L. Root, *Peasants and King in Burgundy: Agrarian Foundations of French Absolutism* (Berkeley, 1987); Le Roy Ladurie, "De la crise ultime à la vraie croissance," pp. 554–75; Jean-Laurent Rosenthal, *Fruits of Revolution*.

22. Bloch, *French Rural History*, pp. 197–234; idem, "La lutte pour l'individualisme agraire"; Le Roy Ladurie, "De la crise ultime à la vraie croissance," pp. 568–75, 581–83.

23. The documents Bloch relied upon include AN H1 1486. For the background, see Bourde, *Agronomie et agronomes*, 2:1077–1192.

24. Saint-Jacob, *Les paysans de la Bourgogne*, pp. 369–71, 450–54.

25. Before the Revolution, Neuviller-sur-Moselle was named Chaumont-sur-Moselle, after its seigneur, but I shall use the modern name, Neuviller.

26. AD Meurthe-et-Moselle, B 11928, B11947, 1 F 10; Jean Peltre, *Recherches métrologiques sur les finages lorrains* (Lille, 1975), pp. 274–84; Bourde, *Agronomie et agronomes*, 408–12. The 441 hectares in Neuviller includes 118 hectares of woodland, 49 of meadow, and 11 of vineyard; most of the strips were in the 263 hectares of arable. While the number of strips come from the eighteenth-century documents, I have taken the area figures from Henri Lepage, *Le département de la Moselle. Statistique, historique et administrative*, 2 vols. (Nancy, 1843), 2:435–36.

27. For a further discussion, see Chapter 5. The rent calculations here come from an analysis of leases and related documents in AD Meurthe-et-Moselle, 1 F 8 and H 852-H 854. The farm in question was the *gagnage* of the Tiercelins in Neuviller. The Tiercelins leased it out for 380 livres de Lorraine in 1748, 372 livres de Lorraine in 1757, and 400 livres de Lorraine in 1765. La Galaizière's project took place in 1768–71, and only one lease for the Tiercelins' farm survives from the period after the project: 620 livres de Lorraine in 1788, a 55 percent increase over 1765. Except for the rearrangement of the parcels, the other characteristics of the *gagnage* had not changed. Rent increases for neighboring communities where there was no rearrangement came from Maurice Lacoste, "La crise agricole dans le département de la Meurthe à la fin de l'ancien régime et au début de la Révolution," Thèse de doctorat, University of Paris, 1951, 2 vols., 2:316–27. I relied on Lacoste's figures for the *gagnage* of Bosserville. To check the sensitivity of my results, I also used figures he gave for another *gagnage* (Bourdonnay) and allowed for slight changes in the size of the Tiercelin's *gagnage*; the results were nearly identical, with a 30 to 34 percent real increase in rent, which could not be attributed to price

changes. An index of rent for Lorraine as a whole led to similar results—a 34 to 36 percent real increase in rent. The index comes from a large sample of *gagnages* in Lorraine in Charles Guyot, "Essai sur l'aisance relative du paysan lorrain à partir du XVe siècle," *Mémoires de l'Académie de Stanislas*, series 5, no. 6 (1888): 1–130. Unfortunately, besides the Tiercelins, there are no other series of leases for Neuviller or Roville. A thorough search of ecclesiastical archives failed to turn up anything, and other sources—notarial registers in AD Meurthe-et-Moselle, 3 E–45 E, and the *contrôle des actes* in C 2750–59—were of no help.

28. Christophe Joseph Alexandre Mathieu de Dombasle, "Des réunions territoriales," in *Annales agricoles de Roville*, 2d ed. (Paris, 1829), 1:264–318.

29. Charles Etienne, ed. *Cahiers de doléances des bailliages des généralités de Metz et de Nancy pour les états généraux de 1789. Première série. Département de Meurthe-et-Moselle*, vol. 3: *Cahiers du bailliage de Vézelise* (Nancy, 1930), pp. 59, 305.

30. AD Meurthe-et-Moselle, Bj 10219 (cote provisoire), Justice de Neuviller (Chaumont-sur-Moselle), Feuilles d'audiences (16 July 1781 to 7 January 1782); 3 B IV (cote provisoire), Parlement de Nancy, arrêts d'audiences, grande chambre (1 May 1783).

31. AD Meurthe-et-Moselle, 3 B IV (cote provisoire), Parlement de Nancy, arrêts d'audiences, grande chambre (1 May 1783); AN H1 1486; Emile Duvernoy, *Inventaire sommaire des archives départementales antérieures à 1790: Meurthe et Moselle*, vol. 9: *Série E supplément, tome troisième: Arrondissement de Nancy* (Nancy, 1912), E supplément 3141; Etienne, *Cahiers du bailliage de Vézelise*, p. 305.

32. Cf. Thompson, *Customs in Common*, pp. 97–184.

33. Duvernoy, *Inventaire sommaire: Meurthe-et-Moselle, Série E supplément*, E supplément 3065; AD Meurthe-et-Moselle, C 320; Hoffman, "Institutions and Agriculture," pp. 252–53; Bourde, *Agronomie et agronomes*, 2:1156, 1183–89.

34. This, even though by 1778 La Galaizière was no longer the intendant of Lorraine.

35. The argument here is due to Donald McCloskey, "The Economics of Enclosure: A Market Analysis," in *European Peasants and Their Markets*, ed. William N. Parker and Eric L. Jones, pp. 132–33. Cf. Lance Davis and Douglass C. North, *Institutional Change and American Economic Growth* (Cambridge, 1971), pp. 17–18; Hoffman, "Institutions and Agriculture," pp. 241–64.

36. AN H1 1486; Arthur Young, *Voyages en France en 1787, 1788 et 1789*, ed. and trans. Henri Sée, 3 vols. (Paris, 1931), 2:727–28; Mathieu de Dombasle, "Des réunions territoriales."

37. The cost figures come from AN H1 1486. One might wonder whether La Galaizière padded his cost figures since he was seeking government reimbursement. Although I cannot be certain, I think that his figures were reasonable. Indeed, he may well have understated his expenses, for he included nothing for his own time, particularly that spent cajoling opponents of his project. This could have been considerable, and it would have pushed his costs even higher. Of the costs, 6,000 livres went for purchases of land at above-market prices or other payments to Monsieur Guenin, Sieur Mirbeck, and a Sieur Rolin, a lawyer in Nancy. After the enclosure, Rolin owned only a tiny amount of land in Neuviller, but he may have sold land to

La Galaizière during the enclosure. Alternatively, he may have been representing others, or perhaps he was particularly threatening because he was an attorney. As for Guenin, if he sold land during the enclosure, he nonetheless remained the second biggest landowner in Roville. Finally, Mirbeck owned property in other parishes and paid twice the average *taille* on the Neuviller tax role of 1782. His family was also quite distinguished. The information about these three individuals here comes from AD Meurthe-et-Moselle, B 11928, 11947, 1 F 8; and Lepage, *Département de la Moselle*, 2:435–36.

38. The range of estimates allows for a ratio of rents to land values of between 0.0353 and 0.0466. The 0.0353 figure was the average ratio of rent to sales prices on local farms; the 0.0466 figure was the interest rate on *rentes*. If we allow the rent increase to vary between 30 and 34 percent, the present values range between 27,000 and 81,000 livres. Local rental figures here come from AD Meurthe-et-Moselle 1 F 8, H 852, H 853, and H 855. All values are stated in livres tournois, as are La Galaizière's expenses. For the necessary conversions from livres de Lorraine and other units and for equivalents of local measures, I relied upon M. de Riocour, "Les monnaies lorraines," *Mémoires de la société d'archéologie lorraine et du musée historique lorrain*, series 3, 11 (1883): 1–106, 12 (1884): 5–43; *Tableau des anciennes mesures du département de la Meurthe comparées aux mesures républicaines* (Paris, An VI [revolutionary year 1797–98]); Jean Peltre, *Recherches métrologiques*; and the indications about measures given in AD 1 F 10, B 11928, B 11947. Total areas of cultivated land for the two villages came from Lepage, *Département de la Moselle*, 2:435–36, 496–97; I assumed that 555 hectares were involved. The ratio of rental rates to land values in Lorraine and the interest rate on *rentes*, I took from Charles Guyot, "Essai sur l'aisance relative du paysan lorrain," pp. 85–86, 96–97. One problem with the calculations was that some of La Galaizière's land had been improved before he undertook the rearrangement of the parcels; furthermore, some property, such as his chateau and his ornamental park, was not involved in the project. Here Charles Gérard, *Histoire d'un village lorrain: Neuviller-sur-Moselle* (Nancy, 1936), was helpful.

39. The calculation assumes a rent increase of 2.4 livres per hectare and costs of 11,141 livres for legal and surveying costs spread over 555 hectares. The long-term loans were *rentes*, which at the time yielded 4.66 percent in Lorraine. Even if we assume that the rents rose by only 2.27 livres per hectare and that the costs were spread over less land (say 443 hectares of arable only), the rate of return is still 9 percent. Obviously, the larger estimates for the rent increase yield higher rates of return—up to 24 percent.

40. AN H1 1486, piece 94.

41. Ibid.

42. In the court cases that Roville appealed and in similar incidents, the actual damages seem to have been on the order of 10 or 20 livres, although the fines levied were higher. How many of them occurred is not clear, but the appeal mentioned four incidents in 1781 in Roville. At four incidents per village per year, the damages would amount to perhaps 160 livres per year for both villages, a small sum by comparison with an increase in rent of at least 1,000 livres per year. Of course, the true number of incidents may have been higher, and they may have been particularly burdensome for certain landowners.

CHAPTER THREE
LABOR MARKETS, RENTAL MARKETS, AND CREDIT IN THE LOCAL ECONOMY

1. Steven Laurence Kaplan, *Provisioning Paris: Merchants and Millers in the Grain and Flour Trade during the Eighteenth Century* (Ithaca, 1984); Meuvret, *Subsistances*, especially volume 3; Georges Durand, *Vin, vigne, vignerons en Lyonnais et Beaujolais* (Paris, 1979); Roger Dion, *Histoire de la vigne et du vin en France* (Paris, 1959; reprint, Paris, 1977); J.-M. Vallez, "Le commerce des bestiaux en Normandie."

2. See Gérard Béaur, *Le marché foncier à la veille de la Révolution* (Paris, 1984); Richard M. Smith, ed., *Land, Kinship and Life-Cycle* (Cambridge, 1984); Levi, *Inheriting Power*, chapter 3; and volume 65 (1987) of *Quaderni Storici*, which is devoted to historical study of the land market in several countries of Europe and Latin America.

3. Pioneering works here include Gilles Postel-Vinay, *La rente foncière dans le capitalisme agricole* (Paris, 1974); Moriceau and Postel-Vinay, *Ferme, entreprise, famille*; Moriceau, *Fermiers*; Bompard, Magnac, and Postel-Vinay, "Emploi, mobilité et chômage"; idem, "Migrations saisonnières de main-d'oeuvre"; Pierre Sicsic, "City-Farm Wages Gaps in Late Nineteenth-Century France," *JEH* 52 (1992): 675–95; and Gilles Postel-Vinay and David Weir, "Frenchmen into Peasants: Myths and Realities of Agricultural Labor Markets in France, 1862–1929," paper delivered at the 15–16 July 1993 Franco-American Conference of the National Bureau of Economic Research. For England, see Allen, *Enclosure and the Yeoman*.

4. See Chapter 1.

5. The major exception here is Meuvret's *Subsistances*.

6. Elizabeth Hoffman and Joel Mokyr, "Peasants, Potatoes, and Poverty: Transactions Costs in Prefamine Ireland," in *Technique, Spirit and Form in the Making of the Modern Economies: Essays in Honor of William N. Parker*, ed. Gary Saxonhouse and Gavin Wright (Greenwich, 1984), Supplement 3 of *Research in Economic History*, pp. 115–45, especially pp. 119–23. One can construct a model in which risk causes trade to make individuals worse off, but it makes unrealistic assumptions about risk aversion, demand elasticities, and gains from trade: David M. G. Newbery and Joseph E. Stiglitz, *The Theory of Commodity Price Stabilization: A Study in the Economics of Risk* (Oxford, 1981), pp. 336–57. Cf. Barbara N. Sands, "Agricultural Decision-Making under Uncertainty: The Case of the Shanxi Farmers, 1931–1936," *Explorations in Economic History* 26 (1989): 339–59.

7. See Chapter 1; Weir, "Markets and Mortality"; and Walter and Schofield, "Famine, Disease and Crisis Mortality." Evidence from England points in the same direction.

8. Chevet, "Le Marquisat d'Ormesson," 2:406–29, 440. Cf. Goubert, *Beauvais et le Beauvaisis*, 1:182; George Lefebvre, *Les paysans du Nord pendant la Révolution française* (Paris, 1924; abridged edition, Bari, 1959), pp. 286–88; Peter J. Bowden, "Agricultural Prices, Farm Profits, and Rents," *AHEW*, 4:657; and Allen, *Enclosure and the Yeoman*, p. 62.

9. *SA 1862*, pp. xiii, xviii. The 1840 yields are 12.45 hectoliters per hectare for wheat and 16.30 for oats; the seeding rates are 2.05 hectoliters per hectare for wheat

and 2.52 for oats. Throughout the calculations I have assumed that the tithe is 8 percent, that a family of four needed 14 hectoliters of wheat per year for food, that each horse required 12.76 liters of oats a day, plus straw and hay; and that taxes amounted to only 2 hectoliters of wheat per year for a family of four. For comparable assumptions about food, see Chevet, "Marquisat d'Ormesson," 2:406–18; George Grantham, "Some Implications of the Level of Agricultural Labour Productivity in Eighteenth and Early Nineteenth-Century France," paper delivered at the Agricultural History Association Conference, April 2–4, 1990; and Goubert, *Beauvais et le Beauvaisis*, 1:165, 180–87. For horses, see Tessier, *Agriculture*, s.v. "Cheval"; Armand Husson, *Les consommations de Paris*, 2d edition (Paris, 1875), p. 119; and Moriceau, *Fermiers*, pp. 272–73. Most of these assumptions are quite optimistic. The taxes rates, for example, were based on a lower bound for central treasury receipts in hectoliters of wheat per person in Philip T. Hoffman, "Early Modern France, 1450–1700," in *Fiscal Crises, Liberty, and Representative Government, 1540–1789*, ed. Philip T. Hoffman and Kathryn Norberg (Stanford, 1994), Table 1. Actual taxes in the countryside could be much higher; Goubert, for example, assumes that taxes (including seigneurial dues, which we have omitted) amounted to 9 hectoliters of wheat per year for a family of *haricotiers* (small-scale peasant farmers). Such a figure would push the level of self-sufficiency even higher. If the draft animals were oxen rather than horses, a peasant could conceivably get by on 5 hectares provided that he fed the oxen not only with his own straw but with grass from the commons. His grain yields would be lower, though, because the straw the animal consumed could not be mixed with its manure, and self-sufficiency would be difficult. Cf. Tessier, *Agriculture*, s.v. "Bêtes à cornes"; M. Hassenfratz "Mémoire sur la comparaison des produits de la culture du Bourbonnais avec celle de la Picardie," in *Mémoires d'agriculture, d'économie rurale et domestique* (Fall, 1786).

10. In the village of La Grande-Paroisse, southeast of Paris, fifty-one probate inventories from the years 1545–1740 showed that farms with one plow had a median size (including both owned and rented land) of 9.5 hectares; the smallest farm with one plow was 5.06 hectares: AN S 468, 471AB, 473B, 474, 475. Among thirty-two inventories from the south of Paris in Jean Jacquart, *La crise rurale en Ile-de-France, 1550–1670* (Paris, 1974), pp. 355–57, the thirty-two farms with one plow had a median size of 12 hectares, with the smallest being 3 hectares. Among the same inventories, horses only appeared in farms above 4 hectares. In Normandy, in the village of Rots, the meticulously constructed tax role of 1740 shows that a single horse became common only on farms over 5 hectares; farms with two horses averaged 17 hectares, counting both owned and rented land.

11. Goubert, *Beauvais et le Beauvaisis*, 1:158; AD Calvados, F 1757 (1687); Le Roy Ladurie, *Les paysans de Languedoc*, 1:241, 2:796.

12. Sée, *Les classes rurales en Bretagne*, pp. 69–71; Jacques Bottin, *Seigneurs et paysans dans l'ouest du pays de Caux: 1540–1650* (Paris, 1983), pp. 83–84; Chevet, "Le Marquisat d'Ormesson," 1:173–74, 186, and 2:421–29, 440; Jacquart, *Crise rurale*, pp. 104, 119, 133–34, 352–57, 724, 749–51; Lefebvre, *Paysans du Nord*, pp. 286–88; Georges Frêche, *Toulouse et la région Midi-Pyrénées au siècle des lumières (vers 1670–1789)* (Paris, 1974), pp. 336, 350; René Baehrel, *Une croissance*, 1:361–62; and Meuvret, *Subsistances*, vol. 1, pt. 1 (*Texte*), p. 88.

13. P. Laboulinière, *Annuaire statistique du département des Hautes-Pyré-nées* (Tarbes, 1807), pp. 321–55, 365–73, 404–10; Mulliez, "Du blé, 'mal néces-saire.'"

14. Werner Rösener, *Bauern im Mittelalter*, pp. 208–14; Allen, *Enclosure and the Yeoman*, pp. 56–77. Western Germany had numerous smallholders who had to work as agricultural laborers in the early modern period. In addition to Rösener, see Wunder, *Die bäuerliche Gemeinde*, pp. 96–97; Wilhelm Abel, "Landwirtschaft, 1500–1648," in *Handbuch der deutschen Wirtschafts- und Sozialgeschichte*, ed. Hermann Aubin and Wolfgang Zorn, 2 vols. (Stuttgart, 1978), 1:391–97; and David Warren Sabean, *Property, Production, and Family in Neckarhausen, 1700–1870* (Cambridge, 1990), p. 97.

15. Hoffman, "Taxes and Agrarian Life."

16. For examples, see Durand, *Vin, vigne et vignerons*, pp. 419–23; and Vardi, *The Land and the Loom*.

17. In four Norman villages near Bretteville-l'Orgueilleuse in 1740, only 41 of 488 families managed to farm more than 10 hectares, counting both rented and owned land. Only 80 managed to farm more than 5 hectares: AD Calvados, 2 C 1191, 1193, 1317, 1345. The evidence here comes from extraordinarily precise tax records established under supervision as part of a program of tax reform; see Jean Piel, *Essai sur la réforme de l'impôt direct au XVIIe siècle: La taille proportion-nelle dans les généralités de Caen et d'Alençon* (Caen, 1937). Even better evidence comes from Chevet's work on a region near Paris, where in 1717 only 12 percent of the farms (including both owned and rented land) exceeded 10 hectares; the situation had not changed greatly in 1789. See Chevet, "Marquisat d'Ormesson," 2:421–22, 440.

18. For work requirements and the size of arable farms, see Allen, *Enclosure and the Yeoman*, p. 57; similar information comes from a sample of death inventories from La Grande-Paroisse. There, only 19 percent of the *exploitations* under 10 hectares mentioned debts to servants; 75 percent of those over 25 hectares did. The sample here consists of fifty-one inventories from the years 1545–1740 in AN S 468, 471AB, 473B, 474, 475; most were from the period 1650–1740. Cf. Chevet, "Marquisat d'Ormesson," 2:423–29; and Meuvret, *Subsistances*, vol. 2, pt. 1 (*Texte*), pp. 167–202.

19. Until their teens, children were of little use on the farm. They could easily be harmed by animals in the courtyard—pigs were a particular danger—and they lacked the strength and skills needed for the heavy tasks such as ploughing. At best they might help a bit at harvesttime. Given high rates of child mortality, the wait for children to reach their teens (particularly boys, who seemed more useful on farms) could be a long one. Cf. Lee Craig, "The Value of Household Labor in Antebellum Northern Agriculture," *Journal of Economic History* 51 (1991): 67–81.

20. Consider, for example, the servants hired in 1691–1705 by the Cairon family in the Norman village of Bretteville-l'Orgueilleuse, a family to be discussed in greater detail below. If we single out the servants who came from Bretteville itself, they rarely appear on the village tax roles, although the roles did contain the poor and also many people who had the same last names as the servants. In all likelihood, the servants from Bretteville were young adults from village families: AD Calvados F 1697, and 2 C 1174 (roles de taille, Bretteville-l'Orgueilleuse, 1691, 1697, 1727).

Cf. Pierre Charbonnier, *Une autre France: La seigneurie rurale en basse Auvergne du XIVe au XVIe siècle*, 2 vols. (Clermont-Ferrand, 1980), 2:804–7.

21. Tessier, *Agriculture*, s.v. "Battage," "Batteurs," "Décembre," "Faucher," "Faucilleur," "Vigne"; Louis Liger, *Oeconomie générale de la campagne ou nouvelle maison rustique*, 2d edition, 2 vols. (Amsterdam, 1701), 1:217–20; Jacquart, *Crise rurale*; Meuvret, *Subsistances*, vol. 2, pt. 2 (*Texte*), pp. 116–18, 147.

22. Marx, *Capital*.

23. In Grillon (Vaucluse), for example, the local cadastres reveal much about landownership, but leases lack areas and complete property descriptions. As for the nineteenth-century censuses, the *enquête* of 1862 noted the lack of information about the size of *exploitations* for previous years and lamented the inaccuracy of its own results, particularly for small farms: *SA 1862*, pp. xcvii, c. For wealthier peasants one could use marriage contracts and probate records.

24. AD Calvados 2 C 1174 (1735). The forty-eight families were mostly *batteurs* (threshers) and *journaliers* (day laborers), but there were a few *domestiques* (servants), *fillassiers* (tow-dressers), and *bergers* (shepherds) as well. On average, they owned 0.02 hectares of land in Bretteville, rented 0.12 hectares, and paid 3.44 livres in taxes, which at average prices in nearby Caen over the years 1730–40 amounted to 0.41 hectoliters of wheat. As above, each family was assumed to require 14 hectoliters of wheat for food and to pay an 8 percent tithe. In the calculations, I considered a family with the average amount of land among the forty-eight: only 0.02 hectares owned and 0.12 rented. I took generous estimates of early-nineteenth-century yields (19.5 hectoliters per hectare) and seeding rates (2.1 hectoliters per hectare) from J. M. Pavard "Productions et rendements céréaliers à Cheux au début du XVIIe siècle," *Annales de Normandie* 26 (1976): 41–65. If yields were in fact lower, then my average family would have to purchase even more of its food. With these assumptions, if the average family paid rent equal to 25 percent of its crops on its rented land—a reasonable figure—then after deducting the rent, taxes, the tithe, and the seed, it would produce only 1.2 percent of its food. It probably grew some food in its garden and perhaps owned some land outside Bretteville, but if we compensate for this by ignoring the rent owed, the family would still produce only 2.4 percent of its food.

25. AD Puy-de-Dôme C 3148, C 3231. The tax roll here did understate peasants' assets, but it did so primarily for the richer peasants. For the poorer ones (including the fifteen families), it was more accurate and might even have exaggerated their wealth. In the words of the government's agent, if the roll were not revised, "the poor of the parish" would be "ruined and the big tenant farmer comforted." Cf. L. A. Sarrauste de Menthière, *La taille tarifée en Auvergne (1733–70)* (Aurillac, 1928), and for local agriculture, James Lowth Goldsmith, *Les Salers et les d'Escorailles: Seigneurs de Haute Auvergne, 1500–1789*, trans. Jacques Buttin (Clermont-Ferrand, 1984).

26. Hoffman, "Taxes and Agrarian Life."

27. Hoffman, "Taxes and Agrarian Life."

28. Le Roy Ladurie, "De la crise ultime à la vraie croissance," pp. 440, 595.

29. Mark R. Rosenzweig, "Labor Markets in Low-Income Countries," in *Handbook of Development Economics*, ed. Hollis Chenery and T. N. Srinivasan, 2 vols. (Amsterdam, 1988), 1:729–33; idem, "Determinants of Wage Rates and Labor

Supply Behavior in the Rural Sector of a Developing Country," in *Contractual Arrangements, Employment, and Wages in Rural Labor Markets in Asia*, ed. Hans P. Binswanger and Mark R. Rosenzweig (New Haven, 1984), pp. 211–41; Sicsic, "City-Farm Wages Gaps in Late Nineteenth-Century France"; Postel-Vinay and Weir, "Frenchmen into Peasants." For Old Regime evidence—most of it admittedly from the heavily commercialized Paris Basin—see Chapter 4, and Appendix A, parts 7 and 10.

30. For Chaionov's work and other similar models, see Frank Ellis, *Peasant Economics: Farm Households and Agrarian Development* (Cambridge, 1988), pp. 106–19. One could go a step further here and separate the peasant family's consumption decisions from the operation of their farm. Indeed, if one ignores problems of uncertainty and assumes that hired labor was a perfect substitute for family labor, then the existence of the labor market implies that the family's consumption decisions can be separated from the operation of their farm. The peasants can then be treated as profit maximizers or cost minimizers, even though their farm is a household operation. For a discussion and parallel evidence from developing countries such as India, see Rosenzweig, "Labor Markets in Low-Income Countries," pp. 729–33; and idem, "Determinants of Wage Rates." Obviously, there are some grave problems with such an approach. In the first place, it glosses over the enormous risks in agriculture, and it ignores the fact that family members required much less supervision than hired hands—issues that I discuss below. Still, it does seem reasonable to treat certain peasants as cost minimizers or profit maximizers—tenant farmers who paid a fixed rent for example—even though their farms were family enterprises. It is at least a good approximation, and it is one that has worked well in analogous situations in developing countries, even though direct tests of separability are as yet inconclusive. Cf. Newbery and Stiglitz, *Commodity Price Stabilization*.

31. Rozier, *Cours complet d'agriculture*, s.v. "Métairie." For the virtues of Rozier's treatise, see Meuvret, *Subsistances*, vol. 1, pt. 1 (*Texte*), pp. 62–63. Although walls about farms had long been common, Rozier's design pushed security farther than was perhaps customary before the eighteenth century. Cf. Moriceau, *Fermiers*, pp. 252–56.

32. For master-servant relations, see the excellent works—all concerned more with urban servants than rural ones—of Sarah C. Maza, *Servants and Masters in Eighteenth-Century France: The Uses of Loyalty* (Princeton, 1983); Cissie Fairchilds, *Domestic Enemies: Servants and Their Masters in Old Regime France* (Baltimore, 1984); and Jean-Pierre Gutton, *Domestiques et serviteurs dans la France de l'ancien régime* (Paris, 1981). For Bentham's Panopticon and Foucault's interpretation of its significance, see Jeremy Bentham, *Panopticon; or, the Inspection-house* (Dublin and London, 1791); and Michel Foucault, *Surveiller et punir; Naissance de la prison* (Paris, 1975).

33. In the 1701 edition of his *Oeconomie générale*, Louis Liger recommended, for instance, that farmers secretly watch over newly hired *charretiers* to see if they mistreated the horses; he also urged farm wives to supervise female servants lest they steal linen or flour: *Oeconomie générale*, 1:15–18, 23, 113–39, 160. Cf. Rozier, *Cours complet d'agriculture*, s.v. "Avoine," "Berger," "Foin," "Froment," and "Métairie"; and L. Rose, *La bonne fermière* (Lille, 1765), pp. 40–42, 47.

34. Charles Estienne, *L'agriculture et la maison rustique* (Paris, 1564), fol. 8; Olivier de Serres, *Le théâtre de l'agriculture* (Paris, 1600), pp. 45–50. The writers of agricultural treatises tended to borrow from one another, but the concern with servants is so widespread that it had to be more than mere repetition of what predecessors had said.

35. AD Calvados, F 1652, F 1697; Abbé Aubert, "Notes extraites de trois livres de raison de 1473 à 1550. Comptes d'une famille de gentilshommes campagnards normands," France. Comité des travaux historiques et scientifiques. Section de philologie et d'histoire. *Bulletin philologique et historique* (Paris, 1898), pp. 447–99. Some of their servants were probably not engaged in farm work—the *laquais* (footman) or the *cocher* (coachman) circa 1700 or a *fille de chambre* (chambermaid)—but the vast majority undoubtedly were.

36. A. Tollemer, *Un Sire de Gouberville: Gentilhomme campagnard au Cotentin de 1553 à 1562* (Paris, 1873; reprint, 1972), pp. xxii, 33, 611; AD Yvelines, 55 J 65, and B non-classé (Bailliage de Brétigny, pièces de greffe, 4 March 1753).

37. W. A. Armstrong, "Labour I: Rural Population Growth, Systems of Employment, and Incomes," *AHEW*, 6:674–75; Wunder, *Die bäuerliche Gemeinde*, p. 135; Gertrud Schröder-Lembke, ed., *Martin Grosser: Anleitung zu der Landwirtschaft: Abraham von Thumbshirn: Oeconomia: Zwei frühe deutsche Landwirtschaftsschriften*, Quellen und Forschungen zur Agrargeschichte, vol. 12 (Stuttgart, 1965), p. 67. Among biblical passages, perhaps the most striking is John 1:11–13. For the rarity of wage labor in agriculture today, see Cadger Otsuka, Hiroyuki Chuma, and Yujiro Hayami, "Land and Labor Contracts in Agrarian Economies: Theories and Facts," *Journal of Economic Literature* 30 (1992): 1974.

38. Jean-Pierre Poussou, "Mobilité et migrations," in Dupâquier, ed., *Histoire de la population française*, vol. 2, pp. 99–143; James Collins, "Geographic and Social Mobility in Early-Modern France," *Journal of Social History* 24, no. 3 (1991): 563–77; Jacques Béaud and Georges Bouchart, "Le dépôt des pauvres de Saint-Denis (1768–1792)," *Annales de démographie historique* (1974): 127–43.

39. Tessier, *Agriculture*, s.v. "Affanures," "Berger," "Chanvre"; Rozier, *Cours complet d'agriculture*, s.v. "Berger"; Liger, *Nouvelle maison rustique*, 1:456–57. Similar problems would presumably have arisen had farmers in early modern France been able to force labor from large numbers of serfs, as in eastern Europe. The serfs would still need supervision; and with more cities in France than in eastern Europe, they might have found escape relatively easy.

40. What follows was inspired by the pattern of wages I found in the Cairon *livres de raison* and other sources. For a formal model of what I describe, see W. Bentley MacLeod and James M. Malcomson, "Reputation and Hierarchy in Dynamic Models of Employment," *Journal of Political Economy* 96 (1988): 832–54.

41. AD Calvados, F 1652. Often the wages above food and lodging came in the form of grain or services instead of coins. But the grain or services (say, plowing the servant's own land) were always converted into a cash equivalent, like many other dealings in the local economy. It should be noted that the Cairon family was in no way exceptional in paying a cash wage in addition to board. Many other farmers did the same, from minor nobles like the Cairon to *laboureurs*; for examples, see Charbonnier, *Une autre France*, 2:804–7, 1089–1106; Edouard Frain de la Gaulayrie,

Un rural de la baronnie de Vitré. Son journal domestique de 1634 à 1671 (Vannes, 1895); Tollemer, *Un Sire de Gouberville*, pp. 28–31, 34, 38; and Moriceau and Postel-Vinay, *Ferme, entreprise, famille*, pp. 251–53. Indeed, although historians have debated whether urban domestics earned a wage—for the debate, see Maza, *Servants and Masters*, pp. 7–20—they generally admit that rural servants were wage earners. See, for instance, Gutton, *Domestiques et serviteurs*, p. 101.

42. Gutton, *Domestiques et serviteurs*, pp. 114–15.

43. Rozier, *Cours complet d'agriculture*, s.v. "Métairie"; Rétif de la Bretonne, *La vie de mon père*, p. 131. Cf. Liger, *Oeconomie générale*, pp. 15–18.

44. AD Yvelines, 55 J 65; Tollemer, *Un Sire de Gouberville*, pp. 28–33; Gutton, *Domestiques et serviteurs*, pp. 103–7, 119. Some of servants of course quit when they married. Local *ordonnances* in the early eighteenth century made it clear that employers could sue servants if they quit before the end of their term, but enforcing the *ordonnances* was extremely difficult.

45. AD Calvados, F 1652, F 1697. I was not able to consult the family's sixteenth-century *livres de raison*, which are in private hands, but they have been excerpted in Abbé Aubert, "Notes extraites de trois livres de raison de 1473 à 1550."

46. Wages were lower for women, higher in summer, and varied with a person's strength and skill. Raises also were affected by the distance to a servant's home. The 31 percent figure here takes into account these differences; it does so via a hedonic wage regression, which demonstrates that the raise was not likely to be a chance result. For details see Appendix D. In Appendix D, I also consider the effect of changes in the wages in the labor market as a whole and address the argument— once common in development economics—that rural wages were rigid and institutionally set.

47. AD Calvados, F 1652.

48. See Appendix D.

49. Gutton, *Domestiques et serviteurs*, pp. 104–5.

50. See Appendix D.

51. Moriceau and Postel-Vinay, *Ferme, entreprise, famille*, pp. 230–31, 245–51, 319. The strategies employed by the tenant farmers north of Paris and by the Cairon were not identical, though, for on average the wages of local servants in Bretteville were no higher than those of servants hired from afar. If one could single out the servants from families that dealt with the Cairon repeatedly, then one could see if these servants were actually the ones who escaped the ordeal of the raise. The test would simply be to see if they (rather than local servants in general) were the ones whose wages stayed the same when they remained with the Cairon. Unfortunately, it is impossible to tell if a family dealt repeatedly with the Cairon. One can note the last names of families that provided numerous servants and the names of families whose other dealings with the Cairon were noted in the family journals, and for what it is worth, a statistical test suggests that such families did not benefit from special treatment. The problem, though, is that singling out such families is not a reliable way to get at repeated dealings and trust, for many families had the same last names and many dealings never figured in the journal.

52. Georges Durand, *Le patrimoine foncier de l'Hôtel-Dieu de Lyon (1482– 1791)* (Lyon, 1974), p. 349.

53. Gutton, *Domestiques et serviteurs*, p. 103; Paul Bastid, *De la fonction so-*

ciale des communautés taisibles de l'ancien droit (Tours, 1916); M. Lugnier, "Les communautés familiales à Roche du XVe siècle à nos jours," *Bulletin de la Diana* 31 (1948): 205–27; Meuvret, *Subsistances*, vol. 1, pt. 1 (*Texte*), pp. 173–85; vol. 2, pt. 1 (*Texte*), pp. 116–18. One other strategy that could be used with servants was to pay them a high wage; they would then presumably work assiduously to avoid being fired. For such a recommendation, see C.J.A. Mathieu de Dombasle, *Annales agricoles de Roville*, 2e édition, livraisons 1–7 (Paris, 1828–39), 2:182–83. Although the indeterminacies of the in-kind pay make it impossible to see if this strategy was used by the Cairon and other agricultural employers, it seems unlikely, for it is hard to reconcile with the large number of servants who quit to move elsewhere.

54. See Gutton, *Domestiques et serviteurs*, pp. 106–7; Fairchilds, *Domestic Enemies*; and especially Maza, *Servants and Masters*, pp. 12–20.

55. Otsuka, Chuma, and Hayami, "Land and Labor Contracts in Agrarian Economies." For the tax system and absentee ownership, see Hoffman, "Taxes and Agrarian Life in Early Modern France."

56. De Serres, *Théâtre de l'agriculture*, pp. 46–47, 53. See also Estienne, *L'agriculture et la maison rustique*, fols. 8–9; and the examples in AN S 273 (La Grande-Paroisse, 1730), and in Philip T. Hoffman, "The Economic Theory of Sharecropping."

57. AN S 247 (1693); LL 337–38 fol. 236–37 (1747); AD Loire-Atlantique, H 275 (1710); *L'art d'augmenter son bien ou règles générales pour l'administration d'une terre* (Amsterdam-Paris, 1784); Rozier, *Cours complet d'agriculture*, s.v. "Bail"; Meuvret, *Subsistances*, vol. 2, pt. 1 (*Texte*), pp. 142–44; Hoffman, "Land Rents and Agricultural Productivity." In 1544, Aymard Nicolaÿ, the *premier président* of the *Chambre de comptes* in Paris, had to leave Paris and undertake a costly journey to Bourg-Saint-Andéol in southeastern France because his tenant had failed to pay Nicolaÿ's salt tax. Nicolaÿ's house in Bourg-Saint-Andéol was seized, forcing Nicolaÿ to sue the tenant and his guarantors in court. Obviously, the tenant here did more than just farm Nicolaÿ's farm property near Bourg-Saint-Andéol, but the principle is the same: Arthur de Boislisle, *Histoire de la maison de Nicolaÿ: Redigée et publiée sous les auspices de M. Le Marquis de Nicolaÿ*, vol. 1: *Titres, correspondances et pièces diverses* (Nogent-le-Rotrou, 1875), pp.176–77. For similar concerns in England and Germany, see J. B. Beckett, "Landownership and Estate Management," *AHEW*, 6:610, 615–17; Schröder-Lembke, *Zwei frühe deutsche Landwirtschaftsschriften*, p. 67.

58. AN LL 337–38 fol. 236–37 (1747); Boislisle, *Histoire de la maison de Nicolaÿ*, 1:176–77.

59. AN LL337–338, s.v. "Orliaco/Orly" (1748); S 154 (26 September 1493); Rozier, *Cours complet d'agriculture*, s.v. "Bail"; Estienne, *L'agriculture et la maison rustique*, fols. 8–9; *L'art d'augmenter son bien*; Tessier, s.v. "Bail"; Boislisle, *Histoire de la maison de Nicolaÿ*, 1:215–16.

60. AD Calvados F 1700, 11 October 1750.

61. The Abbé Tessier, quoted in Meuvret, *Subsistances*, vol. 2, pt. 2 (*Notes*), pp. 182–83.

62. Tessier, quoted in Meuvret, *Subsistances*, vol. 2, pt. 2 (*Notes*), p. 183; see also ibid., vol. 2, pt. 1 (*Texte*), pp. 142–44. For the difficulties of finding such tenants in a region devastated by war, see AN S 154 (26 September 1493).

63. AN K 906, no. 36 (26 December 1760). One issue I shall not deal with here is the identity of landlords who owned the small plots. Whether the owners were peasants or the privileged would not affect my story, but it is a subject that deserves further research.

64. François-René Isambert et al., *Recueil général des anciennes lois françaises depuis l'an 420 jusqu'à la Révolution*, 29 vols. (Paris, 1821–33), 18:171 (Ordonnance touchant la justice civile, April 1667, titre XXXIII, article 16); Moriceau, *Fermiers*, pp. 554, 582. I have benefited here from Jean-Marc Moriceau's discussion of my initial argument about the risk premium (in Hoffman, "Land Rents") and his comments on the peculiarities of the *coutume de Paris* here.

65. Moriceau, *Fermiers*, p. 582, found that defaults were more likely on small plots.

66. Ernest Labrousse, *Esquisse du mouvement des prix et des revenus en France au XVIIIe siècle*, 2 vols. (Paris, 1933; reprint, Paris, 1984), 1:149–56, 176–220, 2:513–41; Michel Morineau, "Budgets populaires en France au XVIIIe siècle," in *Pour une histoire économique vraie* (Lille, 1985), pp. 197–239; Weir, "Life Under Pressure," p. 36; E. A. Wrigley and R. S. Schofield, *The Population History of England 1541–1871: A Reconstruction* (Cambridge, 1989), pp. 319, 639.

67. AN K 906, no. 36.

68. Lefebvre, *Paysans du Nord*, pp. 60–69, 103–6, 111–14, 274–83. Cf. Grantham, "Agricultural Supply during the Industrial Revolution"; Béaur, *Le marché foncier à la veille de la Révolution*, pp. 263–64; Postel-Vinay, *La rente foncière*, pp. 35–54; Jacquart, *La crise rurale*, p. 132; idem, "La rente foncière, indice conjoncturel?" *Revue historique* 514 (1975): 355–76; Hugues Neveux, *Vie et déclin d'une structure économique: Les grains du Cambrésis (fin du XIVe–début du XVIIe siècle)* (Paris, 1980), pp. 45–49; Meuvret, *Subsistances*, vol. 2, pt. 2 (*Notes*), pp. 187–88; Moriceau, *Fermiers*, pp. 107–18; and Scott, *The Moral Economy*, pp. 13–15. For Pierre Saint-Jacob, land hunger in Burgundy derived from the growing practice of leasing land in large consolidated plots to large-scale *fermiers*: *Les paysans de la Bourgogne*, pp. 435–38.

69. A *droit de marché* did exist in certain areas north of Paris: see Postel-Vinay, *La rente foncière*, pp. 44–49, 255–57; and Jean Vinchon, *Le livre de raison d'une famille picarde: Les Vinchon (1488–1947)* (Doullens, 1948), pp. 36–37, 98–103. But it was largely unknown throughout much of the rest of the basin, and even to the north of Paris it was hardly universal. See Jacquart, "La rente foncière," p. 375. It may well have grown up in areas that were far from Paris and less commercialized: Moriceau and Postel-Vinay, *Ferme, entreprise, famille*, p. 321.

70. The sources include the index, AN LL 319–350/351, and the original leases, property descriptions, and land-management records, AN S123–462. Jean-Paul Desaive was first to use AN LL 319–350/51 as a source for leases: "A la recherche d'un indicateur de la conjoncture: Baux de Notre-Dame de Paris et de l'abbaye de Montmartre," in *Fluctuations du produit de la dîme*, ed. Goy and Le Roy Ladurie, pp. 44–57. I have gone over this index myself, and I have also consulted all of the corresponding original documents in AN S123–462. For the eighteenth-century archivist, see Léon Le Grand, "Claude Sarasin, intendant des archives du chapitre de Notre-Dame de Paris et sa collection d'extraits des registres capitulaires de Notre-Dame," *La bibliographie moderne* 4 (1900): 333–71.

71. For a detailed account of how I treated seigneurial dues, *contre-lettres*, rent understatement, *charges*, in-kind payments, *pots-de-vin*, and a host of related problems, see Appendix A, part 1. Cf. Jacquart, "La rente foncière"; Béaur, *Le marché foncier*, pp. 231–46; and Moriceau, *Fermiers*, pp. 37–38.

72. See Chapter 4 and Hoffman, "Land Rents and Agricultural Productivity." All averages here are calculated by counting each lease separately. Weighting each property by its area would not change the results appreciably.

73. Here, readers unversed in statistics may wish to consult a historical work that uses regression, such as Kathryn Norberg's *Rich and Poor in Grenoble, 1600–1814* (Berkeley, 1985), or a simple text, such as Michael S. Lewis-Beck, *Applied Regression: An Introduction* (Beverly Hills, Calif., 1980). The point to keep in mind is that the size of the regression coefficient measures the strength of the relationship between the explanatory variable and the dependent variable, which in this case is the logarithm of the rent. The t statistic or t ratio is simply a measure of the precision with which we can estimate the relationship.

74. Besides surface area, the relevant property characteristics in the regression included soil quality; presence of natural meadow and vineyard, as meadow was scarce and vineyards entailed capital investment; and distance from Paris, which measured the costs of transportation to the major market in the region. Ideally, one would want to have in the regressions a measure of the cost of shipping crops to Paris by the cheapest means available—overland for properties close to Paris, and by river for more distant properties, where the economies of river transport overtook the added costs of shipping crops to a river port and then loading them onto boats. For our properties, however, the shipping costs, as is shown in Appendix A, part 2, were nearly perfectly correlated with simple distance. The regression also included dummy variables for the devastating war years of the League and its immediate aftermath, for the late eighteenth century, when rents seemed to rise, and for repeat tenants, in order to capture the market power of tenant dynasties who would presumably depress the rent; and a time trend, to capture the effects of inflation and changing prices. Using actual prices rather than the time trend is an obvious alternative, but it leads to similar results. Multicollinearity rules out including both variables in the regression.

75. The variable that captures the effects of agricultural prices and the costs of the factors of production other than land is a ratio P/C, where P is a geometric index of the prices of agricultural products weighted by their shares in total revenue and C is a geometric index of the costs of the other factors of production weighted by their factor shares. For an explanation, see Chapter 4; Appendix A, part 5; and Hoffman, "Land Rents and Agricultural Productivity."

76. Admittedly, what might be happening here is that newcomers are only taking over the leases when the old tenants go bankrupt and no one wishes to rent the farm. Market power could then exist (at least until it was destroyed by hard times), yet we would observe no rent increase when the newcomers took over. In that case, however, we would be able to detect rent increases when newcomers took over in good times, when there were few bankruptcies. Restricting the regression to such a period—say to the years after 1725—should then yield different results, but the coefficients turn out to be little changed.

77. Jean-Marc Moriceau, "Un système de protection sociale efficace: Exemple

des vieux fermiers de l'Ile-de-France (XVIIe–début XIXe siècle)," *Annales de démographie historique* (1985), pp. 127–44; idem, *Fermiers*, pp. 107–18, 145–75, 557–78; Moriceau and Postel-Vinay, *Ferme, entreprise, famille*, pp. 97, 112–18, 280–81. Those tenants who did linger were probably the best, retained by the landlord for their mutual benefit.

78. AN S 242 (12 November 1753, 17 March 1761, and 3 February 1762). Like Thezzier, the anonymous author of *L'art d'augmenter son bien* advised keeping old tenants from learning the identity of their replacements, but he, too, did not mention threats or *mauvais gré*.

79. If we regress the change in the logarithm of the rent on a constant and the change in the logarithm of the village population, the coefficient of ln(population change) has a t statistic of 2.09 ($n = 16$) for the period from the 1720s to the 1780s, and 1.41 ($n = 14$) for the period from the 1710s to the 1780s. The first number is significant at conventional levels (a one-sided test yields $p < 0.05$), but the second is not. The rents here are corrected for location, land type, and soil fertility using the method outlined in Chapter 4. The population figures are averages of the reliable figures available for each decade; they are taken from Jacques Dupâquier, *Statistiques démographiques du bassin parisien, 1636–1720* (Paris, 1977); Dupâquier et al., *Paroisses et communes de France: Dictionnaire d'histoire administrative et démographique: Région parisienne* (Paris, 1974); and Marie Le Mée-Orsette and René Le Mée, *Paroisses et communes de France: Dictionnaire d'histoire administrative et démographique: Seine-et-Marne* (Paris, 1988).

80. For the sources here, see Appendix B, part 2.

81. On the Provençal farm of the Sacristie near Avignon, rent increases were actually higher when older tenants retained the lease. The sample only contains eleven leases, but it is hard to reconcile with tenant market power. For the sources used, see Appendix B, part 2.

82. Gérard Béaur, "Prezzo della terra, congiuntura e società alla fine del XVIII secolo: L'esempio di un mercato della Beauce," *Quaderni storici* 65 (1987): 530–31; Guyot, "Essai sur l'aisance relative du paysan lorrain," p. 81.

83. The evidence here comes from two samples of land sales (one from Albi and one from Grillon in the Vaucluse) and two samples that combine leases and sales (one from Cavaillon and the other from Troarn in Normandy). The samples of sales are described in Appendix B, part 2, while the samples of sales and leases were generously furnished by Jean-Laurent Rosenthal, who describes them in his *Fruits of Revolution*, pp. 180–89. For the samples with sales alone, I regressed the logarithm of the sales price on variables like those in table 3.1. For the Albi sample, the coefficient of the logarithm of area, –0.02, was small and essentially indistinguishable from 0 ($t = -0.23$ with 36 degrees of freedom). For Grillon, on the other hand, it was sizable (–0.33) and significantly different from 0 ($t = -3.79$ with 106 degrees of freedom). Near Grillon, therefore, tiny parcels did sell for more, while near Albi they did not. Grillon was an area where sellers frequently provided mortgages; cf. Baehrel, *Une croissance*, 1:600–602. For the samples from Cavaillon and Troarn, I pooled the evidence from sales and leases by multiplying the sales prices by the interest rate. I then ran regressions like those in table 3.1, adding a dummy variable for leases and an interaction term between the dummy variable and the logarithm of the property area. I could thus calculate the relationship between area and per hec-

tare prices separately for leases and sales. For Troarn, both rental and sales prices rose on little parcels, and there was essentially no difference between rentals and sales ($t = 0.46$ with 280 degrees of freedom). Seller mortgages were common in Troarn as well. In Cavaillon, on the other hand, rental prices rose much more sharply than sales prices on tiny plots. The elasticity of the price to the area was only -0.12 for sales and -0.28 for leases, a difference that was highly significant ($t = -2.88$ with 724 degrees of freedom).

84. For England, see Armstrong, "Labour I," *AHEW*, 6: 667. Greg Clark (private communication) has found both higher rents and sales prices on little parcels in England, a relationship that he attributes to a correlation between size and land quality. Such a relationship would imply, however, that sales prices would always be higher on small properties.

85. See also the evidence in Appendix B, part 2. Jean Meuvret has suggested that the short leases in France may have kept mauvais gré at bay in many regions: see his *Subsistances*, vol. 2, pt. 2 (*Notes*), pp. 187–88.

86. AN S 242 (1754–62); S 282 (1746); LL 332 (Larchand, 1762); LL 348–49 (Viersy, 1757).

87. AN LL 329–30 (La Grande-Paroisse, 1618); LL 350–51, fol. 122–24 (Viry, 1761). The example of the posters concerns renting out tithe rights, but posters were used when renting land, too.

88. Moriceau and Postel-Vinay, *Ferme, entreprise, famille*, pp. 280–81.

89. AN S 247 (1693); *L'art d'augmenter son bien*; Rozier, s.v. "Bail."

90. Tessier, *Agriculture*, s.v. "Bail."

91. For examples from other parts of France, see AD Vaucluse, 1 G 611; Jacques Peret, *Seigneurs et seigneuries en Gâtine poitevine: Le duché de la Meilleraye, XVIIe–XVIIIe siècles* (Poitiers, 1976), pp. 175–77.

92. Moriceau, *Fermiers*, pp. 515–16.

93. When his nine-year lease of the farm of Villeroche was renewed in 1724, *fermier* Pierre Vizier offered to split the cost of a new barn with the cathedral. In the aftermath of the Hundred Years' War, cooperation on long-term investments was encouraged by rent reductions and by long leases. In 1483, for example, Notre Dame offered to cut the rent on the Villeroche farm by 1 *setier* of wheat for each *arpent* that tenant Guillot David cleared when he entered into an eighteen-year lease: AN LL 348–49, fols. 190–241 (1724); S 409 (2 June 1483).

94. J. B. Beckett, "Landownership and Estate Management," *AHEW*, 6:615–17. In Lorraine, leases did allow for rent reductions in cases of disasters beyond the tenant's control. To avoid problems of moral hazard, though, the tenant still had to shoulder all the losses up to a certain point: Charles Guyot, *Histoire d'un domaine rural en Lorraine* (Nancy, 1887), pp. 32–33.

95. Otsuka, Chuma, Hayami, "Land and Labor Contracts in Agrarian Economies," p. 1995.

96. Hoffman, "Taxes and Agrarian Life," pp. 42–43; Louis Guibert et al., *Livres de raison, registres de famille et journaux individuels limousins et marchois* (Paris-Limoges, 1888), pp. 370–85. Cf. Bloch, *French Rural History*, pp. 124–26.

97. Durand, *Le patrimoine foncier de l'Hôtel-Dieu*, pp. 204–9.

98. Isambert, *Recueil général des anciennes lois*, 14:401–2 (Ordonnance de Blois, May 1579, article 79); Moriceau, *Fermiers*, pp. 107–18.

99. Tessier, *Agriculture*, s.v. "Bail"; Meuvret, *Subsistances*, vol. 2, pt. 1 (*Texte*), pp. 137–47; vol. 2, pt. 2 (*Notes*), pp. 176–88.

100. Allen, *Enclosure and the Yeoman*, pp. 68–72, 78–85, 230–31; Peter Bowden, "Agricultural Prices, Farm Profits, and Rents," *AHEW*, 4:675, 684–89; idem, "Agricultural Prices, Wages, Farm Profits and Rents, 1640–1750," *CAHEW*, 1:262–69; J. B. Beckett, "Landownership and Estate Management," *AHEW*, 6:611–12.

101. De Serres, *Théâtre de l'agriculture*, pp. 46–48, 53.

102. Another possibility here—prepayment of the rent—seems never to have occurred, perhaps because of the burdens it would have imposed on tenants.

103. Bloch, *French Rural History*, pp. 125, 146–48; Jean Jacquart, "Immobilisme et catastrophes: 1560–1660," *HFR*, 2:230–31; Louis Merle, *La métairie et l'évolution agraire de la Gâtine poitevine de la fin du Moyen Age à la Revolution* (Paris, 1958), pp. 176–85; Tessier, *Agriculture*, s.v. "Bail."

104. What follows is taken from formal models in Otsuka, Chuma, and Hayami, "Land and Labor Contracts in Agrarian Economies"; and Jean-Jacques Laffont and Mohamed Salah Matoussi, "Moral Hazard, Financial Constraints and Sharecropping in El Oulja," Social Science Working Paper 667, California Institute of Technology, Pasadena, California, March, 1988. Cf. Joseph E. Stiglitz, "Economic Organization, Information, and Development," pp. 93–160; and Meuvret, *Subsistances*, vol. 2, pt. 1 (*Texte*): 153–54. The models make landlords the principals and tenants (or wage laborers) the agents. The landlords choose an optimal contract for tenants (from a finite dimensional set of possibilities), given that they cannot observe the tenants' effort. The Otsuka, Chuma, and Hayami model relies on the trade-off with risk aversion; the Laffont and Matoussi model, on financial constraints facing the tenant. For more on sharecropping, including excellent work by economic historians such as Lee J. Alston, Robert Higgs, and Joseph Reid, see my two articles: "Sharecropping and Investment in Agriculture in Early Modern France," *JEH* 42 (1982): 155–59, and "The Economic Theory of Sharecropping."

105. This holds for the sample of rental, share, and wage labor contracts from the Lyonnais described in Hoffman, "Economic Theory of Sharecropping." It is true as well of rental and sharecropping contracts in the village of Grillon in the Vaucluse.

106. Newbery and Stiglitz, *Commodity Price Stabilization*, pp. 96–110, 164–65. For rural credit markets, see below and also Jean-Laurent Rosenthal, "Credit Markets and Economic Change in southeastern France 1630–1788," *Explorations in Economic History* 30 (1993): 129–57.

107. Rétif de la Bretonne, *La vie de mon père*, pp. 83–84.

108. For examples from various parts of France and from the fifteenth century to the eighteenth, see AD Loire-Atlantique, 4E XXIX 34 (26 December 1728, 14 April 1729); AD Vaucluse, 3 E 72, Etude Petit à Valréas, nos. 18, 19, 23 (1588–91, 1599–1600); Guibert, *Livres de raison*, pp. 93–97, 114, 125, 302–20; Louis de Santi and Auguste Vidal, eds., *Deux livres de raison (1517–1550) avec des notes et une introduction sur les conditions agricoles et commerciales de l'Albigeois au XVIe siècle* (Paris, 1896), p. 211; Hoffman, "Economic Theory of Sharecropping," pp. 316–17; Meuvret, *Subsistances*, vol. 2, pt. 2 (*Texte*), p. 156.

109. Laffont and Matoussi, "Moral Hazard, Financial Constraints and Sharecropping."

110. Hoffman, "Economic Theory of Sharecropping."

111. De Serres, *Théâtre de l'agriculture*, pp. 47–50; Meuvret, *Subsistances*, vol. 2, pt. 1 (*Texte*), p. 150.

112. The evidence here comes from a logit model of contract choice detailed in Hoffman, "Economic Theory of Sharecropping," which also describes the sample of leases. Though the sample is small, the results are not likely to be statistical flukes: the relevant logit coefficients all pass the appropriate one-tailed significance tests at the 6 percent level, and most do so at the 3 percent level. For impressionistic evidence of the same sort from the Beaujolais, see Durand, *Vin, vigne et vignerons*, p. 483.

113. See Hoffman, "Economic Theory of Sharecropping"; idem, "Taxes and Agrarian Life."

114. Tessier, *Agriculture*, s.v. "Bail"; Young, *Voyages en France*, 2:606–7, 736; AD Gers, C 357 (1780); BM Avignon, Fonds Chobaut, ms. 5951; Le Roy Ladurie, *French Peasantry*, pp. 339–46; Jacquart, "Immobilisme et catastrophes," pp. 440–41.

115. Otsuka, Chuma, and Hayami, "Land and Labor Contracts in Agrarian Economies," pp. 2005–10. Productivity growth was also rapid in the southeastern village of Grillon in the sixteenth century, although sharecropping was quite common at the time. For Grillon and the examples of the Beaujolais and the Albigeois, see Chapter 4. One theoretical reason why sharecropping leads to little allocational inefficiency is that landlords can choose the appropriate contract on the basis of their comparative advantage in monitoring.

116. AD Calvados, F 1652, F 1697. Cf. Tollemer, *Un Sire de Gouberville*, pp. 28, 34, 38; Frain de la Gaulayrie, *Un rural de la baronnie de Vitré*; de Santi and Vidal, *Deux livres de raison*, p. 209; Gutton, *Domestiques et serviteurs*, pp. 112–13.

117. AD Calvados, F 1697, fol. 14. For other examples of the conversion of in-kind or share rent to cash, see Guibert et al., *Livres de raison*, pp. 96–97, 302–20, 426–34; and the discussion of how Notre Dame evaluated in-kind dues in Appendix A, parts 1 and 8.

118. Near Bretteville, in the village of Rots, there were 120 *journaliers* on the highly detailed 1740 tax role. They owned fifty-six horses whose services were at least in part rented out. The same was true in other nearby villages. See AD Calvados, 2 C 1317 (1740), 2 C 1191 (1740), 2 C 1193 (1740), and 2 C 1345 (1740).

119. AD Calvados, F 1697, fols. 29–30.

120. Frain de la Gaulayrie, *Un rural de la baronnie de Vitré*, pp. 9–14; Guibert et al., *Livres de raison*, pp. 427–28; Tollemer, *Un Sire de Gouberville*, pp. 28, 34; Gutton, *Domestiques et serviteurs*, pp. 112–13; Meuvret, *Subsistances*, vol. 2, pt. 1 (*Texte*), p. 160; vol. 2, pt. 2 (*Notes*), pp. 199–200; vol. 3, pt. 2 (*Notes*), p. 96.

121. AD Vaucluse, 3 E 72, nos. 18–23; Roland Sicard, *Paroisses et communes de France. Dictionnaire d'histoire administrative et démographique. Vaucluse* (Paris, 1987). Notaries in neighboring communities undoubtedly registered additional loans. Cf. Rosenthal, "Credit Markets and Economic Change in Southeastern France." For the use of obligations to consolidate debts or when borrowers fell in arrears, see Moriceau and Postel-Vinay, *Ferme, entreprise, famille*, pp. 222–23; and AD Pas de Calais, 4 E 58/15 (7 May 1772).

122. Aubert, "Notes extraites de trois livres de raison de 1473 à 1550," pp. 463–66; Meuvret, *Subsistances*, vol. 2, pt. 1 (*Texte*), pp. 159–65; vol. 3, pt. 1 (*Texte*), pp. 159–62; de Santi and Vidal, *Deux livres de raison*, p. 108.

123. For the *inventaires après décès*, see note 10. One of the *inventaires* is from 1545, and the rest are from the years 1669–1740. Of the 493 livres of debt in the average *inventaire*, only 134 livres on average was for *rentes, obligations*, or endorsable promissory notes (*billets de commerce*). The rest was informal, including debts to landlords. Similarly, only 13 livres of the 82 livres credit due the estates was formal. I have counted family debts as informal credit here.

124. AN S 468 (14 June 1740); S 474. Lending, it should be stressed, was not peculiar to the Paris Basin or Normandy. It was common even in the most remote corners of the kingdom. For examples, see Jean-Charles Rivière, "Economie et société en Barèges au XVIIIe siècle," *Lavedan et pays Toy* 5 (1978–79): 106–15; Claverie and Lamaison, *L'impossible mariage*, pp. 46–47, 113–15.

125. What follows is taken from the model in Dan Bernhardt, "Money and Loans," *Review of Economic Studies* 56 (1989): 89–100. Although Bernhardt's is not the only model applicable here, it does focus precisely on the sort of credit that facilitated trade in the local economy. It also explains why that sort of credit would not operate in larger economies.

126. The conditions here involve, among other things, the nature of utility functions, the size of the economy, and the discount rate that households use to evaluate the gains from trading in the future. I also make the reasonable assumption that there were some costs to relocating, so that a borrower could not simply default and then move on to do the same in other villages.

127. Here a game theorist would probably prefer a much more careful definition of reputation. He would want to reformulate our model of the local economy in a way that would make explicit what villagers learned through their past dealings with one another. The typical way of doing so is to imagine the villagers divided into two types. Each type of villager faces a different set of payoffs or incentives, and each type is thus associated with a different sort of behavior. One type, for example, may face the typical incentives that any villager would, while the others may be wedded to a particular sort of behavior. In the resulting model, villagers eventually learn one another's types and style of play through their dealings with one another. Unfortunately, such a reformulation, which reduces villagers to two types, seems terribly simplistic. It does not really seem to make previous dealings any more important than they already are in the original model, and, most important of all, it does nothing to limit the enormous number of possible equilibria, because the game has many long-run players. For a discussion, see Drew Fudenberg and Jean Tirole, *Game Theory* (Cambridge, 1991), pp. 368–95.

128. Cf. Hoffman, Postel-Vinay, and Rosenthal, "Private Credit Markets"; Norberg, *Rich and Poor in Grenoble*, pp. 46–48; Thomas Brennan, *Public Drinking and Popular Culture in Eighteenth-Century Paris* (Princeton, 1988), pp. 70–71; Elizabeth S. Cohen, "Honor and Gender in the Streets of Early Modern Rome," *Journal of Interdisciplinary History* 22 (1992): 597–625. For anthropological views, see J. G. Peristiany, ed., *Honour and Shame: The Values of Mediterranean Society* (Chicago, 1966), and J. G. Peristiany and Julian Pitt-Rivers, eds., *Honor and Grace in Anthropology* (Cambridge, 1992). For the evolution of the French and

English words for credit, see Alain Rey, ed., *Dictionnaire historique de la langue française* (Paris, 1992), s.v. "Crédit"; and the *Oxford English Dictionary*, s.v. "Credit."

129. John Bossy, *Christianity in the West, 1400–1700* (Oxford, 1985), p. 169.

130. Rétif de la Bretonne, *La vie de mon père*, pp. 79, 88, 129; Tessier, *Agriculture*, s.v. "Cheval."

131. What follows is based on a number of criminal and civil court records, including AD Rhône, 3 B 502 (Bailliage de Beaujolais, plaintes criminelles, 1604–23); 10 G 2808 (Justice de Saint-Genis-Laval, 1524–1774); AD Yvelines, B non-classé (Bailliage de Brétigny, liasses 85–105, pièces de greffe, 1615–1790); and AD Cantal 7 B 189 and 7 B 200 (Bailliage de Vic, dossiers criminels, 1584–1666 and 1776–78).

132. AD Yvelines, B non-classé (Bailliage de Brétigny-sur-Oise, pièces de greffe [henceforth AD Yvelines, B Brétigny], liasse 86 [18 July to 29 August, 1619]).

133. AD Rhône, 10 G 2808 (25 June, 1601).

134. AD Yvelines, B Brétigny, liasse 87 (14 April 1624).

135. In Bernhardt's model there is a continuum of sequential equilibria. Changes in other conditions—in the discount rate, for instance—could eliminate cooperation altogether. Cooperation would diminish, too, with other modifications of the model—introducing noise so that it is no longer clear whether a default was willful or so that players could make mistakes. With noise, strategies would change as well, shifting to punishment of limited duration.

136. AD Cantal, 7 B 189 (11 March 1661). For other examples of soured relationships between masters and servants, see AD Yvelines, B, Brétigny, liasse, 99 (24 December 1712: having been paid in advance, Antoine Feraud's household servants loot his country home while he is in Paris); and AD Rhône, 10 G 2808 (2 April 1602: a maidservant is beaten when she asks for her wages).

137. AD Yvelines, B, Brétigny, liasse 89 (22 September 1630). If Brétigny's seigneur did cheat Briberon, it may have been motivated by financial problems he faced.

138. AD Rhône, 3 B 502 (18 August 1620). Rabbin may have been closer to a *fermier-général* than to a tenant farmer, but the document and the opinion of local *laboureurs* does not permit a clear distinction.

139. Polanyi, *The Great Transformation*; Marcel Mauss, *The Gift: Forms and Functions of Exchange in Archaic Societies*, trans. Ian Cunnison (New York, 1967); Sahlins, *Stone Age Economics*. For examples of the use of such sources in history and political science, see Levi, *Inheriting Power*, pp. 66–99, 181–85; Scott, *The Moral Economy*, pp. 5, 9, 167–70. For the debate over colonial New England, see Gordon S. Wood, "Inventing American Capitalism," *New York Review of Books* 41, no. 11 (June 9, 1994): 44–49, which discusses works by such authors such as James Henretta and Winifred Rothenberg.

140. For one example from a burgeoning literature, see Olga Linares, *Power, Prayer, and Production: The Jola of Casamance, Senegal* (Cambridge, 1992). I wish to thank Ted Scudder for this reference. For additional problems with historians' borrowing from anthropology, see John W. Adams, "Anthropology and History in the 1980s," *Journal of Interdisciplinary History* 12 (1981): 253–65.

141. Cf. Sahlins, *Stone Age Economics*, pp. 149–280; Polanyi, *The Great Transformation*, pp. 43–55; and Annette B. Weiner, *Inalienable Possessions: The Paradox of Keeping-While-Giving* (Berkeley, 1992).

142. Bossy, *Christianity in the West*.

143. Cf. Chapter 2 and Sabean, *Power in the Blood*.

144. Ronald Coase, "The Nature of the Firm," *Economica* 4 (1937): 386–405.

145. The calculations exclude debts to absentee landlords. They are based upon the sample of notarial records from Grillon and the sample of death inventories from La Grande-Paroisse, both of which are discussed above. In Brétigny, the credit extended by a local épicier was equally limited: AD Yvelines, B Brétigny (7 November 1775).

146. In La Grande-Paroisse, for example, the *laboureur* Bonnaventure Langlois purchased livestock at considerable distance (22 kilometers) and then sold it on credit to local *laboureurs* and *voituriers*: AN S 474A (12 October 1684).

147. In a study of an Italian village, Giovanni Levi discovered that the sales price of land was low when the buyer lived outside the village, high when he came from the village, and higher still when he belonged to the seller's own family. Levi has his own explanation for the pattern involving "ties of dependence" that linked villagers and outsiders. But several economic explanations are just as plausible. Among them might be the difficulties of determining the quality of land. Locals might be able to determine the quality of land themselves. They might also be able to rely upon the seller to communicate the true value of the land since he was a neighbor (or perhaps even a family member) with whom they had repeated dealings. But an outside buyer would be in the dark with no one to trust. With no way to distinguish good land, he might expect that only mediocre land would be sold to outsiders, and under the right conditions his expectations could become reality. One hesitates to test this and Levi's explanation, though, because Gérard Béaur has found a very different pattern in the Beauce in France. See Levi, *Inheriting Power*, pp. 79–99, 183–85; Béaur, "Prezzo della terra," pp. 523–48.

148. Philip T. Hoffman, Gilles Postel-Vinay, and Jean-Laurent Rosenthal, "What Do Notaries Do? The Social Dimension of Credit in Eighteenth-Century Paris," Economics Department Working Paper, UCLA, Los Angeles, California 1994; Avner Greif, "Contract Enforceability"; idem, "Reputation and Coalitions"; and idem, "Cultural Beliefs."

149. The following draws on Greif's "Cultural Beliefs."

150. Cf. de Santi and Vidal, *Deux livres de raison*, pp. 110–20, 216.

CHAPTER FOUR
AGRICULTURAL PRODUCTIVITY IN FRANCE, 1450–1789

1. Bourde, *Agronomie et agronomes*, 2:1099–1100; Bloch, *French Rural History*, pp. 216–18.

2. Olivier Marchand and Claude Thélot, *Deux siècles de travail en France* (Paris, 1991); for further difficulties, see Bompard, Magnac, and Postel-Vinay, "Emploi, mobilité et chômage." If one ignores exports and imports and assumes that food consumption did not vary greatly over time, then a crude measure of agricultural labor productivity can be derived from the ratio of the total population to the

agricultural labor force: E. Anthony Wrigley, "Urban Growth and Agricultural Change: England and the Continent in the Early Modern Period," *Journal of Interdisciplinary History* 15 (1985): 683–728.

3. For difficulties with comparisons of yields, see Meuvret, *Subsistances*, vol. 1, pt. 1 (*Texte*), pp. 207–11. The best-known attempt to compare French yields is Michel Morineau, *Les faux-semblants*. One might object that productivity estimates calculated from leases would also vary drastically from year to year and place to place, but there are so many leases over which we can average that the problem is less severe than it seems. Furthermore, with the leases we can at least follow the same properties over time and thus control for differences in land quality, something practically impossible with yields.

4. Goy and Le Roy Ladurie, eds., *Fluctuations du produit de la dîme*, pp. 44–57; idem, *Prestations paysannes*.

5. AN S 273 (21 May 1588); LL 327–28, fols. 12–17; LL 331, fols. 210–50; Garnier, "La mise en herbe"; idem, "Pays herbagers"; idem, "Production céréalière et mise en herbe: Lieuvin et pays d'Auge aux XVIIe et XVIIIe siècles," *Annales de Normandie* 21 (1971): 33–53. For additional examples, see AN S 259–60 (6 September 1682); L. Michel, "Quelques données sur le mouvement de la rente foncière en Anjou, du milieu du XVIIe siècle à la Révolution," in Goy and Le Roy Ladurie, *Prestations paysannes*, 2:607–24; and Meuvret, *Subsistances*, vol. 2, pt. 1 (*Texte*), pp. 51–54.

6. Cf. Mulliez, "Du blé, 'mal nécessaire'"; Hickey, "Innovation and Obstacles to Growth." In some regions, tithe records did include animal output; for an excellent example, see Le Roy Ladurie, *Les paysans de Languedoc*, 1:526–28, 2:982–89.

7. McCloskey, "The Economics of Enclosure"; Robert C. Allen, "The Efficiency and Distributional Consequences of Eighteenth-Century Enclosures," *Economic Journal* 92 (1982): 927–53.

8. The definition of TFP is from Robert G. Chambers, *Applied Production Analysis* (Cambridge, 1988), pp. 235–39. For a derivation of equations (1) and (2), see Appendix A, part 5.

9. Imagine, for example, that a growing population drove wages down relative to agricultural prices and pushed rents up, while TFP remained constant. The cost index C would decline relative to the price index P, while rent and hence $(r + t)$ rose, but the change in rent would be just enough to compensate for the change in prices and wages, leaving TFP = $(r + t)^s C/P$ constant. Note that measuring the prices here either in money of account, as I have done, or in precious metal would yield the same answer for TFP and for its rate of change. Converting prices to silver, for instance, would simply multiply the numerator and the denominator in equation 2 by the same number, because the product and factor shares sum to 1. TFP would thus be unchanged.

10. Throughout this chapter, the price of all capital goods such as livestock is a rental price, which equals the sales prices multiplied by interest plus depreciation. For instance, if interest rates are 5 percent and horses sell for 200 livres and last nine years, then the rental rate for horses is $(0.05 + 1/9)200$, or very nearly 32 livres a year. When available actual rental rates are close to these imputed rental rates; see Appendix A, part 6, for details.

11. For a detailed account of how I treated seigneurial dues, contre-lettres, rent

understatement, *charges*, in-kind payments, pots-de-vin, and a host of related problems, see Appendix A, part 1. Cf. Jacquart, "La rente foncière"; and Béaur, *Le marché foncier*, pp. 231–46.

12. Although the independent variables include both property attributes and time attributes, only the time attributes were used in adjusting the rents for quality. See table 4.2 and Appendix A, part 3, for details.

13. For a discussion, see Appendix A, part 3.

14. Emmanuel Le Roy Ladurie and Béatrice Veyrassat-Herren, "La rente foncière autour de Paris au XVIIe siècle," *AESC* 23 (1968): 541–55. Because these scholars deflated their rent series, I multiplied their numbers by the moving average wheat price that they used for deflation. Other ways of comparing the two series (converting both to bushels of wheat, for example) led to similar results. See Appendix A, part 4, for details. For other local rent figures that parallel ours, both for lay and clerical property, see Béaur, *Le marché foncier*, pp. 262–68; Jacquart, *La crise rurale*, pp. 616, 638, 699; M. Bertrandy-Lacabane, *Brétigny-sur-Orge, Marolles-en-Hurepoix, Saint-Michel-sur-Orge* (Versailles, 1886), pp. 314–15; Jean-Marie Constant, *Nobles et paysans en Beauce aux XVIe et XVIIe siècles* (Service de reproduction des thèses de l'Université de Lille, 1981), pp. 104–30; Moriceau, *Fermiers*, pp. 102–5, 549–55, 904–7. One might worry that small properties trace out a different rental pattern, but the regressions performed in Chapter 3 suggest otherwise.

15. See Appendix A, part 5.

16. Hoffman, "Land Rents and Agricultural Productivity," p. 781.

17. The Bernonville shares included fourteen inputs and thirteen outputs; see Appendix A, part 6, for details.

18. The reason demographic data are useful here is that under constant factor shares the ratio of rent to wages will be proportional to the ratio of labor to land, which we can approximate by the rural population. An analogous argument holds for livestock, the most important form of agricultural capital, and there too the evidence points to constant shares. For details concerning this and the following paragraph, see Appendix A, part 6.

19. One should not forget the importance of vineyards in certain parts of the Paris Basin; they remained important up to the nineteenth century.

20. Most of the difference between the Chartier shares and mine results from aggregating inputs and outputs and treating seed as an intermediate product when calculating shares from their records. Had we followed the same procedure with the Bernonville accounts, the shares would be nearly identical. The evidence thus suggests that shares in the Paris Basin did not vary, and the alternative shares used here really gauge the effects of aggregating and netting out seed. See Appendix A, part 6, for details.

21. In the model used in Chapter 3, servants eventually earn their marginal product. Hence, the wage-tenure profile does not end the relationship between wages and productivity, a relationship that we need for our productivity calculations.

22. Micheline Baulant, "Prix et salaires à Paris au XVIe siècle: Sources et résultats," *AESC* 31 (1976): 954–95; Guy Fourquin, *Les campagnes de la région parisienne à la fin du Moyen Age* (Paris, 1964), p. 496; Goubert, *Beauvais et le Beauvaisis*, vol. 1, pp. 139–40, 547–60; and Gutton, *Domestiques et serviteurs*, pp. 111–17.

23. Micheline Baulant, "Prix et salaires," pp. 980–86; and idem, "Le salaire des ouvriers du bâtiment à Paris de 1400 à 1726," *AESC* 26 (1971): 463–83. This is sixteenth-century evidence; for evidence for later periods, see Appendix A, part 7. Even in 1852 there was little gap between urban and rural wages in France, once one adjusts for costs of living: Pierre Sicsic, "City Farm Wage Gaps." One might worry that the cash wages paid in Paris and the in-kind wages paid in the surrounding countryside could diverge, but evidence from the eighteenth and early nineteenth centuries argues against such divergence. See Appendix A, part 7, and Labrousse, *Esquisse*, 2:455–56, n. 33. For the sources of the wages and the prices that enter into the calculation of the indexes C and P, see Appendix A, part 14.

24. See Baulant, "Le salaire des ouvriers," p. 472; idem, "Prix et salaires," pp. 980–87; Marcel Lachiver, *La population de Meulan du XVIIe au XIXe siècle* (Paris, 1969), pp. 91–122; Béaud and Bouchart, "Le dépôt des pauvres," pp. 127–43; and Appendix A, part 7.

25. Because much grain reached the consumers in the form of in-kind payments or self-production, one might suppose that the farm gate price of grain bore no relationship to the market price, but such was not the case near Paris. On this point, see Appendix A, part 8.

26. See Appendix A, part 9. Prices were too fragmentary to calculate P/C before 1520.

27. Kaplan, *Provisioning Paris*, pp. 206, 215–16; Jacquart, *La crise rurale*, pp. 764–66; Jacques Dupâquier et al., *Mercuriales du pays de France et du Vexin français (1640–1792)* (Paris, 1968), p. 233; Micheline Baulant and Jean Meuvret, *Prix des céréales extraits de la mercuriale de Paris (1520–1698)*, 2 vols. (Paris, 1960–62), 1:12, 25. For details about the prices used, see Appendix A, part 14. As we shall discuss below, hinterland prices did rise relative to the Paris price between the seventeenth and the eighteenth centuries: see Micheline Baulant, "Le prix des grains à Paris de 1431 à 1788," *AESC* 23 (1968): 520–40. All of the evidence suggests that the gap between the farm gate price and the Paris price did indeed reflect transportation costs: the behavior of prices as one moved away from Paris; the competition among grain transporters, who regularly imported grain into Paris from practically all the region where our farms were located; and the existence of extensive intermarket arbitrage, which tied the Paris price to the price in regions too distant to export grain directly to Paris. See Meuvret, *Subsistances*, vol. 3, pt. 2 (*Notes*), pp. 116–21; Kaplan, *Provisioning Paris*, pp. 88–92; and Chevet, "Le Marquisat d'Ormesson," 1:101–2.

28. Charles Rebeyrol, *De la grande et de la petite culture chez les physiocrates* (Paris, 1912), pp. 35–44; Tessier, *Agriculture*, s.v. "Bail"; and Moriceau and Postel-Vinay, *Ferme, entreprise, famille*, pp. 152–56, 199, 334–40. In the middle to late eighteenth century, estimates for the tenants' capital in the Paris Basin ranged from 75 livres per hectare for livestock and equipment up to 120 livres per hectare if seed and feed were included: A return of only 5 percent then implies income of 4 to 6 livres per hectare. I have also assumed a range for the compensation due the tenant and his family members for their labor of 360 to 740 livres. The lower end of the range was determined by the pay to a *charretier* and a female farm servant in wages and in-kind payments. The upper end was determined by assuming that the fermier's family would furnish the equivalent of two male adults, earning what

skilled masons were paid. The high-end assumption of a mason's wage is not consistent with my use of unskilled wages in the index C, but the error is minor, as I show in Appendix A, part 10.

29. Moriceau and Postel-Vinay, *Ferme, entreprise, famille*, pp. 136–41, 154, 177–88, 279–89; Moriceau, *Fermiers*, pp. 515–56, 579–612.

30. AN S 242 (Dampmart, 1744–62); S 282 (La Grande-Paroisse, 1746). There is another reason why entrepreneurial profits may have come back down relative to wages in the late eighteenth century. In the eighteenth century, as more tenant farmers sent their sons to *collèges* and taught their daughters to read, it is possible that more of the children learned to manage large farms. In the end, competition among the children when they became tenants brought entrepreneurial profits down. See Moriceau and Postel-Vinay, *Ferme, entreprise, famille*, pp. 296–99; Moriceau, *Fermiers*, pp. 196–218, 731–41.

31. Short-term entrepreneurial profits would presumably rise when higher agricultural prices drove up profits, before rents had a chance to move upward. Since agricultural demand would in all likelihood be price-inelastic and vary little in the short run, higher prices would in all likelihood mean higher revenues in the short run—unless crops failed—because rents and wages would be slower to adjust. In that case, as I explain in part 10 of Appendix A, TFP as calculated from equation 2 would be negatively correlated with the rate of increase in agricultural prices, for when prices rose we would underestimate the cost of the entrepreneurial input by setting it equal to the wage rate, and the higher agricultural prices would then push down our estimate of TFP. Fortunately, we can test for such a phenomenon by adding the agricultural inflation rate to regressions with ln(TFP). We would expect to find a negative and significant coefficient for the inflation rate, but in fact that never occurs, even if we vary the way we measure inflation. Moreover, the regression coefficient of the inflation rate implies only a small correction to TFP. It is worth noting here that equation 2 does not assume that the land supply is fixed or that the tenant farmers were profit maximizers, though without profit maximization, our definition of TFP has no necessary connection with technical change. We do have to assume the existence of a large number of risk-neutral tenants, but risk neutrality is not an absurd assumption for the sort of wealthy *fermiers* who rented Notre Dame's farms. For them, even profit maximization is not unrealistic. For a discussion and other assumptions, see Appendix A, part 5.

32. For details, see Appendix A, part 11.

33. One alternative would be to average $s\ln(r)$ and $\ln(P/C)$ separately, taking the mean of $s\ln(r)$ over all the leases in each twenty-five-year period and then subtracting $\ln(P/C)$ averaged over all the years in the period, rather than over all the leases. This procedure, though, yields results nearly indistinguishable from simply averaging ln(TFP) lease by lease; see Appendix A, part 12, for a discussion. We could also average ln(TFP) by decade, but the decennial averages obscure the trend. Finally, although it might seem promising to chart TFP for clusters of properties (the landlocked ones north of Paris, for example) or to single out farms with high rates of TFP growth, in the end neither technique proved illuminating.

34. In 1650–74, the TFP index with alternative prices is inflated—perhaps artificially—because it employs prices eight years into the future; it thus incorporates the depressed prices of the 1670s, when P/C is very low (table 4.2, column five). Its

jump in 1775–89 may also be a fluke. Since our prices series stop in 1789, we cannot really incorporate prices eight years forward; rather, we have to calculate P/C in the late 1780s, with prices from only a few years from the late 1780s, making the alternate price estimates suspect.

35. As TFP equals $(r + t)^s C/P$, omitting taxes t, as we have, would tend to understate both the level and the growth rate of TFP, if taxes were rising relative to rents. The precise taxes t for each piece of property will never be known precisely, but one reasonable assumption is that for the i-th property the fraction of gross rent (that is, rent plus taxes) going to the landlord rather than to the fisc is g, where $\ln(g)$ equals $b\ln(t_a/r_a) + c_i$. Here b is a negative constant, t_a is the average per-capita tax assessment, r_a is the average per hectare rent, and c_i is a constant that varies from property to property. Under this assumption, which amounts to saying that taxes were apportioned with an eye toward average rent and population levels, we can estimate the magnitude of the error involved in omitting taxes from the formula for TFP. The way to do so, as shown in Appendix A, part 13, is to regress the growth rate of TFP measured without taxes on the growth rate of t_a/r_a, which we can derive from tax receipts, population statistics, and average rent levels. We then subtract the product of the growth rate of t_a/r_a and its regression coefficient from the measured growth rate of TFP in order to correct the measured growth rate of TFP for the omission of taxes. To adjust the measured level of TFP, we subtract the same regression coefficient times $\ln(t_a/r_a)$. Table 4.4, column one, contains the necessary regression; the error involved in ignoring taxes turns out to be very small, particularly in the case of the growth rate of TFP. See Appendix A, part 13, for details.

36. See AN S407 (1464); S 272 (1522, 1545); and S 409 (1479, 1482, 1483, 1498, 1511). Cf. Fourquin, *Les campagnes*, pp. 389–97, 430–531, map five; Moriceau, *Fermiers*, pp. 74–105.

37. The 0.3 to 0.4 percent range covers the growth rates one gets with all the various shares and prices.

38. Fourquin, *Les campagnes*, pp. 389–97, 430–531; Jacquart, *La crise rurale*, pp. 42–47; Moriceau, *Fermiers*, pp. 74–105.

39. See Appendix A, figure A-3.

40. See AN LL 329–30, La Grande-Paroisse (1594); S 242 (25 June 1597); and Jacquart, *La crise rurale*, pp. 171–207. The 25 percent decline in TFP comes from table 4.3, regression one, which is discussed below.

41. The regression with ln(rent) also suggests that rising prices, rather than declining rents, lay behind the drop in TFP, as the dummy variable for the war years 1589 to 1597 does not have a large or significant coefficient (table 3.1). The chief argument against the reality of the TFP drop would run something like this: The 1589–90 siege of Paris disrupted transportation and temporarily drove up the Paris grain prices that figure in our index P (thereby depressing TFP), even though farm-gate prices and true TFP in fact remained the same. It is true that transportation was disrupted, particularly over long distances: that much is apparent from the ratio of grain prices in Paris to prices in Chartres, nearly 100 kilometers away. But local markets closer to Paris—markets relevant to our sample—show the same spike in prices in 1589–90 as does Paris, suggesting that the price increase was not confined to the city: Jacquart, *La crise rurale*, pp. 764–65. Furthermore, the index P averages

prices for the current year and for the eight years of the previous lease; it is therefore unlikely to be swayed unduly by any single year of siege.

42. Jacquart, *La crise rurale*, pp. 616, 623–99. Cf. Moriceau, *Fermiers*, pp. 515–56, 579–612.

43. Meuvret, *Subsistances*, vol. 3, pt. 2, pp. 116–34; Baulant, "Le prix des grains"; AN F11 207 (Soissons price, corrected following the indications in Goubert, *Beauvais et le Beauvaisis*, 1:408); and Dupâquier, *Mercuriales*. Graphs of the Soissons and Pontoise prices show that they rose roughly 5 to 10 percent relative to the Paris price between 1650 and 1750, with more of an increase in distant Soissons than in Pontoise. Available prices from before 1650 suggest that transportation costs were relatively stable in the sixteenth and early seventeenth centuries.

44. For direct evidence of declining costs of transportation, see Letaconnoux, "Les transports en France au 18e siècle," *Revue d'histoire moderne et contemporaine* 11 (1908–9): 97–114, 269–92. The separation of transportation and farming is somewhat artificial since the cheaper transportation near Paris was in part the work of prosperous tenant farmers who invested in large *charrettes* (carts) after 1650; see Moriceau, *Fermiers*, pp. 286–99.

45. Prices at Rozay-en-Brie suggest a similarly large role for transportation in the period between 1650–74 and 1725–45, when the Rozay price series unfortunately stops.

46. See N.F.R. Crafts, *British Economic Growth during the Industrial Revolution* (Oxford, 1985), pp. 83–85; Robert C. Allen, "The Growth of Labor Productivity in Early Modern English Agriculture," *Explorations in Economic History* 25 (1988): 117–46; idem, *Enclosure and the Yeoman*, pp. 211–31. In "Agriculture during the Industrial Revolution, 1700–1850" (paper delivered at the November 8–10, 1991, All–University of California Group in Economic History Conference at Davis, California), Allen estimates somewhat higher TFP growth rates for the period 1700–1850—0.6 percent per year. These would still be within the reach of the peak rates of growth in the Paris Basin.

47. AN S 242, 1754–62 (Dampmart); S 282, 1746–55; and S 460, 1782 (La Grande-Paroisse).

48. In addition to Chapter 3, see the examples in AN LL 329–30 (La Grande-Paroisse, 1636 and 1689) and AN S 247 (1693). For tighter estate management during the seigneurial reaction, see Forster, *The House of Saulx-Tavanes*.

49. Béaur, *Le marché foncier*, pp. 262–68; Bertrandy-Lacabane, *Brétigny-sur-Orge*, pp. 314–15; Constant, *Nobles et paysans en Beauce*; and Le Roy Ladurie and Veyrassat-Herren, "La rente foncière."

50. For the regressions with alternative shares and prices, see Appendix A, parts 6 and 9. In table 4.3, the level of TFP includes a correction for taxes, but in table 4.4 the TFP growth rate does not. The coefficients in table 4.4 will not be affected by the failure to correct for taxes, because the growth rate of taxes relative to rents appears among the explanatory variables. See Appendix 4, part 13, for an explanation. The TFP growth rate regressions also include a dummy variable for ongoing repairs and for tenants who repeat from previous leases, which corrects for any market power that repeat tenants may have exercised.

51. One cause for worry is the large value of the condition number, a sign of multicollinearity. Although multicollinearity may therefore cast some doubt on the

results with ln(TFP), it does not afflict the regression with the TFP growth rate, which points to the same dip in 1589 to 1597 and to the same sharp increase after 1775 (table 4.4, regression one). For the condition number and multicollinearity, see George G. Judge et al., *The Theory and Practice of Econometrics* (New York, 1985), pp. 896–904. The regressions showed no signs of heteroscedasticity or autocorrelation.

52. Sharecropping agreements abounded, for example, in the leases of ecclesiastical property at the AD Gers; cf. AD Gers, C 357, G 183, G 227, G 293. Sharecropping was also common near our village of Grillon: BM Avignon, mss. 1131, 5951 (fonds Chobaut); AD Vaucluse, 3 E, études Evesque and Petit à Valréas. In addition, agricultural leases near Grillon often omitted property descriptions and areas, both landlord and tenant merely saying that they knew the property well.

53. Neveux, *Vie et déclin*. As Michel Morineau has pointed out, mauvais gré also casts doubt on the tithe series Neveux has amassed, because the tithe farmers developed proprietary rights to the tithe rights they leased out. See Morineau, "Cambrésis et Hainaut."

54. Garnier, "La mise en herbe," pp. 157–80; idem, "Pays herbagers," pp. 493–525; idem, "Production céréalière et mise en herbe," pp. 33–53; Durand, *Vin, vigne et vignerons*, pp. 210–24; Edouard Gruter, *La naissance d'un grand vignoble: Les seigneuries de Pizay et Tanay en Beaujolais au XVIe et au XVIIe siècles* (Lyon, 1977); Dion, *Histoire de la vigne*, pp. 576–607; and Baehrel, *Une croissance*.

55. See Appendix B, part 1. Intuitively, the use of average shares involves a better approximation to the integral of the expression on the right- or left-hand side of equation (1) when the shares change.

56. For the French printed sources, the essential research tool is Jean-Yves Grenier's extraordinary bibliography, *Séries économiques françaises (XVIe–XVIIIe siècles)* (Paris, 1985). Appendix B, part 2, contains a complete list of the sources I used for rental figures, prices, and wages for each locality.

57. For details about the shares and price averages for each site, see Appendix B, part 2.

58. The exceptions include the farms in Lorraine, where the shares mattered slightly, and the properties in Nantes and in the Ille-et-Vilaine, where price averages made a difference. The case of Lorraine is discussed below; the results for Nantes and the Ille-et-Villaine are taken up in Appendix B, part 2. The alternative price averages involved averaging prices over the new lease instead of the old, just as with the Notre Dame properties.

59. Pierre Deyon, *Contribution à l'étude des revenus fonciers en Picardie: Les fermages de l'Hôtel-Dieu d'Amiens et leurs variations de 1515 à 1789* (Lille, 1967), pp. 74–75; and idem, *Amiens, capitale provinciale: Etude sur la société urbaine au 17e siècle* (Paris, 1967), pp. 21–22.

60. Bourde, *Agronomie et agronomes*, 2:1036.

61. For calculating TFP with rents measured relative to a base period—a standard technique in panel studies—see Appendix B, part 3. Another way to estimate the growth of TFP is to regress its rate of change (without a tax correction) on a constant, property characteristics, and the rate of change of per-capita taxes relative to average rents. The coefficient of the constant will then be the growth rate of TFP, corrected for taxes. See Appendix B, part 2, table B.1, for the regression with the

standard shares and prices; it yields a TFP growth rate that is even lower, although it is not statistically significant. The rate of change regressions also suggests that the local productivity growth was not the result of declining transportation costs, which would boost the rent—and hence the measured TFP—on far-flung properties. Other ways of correcting for differences among the Amiens properties—via regressions with dummy variables for each property or by using the property characteristics that are known—tell much the same story about the trend of TFP.

62. The reason is that the twenty-five-year averages rule out a regression with the growth rate of TFP on the individual properties; this sort of regression is what provides the tax correction for the Notre Dame properties. See Appendix A, part 2.

63. The TFP growth between 1650 and 1750 in Lorraine is not the result of declining transportation costs, for the prices in our index P are from Lorraine. In addition, there is no reason to believe that transportation costs diminished in Lorraine. Between 1650 and 1750, the price of grain in Lorraine did not rise relative to the price in Paris, contrary to what one might expect if local transport costs were falling.

64. Garnier, "Pays herbagers"; Pavard, "Productions et rendements céréaliers." The tithe does show an upturn in the eighteenth century, but this may be a result of the way the tithe returns were deflated.

65. The high value of the condition number points to multicollinearity when the regressions are done for single centuries, but the multicollinearity does not seem to have affected the coefficient of the year.

66. The TFP estimates were not corrected for taxes, but the correction would in all likelihood be small.

67. Garnier, "La mise en herbe"; idem, "Pays herbagers"; idem, "Production céréalière et mise en herbe"; Musset, *L'Elevage du cheval en France*; Vallez, "Le commerce des bestiaux en Normandie"; Mulliez, "Du blé, 'mal nécessaire.'" For conversion to pasture and grain yields, see Gregory Clark, "The Economics of Exhaustion, the Postan Thesis, and the Agricultural Revolution," *JEH* 52, no. 1 (March 1992): 61–84. I took farmland to include sown fields, meadow, and pasture; and I adapted the estimates of the amount of land converted from Garnier, "La mise en herbe," assuming that Garnier's table has two reversed rows.

68. See Appendix B, part 1. A more precise calculation of the TFP increase would take into account the cost of the labor and capital expended in the conversion by including these costs in the computation of postconversion factor shares. One additional difficulty here is a problem of self-selection: we do our calculations with the rent of land that is not yet converted to pasture. Land that was actually converted would presumably give a higher ratio of the rental price of pasture to the rental price of arable. For a discussion, see Appendix B, part 2.

69. For more detailed calculations, see Appendix B, part 2.

70. Bloch, *French Rural History*, p. 56.

71. Young, *Voyages en France*, 1:229–32, 2:569–76; 3:1168–89. François Le Brun, *Les hommes et la mort en Anjou aux 17e et 18e siècles* (Paris, 1971), pp. 39–78; Mulliez, "Du blé, 'mal nécessaire,'" pp. 28–38; Merle, *La métairie*; Meyer, *La noblesse bretonne*, 1:452–58, 501–2; 2:605; Sée, *Les classes rurales en Bretagne*, pp. 373–99; Peret, *Seigneurs et seigneuries en Gâtine poitevine*, pp. 132–34; Michel Le Mené, *Les campagnes angevines à la fin du Moyen Age (vers 1350–vers*

1530) (Nantes, 1982), pp. 185–92, 232–73; O. Leclerc-Thoüin, *L'agriculture dans l'ouest de la France* (Paris, 1843).

72. AD Loire-Atlantique, H 275, pièce 19; Merle, *La métairie*, pp. 108–21. The farm near Nantes resembled western farms in other ways as well—its access to *landes* for example; see AD Loire-Atlantique, H 274, H 275; and Jean de Malestroit and R. P. Emile Laure, *Histoire de Vallet* (Maulévrier, 1985), pp. 101–27.

73. The shares for the farm near Laval could be estimated in a different way; the calculation that I made exaggerated the difference between the shares from Laval and the shares from the Gâtine. The other way of computing shares from Laval in fact produced numbers very close to those from the Gâtine. See Appendix B, part 2, for details.

74. Tessier, *Agriculture*, s.v. "Bêtes à laine," "Bêtes à cornes," and "Consommation de Paris"; Meyer, *La noblesse bretonne*, 1:453–58; Musset, *L'élevage du cheval en France*; and Appendix A, part 14. Appendix B, part 2, discusses the shortcomings of the price data, establishes the parallel movement of grain prices in Rennes and Angers, and shows that using grain prices from other markets does not disturb the trend of TFP.

75. In table 4.6, as in figure 4.7 (parts A and B), the rents that enter into TFP are measured relative to a common base period for each property in a sample so as to control for differences among property characteristics. The regressions with the alternative shares and price averages yield TFP growth rates of 0.1 percent per year for the eight farms near Angers and between –0.7 and 0.0 percent per year for the other samples. Regressions with the rate of change of TFP suggest much the same; for them, see Appendix B, part 2, table B.1. For the TFP trend with prices taken from Rennes, see Appendix B, part 2.

76. For the practice of additions to the rent in the west, see Meyer, *La noblesse bretonne*, 2:695–701. The problem is less likely to afflict our rental figures, nearly all of which derive from ecclesiastical records, for the clergy usually included all the additions to the rent (for example, the entry fines known as pots-de-vin) in the lease rather than in secret contre-lettres. In addition, for some of our samples we know that the problems are minimal. For the leases in the Gâtine, it was possible to evaluate the additions to the rent, and the farms in the Ille-et-Vilaine were specifically chosen so that seigneurial dues and in-kind payments would be small. For the three farms near Nantes, it proved possible to evaluate all the additional payments for La Chapelle-aux-Moines, where they amounted to 6 percent of the rent in both the seventeenth and the eighteenth centuries. For the other two farms, the additions (minuscule in-kind payments, a tiny corvée, and no pots-de-vin) could not be evaluated exactly, but they were nevertheless small, so small in fact that they could not account for a TFP increase over the course of the eighteenth century.

77. Although access to the commons may have changed in 1633 for the three farms near Nantes, I have not used leases before that date; conflicts over nearby *landes* after 1744 did not diminish their access to the commons—indeed, it may have increased it. See AD Loire-Atlantique, H 274, H 275; and Malestroit and Laure, *Histoire de Vallet*, pp. 101–27. Land reclamation in the west may have been somewhat more important near western cities, where most of our sample properties are located; see E. Labrousse, "L'expansion agricole: La montée de la production," in *HESF*, 2:427–30. But overall, very little of the commons was put into cultivation:

perhaps 2 percent of the commons in Anjou and 10 percent in Brittany. Of that, much quickly returned to waste. See Le Brun, *Les hommes et la mort en Anjou*, pp. 90–104; Meyer, *La noblesse bretonne*, 1:533–69; Young, *Voyages en France*, 3:1174–76, 1182–83.

78. Le Brun, *Les hommes et la mort en Anjou*, pp. 39–78; Mulliez, "Du blé, 'mal nécessaire' "; Dion, *Histoire de la vigne*, pp. 448–60; Malestroit and Laure, *Histoire de Vallet*, pp. 54–60. The landscape was also diverse near Le Mans: Paul Bois, *Paysans de l'Ouest: Des structures économiques et sociales aux options politiques depuis l'époque révolutionaire dans la Sarthe* (Le Mans, 1960), pp. 36–40.

79. Chavais was located in the parish of Dénéze-sous-Doué. For descriptions of the surrounding region, see Le Brun, *Les hommes et la mort en Anjou*, pp. 58–63, 70; Le Clerc-Thoüin, *L'agriculture de l'Ouest de la France*, map, page 1. The calculation of TFP here was done without a correction for taxes.

80. AD Loire-Atlantique, H 274, H 275; Malestroit and Laure, *Histoire de Vallet*, pp. 101–6. The recalculation of the shares was based on evidence about the costs and revenues of local vineyards taken from Young, *Voyages en France*, 2:692. See Appendix B, part 2, for details. As with Chavais, TFP here is not corrected for taxes.

81. If we regress the rate of change of TFP on taxes and characteristics of the three farms near Nantes, we find no higher rate of productivity growth when vineyards are present. See Appendix B, part 2, table B.1.

82. T.J.A. Le Goff, "Autour de quelques dîmes vannetaises XVIIe–XVIIIe siècle," in Goy and Le Roy Ladurie, *Prestations paysannes*, 2:583–98.

83. Although most leases of the Sacristie lasted six years or less, I averaged prices over the current year and the previous eight, because doing so helped fill in a few gaps in the price data. Performing the calculations with six-year averages leads to nearly identical results, as does averaging prices over the next eight years or using the alternative shares.

84. I was forced to use the sales prices for Grillon, since most local leases either involved sharecropping or omitted essential information such as the property area. Obviously, because the sales prices incorporate expectations concerning capital gains, the TFP figures derived from them may exaggerate slightly the amount of TFP growth in the seventeenth century; any error, however, is likely to be small. More worrisome are the complicated monetary conversions that both the Grange de la Sacristie leases and the Grillon land sales contracts entailed, which may cast doubt on the results. Also troublesome is the fact that the sales prices, unlike rental rates, would be affected by taxes. Unfortunately, the complications of local fiscal system—Grillon was part of the papal Comtat Venaissin—make it impossible to adjust the sales prices for taxes. It was also impossible to check the TFP indices derived from the sales contracts for entrepreneurial profits.

85. Hickey, "Innovation and Obstacles to Growth."

86. As with the TFP estimates derived from land sales in Grillon, the figures based on Rosenthal's data ignore taxes and tend to exaggerate TFP increases slightly because of capital gains. Vineyards spread in parts of this region in the eighteenth century, but their spread ought to have boosted our TFP estimates by raising rents.

87. Le Roy Ladurie, *Paysans de Languedoc*, 1:296–97, 491.

88. Le Roy Ladurie, *Paysans de Languedoc*, 1:431–37, 526–30, 633–38, 645;

2:978–79. The onset of the crisis coincided, at least approximately, with the opening of the Canal des Deux-Mers in 1681, which flooded southeastern Languedoc with grain from as far away as Toulouse: George and Geneviève Frêche, *Les prix des grains, des vins et des légumes à Toulouse (1486–1868)* (Paris, 1967). Naturally, one might wonder if the two events were linked. The influx of grain via the canal would have depressed the local price of grain and thus local rents, but because the TFP calculation takes into account both the rents and the local grain prices—the price of wheat in the index *P* is from Béziers itself—the TFP index should be unaffected. The low prices may have cut investment in improvements to the soil, though, a subject taken up in Chapter 5.

89. See, for example, Goldsmith, *Les Salers*, pp. 193–207; and P. Laboulinière, *Annuaire statistique du département des Hautes-Pyrénées*, pp. 322, 367.

90. Goldsmith, *Les Salers*, pp. 193–207. For details, see Appendix B, part 2.

91. Dion, *Histoire de la vigne*, pp. 576–93; Durand, *Vin, vigne, vignerons*, pp. 210–24; Gruter, *La naissance d'un grand vignoble*, pp 67–70.

92. For details and sources, see Appendix B, part 2. As with the Auge, there is a problem of self-selection here: we do our calculations with rents from land that is not yet converted to vineyard. Land that was actually converted would presumably give a higher ratio of the rental price of vineyard to the rental price of arable, and that, too, would tend to reduce the amount of exaggeration in our estimates.

93. Cf. Robert C. Allen and Cormac Ó Gráda, "On the Road Again with Arthur Young: English, Irish, and French Agriculture during the Industrial Revolution," *JEH* 48, no. 1 (March, 1988): 93–116.

94. The calculation uses rents for 1852 and a land share of one-half for unknown crops in order to exaggerate the impact on TFP: *SA 1852*, 2:402, 410, 417. Evidence from 1862 gives similar results.

95. Young, *Voyages en France*, 1:89–91, 2:615, 727, 732–58, 784–91; 3:1224, 1330. For Brenner and the works of synthesis, see Chapter 1.

96. Morineau, *Les faux-semblants*; idem, "Cambrésis et Hainaut" and "Dîmes, rente foncière et mouvement de la production agricole à l'époque préindustrielle," in Goy and Le Roy Ladurie, *Prestations paysannes*, 2:625–43.

97. Bourde, *Agronomie et agronomes*, 1:253–424.

98. The coastal strip from the Netherlands to Denmark witnessed an intensification of pastoral farming in the early modern period—in particular, increasing production of livestock, butter, and cheese for sale in northwestern Europe. The TFP growth rates result from a study of price and rental rates for one portion of this coastal strip—Eiderstedt, along the western coast of Schleswig-Holstein. The TFP calculations were done with a variety of product and factor shares derived from descriptions of local farming, but they are still subject to caution because they are not adjusted for taxes. In addition, the specialization in livestock, butter, and cheese production may have shifted the product and factor shares. For details and sources, see Appendix B, part 2.

99. Robert C. Allen estimates that TFP in the Midlands advanced 58 percent between roughly 1600 and 1800: see his *Enclosure and the Yeoman*, pp. 211–31. In the Paris Basin it took almost a century longer—from 1520–24 to 1775–89—to grow roughly the same amount (39 to 64 percent, depending upon the shares and prices used).

100. Here, we are aggregating all farm products together, weighting them by their factor shares in farm revenue.

101. The agricultural labor force estimates are from Wrigley, "Urban Growth and Agricultural Change," table 9. For land, the optimistic assumption is that throughout the early modern period land reclamation proceeded at the same pace as in the years 1730–89, when it added at most 4 percent to the land supply, or 0.08 percent per year: E. Labrousse, "L'expansion agricole: La montée de la production," in *HESF*, 2:427–30. As for livestock and equipment, it seems reasonable to assume that the supply of livestock did not increase. The data concerning shares argue against much growth in the amount of livestock and equipment even in the Paris Basin, and there is similar evidence for stock-raising areas such as the Gâtine Poitevine. For evidence both for and against this assumption, see, Merle, *La métairie*, pp. 109, 114–15; Meuvret, *Subsistances*, vol. 1, pt. 1 (*Texte*), p. 125, and pt. 2 (*Notes*), pp. 92–93; and Moriceau, *Fermiers*, pp. 402–3.

102. The alternative population growth rates are derived from Dupâquier, *Histoire de la population française*, 1:513–24, 2:51–68; and Wrigley, "Urban Growth and Agricultural Change," table 9. For rents and wages in the eighteenth century, see Weir, "Les crises économiques."

103. Wrigley, "Urban Growth and Agricultural Change," p. 720; Allen, *Enclosure and the Yeomen*, pp. 169, 226.

104. Emmanuel Le Roy Ladurie and Joseph Goy, "Présentation" and "Première esquisse d'une conjoncture du produit décimal et domanial: Fin du Moyen Age–XVIIIe siècle," in their *Les fluctuations du produit de la dîme*, pp. 9–24, 335–74. Unfortunately, their figures are not precise enough to permit a comparison over the longer period from 1500 to 1800. Both their figures and my own are well below the 1 percent a year growth in output proposed for the years 1701–80 by J.-C. Toutain, *Le produit de l'agriculture française de 1700 à 1958*, vol. 2, *La croissance* (Paris, 1961), table 99.

105. In making the calculations for the Paris Basin, I assumed no growth in the land supply but I did allow for some increase in capital. Although farm accounts suggested that the total number of animals did not change greatly, there was evidence from a small number of parishes in the *élection* of Melun that implied capital growth of 0.5 percent per year between 1717 and 1783; see Meuvret, *Subsistances*, vol. 1, pt. 1 (*Texte*), p. 125. And north of Paris, the number of animals per hectare grew at 0.2 percent per year between 1550 and 1650 and roughly 0.5 percent between 1650 and 1730: Moriceau, *Fermiers*, pp. 402–3, 643. To cover this range of possibilities, I therefore performed the Paris Basin calculations—both for 1450–1789 and for 1750–1789—with capital growth rates of 0.0 percent and 0.5 percent. I also assumed a range for labor-supply growth in the Paris Basin, based on a number of experiments. The experiments ranged from assuming that the labor supply in the Paris Basin grew at the same rate as it did elsewhere in France to deriving estimates from evidence about the rural and urban populations of the *généralités* of Paris and Orléans. The evidence about the populations of these two généralités was taken from Philip Benedict, "Was the Eighteenth Century an Era of Urbanization in France?" *Journal of Interdisciplinary History* 21 (1990): 179–215; and Jacques Dupâquier, *La population rurale du Bassin Parisien à l'époque de Louis XIV* (Paris, 1979). My values for the increase in the food supply are close to estimates derived

from the tithe returns, which were about 0.50 percent per year in the eighteenth century: Le Roy Ladurie and Goy, "Première esquisse," p. 373.

106. For the Paris population, see Appendix A, part 14. For the widening of the Paris food supply, see George Grantham, "Urban Provisioning Zones Before the Industrial Revolution," manuscript, Department of Economics, McGill University, 1992. The estimate of the growth of the food supply near Paris after 1750 fit those derived from local tithe figures by Goy and Le Roy Ladurie.

107. See the detailed discussion of yields, capital per hectare, and labor per hectare in Bretteville in Appendix B, part 2. The idea here is that if Y is aggregated output, then for an arable farm Y is nearly all grain. If K, L, and C are land, labor, and capital, then the productivity of land—essentially grain yields—is Y/K, while the productivity of labor is Y/L, and the productivity of capital is Y/C. If the yields Y/K near Paris and Bretteville are the same and if farms use the same number of workers per hectare L/K, then the productivities of labor in the two regions must be the same because

$$\frac{Y}{L} = \frac{\frac{Y}{K}}{\frac{L}{K}}$$

Similarly, if the use of capital per hectare C/K is the same in the two regions, then the productivities of capital must be the same.

108. Circa 1600 wheat yields near Bretteville were at least 14 to 16.5 hectoliters per hectare, or roughly 16 to 19 bushels per acre, according to evidence from champart records in the nearby village of Cheux: Garnier, "Pays herbagers"; Pavard, "Productions et rendements céréaliers." My own analysis of some of the same champart records (AD Calvados, H 2873) suggests that these estimates are quite conservative: in 1603–8, wheat yields could have ranged as high as 18 to 27 hectoliters per hectare. As for yields a century earlier, we know much less. If we calculate an area weighted average yield from fragmentary evidence in Cairon family diaries, then yields were only 11 hectoliters per hectare circa 1500; apparently, they had increased over the sixteenth century, just as our TFP numbers would suggest. Unfortunately, the estimate of the yield in 1500 is far from certain: indeed, an unweighted average of the same evidence gives yields of 15 hectoliters per hectare in 1500 with a standard deviation of nearly 8 hectoliters per hectare. The yields in 1600, though, do merit our confidence, and they compare favorably with contemporary figures from England: Paul Glennie, "Measuring Crop Yields in Early Modern England," in *Land, Labour, and Livestock*, ed. Bruce M. S. Campbell and Mark Overton (Manchester, 1991), pp. 273, 278. Because yields were high near Bretteville, the productivities of labor and capital would be elevated in 1600 as long as workers and livestock per hectare remained low. That seems to have been the case, although the evidence is of course fragmentary. The evidence here comes from the records cited in the discussion of the shares used for the Paris Basin and the Bretteville farms; see Appendix A, part 6, and Appendix B, part 2, for further details.

109. In mathematical terms, the ratio of TFP on one farm to TFP on another will be:

$$\frac{(\frac{w_1}{\bar{w}_1})^{v_1} \dots (\frac{w_n}{\bar{w}_n})^{v_n}}{(\frac{p_1}{\bar{p}_1})^{u_1} \dots (\frac{p_m}{\bar{p}_m})^{u_m}}$$

Here the w's are the rents, wages, and prices as in equation (2), all measured in the same units; the prices without the tildes refer to one farm and the prices with the tildes refer to the other; and the v's are the average of the factor shares on the two farms, and the u's the average of the product shares on the two farms. This formula works for the same reason that we can compute a relative index of TFP when shares change merely by using average product and factor shares. For details, see Appendix B, part 1.

110. Given the low costs of transporting livestock, I assumed that meat and livestock prices were the same for both farms. The calculations were done using the Chartier shares and prices averaged over the current year and the previous eight years. I made the reasonable assumption that taxes took the same fraction of the rent at any given time in Normandy and the Paris Basin, and for each fifty-year period I adjusted the Paris Basin rents to give the cost of leasing property of the same average size as in Bretteville and the same distance from the relevant markets of Bayeux and Caen, which provided the prices for the Bretteville index P. Bretteville was 15 kilometers from Bayeux and 11 from Caen; I assumed that the Parisian property was 15 kilometers from market.

111. The comparison uses twenty-five-year price and wage averages (without any lags or averaging over the previous lease) for all inputs and outputs. It employs the Chartier shares for the Paris Basin and the Ladurie shares for Grillon. The outputs for both regions are grain, other crops, and animal products; the prices of these outputs are—again for both regions—taken to be the prices of wheat, wine, and mutton, respectively. The factors of production for both regions are labor, land, and capital, with the price of capital in both regions being the rental price of sheep. The rents for the Paris Basin are adjusted using the rent regressions in table 3.1 to put them on an equal footing with the Grillon properties in terms of area, percent meadow and vineyard, and distance from market, which in the case of the Grillon properties was the market in Aix. Again, I assumed that tax rates as a percentage of rent were similar for both properties, but this assumption is a bit dubious. The Grillon rental rates were taken from sales prices and so would reflect taxes, but Grillon was not part of the kingdom of France. A similar comparison was not possible for the Grange de la Sacristie because of uncertainties about the farm's area; for Cavaillon it was clouded by taxes: tenants in Cavaillon did not pay taxes on rental property, whereas in the Paris Basin they did. For yields, see Allen and Ó Gráda, "On the Road Again with Arthur Young," who use Arthur Young's evidence to reconstruct grain yields for France. Young's evidence is problematic, as they and other historians have noted, but the errors can be reduced by using the yields implied by his seed-yield ratios. These are much lower near Grillon, and the difference is borne out by early-nineteenth-century data.

112. The comparison corrects for property size and distance to the market, but it does not adjust for soil quality, which was poorer in the west. It also assumes that taxes were the same fraction of rent in both areas and compares TFP for twenty-five-year periods. The shares are the Merle shares for the farms near Nantes, and the Chartier shares for the Paris Basin. Prices are twenty-five-year averages for all inputs and outputs without lags or averaging over old leases. Inputs for both regions were land, labor, and capital, with capital prices in both areas computed from a rental price based on the interest rate, depreciation rates, and the sales price, which

was taken to be the price of meat. I used the price of meat as the sales price to avoid comparing cattle and sheep. Outputs in both areas were aggregated to animal products and crops, with the price of crops in both areas being the price of rye. Employing rye prices biased the results against the Paris Basin, as did the existence of extensive commons in the west. On the other hand, the lack of a correction for soil quality would stack the results against the west, for some of the low productivity there simply reflected poor soil. For yields, see Allen and Ó Gráda, "On the Road Again with Arthur Young." A productivity comparison based on prices and rents in the 1852 agricultural census led to analogous results for other parts of the west: the département of the Deux-Sèvres, for example, lagged behind the Seine-et-Marne by 40 to 58 percent.

113. Wrigley, "Urban Growth and Agriculture," table 10; Allen and Ó Gráda, "On the Road Again with Arthur Young." As Allen and Ó Gráda point out, Young took too many measurements in fertile river valleys in France. On the other hand, his itinerary may have also biased his estimates downward in the west or the southwest of France; see Morineau, *Les faux-semblants*, pp. 21–22. Fortunately, Allen and Ó Gráda can correct for some of the errors by using Young's seed-yield ratios and nineteenth-century evidence. As for meat, wool, and dairy products, a comparison of estimates made by Young and Antoine Lavoisier suggests that England had roughly twice as much livestock per hectare as France in the late eighteenth century: roughly forty head per 100 hectares in England versus only twenty head in France. The comparison here assumes that larger animals such as cattle and horses were worth one head, while sheep were only a tenth of a head. See Antoine Lavoisier, *Oeuvres de Lavoisier*, 6 vols. (Paris, 1864–93), 6: 420–21, and, for Young's estimates, A. H. John, "Statistical Appendix," in *AHEW*, 6:1045. However dubious such estimates may be, it is still hard to imagine England producing less from its animals. For another interesting comparison of England and France, see Jack A. Goldstone, "Regional Ecology and Agrarian Development in England and France," *Politics and Society* 16 (1988): 287–334.

114. Allen and Ó Gráda, "On the Road Again with Arthur Young," pp. 102, 111–12. The yields for northern France are actually for Young's loam district, which included Picardy, Flanders, Artois, Ile-de-France, and parts of Normandy, Alsace, and Auvergne—in other words, much more than the Paris Basin, where yields might have been higher still. George Grantham has proposed somewhat lower yields for the Paris Basin, but his Paris Basin is actually quite larger than the area I am considering. Closer to Paris, his yields are actually much higher. In any case, it seemed best to use Young's figures to compare England and France, because both sets of observations would then be made by the same observer. See Grantham's "The Growth of Labour Productivity in the *Cinq Grosses Fermes* of France, 1750–1929," in *Land, Labour, and Livestock*, ed. Bruce M. S. Campbell and Mark Overton (Manchester, 1991), pp. 340–63, especially p. 362. Because our interest is the late eighteenth century, it also seemed best not to compare English yields from the years 1835–37 with French yields from 1840, as Michel Morineau did in *Les faux-semblants*, pp. 73–85. The reason is that English yields increased considerably in the early nineteenth century, while French yields stood still; on this point, see Allen and Ó Gráda, "On the Road Again with Arthur Young." A comparison of yields in the nineteenth century might therefore lead to an erroneous conclusion about late-eighteenth-century agriculture.

115. In the late eighteenth century, the *généralité* of Paris had roughly forty head per 100 hectares, if we count large animals as one head and smaller ones such as sheep at a tenth of a head. This was the same as Young's estimates for England and Wales, and it fit the number of animals in English regions that resembled the Paris Basin—Hertfordshire, for example. See Meuvret, *Subsistances*, vol. 1, pt. 1 (*Texte*), pp. 124–25; John, "Statistical Appendix," *AHEW*, 6:1045, 1065. Evidence about typical arable farms in England also fits what we know about the Paris Basin; see Peter J. Bowden, "Agricultural Prices, Wages, Farm Profits and Rents," in *CAHEW*, 1:275.

116. Evidence that Arthur Young collected circa 1770 suggests that English farms hired about one permanent male laborer for every 30 to 40 hectares, with the precise number depending on the size and the nature of the farm. Not all the male laborers were necessarily plowmen, so that there might have been somewhat more land for each plowman on a farm. The number of plowmen on farms in the Paris Basin was in any case similar. It varied between one for every 30 hectares and one for every 60 hectares in the early modern period. North of Paris, it was perhaps one plowman for every 33 hectares in 1700 and one for every 45 hectares at the end of the century. See Armstrong, "Labour I," *AHEW*, 6:673, and the discussion in Appendix A, part 6. As for harvest operations, in the Paris Basin, the number of man-days it took to thresh grain and to cut it (with a sickle or the more efficient scythe) was similar to what it took in England: Grantham, "The Growth of Labour Productivity," p. 363; Tessier, *Agriculture*, s.v. "Faucheur"; G. E. Mingay et al., "Farming Techniques," *AHEW*, 6:291–92; and Gregory Clark, "Productivity Growth without Technical Change in European Agriculture before 1850," *JEH* 47, no. 2 (June 1987): 419–32.

117. For details, sources, and a justification of the choice of Hertfordshire, see Appendix B, part 2. The Paris Basin rents were adjusted slightly to take into account the distance between Hertfordshire and London.

118. Allen, "The Efficiency and Distributional Consequences"; for sources and further details of the comparisons here, see Appendix B, part 2.

119. The evidence about yields, workers per hectare, and livestock per hectare in eastern Germany comes from Abel, *Geschichte der deutschen Landwirtschaft*, pp. 215, 236–38, 251.

CHAPTER FIVE
EXPLAINING PRODUCTIVITY IN A TRADITIONAL ECONOMY

1. Polanyi, *The Great Transformation*.

2. François Quesnay, in Denis Diderot et al., eds., *Encyclopédie ou dictionnaire raisonné des sciences, des arts et des métiers par une société des gens de lettres*, 17 vols. (Paris-Neuchâtel, 1751–65), vol. 6, s.v. "Fermier"; Young, *Voyages en France*. For the debate over the issue among agronomists, see Bourde, *Agronomie et agronomes*, 2:1038–47. For modern historians, see Bloch, *French Rural History*; Robert Brenner, "Agrarian Class Structure and Economic Development in Pre-Industrial Europe" and "The Agrarian Roots of European Capitalism," in *The Brenner Debate*, ed. T. H. Aston and C.H.E. Philpin, pp. 10–63, 213–327. See also Hickey, "Innovation and Obstacles to Growth," and Allen, *Enclosure and the Yeoman*.

3. Brenner, "Agrarian Class Structure," pp. 30, 46, 49, 50–51, 59; idem, "Agrarian Roots," pp. 303–17. For the demographic argument, see Emmanuel Le Roy Ladurie, "Les masses profondes: La paysannerie," *HESF*, vol. 1, pt. 2, pp. 483–865.

4. For two striking dissents, see Robert Forster, "Obstacles to Agricultural Growth in Eighteenth-Century France," *American Historical Review* 75, pt. 2 (1970): 1600–1615; and Daniel Hickey, "Innovation and Obstacles to Growth."

5. Moriceau, *Fermiers*, pp. 363–93.

6. Jean-Michel Chevet, "Le Marquisat d'Ormesson"; Grantham, "The Diffusion of the New Husbandry"; idem, "Agricultural Supply during the Industrial Revolution"; Jacquart, *La crise rurale*, pp. 321–30; Meuvret, *Subsistances*; and Moriceau and Postel-Vinay, *Ferme, entreprise, famille*. Cf. Moriceau, *Fermiers*, pp. 342–73; idem, "Au rendez-vous de la 'révolution agricole.' " That soil quality has no effect on rent or on TFP (tables 3.1 and 4.3) is consistent with this story: near Paris, enough manure was available to make up for soil differences. For carriages in Paris, see Leon Bernard, *The Emerging City: Paris in the Age of Louis XIV* (Durham, 1970), pp. 56–68.

7. Jan de Vries, *European Urbanization 1500–1800* (Cambridge, 1984), pp. 137–42, 242.

8. Hanoteau died in 1785 and, according to the tax roll of that year, farmed 224 hectares. Records of his estate suggest that he farmed even more—some 400 hectares. I thank Gilles Postel-Vinay and Jean-Marc Moriceau for furnishing this information.

9. See Jacquart, *La crise rurale*, pp. 340–48; Moriceau, *Fermiers*, pp. 613–62; and for an excellent example, Moriceau and Postel-Vinay, *Ferme, entreprise, famille*. In the eighteenth century, Notre Dame wanted to suppress the buildings on properties no longer large enough to be economical farms: see AN LL 332 (1761–62, Larchant); and S 320 (26 June 1780, Lizy-sur-Ourcq). One sign of the greater frequency of *cumul de baux* was that the leases began to carry a clause acknowledging it: see AN S324A (Le Mesnil-Amelot, 25 June 1781); and S 407 (Viercy, 25 August 1785).

10. AN LL 329–30; S 272; and S 273 (1636–54).

11. For the tax rolls, see Jean Guerout, ed., *Rôles de la taille de l'élection de Paris conservés aux Archives Nationales (sous séries Z 1G) et dans les archives départementales* (Paris, 1981). A search at the Archives Nationales turned up tax assessments for forty-four tenants in the series Z 1G, and those assessments bore out the close relationship between the amount of the assessment and the number of hectares the tenant farmed. Tax assessments may have been misleading in earlier periods and in other regions, but here they seem a reliable guide to the acreage farmed. Unfortunately, I was able to get leases and usable tax assessments in both 1740–41 and 1783–89 for only seven of the properties. When more than one tax assessment was available for a property in 1740–41 or in 1783–89, I averaged the logarithm of the different assessments for each period. No tax correction is needed in figure 5.1; for an explanation, see Appendix A, part 13.

12. One might worry that the tax levies would mix scale effects with major capital improvements such as new buildings, but there were no such improvements between 1740 and 1789 on the properties in figure 5.1.

13. AN Z 1G 291B (1740), 292B (1741), 431A (1786), and 451B (1789). Hanoteau died in 1785, forcing me to use his widow's tax assessment for 1786 and 1789; using his own assessment for 1785 would not have changed matters appreciably. As with all the properties, the change in ln(TFP) here was computed between the years 1732–45 and 1777–89. Such long periods had to be chosen because of the volatility of rent payments and because the leases in force in the years 1740–41 and 1783–89 had been drawn up as early as 1732 and 1777.

14. Moriceau, *Fermiers*, pp. 613–62.

15. For a range of estimates for the evolution of the number of animals per hectare, see Meuvret, *Subsistances*, vol. 1, pt. 1 (*Texte*), p. 125; Moriceau, *Fermiers*, p. 643. Heavier animals—a possibility discussed below—would have a similar effect.

16. On the Chartier farm, the number of males hired to work per 100 hectares dropped 13 percent between the late seventeenth and the late eighteenth century: Moriceau and Postel-Vinay, *Ferme, entreprise, famille*, pp. 197–98, 208–9. I assumed that labor by women and by the tenant farmer fell by the same amount. The 13 percent decline implies a 5 percent increase in TFP, but this is likely to have occurred over the entire eighteenth century, rather than over the shorter period from 1725–49 to 1775–89. If we prorate the 13 percent decline in the use of labor over the forty-five years separating the midpoints of the periods 1725–49 and 1775–89, we get a 6 percent drop in the use of labor and a 2 percent increase in TFP between 1725–49 and 1775–89.

17. Meuvret, *Subsistances*, vol. 1, pt. 1, (*Texte*), pp. 194–203; Grantham, "The Growth of Labour Productivity," pp. 344–45, 362. Grantham's yield increase actually concerns a much larger area than my Paris Basin, and the absolute yields that he reports (15 hectoliters per hectare in 1800) are lower than the ones I employed in Chapter 4. Closer to Paris, though, in the area that is my Paris Basin, Grantham reports yields nearly identical to mine—20 hectoliters per hectare in 1750. In any event his yield increase seems reliable, and it should be noted that Chevet, "Le Marquisat d'Ormesson," 2:476–87, proposes even larger yield increases than does Grantham. Cf. Moriceau, "Au rendez-vous de la 'révolution agricole.'"

18. Moriceau and Postel-Vinay, *Ferme, entreprise, famille*, pp. 211, 243–44, 287, 323; Moriceau, "Au rendez-vous de la 'révolution agricole'"; Chevet, "Marquisat d'Ormesson," 2:476–510; idem, "Progrès techniques et productivité dans les fermes de la région parisienne aux 18e et 19e siècles" manuscript, Institut National de la Recherche Agronomique, Paris, 1989; Jacquart, *La crise rurale*, pp. 293–94; Emile Mireaux, *Une province française au temps du grand roi: La Brie* (Paris, 1958), p. 124; Goubert, *Beauvais et le Beauvaisis*, 1:97–98; Meuvret, *Subsistances*, vol. 1, pt. 1 (*Texte*), pp. 147–51; vol. 1, pt. 2 (*Notes*), pp. 147–52. Figures given by Meuvret suggest that the shift from maslin to rye affected up to 30 percent of the arable. Such a shift would increase TFP by 2 percent or less.

19. Paul Glennie, "Continuity and Change in Hertfordshire Agriculture 1550–1700: II-Trends in Crop Yields and their Determinants," *Agricultural History Review* 36 (1988): 145–61; George Grantham's estimates for the labor inputs involved in wheat farming do not reveal any additional soil preparation in the Paris area between 1750 and 1800. On the other hand, if more intensive soil preparation were restricted to small areas, the contemporary authorities that are Grantham's sources

may have not noticed it. See George Grantham, "The Growth of Labour Productivity," pp. 362–63. Unfortunately, Moriceau's *Fermiers* does not have enough evidence on the late eighteenth century to shed light on the matter.

20. Moriceau, "Au rendez-vous de la 'révolution agricole.' "

21. In "The Economics of Exhaustion," Greg Clark makes a persuasive case for nitrogen fixing, but recently George Grantham (personal communication) has contested his calculations. See also the discussion of artificial meadows below. For arguments involving larger herds or heavier animals, see Moriceau, "Au rendez-vous de la 'révolution agricole,' " and Chevet, "Marquisat d'Ormesson," 2:508–10. For the meager record of animal weights, see Husson, *Les consommations de Paris*, pp. 200–202.

22. Young, *Voyages en France*; Allen, *Enclosure and the Yeoman*, pp. 191–234.

23. Moriceau's *Fermiers* is a welcome first step in the right direction here.

24. Bloch, *French Rural History*, pp. 136–38, 207–8.

25. AD Calvados, F 1757, pp. 32, 81–82; H 3226, fols. 200–201, 244; H 3229; H 3551, pp. 10, 19–29, 43–52. See also M. Boudin, "Du laboureur aisé au gentilhomme campagnard: Les Perrote de Cairon, de Bretteville-l'Orgueilleuse (1380–1480)," *Annales de Normandie* 13 (1963): 237–68. For evidence that the process of consolidation began early, see H 3226, fol. 271, and H 3351, pp. 271–72. On the basis of a 1748 comparison of the two land surveys (H 3551), Boudin lists the Clos de la Perrelle as one of the few enclosures dating back to 1482, but the original 1482 survey (H 3226) demonstrates that it was consolidated and enclosed after 1482. For examples of exchanges of land that helped consolidate the Cairon holdings, see AD Calvados, F 1773 (19 October 1667), and F 1776 (2 November 1508).

26. The property ownership records include AD Calvados, F 1650, F 1757, H 3226, H 3229, and H3351. The account books include F 1652, which covers the years 1473–85; F 1697, which concerns the period 1691–1705; and the excerpts from two early-sixteenth-century account books published in Aubert, "Notes extraites de trois livres de raison de 1473 à 1550," pp. 447–99. The calculations below depend on these sources and on the 1673 probate inventory of Jean de Cairon in F 1665.

27. Cf. Madeleine Foisil, *Le Sire de Gouberville, un gentilhomme normand au XVIe siècle* (Paris, 1981), pp. 108–10.

28. I have omitted carriage horses listed in the 1673 probate inventory I used, and assumed that family members farmed all of the land they owned. Had they leased any out, the number of horses used per acre might have been higher in the late fifteenth century. The number of horses used was similar to that on large farms near Paris.

29. Moriceau and Postel-Vinay, *Ferme, entreprise, famille*, pp. 197–98, 208–9.

30. Restricting the regressions to farms that actually had horses may involve a rather subtle problem of truncation, but we are only interested in farms with horses. Furthermore, if we include in the regressions the farms over 5 hectares without horses, we get nearly the same results. Similarly, if we restrict the regressions to farms over 10 or 20 hectares—all of these had horses—the regressions are once again nearly the same.

31. Piel, *Essai sur la réforme de l'impôt direct*. For consolidation in Rots, see AD Calvados, H 3229.

32. See also Moriceau and Postel-Vinay, *Ferme, entreprise, famille*, pp. 197–98.

33. AD Calvados, F 1652, F 1697; Allen, *Enclosure and the Yeoman*, pp. 211–31.

34. In *Enclosure and the Yeoman*, pp. 224–29, Allen finds a 58 percent increase in TFP between 1600 and 1800, three-fourths of which (a 44 percent increase) was realized in the seventeenth century, primarily from higher yields. The remainder was the result of eighteenth-century farm amalgamation.

35. The calculation here involved a Törnqvist productivity index—the same sort of index we used to compare our method of measuring productivity in the Paris Basin with evidence about physical inputs and outputs. See Chapter 4 and Appendix A, part 11, for this earlier use of the Törnqvist productivity index. In making the calculation, I relied on the Bernonville shares rather than the Chartier shares used in the lease regressions, because the disaggregated Bernonville shares allowed me to separate out the effects of oat feed and equipment such as harnesses. Since both sets of shares gave similar TFP results, the choice of shares should not matter. The regressions in table 5.2 lead to similar results. Doubling the average farm—a generous allowance for the increase in size one might expect from consolidation—leads to an 18 percent decrease in the number of horses and plowmen, very close to the 17 percent figure derived from the Cairon accounts.

36. Although multicollinearity afflicts the sixteenth-century regression used here (table 4.7), it does not affect the coefficient of the year. Indeed, varying the specification—omitting the fraction of land enclosed, or including the property area or the fraction of the land that is pasture—leads to coefficients for the year that are nearly identical: they range from .42 to .44. If instead of relying upon the regression in table 4.7, we simply take the difference between the average productivity of all the plots in our sample in 1520–49 and the productivity of all the plots in 1550–99, then we do get a lower figure for the productivity increase over the sixteenth century—roughly 12 percent. I would argue, though, that the regression gives us a better measurement of TFP growth, because we are not sampling the same properties in both periods.

37. The estimate here begins by adding a dummy variable for major repairs to the rental regression in table 3.1. The coefficient of the dummy variable implies that major repairs amounted to 39 percent of the average rent. Such major repairs—rebuilding a barn, for example—did not happen every year, though; they were a sizable investment, which would be stretched out over the life of a building. On average, major repairs happened only one year in 20; or on the properties over 20 hectares, which were more likely to have buildings, only one year in eleven. If we spread out the 39 percent of the rent over eleven years and add 5 percent interest cost, we get a generous estimate for the imputed rental cost of buildings of 8 percent of the rent. (For a real example where the imputed rent is very close to this—9 percent—see AN LL 332, Larchant, 1761.) Consolidating two properties might cut this in half and thus increase TFP by perhaps 1.5 percent or less, depending on the shares we use in our calculation. Even if consolidation completely eliminated the costs of maintaining buildings—an impossibility—the TFP increase would be at most 3 percent.

38. In the first place, there is no clear evidence that the number of sheep had diminished. I estimate that there were at least 339 sheep per 100 hectares on

Nicolas de Cairon's farm in 1473–84; it is not clear whether the figure includes lambs or not. When Jean de Cairon died in 1673, his farm had roughly the same number of sheep, or perhaps more: between 342 and 406 sheep per 100 hectares, depending on which death inventory one uses and whether one counts lambs as one-half or as one full head. On the other hand, by the turn of the century Jean de Cairon's son farmed with a slightly smaller number of sheep—perhaps as low as 224 per 100 hectares, if we count lambs as one-half head and ignore the possibility that he was renting additional sheep for part of the year. The trend is simply not clear, although the average of the two seventeenth-century figures would seem about the same as the late fifteenth-century one. See AD Calvados, F 1652; F 1665, pièces 16 and 18; F 1697; H 3351. Second, even a considerable drop in the number of sheep would translate into only a minuscule increase in TFP. With the Bernonville shares, for example, a 50 percent decline in the number of sheep would increase TFP by less than 4 percent; and if there was indeed greater efficiency in the use of sheep, it was probably much less than this. As for farm size, in the late fifteenth century the Cairon family farmed as much as 88 hectares. By the late seventeenth century, their land was split up among several branches of the family, so that Jean de Cairon's holdings, for example, were a bit under 50 hectares—relatively small compared to the gigantic farms then emerging near Paris. For economies of scale in sheep raising, see Rozier, *Cours complet d'agriculture*, s.v. "Mouton, bélier, brebis."

39. AD Calvados, F1697 (1702, 1703); C 277 (1727), C 278 (1731–34, 1764); 2 C 1174 (1735); Aubert, "Notes extraites de trois livres de raison de 1473 à 1550," p. 471; Jean-Claude Perrot, *Genèse d'une ville moderne: Caen au XVIIIe siècle,* 2 vols. (Paris, 1975), 1:193–204, 230–32.

40. For the yields in Bretteville, see Chapter 4.

41. Chevet, "Marquisat d'Ormesson," 2:520–29; Allen, *Enclosure and the Yeoman*, pp. 193–200. Large, consolidated farms did enjoy advantages in keeping sheep and spreading their fertilizer—folding sheep (*parcage*) was easier on big farms—but small farms had more livestock overall. Cf. Tessier, *Agriculture*, s.v. "Bêtes à laine"; Rozier, *Cours complet d'agriculture*, s.v. "Mouton, bélier, brebis." Moriceau, *Fermiers*, pp. 379–86, 403, 643, 870, finds more livestock by 1700 than in table 5.3 and more sheep on large farms. However, his figures for agricultural capital as a whole per hectare—chiefly livestock—show no tendency to rise with farm size.

42. One might argue that small parcels would be worked more intensely and hence show higher yields, but the regression coefficients and *t* statistics are not large enough to support such an argument.

43. The champart records used here are from AD Calvados, H 2873, which records the champart receipts for 1603–8; H 2874 contains additional receipts for the early 1630s, which I did not use because the farmers were completely different. To see if the parcels subject to the champart were scattered throughout the village, I used the nineteen maps drawn up for a 1674 *terrier* in AD Calvados, H 2892, to divide the village up into nineteen sections. Since the maps were each of the same size and had the same scale, each section was roughly of the same size, and using the parcel descriptions in the champart receipts, I could place over two-thirds of the parcels in one of nineteen sections. One section had no champart parcels, and four

others had four or fewer champart parcels, but otherwise the champart seemed relatively evenly distributed over the fields of Cheux. I also used the sections to control for variations in microclimate and soil fertility by simply assigning a dummy variable to the parcels in each section. For the champart in Cheux, see Pavard, "Productions et rendements céréaliers."

44. Allen, *Enclosure and the Yeoman*, pp. 13–21, 200–210; Mark Overton, "The Determinants of Crop Yields in Early Modern England," in *Land, Labour, Livestock*, ed. Bruce M. S. Campbell and Mark Overton (Manchester, 1991), pp. 284–322, especially pp. 309–10.

45. Chevet, "Marquisat d'Ormesson," 2:498–502.

46. Moriceau and Postel-Vinay, *Ferme, entreprise, famille*, pp. 191, 241–43; Meuvret, *Subsistances*, vol. 1, pt. 1 (*Texte*), pp. 127–36; Chevet, "Marquisat d'Ormesson," 2:519–20; Rozier, *Cours complet d'agriculture*, s.v. "Mouton, bélier, brebis"; Moriceau, *Fermiers*, pp. 423–24.

47. Moriceau, *Fermiers*, pp. 613–35.

48. Southeast of Paris, in the villages of Guignes and Yèbles, the size of farms grew 34 percent between 1717 and 1789, according to tax roles analyzed by Chevet, "Le Marquisat d'Ormesson," tables 6 and 7. Chevet's figures here are restricted to farms over 10 hectares. Unfortunately, it is difficult to find tax rolls or fiscal investigations that record the farm size both in the early eighteenth century and at the century's end. Cf. Meuvret, *Subsistances*, vol. 2, pt. 1 (*Texte*), p. 126; and Moriceau, *Fermiers*, p. 631. As for converting these size figures into productivity, a regression of the data in figure 5.1 suggests that tripling farm size raises TFP by 2.9 percent; increasing farm size by 34 percent boosts it by merely 0.8 percent.

49. Grantham, "The Persistence of Open-Field Farming"; Dombasle, "Des réunions territoriales"; François de Neufchâteau, *Voyages agronomiques dans la sénatorie de Dijon* (Paris, 1806); Georges Hottenger, *La propriété rurale: Morcellement et remembrement* (Paris-Nancy, n.d.); Alfred de Foville, *Le morcellement* (Paris, 1885), pp. 165, 179; Henri Boulay, *De la dispersion des propriétés et des moyens d'y remédier* (Nancy, 1902).

50. Young, *Voyages en France*; Bourde, *Agronomie et agronomes*, 1:253–368. Among the numerous modern historians who make similar arguments, one should note Bloch, *French Rural History*; Neveux, *Vie et déclin*; and Clark, "The Economics of Exhaustion."

51. In AD Calvados, H 3348, a tithe dispute in 1573 shows peas and vetch on 2 to 3 acres of the 24 acres involved in the dispute. Because tithe disputes were more common when crops were new, these 24 acres may not have been representative of the rest of the village. Tithe records from the late fifteenth century did not mention vetch or peas, but they do appear in the Cairon diaries in the 1490s: Aubert, "Notes extraites de trois livres de raison de 1473 à 1550," p. 471. In all likelihood, the pulses in Bretteville were not sown on the fallow. Rather, they were probably part of a crop rotation that retained the fallow and yet coaxed more wheat out of the ground at the expense of spring grains, just as in the Paris Basin. Evidence from nearby Cheux has been used to argue for planting on the fallow, but the figures cited undercut the argument: Pavard, "Productions et rendements céréaliers"; and Garnier, "Pays herbagers." Cf. Moriceau, *Fermiers*, pp. 363–69. Sainfoin in Bretteville and neighboring villages: AD Calvados, H 3229 (1666–67).

52. Bourde, *Agronomie et agronomes*, 1:537–57. For one example among many, see Young, *Voyages en France*, 2:722–31.

53. Bloch, *French Rural History*, pp. 42–46, 219–34; idem, "La lutte pour l'individualisme agraire"; Meuvret, *Subsistances*, vol. 2, pt. 1 (*Texte*), pp. 12–45. For the hedges and ditches in Bretteville, see AD Calvados, H 3229; contemporary leases also specified that they be maintained: 7 E 162, 7 E 175, H 3364. For Gorze and similar incidents in Lorraine, see AD Moselle, B 5058 (15 to 19 October 1787); E dépôt 257, Gorze, liasse 4; B 5716 (21 June 1790) and B 5693, *passim*. For contemporary warnings of the damage animals could do to artificial meadows and natural pasture, see Tessier, *Agriculture*, s.v. "Bêtes à laine," "Clôture," "Luzerne," "Sainfoin," "Trèfle"; Nicolas Durival, *Mémoire concernant la clôture des heritages, le vaine-pâturage et le parcours en Lorraine* (Nancy, 1763).

54. Allen, *Enclosure and the Yeoman*, pp. 137–38; Overton, "The Determinants of Crop Yields," p. 310. In "Measuring Crop Yields in Early Modern England," p. 275, Paul Glennie maintains that fodder crops did raise grain yields somewhat, but he argues that among the fodder crops artificial grasses had little to do with the yield increases.

55. AN F10 351 (1811–12: artificial meadows of sainfoin, clover, and alfalfa for over sixty years near Saint-Quentin, without enclosures); Ministère de l'instruction publique et des beaux-arts. Comité des travaux historiques et scientifiques, *La statistique agricole de 1814* (Paris, 1914), p. 470; AN S 471 A (6 February 1664), S 474 (6 May 1690), S 475 (30 April 1700): sainfoin in La Grande-Paroisse. Incursions by animals into the sainfoin in La Grande-Paroisse were generally rare. Indeed, the *registre de greffe* of the local seigneurial court, which seems complete from 1723 to 1792, lists only seven *délits champêtres* of any sort—not just sheep grazing in sainfoin but other problems as well: AN Z2 4604. See also Jacquart, *La crise rurale*, pp. 328–30; Chevet, "Marquisat d'Ormesson," 2:493–510; and Moriceau, *Fermiers*, pp. 344–50. For sainfoin in Lorraine, see AD Moselle, B 5716 (21 June 1790) and B 5693.

56. Gorze: AD Moselle, B 5058 (15 to 19 October 1787); E dépôt 257, Gorze, liasse 4. For the edicts in Lorraine and enclosures in their aftermath, see AN H1 1515; Bourde, *Agronomie et agronomes*, 2:1151–68; AD Moselle, E dépôt 453 (Marsal), liasse 120; E dépôt 609 (Saint-Avold), liasses 27 and 332. Despite the enclosures in Saint-Avold, a tax document drawn up in 1791, and covering a quarter of the village (contribution foncière, section A), shows that only 13 of 1,098 pieces of land were enclosed; none of the 13 were large. Arthur Young also commented that the effect of the edicts in Lorraine was minimal: *Voyages en France*, 2:727–28.

57. Donald N. McCloskey, "The Open Fields of England: Rent, Risk, and the Rate of Interest, 1300–1815," in *Markets in History*, ed. David Galenson (Cambridge, 1989), pp. 20–21; George Boyer, "England's Two Agricultural Revolutions," *JEH* 53 (1993): 919.

58. As I explain in Chapter 2, the rent increase here is that attributed to the project alone and not to changing prices or other increases in productivity. The TFP calculation assumes the medium-yield shares for Lorraine. For the difficulties of establishing artificial meadows on undrained soil, see Tessier, *Agriculture*, s.v. "Trèfle"; Boulay, *De la dispersion des propriétés*, pp. 9–11; Grantham, "The Dif-

fusion of the New Husbandry." For the English evidence, see Robert Allen, *Enclosure and the Yeoman*, pp. 165–66, 176–77.

59. Dombasle, "Des réunions territoriales," p. 270; Grantham, "Persistence of Open-Field Farming," pp. 527–30; Hottenger, *La propriété rurale*; Peltre, *Recherches métrologiques*, pp. 175–221, 259–84; Bourde, *Agronomie et Agronomes*, 3:1408–12; Boulay, *De la dispersion des propriétés*, pp. 1–26,114–31. By the late nineteenth century, the general enclosures came to be known as *remembrements*. There were many remembrements after the Thirty Years' War in Lorraine, but these earlier remembrements were merely attempts to restore the old layout of the fields. They changed little or nothing in the agricultural landscape.

60. See Chapter 2; and for the nineteenth-century evidence, see Grantham, "Persistence of Open-Field Farming."

61. Joan Thirsk, "Agricultural Policy: Public Debate and Legislation," *AHEW*, vol. 5, pt. 2: 378–82; J. M. Martin, "Members of Parliament and Enclosure: A Reconsideration," *Agricultural History Review* 27, no. 2 (1979): 101–9; W. H. Hosford, "Some Lincolnshire Enclosure Documents," *Economic History Review*, 2d series, vol. 2, no. 1 (1949): 73–79. Donald McCloskey was the first to stress the importance of the enclosure acts in overcoming the unanimity problem: "The Economics of Enclosure."

62. Hoffman, "Early Modern France, 1450–1700," p. 250.

63. AN H1 1624, pièce 18: mémoire du sieur Boutier; Hoffman, "Institutions and Agriculture." Cf. Root, *Peasants and King*.

64. The same was true of nearly every other general enclosure in the eighteenth century: Grantham, "Persistence of Open-Field Farming," pp. 527–28; Peltre, *Recherches metrologiques*, pp. 259–84; Boulay, *De la dispersion des propriétés*, pp. 114–31.

65. Rosenthal, *Fruits of Revolution*.

66. Grantham, "The Persistence of Open-Field Farming," pp. 528–31.

67. Hugh D. Clout, *The Land of France* (London, 1973), pp. 67–68.

68. Clout, *The Land of France*, pp. 33, 49, 67–68; Dombasle, "Des réunions territoriales," pp. 282–83; de Neufchâteau, *Voyages agronomiques*, pp. 30–35; de Foville, *Morcellement*, pp. 177–87; Hottenger, *La propriété rurale*, pp. 87–110; Boulay, *De la dispersion des propriétés*, pp. 9, 161; [French] Ministère des finances, *Procès-verbaux de la commission extraparlementaire du cadastre institué au Ministre des finances (décret du 30 mai 1891). Documents annexes aux procès-verbaux*, Fascicule 4 (Paris, 1893). The estimate that one-sixth of Lorraine's arable needed drainage is based on figures for the department of the Moselle only: Agriculture, commerce, travaux publics, Ministère, *Enquête agricole*, 2e série: *Enquêtes départementales: 12e circonscription: Meuse, Ardennes, Moselle, Meurthe* (Paris, 1867), p. 376.

69. See the discussion in de Vries, *European Urbanization*, pp. 246–49, and also David Ringrose, *Madrid and the Spanish Economy, 1560–1850* (Berkeley, 1983); Paul Bairoch, *Cities and Economic Development: From the Dawn of History to the Present* (Chicago, 1988); Paul M. Hohenberg and Lynn H. Lees, *The Making of Urban Europe, 1000–1950* (Cambridge, 1985); Bernard Lepetit, *Les villes dans la France moderne (1740–1840)* (Paris, 1988); idem, "Urbanization in Eighteenth-Century France: A Comment," *Journal of Interdisciplinary History* 23 (Summer,

1992): 87–95; Philip Benedict, "Urbanization in Eighteenth-Century France: A Reply," *Journal of Interdisciplinary History* 23 (Summer, 1992):73–85; E. A. Wrigley, *People, Cities and Wealth: The Transformation of Traditional Society* (New York, 1987), pp. 133–56; Jean-Yves Grenier et al., "Croissance et déstabilisation," in *Histoire de la population française*, ed. Jacques Dupâquier, 2:438–51.

70. To decide whether it is productivity growth that leads to urbanization or whether the reverse is in fact the case, we can use regressions like those in table 4.4. Instead of calculating the growth rate of TFP and of the Paris population over the same periods (the course of the previous lease), we instead run the regressions with the growth rate of the Paris population lagged or led by one period—typically nine years. If the Paris population growth rate one period after the lease is signed has a large, positive, and significant coefficient, then TFP growth is associated with subsequent population growth, and it is reasonable to assume that the effect we observe is simply the urbanization that ensues from higher agricultural productivity. Similarly, if urban growth two leases back into the past has such a coefficient, then it clearly causes higher productivity. Unfortunately, both regressions yield coefficients that are negative, small in absolute value, and statistically insignificant. The tests simply do not let us resolve the matter. We can, though, dismiss one possible interpretation of the relationship between TFP growth and urbanization in the Paris Basin: that it simply reflects declining transportation costs, lower transportation costs that made feeding a larger city possible but which our TFP measure would erroneously measure as greater agricultural productivity. If so, then the relationship should disappear when we run the regression for the years after 1750, when transportation costs were nearly constant. However, far from disappearing, the relationship appears to be even stronger after 1750.

71. Meuvret, *Subsistances*, vol. 3, pt. 2 (*Texte*), pp. 60–61.

72. The tests involved regressing the average growth of TFP on the increase of the city's population. In performing the regressions, I corrected for the heteroscedacticity caused by the differing variances of the TFP growth rates. One might worry here that proximity to cities would create higher opportunity costs for land outside of agriculture and thus distort my TFP figures. However, all of my TFP estimates derived from land that was in agricultural use; the opportunity costs outside agricultural would therefore not be high enough to affect the rent.

73. Unfortunately, it is as yet impossible to use rental series to investigate London's analogous effects on nearby agriculture. The necessary long-rental series are rare for England, and those that do exist are complicated by enclosures and changing property rights. Furthermore, until rack renting became common—typically, in the eighteenth century—it is hard to argue that rental payments reflected the true value of the land. Gregory Clark's current research will undoubtedly change this situation.

74. Jean Meyer, "Le commerce Nantais du XVIe au XVIIIe siècle," in *Histoire de Nantes*, ed. Paul Bois, pp. 117–54; idem, "L'agriculture bretonne au 18e siècle," in *Irlande et France. Pour une histoire rurale comparée. Actes du 1er colloque franco-irlandais d'histoire économique et sociale*, ed. Louis M. Cullen and François Furet (Paris, 1980), pp. 21–35. Bordeaux again furnishes an obvious contrast here; it had an enormous effect on agriculture in the surrounding region, an effect that, for lack of leases, we cannot measure.

75. Cf. Ken Sokoloff, "Inventive Activity in Early Industrial America: Evidence from Patent Records," *JEH* 48 (1988): 813–50; Joel Mokyr, *The Lever of Riches: Technological Creativity and Economic Progress* (Oxford, 1990), pp. 191, 251.

76. Grantham "The Diffusion of the New Husbandry"; idem, "Agricultural Supply during the Industrial Revolution."

77. Grantham's Paris region includes Normandy, where artificial meadows were also profitable. I could not do a separate calculation of costs and implicit prices for Normandy because I had only price indexes and not the necessary prices themselves.

78. See the observations of the Venetian ambassador in 1577, quoted in Husson, *Les consommations de Paris*, pp. 113–14; even then hay was being shipped over long distances to Paris by river. For evidence from the middle of the seventeenth century, see Meuvret, *Subsistances*, vol. 2, pt. 2 (*Notes*): pp. 59–60; AN AD IX 400, numéro 6 (1649); and Moriceau, *Fermiers*, pp. 347–500. Cf. Liger, *La nouvelle maison rustique*, 2:728–29; and F. H. Gilbert, *Traité des prairies artificielles* (Paris, 1789).

79. The calculation assumes that 80 percent of the land around Paris was arable, that fertilizer was supplied by animals, that farmers had forty head of livestock for every 100 hectares of arable, and that horses equaled one head of livestock. The forty head of livestock per 100 hectares was the average of all *élections* in the généralité of Paris in 1788. See Meuvret, *Subsistances*, vol. 1, pt. 1 (*Texte*), pp. 121–27. For a similar calculation, see Chevet, "Progrès techniques," which documents the eighteenth-century use of urban manure. See also Chevet, "Marquisat d'Ormesson," 2:508–510; Grantham, "Agricultural Supply during the Industrial Revolution," pp. 48–52; and Gilbert, *Traité des prairies artificielles*, pp. 19–21.

80. The urban population figures here are taken from a data base assembled by Philip Benedict. For a discussion, see Benedict, "Was the Eighteenth Century an Era of Urbanization?"; Lepetit, "Urbanization in Eighteenth-Century France: A Comment"; Benedict, "Urbanization in Eighteenth-Century France: A Reply." As for the number of urban horses and other animals, precise figures for the Old Regime are lacking, but Lavoisier made some credible guesses for the number of horses circa 1789. According to his estimates, there were 21,500 horses in Paris; another 160,000 could be found in the other cities of France and in large-scale transportation (*roulage*): *Oeuvres de Lavoisier*, 6:420. If we ignore the roulage, then the number of horses in cities turns out to be roughly proportional to the urban population. If so, Paris undoubtedly had far more horses than other cities, simply because it was so much larger. Furthermore, the difference was probably even greater than the population figures suggest, because the roulage was not insignificant.

81. Grantham, "Agricultural Supply during the Industrial Revolution," p. 51.

82. For a more elaborate economic argument, see Appendix C.

83. Bernard Lepetit, *Chemins de terre et voies d'eau* (Paris, 1984); Henri Cavaillès, *La route française, son histoire, sa fonction: Etude de géographie humaine* (Paris, 1946); Pierre Léon and Charles Carrière, "L'appel des marchés," *HESF*, 2:166–80; Meuvret, *Subsistances*, vol. 3, pt. 1 (*Texte*), pp. 64–72, 93–94; Guy Arbellot "La grande mutation des routes de France au milieu du XVIII siècle," *AESC* 28 (1973): 765–91.

84. For the economic argument, see Appendix C. For eighteenth-century evidence that high transportation costs ruled out the use of urban waste as fertilizer, see L. Rose, *Le bon fermier ou l'ami du laboureur* (Lille, 1767), p. 395.

85. Kaplan, *Provisioning Paris*, pp. 83–87, 342–45, 473, 482, 599; Meuvret, *Subsistances*, vol. 3, pt. 1 (*Texte*); Moriceau, *Fermiers*, pp. 286–99.

86. Kaplan, *Provisioning Paris*, p. 344. Information about grain merchants in France was limited because of the illegality of their dealings; for a survey of the meager information available from a registration law of 1770, see Kaplan, *Bread, Politics and Political Economy*, 1:283–93.

87. Cf. Meuvret, *Subsistances*, vol. 3, pt. 2 (*Notes*): 118–20, 131–34.

88. "Mémoire sur la navigation des rivières, par Vauban," in *Mémoires des intendants sur l'état des généralités dressés pour l'instruction du Duc de Bourgogne*, ed. A. M. Boislisle, vol. 1: *Mémoire sur la généralité de Paris* (Paris, 1881), p. 402. Such sentiment was more common later in the eighteenth century: Tessier, *Agriculture*, "Discours préliminaire"; Frêche, *Toulouse et la région Midi-Pyrénées*, p. 563.

89. Merle, *La métairie*; Peret, *Seigneurs et seigneuries en Gâtine Poitevine*; Vallez, "Le commerce des bestiaux en Normandie; Mulliez, "Du blé, 'mal nécessaire.'"

90. For the Auge and the plain of Caen, in addition to Chapter 4, see Mulliez, "Du blé, 'mal nécessaire'"; Garnier, "La mise en herbe"; Vallez, "Le commerce des bestiaux en Normandie"; Perrot, *Genèse d'une ville moderne*, 1:204. For problems with transportation and trade in the west, see Lepetit, *Chemins de terre et voies d'eau*; Cavaillès, *La route française*; Léon and Carrière, "L'appel des marchés,"*HESF*, 2:166–80; Meyer, *La noblesse bretonne*, 2:700; Le Brun, *Les hommes et la mort en Anjou*; Alain Croix, *La Bretagne aux 16e et 17e siècles: La vie—La Mort—La foi*, 2 vols. (Paris, 1981), 1:22–23, 38–39; and also the demographic evidence in Dupâquier, *La population rurale du Bassin Parisien*, pp. 153–54. For early livestock breeding in Anjou and its limits, see Le Mené, *Les campagnes angevines*, pp. 323–57.

91. Cf. Jean Bourgeon, *La vie est dans le pré* (Nantes, 1986); Croix, *La Bretagne aux 16e et 17e siècles*, 1:42.

92. The case here is at best circumstantial. It consists of evidence that per-capita meat consumption in Paris continued to rise for most of the eighteenth century, a sign that Paris was perhaps buying more meat from regions besides the west. See Marcel Lachiver, "L'approvisionnement de Paris en viande au XVIIIe siècle," in *La France d'ancien régime: Etudes réunies en l'honneur de Pierre Goubert*, 2 vols. (Paris, 1984), 1:345–54; Lebrun, *Les hommes et la mort en Anjou*, pp. 49–58.

93. See Chapter 4; Durand, *Vin, vigne, vignerons*, pp. 93–101, 111–14, 128–32; and especially Dion, *Histoire de la vigne*, pp. 576–93.

94. Frêche, *Toulouse et la région Midi-Pyrénées*, pp. 6–7, 213–43, 580–86, 639–62.

95. In addition to Chapter 4, see H. Wiese and J. Bölts, *Rinderhandel und Rinderhaltung in nordwesteuropaischen Küstengebiet vom 15. bis zum 19. Jahrhundert* (Stuttgart, 1966), pp. 9, 112; Wilhelm Abel, *Geschichte der deutschen Landwirtschaft*, pp. 180–83; de Vries, *The Dutch Rural Economy*. The local herds of cattle provided abundant fertilizer for the local arable, so that the area could easily

feed itself and even export some grain. As a result, it was not held back by the need to keep large amounts of land in cereals, as was the case in much of the west of France.

96. Cavaillès, *La route française*; Lepetit, *Chemins de terre et voies d'eau*; Meuvret, *Subsistances*, vol. 3, pt. 2 (*Notes*): 26.

97. Baehrel, *Une croissance*, pp. 29–30, 78, 104–8, 217–23; Le Roy Ladurie, *Les paysans de Languedoc*, 1:645; idem, "De la crise ultime à la vraie croissance," *HFR*, 2:359–599; Rosenthal, *Fruits of Revolution*.

98. Cf. Bowden, "Agricultural Prices, Wages, Farm Profits and Rents, 1640–1750," *CAHEW*, 1:195–97; Abel, *Geschichte der deutschen Landwirtschaft*, pp. 174–90, 231; Le Roy Ladurie, "De la crise ultime à la vraie croissance."

99. Cf. Douglass C. North and Robert Paul Thomas, *The Rise of the Western World: A New Economic History* (Cambridge, 1973), p. 93.

100. Frêche, *Toulouse et la région Midi-Pyrénées*, pp. 579–637, presents costs and revenues from the Canal du Midi and evidence about transportation costs. But estimates of the tonnage transported are too rare to estimate the social savings from the canal, and the prevalence of sharecropping on local farms means we cannot measure the increase in rent it generated. For a more skeptical view of the canal, see Jan de Vries, *The European Economy in an Age of Crisis* (Cambridge, 1976), pp. 168–75.

101. Rosenthal, *Fruits of Revolution*. For examples of the difficulties that private entrepreneurs encountered when they tried to improve water transportation, see Kaplan, *Provisioning Paris*, pp. 83–87. For the political problems of road building, see Cavaillès, *La route française*.

102. Richard Perren, "Markets and Marketing," *AHEW*, 6:190–274; Moriceau and Postel-Vinay, *Ferme, entreprise, famille*, pp. 263–67.

103. Le Roy Ladurie, *Paysans de Languedoc*, 1:527–29, 588–89; Moriceau, *Fermiers*, pp. 515–16. Lower prices should not change the TFP index, but if they caused farmers to cut back on maintenance, then rents would fall to levels reflecting not only the lower prices but the deterioration of the property. Measured TFP would thus drop.

104. John Fortescue, *De laudibus legum Anglie*, ed. and trans. S. B. Chrimes (Cambridge, 1949); Peter Mathias and Patrick O'Brien, "Taxation in Britain and France, 1715–1810. A Comparison of the Social and Economic Incidence of Taxes Collected for the Central Governments," *Journal of European Economic History* 5 (1976): 601–50; Philip T. Hoffman and Kathryn Norberg, "Conclusion," in their *Fiscal Crises*, pp. 299–302. For Lavoisier, the tax system discouraged agriculture: Henri Pigeonneau and Alfred de Foville, eds., *L'administration de l'agriculture au contrôle général des finances (1785–87): Procès-verbaux et rapports* (Paris, 1882), pp. 409–10. Many other eighteenth-century commentators shared his opinion.

105. AN Z1G 440, 451B; AD Calvados, C 277, 2 C 1191 (Carpiquet, 1740), 2 C 1193 (Cheux, 1740), 2 C 1317 (Rots, 1740), 2 C 1345 (Secqueville-en-Bassin, 1740); Bowden, "Agricultural Prices, Wages, Farm Profits and Rents, 1640–1750," *CAHEW*, 1:260–61; James Collins, *The Fiscal Limits of Absolutism* (Berkeley, 1988) pp. 199–200. Cf. Moriceau, *Fermiers*, pp. 542, 551. For an example of higher taxes in Germany, see Abel, *Geschichte der deutschen Landwirtschaft*, p. 218.

106. Clément, ed., *Lettres, instructions et mémoires de Colbert*, vol. 2, pt. 1 (*Finances, impôts, monnaies*): 71, 73, 89, 120, 126, 168; Yves-Marie Bercé, "Notes sur les procédés de recouvrement au XVIIe siècle," in *La fiscalité et ses implications sociales en Italie et en France aux XVIIe et XVIIIe siècles* (Rome, 1980); Hickey, "Innovation and Obstacles to Growth"; Collins, *The Fiscal Limits of Absolutism*, p. 207; Meuvret, *Subsistances*, vol. 2, pt. 1 (*Texte*), pp. 56–62; Boris Porchnev, *Les soulèvements populaires en France de 1623 à 1648* (Paris, 1963), pp. 422–38; Roland Mousnier, *Peasant Uprisings in Seventeenth-Century France, Russia, and China*, trans. Brian Pearce (New York, 1972), pp. 87–88; Edmond Esmonin, *La taille en Normandie au temps de Colbert (1661–1683)* (Paris, 1913), pp. 424–28, 451–500; Paul de Longuemare, *Etude sur le canton de Tilly-sur-Seulles* (Caen, 1907), pp. 44–45; Moriceau, *Fermiers*, 515–612.

107. Esmonin, *La taille en Normandie*, pp. 465–90.

108. See Chapter 4 and AN S 154 (15 February 1449); Hickey, "Innovation and Obstacles to Growth"; Bottin, *Seigneurs et paysans*, pp. 190–97; J. Brun-Durand, ed., *Mémoires de Eustache Piémond: Notaire royal-delphinal de la ville de Saint-Antoine en Dauphiné (1572–1608)* (Valence, 1885; reprint, Geneva, 1973), pp. xxiv–xxix, 62, 133–34, 263, 267. For examples from the Paris region of the damage done during the Fronde and by French troops mobilized to fight the Spanish troops in northern France in the 1630s, see M. Bertrandy Lacabane, *Brétigny-sur-Orge*, pp. 361–62; and Moriceau, *Fermiers*, pp. 516–22. The best study of the economic effects of warfare in early modern Europe is Myron Gutmann, *War and Rural Life in the Early Modern Low Countries* (Princeton, 1980).

109. Brun-Durand, ed., *Mémoires de Eustache Piémond*, p. 62.

110. Jacquart, *Crise rurale*, p. 399.

111. AN S 242 (25 June 1597); LL 327–28, fol. 1–71 (1595, 1612). For an example of the difficulties of clearing overgrown land in the era before strong steel plows, see Tollemer, *Un sire de Gouberville*, p. 324.

112. Musset, *L'Elevage du cheval en France*, p. 75. For examples of the requisitioning of horses near Lyon, see AD Rhône, 3 E 8721 (10 February and 11 March 1568).

113. A fundamental work here is Robert Forster, "Obstacles to Agricultural Growth"; see also his account of the Saulx-Tavanes, *The House of Saulx-Tavanes*, especially pp. 87–108. Cf. Tessier, "Discours préliminaire," *Agriculture*, 1:28–30; J. P. Cooper, "In Search of Agrarian Capitalism," in *The Brenner Debate*, ed. T. H. Aston and C.H.E. Philpin, pp. 139–91; Brenner, "Agrarian Class Structure," p. 51; idem, "Agrarian Roots," pp. 300, 314–15; and Hoffman, "The Economic Theory of Sharecropping."

114. See, for example, AN LL 348–49 (Viersy, 1757; Villeroche, 1481, 1512, 1724); S 407 (Viersy, 1464).

115. At times, English landlords failed to cooperate with their tenants, and despite advice to the contrary, they often hired lawyers as stewards—the same sort of tactics that earn French landlords condemnation: J. B. Beckett, "Landownership and Estate Management," *AHEW*, 6:545–640.

116. Hoffman, "Taxes and Agrarian Life"; Forster, *House of Saulx-Tavanes*, pp. 9–11.

117. Polanyi, *The Great Transformation*, pp. 37–76.

118. Tessier, *Agriculture*, s.v. "Faucher," "Faucheur," "Faucilleur"; Meuvret, *Subsistances*, vol. 1, pt. 1 (*Texte*), pp. 165–85; Rozier, *Cours complet d'agriculture*, s.v. "Avoine," "Faulx ou faux"; Rösener, *Bauern im Mittelalter*, pp. 126–27; Abel, *Geschichte der deutschen Landwirtschaft*, pp. 47, 235, 328.

119. Donald N. McCloskey, "The Persistence of English Common Fields," in *European Peasants and Their Markets*, ed. William N. Parker and Eric L. Jones (Princeton, 1975), pp. 73–119; Popkin, *The Rational Peasant*, p. 49. See also Chapter 2.

120. Bossy, *Christianity in the West*; Hoffman, *Church and Community*.

121. Brenner, "Agrarian Roots," pp. 303–6.

122. Brenner, "Agrarian Roots," p. 304. Brenner acknowledges the existence of a rental market, but he dismisses its significance, arguing that rents were set by small-scale peasants, who were willing to pay far more to rent land in order to ensure their subsistence. I have argued against such a belief in Chapter 3. In his "Marquisat d'Ormesson," 2:672, Chevet collected data on farm size in twenty parishes near Paris circa 1750. His figures concern farms that have animals and are over 10 hectares in size; such farms averaged 85 hectares. In his view, smaller holdings were simply not full-time farms. Chevet's figures compare favorably with Allen's evidence from 636 villages in the South Midlands circa 1790: *Enclosure and the Yeoman*, pp. 81–82. To be fair, we must eliminate small farms from Allen's data, too—say farms under 30 acres, or roughly 12 hectares. Allen's remaining farms still have a smaller average size than Chevet's farms: only 65 hectares. The comparison is not perfect, but it suggests that English farms were not enormously larger than ones in the Paris Basin.

123. Chevet, "Marquisat d'Ormesson," 2:498–502. For a similar pattern from the area of Mantes-la-Jolie, to the west of Paris, see Gilbert, *Traité des prairies artificielles*, pp. 22–23; cf. Meuvret, *Subsistances*, vol. 2, pt. 1 (Texte), p. 122.

124. Allen, *Enclosure and the Yeoman*; Albert Berry and William R. Cline, *Agrarian Structure and Productivity in Developing Countries* (Baltimore, 1979).

CHAPTER SIX
CONCLUSION

1. Jones, *Peasantry*, pp. 257–59.

2. Rosenthal, *The Fruits of Revolution*.

3. Ibid., pp. 51–58.

4. Postel-Vinay, "A la recherche de la révolution économique."

5. Le Goff and Sutherland, "The Revolution and the Rural Economy."

6. There were problems with troop movements in 1811–12 and 1814–15, and in the latter period livestock herds were struck by murrain and military requisitions. In addition, harvests were low in 1810–12 (particularly in 1811). Nonetheless, Le Goff and Sutherland suggest that cereal production in the years 1810–13 was probably close to what it was in the periods 1800–1809 and 1815–25. One cannot simply jump to 1815–20, for the early years of the Bourbon restoration (especially 1815–17) were lean years as well. See Le Goff and Sutherland, "The Revolution and the Rural Economy," pp. 57–59; Postel-Vinay, "A la recherche de la révolution éco-

nomique," pp. 1020–22, 1027; Louis Bergeron, *L'épisode napoléonien* (Paris, 1972), pp. 122–23, 180–88.

7. Postel-Vinay, "A la recherche de la révolution économique," pp. 1034–35.

8. Le Goff and Sutherland, "The Revolution and the Rural Economy," pp. 60–63.

9. The optimistic assumption also involves assigning a large factor share to capital, so that lower amounts of agricultural capital would have a greater impact. Note too that table 6.2 assumes a very different agricultural technology than table 6.1. In table 6.2 it is the production function for agriculture as a whole that can be approximated by a Cobb-Douglas function, rather than the dual.

10. Allen and Ó Gráda, "On the Road Again with Arthur Young."

11. Often historians conceive of self-sufficiency in isolation from markets, transportation costs, and prices. A much more fruitful way to think of it has been outlined by de Vries, *Dutch Rural Economy*, pp. 1–21.

12. Meuvret, *Subsistances*, vol. 3, pt. 1 (*Texte*), pp. 13–187; Kaplan, *Bread, Politics and Political Economy*, 1:1–4, 52–96. For a discussion of the economies of scale among agricultural middlemen—economies of scale that reflect inadequate insurance markets and the advantages of pooling risks—see Newbery and Stiglitz, *Theory of Commodity Price Stabilization*, pp. 54–55.

13. Charles Woolsey Cole, *Colbert and a Century of French Mercantilism*, 2 vols. (New York, 1939; reprint, Hamden, Conn., 1964), 1:374–83; Lepetit, *Chemins de terre et voies d'eau*; Cavaillès, *La route française*; Léon and Carrière, "L'appel des marchés," *HESF*, 2:166–80; Meuvret, *Subsistances*, vol. 3, pt. 1 (*Texte*), pp. 64–72, 93–94; Arbellot, "La grande mutation des routes."

14. I say may, because there were obviously exceptions here, such as the Netherlands, with its canals, and Sicily, with its poor roads and lack of ports. See de Vries, *The European Economy in an Age of Crisis* (Cambridge, 1976), pp. 168–75.

15. Kenneth L. Sokoloff and David Dollar, "Agricultural Seasonality and the Organization of Manufacturing during Early Industrialization," unpublished manuscript, UCLA, 1993; Bompard, Magnac, and Postel-Vinay, "Emploi, mobilité et chômage"; Jan de Vries, "The City Thrice Considered," paper delivered at the Center for Social Theory and Comparative History, UCLA, Los Angeles, California, 1994. Yet another fruitful form of exchange is the purchase of urban manufactures; cf. de Vries, *Dutch Rural Economy*, which explores the peasants' role as consumers.

16. Cf. Ferejohn, "Rationality and Interpretation."

Appendix A
The Method and Sources Used with the Notre Dame Sample

1. AN S 324A, 25 June 1781.

2. Information on the cost of transportation was taken from Meuvret, *Subsistances*, vol. 1, pt. 1 (*Texte*), pp. 53–58; vol. 1, pt. 2 (*Notes*), pp. 21–23, 58–62.

3. See, for example, AN LL 329–30 (La Grande-Paroisse, 1594); LL 332 (Larchant, 1596); LL 341–42 (Rungis, 1588); and S 242 (Dampmart, 1597).

4. Béaur, *Marché foncier*, pp. 262–68; Le Roy Ladurie and Veyrassat-Herren, "La rente foncière"; Bertrandy-Lacabane, *Brétigny-sur-Orge*, pp. 314–15.

5. For an example, see Robert E. Evenson and Hans P. Binswanger, "Estimating

Labor Demand Functions for Indian Agriculture," in *Contractual Arrangements, Employment, and Wages in Rural Labor Markets in Asia,* ed. Hans P. Binswanger and Mark R. Rosenzweig (New Haven, 1984). Cf. the criticisms in G.R.E. Lopez, "Estimating Substitution and Expansion Effects Using a Profit Function Framework," *American Journal of Agricultural Economics* 66 (1984): 358–67.

6. Furthermore, if we ignore the problems of uncertainty, then the existence of a labor market allows us to separate the operations of the farm from the utility function of the farmer's family. See the discussion in Chapter 3.

7. For the necessary assumptions, see Chambers, *Applied Production Analysis,* pp. 260–61. Except for the land-rental market, all the other price and factor markets had so many actors that competition seems very reasonable.

8. Alternatively, if the technology does not exhibit constant returns to scale, then we can let the amount of land vary in the short run and allow the farmer to maximize long-run profits. We will in any case end up with the same identity between TFP and technical change. We need not assume, it is worth stressing, that the supply of land is fixed.

9. For the form of the profit function with constant shares, see Allen, "Efficiency and Distributional Consequences." On multioutput profit functions, see Chambers, *Applied Production Analysis,* pp. 268–81; Lawrence J. Lau, "Applications of Profit Functions," in *Production Economics: A Dual Approach to Theory and Applications,* ed. Melvyn Fuss and Danield McFadden, 2 vols. (Amsterdam, 1978), 1:133–310; W. E. Diewert, "Applications of Duality Theory," in *Frontiers of Quantitative Economics,* ed. Michael D. Intriligator and David A. Kendrick, (Amsterdam, 1974), 2:107–71. In practice it is easier to estimate demand equations derived from profit functions rather than the profit function directly; for examples, see Lopez, "Estimating Substitution and Expansion," and Evenson and Binswanger, "Estimating Labor Demand Functions for Indian Agriculture." Part 11 takes up the issue of superlative index numbers—another way to calculate TFP and one equivalent to the use of flexible functional forms—but they, too, require information on quantities.

10. Bourde, *Agronomie et agronomes,* 3:1513–14; Jean-Claude Perrot, "La comptabilité des entreprises agricoles dans l'économie physiocratique," *AESC* 33 (1978): 559–79, where the farm is called Bernoville.

11. Sources for the *rente* interest rates were as follows: Bernard Schnapper, *Les rentes au XVIe siècle: Histoire d'un instrument de crédit* (Paris, 1957), pp. 68–72, 100–102, 279; Pierre Goubert, "Le tragique 17e siècle," *HESF,* 2:343–44; Le Roy Ladurie, *Les Paysans de Languedoc,* 2:1024–25. The rates I used, which were medians for each twenty-five-year period, were as follows: 0.0833 (1500–99), 0.0625 (1600–49), 0.05 (1650–99), 0.0455 (1700–1724), 0.03 (1725–74), 0.0427 (1775–89). Except for Le Roy Ladurie's rates, these were all rates from the Paris area, but the rates Ladurie gave (for Languedoc) tended to agree with the evidence in Schnapper and Goubert. Furthermore, all three sources yield rates that agree with those I have found in rural notarial archives from the Paris Basin, including AN S 468–69, 473–75 (La Grande-Paroisse); AD Yvelines, E notaires (Brétigny-sur-Orge).

12. Abel, *Geschichte der deutschen Landwirtschaft,* p. 26.

13. For example, raising our interest rates to the legal maximum (they were generally a bit below the legal maximum) would have very little effect on the overall trend of TFP. If we recalculate the index of TFP using the legal maximum interest

rates and normalize the resulting index to have the same value as the old index in the years 1750–74, then our TFP figures would be almost uniformly 2 percent lower for the years before 1700, 1 percent lower in 1700–1724 and 1775–89, and essentially unchanged in 1725–74.

14. Meuvret, *Subsistances*, vol. 1, pt. 1 (*Texte*), pp. 196–97.

15. If one were to assume, for example, that the Bernonville accounts were wrong and that the farm actually imported twice the quantity of oats shown in the accounts, the TFP figures would still be practically unchanged. Making the farm a net exporter of oats (a possibility because of its artificial meadows) would have an equally small effect on TFP.

16. Sources for the following discussion include Tessier, *Agriculture*, s.v. "Bail" and "Andonville"; Moriceau and Postel-Vinay, *Ferme, entreprise, famille*, pp. 177–276; Mireaux, *Une province française au temps du grand roi*, pp. 97–164, 322–41; and Jacquart, *Crise rurale*, pp. 289–408. The evidence in Moriceau, *Fermiers*, pp. 321–403, 441–74, 644, is similar; it reaches back to the early sixteenth century.

17. Chevet, "Marquisat d'Ormesson," 493–508.

18. The figures here are for farms with two or more plows only.

19. The Bernonville accounts used the *arpent de Paris* measure, equal to 0.34 hectares: Perrot, "Comptabilité," pp. 578–79.

20. The evidence from the Hurepoix comes from Jacquart's death inventories for *grandes exploitations*, in *Crise rurale*, pp. 355–56. Moriceau, *Fermiers*, pp. 375, 384, 644, has similar figures for the period 1550–1650.

21. Moriceau, *Fermiers*, pp. 375, 384, 402–3. We can check for a constant factor share for sheep by seeing if the ratio of the rent to the price of sheep is proportional to the number of sheep per hectare. It is, and an analogous calculation supports a constant factor share for horses. The evidence here is taken from Moriceau, *Fermiers*, pp. 271, 375, 900.

22. On attempts to reform breeding and stock raising, see Bourde, *Agronomie et agronomes*, 2:743–898.

23. For the sharecropping contracts, see Mireaux, *Une province française au temps du grand roi*, pp. 109–11; none of the sharecropping contracts here involved Notre Dame. The factor and product shares from the farm described by Moriceau and Postel-Vinay in *Ferme, entreprise, famille*, also satisfy the sharecropping inequalities.

24. The baptism figures are derived from Dupâquier, *La population rurale du Bassin Parisien*, p. 239. The baptisms come from an area that extends over 300 kilometers from Paris—much further than any of our properties. Both the rent-wage ratio and the baptism series have been normalized to have mean 1, and both series are averages over the current year and the previous eight years.

25. Moriceau and Postel-Vinay, *Ferme, entreprise, famille*.

26. Because of the aggregation of inputs and outputs, I relied on the following prices with the alternative shares: the rental price of horses for the price of livestock, the price of oats for oats and straw, the price of beans and peas for other crops, and the price of meat for animal products.

27. Moriceau and Postel-Vinay, *Ferme, entreprise, famille*, pp. 245–51, 267–73.

28. Baulant, "Le salaire des ouvriers"; idem, "Prix et salaires," pp. 980–86. Baulant notes one major exception to the pattern of wage equality—*vignerons* (vine

dressers)—but she relates the peculiar behavior of their wages to their situation and to the way in which they were paid.

29. Goubert, *Beauvais et le Beauvaisis*, 1:551; Baulant, "Prix et salaires," pp. 954–55, 977–79. Cf. Labrousse, *Esquisse*, 2:470–74. In the Paris Basin we also lack wage data from the sort of detailed communal archives that exist in market towns and even villages in Provence. Cf. Moriceau, *Fermiers*, pp. 908–16.

30. Bertrandy-Lacabane, *Brétigny-sur-Orge*, pp. 340–43; Baulant, "Le salaire des ouvriers," pp. 463–83; idem, "Le prix des grains"; Yves Durand, "Recherches sur les salaires des maçons à Paris au XVIIIe siècle," *Revue d'histoire économique et sociale* 44 (1966): 468–80. For the number of workdays in the year, see Labrousse, *Esquisse*, 2:501–3.

31. AD Yvelines, 55 J 65, 67.

32. AD Val d'Oise, 72H 30, 32, 33; Durand, "Recherches sur les salaires." Wages for the workers who fished and cleaned the fish pond varied considerably in Saint-Ouen as well: between 14 and 35 *sous* in 1759. The high figure of 35 sous suggests that there was probably considerable skill or difficulty involved, which further complicates the comparison. As for evidence that rural wages were lower, consider the Abbey of Maubuisson's payments for work on its dovecote. In 1739, the abbey paid day laborers an average of 13.4 sous a day for work on the dovecote, considerably lower than the Paris mean wage for unskilled workers of 19 sous. In 1740, the abbey paid an average of 17.7 sous, while the Paris mean was 20. Unfortunately, we do not know if the abbey fed its workers (it may well have done so in 1739), and the comparison is further clouded by the seasonality of wages. Work on the dovecote might have been done off season, and in that case the difference between the Paris wage and what the abbey paid would be much smaller indeed and hardly conclusive. The accounts of the Abbey of Maubuisson in AD Val d'Oise, 72 H 22–33 cited here seemed a promising source for rural wages in the Paris Basin, and I examined them for the late seventeenth and eighteenth centuries. Unfortunately, most of the records were silent on essential details, such as in-kind payments to workers or the precise types of workers employed, and worst of all, the usable information was simply too fragmentary to permit the construction of a homogenous rural wage series. The same was true of the records of the Seigneurie de Rueil-Seraincourt in AD Yvelines, 55 J 65–68.

33. Moriceau and Postel-Vinay, *Ferme, entreprise, famille*, Annexe 8, contains a table of cash payments to male domestics on a single farm during the years 1731–51. If we assume that their in-kind wages amounted to 3 *setiers* of wheat a year, and if we restrict ourselves to years when figures for both Paris wages and the domestics' wages are available, then we find that the domestics' compensation increased 12.5 percent between 1731–37 and 1738–51, while Paris wages grew only 7.1 percent. The in-kind wages here have been evaluated using local prices from Soissons. The difference would suggest that rural wages were rising more rapidly than urban wages, but if we look at evidence from the Abbey of Maubuisson, the reverse seems to have been the case. There, if we make the same assumptions concerning in-kind compensation, we find that the earnings of the same sort of domestic decreased 3.5 percent between 1727–41 and 1755–64, whereas Paris wages grew 9.9 percent. Given the disparate results and the uncertainties surrounding the in-kind compensation, none of the evidence seems conclusive.

34. AN S320, 27 November 1486; S324A, 25 June 1781; S 359, 22 November 1496; S380B; Dupré de Saint Maur, *Essai sur les monnoies ou reflexions sur le rapport entre l'argent et les denrées* (Paris, 1746), p. 127 (1644).

35. AN LL 348–49 (Viersy, 1757); LL 329–30 (La Grande-Paroisse, 1618 and 1689); LL 332 (Larchand, 1762); LL 350–51 (Viry, 1757); S 267, S 457 (Ferrières, 1775); S 247 (Epiais, 1693).

36. AN S 242 (Dampmart, 1744–62); S 282 (La Grande-Paroisse, 1746).

37. Tessier, *Agriculture*, s.v. "Bail."

38. Ibid., especially pp. 24–26.

39. For beans and peas, flax, livestock, and animal products, there were too many missing data to construct annual price series. For these items, I first took twenty-five-year averages, which I assumed to be the price at the midpoint of each twenty-five-year period. I then constructed annual series by interpolating between the midpoints; the interpolation was linear in the logarithm of the prices. Since averaging an interpolated price over the life of the previous lease would involve averaging what was already an average, I simply used the price at the midpoint of the previous lease.

40. Rousselot de Surgy, *Encyclopédie méthodique ou par ordre de matières. Finances*, 3 vols. (Paris, 1784), s.v. "Charges publiques," by M. Boullanger, *ingénieur des ponts et chaussées*.

41. Ibid., especially p. 288. Cf. Perrot, "Comptabilité," pp. 573–74; and Moriceau, *Fermiers*, pp. 441–74, whose profit figures are similar once one corrects for the low cost (3 percent) he assigns capital.

42. Lavoisier, *Oeuvres de Lavoisier*, 6:451. The assertion is made in a careful attempt to calculate French income, in which Lavoisier allows for the alternative possibility of small entrepreneurial profits from raising livestock.

43. AN S 242 (Dampmart, 1744–62); S 282 (La Grande-Paroisse, 1746); Moriceau and Postel-Vinay, *Ferme, entreprise, famille*; Moriceau, *Fermiers*, pp. 515–612.

44. Baulant, "Les salaires des ouvriers," pp. 480–81.

45. The farm had changed somewhat between the 1740s and the 1780s, but the kernel of the operation remained the same and the same family operated it.

46. For this and the following paragraph, see Robert C. Allen, "Recent Developments in Production, Cost and Index Number Theory, with an Application to International Differences in the Cost and Efficiency of Steelmaking in 1907/09," in *Productivity in the Economies of Europe*, ed. Rainer Fremdling and Patrick O'Brien (Stuttgart, 1983), pp. 90–99; Robert C. Allen and W. E. Diewert, "Direct versus Superlative Index Number Formulae," *Review of Economics and Statistics* 53 (1981): 430–35; Douglas W. Caves et al., "Multilateral Comparisons of Output, Input and Productivity using Superlative Index Numbers," *Economic Journal* 92 (1982): 73–86; idem, "The Economic Theory of Index Numbers and the Measurement of Input, Output, and Productivity," *Econometrica* 50 (1982): 1393–1414; W. E. Diewiert, "Exact and Superlative Index Numbers," *Journal of Econometrics* 4 (1976): 115–45; and Chambers, *Applied Production Analysis*, pp. 239–49.

47. Some of the inputs and outputs are aggregates, and so we have to rely on prices to get the composite commodities; in other cases, the farm records mentioned only revenues and costs, not quantities.

48. For equipment, the sales price was taken to be proportional to wages, as elsewhere in this book. All prices were averages over the 1740s and the 1780s.

49. If we were to assume constant shares yet use local prices and factor and product shares from the Chartier farm itself, we would calculate a TFP increase of either 9.72 or 10.09 percent, depending on whether we chose the shares from the 1740s or the 1780s. The minuscule gap between these two numbers and the 9.79 figure is what is properly due to the constant-shares assumption.

50. We could also calculate the average value of P/C for the twenty-five-year period and take its logarithm, but the result turns out to differ little from averaging $\ln(P/C)$ over the same period.

51. In figure A.3, the adjustment for taxes is applied using the Bernonville shares and prices averaged over the outgoing lease. The growth-rate curves plotted for alternative shares and alternative prices have not been corrected for taxes.

52. If properties jump in and out of the sample, the effect of the sc_i terms may vary from period to period, depending on what properties remain in the sample. The effect should be relatively minor, though.

53. An alternative is to look at changes in $\ln(\text{TFP})$ relative to the same base period for each property, a standard technique with panel data. It leads to similar results.

54. I have also made the assumption that we can simply fold the sc_i terms (or their deviations from their means) into the regression error term. While this is defensible, one could argue that it is somewhat restrictive.

55. The rye, barley, and oats proxies in the index P differed slightly from the prices I used for the in-kind payments. For in-kind payments of rye made in Paris, I used a proxy constructed by regressing the Saint-Martin Paris price of rye on the annual Paris price of wheat. I did so because to convert in-kind payments to cash in leases before 1520 I needed rye prices before 1520, when the Pontoise prices were not available. For in-kind payments of barley and oats made in Paris, I used the Saint-Martin prices; when they were unavailable—before 1520 and after 1698—I relied on twenty-five-year averages. The twenty-five-year averages were calculated using the Pontoise prices and Paris prices in Henri Hauser, *Recherches et documents sur l'histoire des prix en France de 1500 à 1800* (Paris, 1936), pp. 114–17, 124–25. For before 1500, I constructed the twenty-five-year average price of oats by multiplying the twenty-five-year average annual price of Paris wheat by the ratio of oat prices to wheat prices in the years 1500–1524. I did the same for barley before 1525. The difference between the in-kind conversion price and the price in the index P is slight, and it cannot affect the results appreciably, for most in-kind payments involved not rye, barley, or oats, but wheat. As for in-kind payments of grain made outside Paris and for miscellaneous in-kind payments, I evaluated them as outlined in Appendix A, part 1; my sources included Hauser, *Recherches et documents*; Dupré de Saint Maur, *Essai sur les monnoies*; Dupâquier, *Mercuriales*; the Paris wage series to be described below; and, for wine prices, Bertrandy-Lacabane, *Brétigny-sur-Orge*, p. 329; Baulant, "Prix et salaires"; and P. Mantellier, *Mémoire sur la valeur des principales denrées et marchandises qui se vendaient ou se consommaient en la ville d'Orléans* (Orléans, 1861), pp. 179–86.

56. In Baulant, "Le prix des grains à Paris," the year 1708 is repeated twice, but

the second price is clearly that in 1709. In 1734, the price should be 12.13 livres rather than 17.13; I thank David Weir for providing me with this information. Baulant and Meuvret, *Prix des céréales*, 1:18–22, give Saint-Martin prices for a setier of constant volume (2.73 hectoliters for oats, 1.56 hectoliters for other grains). They adjust their prices for changes in the size of the oats setier, but they do not correct grain prices for what they admit was probably an 8 percent increase in the size of both setiers between 1573 and 1586, an increase that seems to have been caused by wear of the physical measure. To ensure that the prices in the index *P* would represent a constant volume, I assumed that the 8 percent increase was spread out evenly over the period 1573–86. It is worth pointing out that the prices used to convert the in-kind payments made in Paris were not adjusted for this change in the setier. Since the in-kind payments were always specified in setiers themselves, un-adjusted figures were appropriate. For a different argument about the 8 percent increase, see Moriceau, *Fermiers*, p. 839.

57. For the interpolation procedure, see part 9.

58. For d'Avenel, see the remarks of Labrousse, *Esquisse*, 1:12–15, especially pp. 14–15. When using d'Avenel, I have tried to work with his raw data rather than his averages. Where I had to use his averages, I checked the results against other available figures. For evidence concerning the long-distance trade in livestock, particularly in the region about Paris, see Tessier, *Agriculture*, s.v. "Bêtes à laine," "Bêtes à cornes," "Consommation de Paris"; Meyer, *La noblesse bretonne*, 1:453–58; and Musset, *L'élevage du cheval en France*.

APPENDIX B
MEASURING TFP WITH OTHER SAMPLES OF LEASES

1. For a discussion, see Chambers, *Applied Production Analysis*, pp. 203–49.

2. For a description of local farming, see Nottin, *Recherces sur les variations des prix*, pp. 25–36. For the local shift to stock raising in the early nineteenth century, see Mulliez, "Du blé, 'mal nécessaire,'" p. 40.

3. For the use of relative rents, see Appendix B, part 3.

4. For problems with *mauvais gré* in the rental market, see Chapter 4.

5. One of the property characteristics is the distance not to Amiens, but to Montdidier, the market that provided the grain prices. Employing the distance to Amiens leads to similar results. The other characteristic was the logarithm of the property area.

6. Guyot's rental rates did not diverge from those in Guy Cabourdin, *Terre et hommes en Lorraine (1550–1635)*, 2 vols. (Nancy, 1977), 1:363, as long as we follow Cabourdin's text and not his table, which disagrees with the text. Local leases were not complicated by large pots-de-vin or any of the other problems often encountered with early modern leases: Guyot, *Histoire d'un domaine rural*, pp. 32, 34.

7. Livestock in Old Regime Lorraine may have also been smaller or weaker, a difference I have ignored. It should not change the calculations greatly.

8. Moriceau and Postel-Vinay, *Ferme, entreprise, famille*, p. 211. The wheat yields for Lorraine were calculated on the basis of contemporary information either about yields or about seed-yield ratios.

9. To adjust the Chartier shares, I calculated wheat outputs net of seed in Lorraine with the various yield assumptions and then computed the ratio of these wheat outputs net of seed to that on the Chartier farm. I then assumed that oat output net of seed was smaller by the same proportion as wheat.

10. Guyot's wage data parallel the evidence in Cabourdin, but Guyot's wheat prices seem slightly different in 1600–1625. See Cabourdin, *Terre et hommes en Lorraine*, 1:351, 354.

11. AD Calvados, 7 E 162, 7 E 163, 7 E 174, 7 E 175, F 1650, F 1697, F 1778, H 3364.

12. AD Calvados, H 3226, marchement, 1479–82; H 3229, arpentage et terrier, 1666–67; F 1757, copy (1757) of the *arpentement* of 1666–67. I also used the related documents H 3351, H 3353, H 3369, and H 3371.

13. Hugues Neveux and Bernard Garnier, "Valeur de la terre, production agricole et marché urbain au milieu du XVIIIe siècle: L'exemple de la Normandie entre la baie de Seine et la baie des Veys," in *Problèmes agraires et société rurale: Normandie et Europe du Nord-Ouest (XIVe–XIXe siècle)*, ed. G. Desert et al. (Caen, 1979), Cahier des Annales de Normandie, no. 11, pp. 44–99. Had contre-lettres revised the rent, we would have found evidence of it in the Cairon account books, but nothing of the sort turned up.

14. The tenants of privileged owners may well have escaped much taxation, particularly before 1720. I tried taking this into account by computing different tax burdens for the tenants of the privileged before 1720, but the results were much the same.

15. AD Calvados, C 277, C278, H 2873, H 2874, H 2892, H 3226, H 3229, 3 P 1973. See also Neveux and Garnier, "Valeur de la terre," pp. 44–99; and Gabriel Desert, *Une société rurale au XIXe siècle: Les paysans du Calvados, 1815–95* (New York, 1977).

16. Yields for the surrounding canton were 19.5 hectoliters per hectare in 1817, a bad year. In an average year, yields must therefore have been a bit higher and close to the 23 to 24 hectoliters per hectare achieved on the Chartier farm in the early nineteenth century: Moriceau and Postel-Vinay, *Ferme, entreprise, famille*, p. 211. They were also close to what Arthur Young found for the Paris Basin. The number of sheep found was also comparable to what was reported for the Paris Basin: roughly 220 and 340 head per 100 hectares (counting lambs as half a head) in the seventeenth and eighteenth centuries. Since grain yields and livestock per hectare resembled those in Paris, animal output would presumably be similar, too. The evidence about yields, capital, and labor in Bretteville and the surrounding region came from AD Calvados, F1650, F 1652, F 1665, F 1697, F 1757, H 3226, and H 3351; Aubert, "Notes extraites de trois livres de raison de 1473 à 1550"; Garnier, "Pays herbagers"; Pavard, "Productions et rendements céréaliers."

17. Hauser's price data—particularly for Paris—have been criticized, but though justified in some cases, most of the criticisms do not affect our index P. His use of the calendar year for grain prices, for instance, would not affect our long-term trends based on moving averages, and in any event the Coutances prices appear fairly reliable.

18. Since both Bois's and Bottin's wages were nearly identical, I spliced them without a regression. As for Bois's and Hauser's wages, they were both summer

wages, and regressions on the Paris wages series revealed that they were both were nearly the same fraction of wages in Paris, even though Bois's figures came from the fifteenth and sixteenth centuries and Hauser's from the eighteenth. I therefore felt justified in splicing them without a regression, too.

19. Bois, *Crise du féodalisme*, pp. 93–94.

20. Lemarchand omitted certain additional payments by tenants. Adding them might flatten out the TFP decline in the eighteenth century, but the correction would probably be small.

21. The sources here are the accounts for a farm in Bas Maine, in Morineau, *Faux-semblants*, pp. 38–38, 49–50, 233–74, and accounts and information about farms in the Gâtine in Merle, *La métairie*. For details, see the discussion of western shares below. Farms in the Auge were more likely to fatten livestock for market, but the land share should not be greatly different.

22. These are the shares for the Chartier farm and the Bernonville farm, with seed netted out.

23. *SA 1852*, 1:249, 382–83; Desert, *Une société rurale*, 311–21; Neveux and Garnier, "Valeur de la terre," p. 44–99; Young, *Voyages en France*, 2:356–57.

24. For a single field, of course, the results are much more dramatic: with the 2.42 ratio and a .48 average land share, the TFP increase is 54 percent; with the 3.00 ratio, it is 69 percent.

25. One virtue of the farms in the Ille-et-Vilaine was that they were specifically chosen so that seigneurial dues and in-kind payments would be minimal; in addition, they were taken from ecclesiastical sources, which, as Meyer points out, tended not to hide the rent in secret contre-lettres.

26. Michel, "Quelques données sur le mouvement de la rente foncière," 2:607–24; Meyer, *La Noblesse bretonne*, 2:673; Peret, *Seigneurs et seigneuries en Gâtine poitevine*, pp. 175–77; Meuvret, *Subsistances*, vol. 2, pt. 2 (*Notes*), p. 188. For the rent increases on the three farms near Nantes, see Chapter 3. As with the Paris Basin sample, the search for short-lived entrepreneurial profits was done by adding the rate of change of agricultural output prices to regressions with ln(TFP) as the dependent variable. The only instances where the coefficient was sizable and significant were in all likelihood results of multicollinearity.

27. Additional information about local seeding rates was taken from *SA 1840*, 4:579, 584. Necessary information about prices was taken from Labrousse, *Esquisse*, 1:173; and from a series of eighteenth-century prices kindly furnished by David Weir. Information about local tax rates and the value of agricultural equipment was taken from accounts for a farm in the region published by Rebeyrol, *De la grande et de la petite culture*, pp. 52–55.

28. Additional information was taken from AD Loire-Atlantique, F1388, H 274, H 275; and Malestroit and Laure, *Histoire de Vallet*, pp. 24–26, 395–96.

29. Le Mené, *Les campagnes angevines*, pp. 185–92, 283–90, 323–29; Merle, *La métairie*.

30. I calculated the rent-wage ratio for the eight farms of the Saint-Jean Hospital of Angers; the farms of Chavais and L'Epinay, also near Angers; and each of the three farms near Nantes. I compared the rent-wage ratios with the rural population of the west, as depicted in Dupâquier, *Histoire de la population française*, 2:159. The graphs of the rent-wage ratios and of the population trend tended to parallel one

another fairly closely, and the only discrepancies could easily be the result of variations in the local population and the health of rural industry.

31. In the regression the year has a coefficient of only 0.00028, with a t statistic
of 0.80, evidence that there was no movement of the Angers price relative to the
Rennes price. Although prices in the west seem to have moved together, they may
have all moved closer to the Paris price; see Meyer, *La noblesse bretonne*, 1:489–
93. When I recalculated TFP for the Ille-et-Vilaine farms with Rennes grain prices,
I was obliged to use the price of wheat in Rennes rather than the price of rye.

32. Other scholars have remarked on the difficulty of putting together homogenous wage series in the west, particularly in Brittany: Léon Vignols, "Salaires des
ouvriers et prix des matériaux employés aux travaux publics, à Saint-Malo de 1737
à 1744 et 1755 à 1762," *Annales de Bretagne* 39 (1930–31): 351–69; and Sée, *Les
classes rurales en Bretagne*, p. 308. In Nantes, one excellent source—municipal
comptes des miseurs—ends before the eighteenth century.

33. Sée, *Les classes rurales en Bretagne*, pp. 306–13.

34. By the same token, if varying transportation costs were distorting our TFP
indices in the west, then the graphs should be very different for the farms near
Angers, the market from which the grain prices were taken. But as we saw, the trend
near Angers was the same as elsewhere in the west.

35. These interest rates, which came from a decennial sample of local notarial
records, were kindly provided by Jean-Laurent Rosenthal. In-kind payments for the
Grange de la Sacristie were converted using the same prices that figured in the index
P. Here and elsewhere in the Vaucluse, I took necessary information units of measure and on the complicated monetary situation from AD Vaucluse, I, ms. Monteux,
and "Poids et mesures," *Annuaire administratif, statistique et historique du département de Vaucluse pour l'année 1857*, pp. 350–63.

36. My original plan was to choose a notarial register covering each twentieth
year beginning in 1560 and then to read all the land-sale contracts in the register
concerning Grillon, including those not in the twentieth year. Each register usually
covered a number of years, and when there was no register covering a twentieth
year, I chose the register closest to that year. Unfortunately, the loss of certain
notarial records for Grillon left gaps in my sample.

37. The property characteristics included the percentage of the property that was
vineyard, the percentage *herme*, the percentage garden, and the percentage *pré*
(meadow). A constant term was included in the regression, but no year.

38. Baehrel, *Une croissance*, 1:367. The average lease length for the Grange de
la Sacristie over the course of the seventeenth and eighteenth century was 5.6 years.
Regressions suggest that on the farm of the Sacristie continuing tenants did not
experience lower rent increases than new renters. Given the small number of leases,
it was not possible to check for entrepreneurial profits.

39. For the similarity of crops and agricultural techniques throughout the Midi,
see Le Roy Ladurie, *Les Paysans de Languedoc*, 1:53–90.

40. Hickey, "Innovation and Obstacles to Growth," pp. 208–40; Baehrel, *Une
croissance*, 1:29–30, 78, 122–41, 170–88, 224–28, 381.

41. The evidence about sharecropping contracts comes from contracts I collected
in the notarial registers used for the Grillon sample of land sales and from Baehrel,
Une croissance, 1:368–70.

42. Cf. Frêche, *Toulouse et la région Midi-Pyrenées*. Despite the problems with Rascol, it is unlikely that the TFP index would change considerably. TFP could go up or down, but the most likely effect would be a slight reduction from 0.3 percent per year to 0.2 percent per year.

43. The interest rates were decennial medians, read off from the graph in Le Roy Ladurie, *Les Paysans de Languedoc*, 2:1024–25.

44. In-kind payments in small grains were converted to wheat using the equivalents given in Le Roy Ladurie, *Les Paysans de Languedoc*, 2:845, and then to cash using the price of wheat.

45. Le Roy Ladurie, *Les Paysans de Languedoc*, 1:275–76, 308–9, 431–37, 529.

46. I compared the rent-wage ratio with the graphs of baptisms and the local population estimates derived from *cadastres*, in Le Roy Ladurie, *Les Paysans de Languedoc*, 2:922–37.

47. The interest rates were decennial medians, from Le Roy Ladurie, *Les Paysans de Languedoc*, 2:1024–25.

48. Zolla, "Les variations du revenu et du prix des terres en France," *Sciences politiques* (1894): 422–30; Labrousse, *Esquisse*, 2:480–81.

49. If TFP is calculated using a similar series of skilled urban wages, it rises somewhat in the seventeenth century before falling after 1680. The overall rate of decline is then attenuated: only -0.1 percent per year. But the skilled wage series suffer from their own serious problems, and they seem much less appropriate to agriculture than our unskilled wages.

50. For the precise formula, see Appendix A, part 11.

51. Goldsmith, *Les Salers*, pp. 193–207.

52. *SA 1840*, 2:568–69, 598–99, 602–33. For the problems with the census, see *SA 1840*, 1:xxxvii, xxxix, and Bertrand Gille, *Les sources statistiques de l'histoire de France* (Geneva, 1980), pp. 196–200.

53. The accounts, which are from the eighteenth century, are for the ferme de la Tête d'Or and the grange de Brouillat; they are taken from Georges Durand, *Le patrimoine foncier de l'Hôtel-Dieu*, pp. 186–89, 305–7, 314–15, 366–78. The product revenue share for wine on the grange de Brouillat, where viticulture dominated, was 0.89. These two farms were actually not in the Beaujolais, but rather next door in the Lyonnais. The technology, though, was essentially the same.

54. Durand, *Le Patrimoine foncier de l'Hôtel-Dieu*, pp. 201–9.

55. The evidence from 1840 was from *SA 1840*, vol. 2.

56. Using the price of oxen from Hamburg alone (in Abel, *Geschichte der deutschen Landwirtschaft*, pp. 128–29) led to nearly identical results. One other source of prices, E. Waschinski, *Währung, Preisentwicklung und Kaufkraft des Geldes in Schleswig-Holstein von 1226–1864* (Neumünster, 1959), proved of little value, as did M. J. Elsas, *Umriss einer Geschichte der Preise und Löhne in Deutschland*, 2 vols. (Leiden, 1936–49).

57. Young's rents are in John, "Statistical Appendix," *AHEW*, 6:1112. For farming in the Home Counties, see Joan Thirsk, "The Farming Regions of England and Wales," *AHEW*, 4:4; Hugh C. Prince, "The Changing Rural Landscape, 1750–1850," *AHEW*, 6:7–83; Mingay, "Farming Techniques," *AHEW*, 6:275–383; and Glennie, "Continuity and Change." Since the distance between London and Hertfordshire was slightly greater than that between Paris and the average farm in the

Notre Dame sample, I adjusted the Notre Dame rents downward slightly, as if for a farm 50 kilometers outside of Paris. That put Hertfordshire and the Notre Dame sample on an equal footing.

58. The Norfolk accounts and the rule of thumb shares are from B. A. Holderness, "Prices, Productivity, and Output," *AHEW*, 6:179–81; J. B. Beckett, "Landownership and Estate Management," *AHEW*, 6:609.

59. Because the Norfolk accounts and the rule of thumb shed no light on depreciation, I used the Chartier depreciation rates for all three sets of shares when calculating the rental price of livestock and equipment in England. I assumed a 4 percent interest rate in England versus 5 percent in France. The Pontoise price of wheat and oats was taken from Dupâquier, et al. *Mercuriales du pays de France*; the price of peas in Paris, from Hauser, *Recherches et documents*, p. 130; the price of mutton (a national average), from Labrousse, *Esquisse*, 1:301–3; and the price of horses near Paris, from Bertrandy-Lacabane, *Brétigny-sur-Orge*, pp. 331–35.

60. Sources for the English prices were A. H. John, "Statistical Appendix," *AHEW*, 6:976, 998, which provided prices for wheat, oat, and peas in Reading and mutton prices in London. The price of horses was Arthur Young's price from Norfolk in 1782, from Richard Perren, "Markets and Marketing," *AHEW*, 6:265–66. The mutton prices were from the years 1765–72, the crop prices from 1766–72, and the horse price from 1782. Earlier prices for the crops and additional prices for horses were not available—again, reason to try a second sales price for capital.

61. The French wages for the 1760s came from AD Yvelines, 55 J 67, and for the 1780s from Bertrandy-Lacabane, *Brétigny-sur-Orge*, pp. 340–43. The English wages were from John, "Statistical Appendix," *AHEW*, 6:1075–79, 1095.

62. Peter J. Bowden, "Agricultural Prices, Wages, Farm Profits and Rents, 1640–1750," *CAHEW*, 1:260–61; Holderness, "Prices, Productivity, and Output," *AHEW*, 6:179–81; Beckett, "Landownership and Estate Management," *AHEW*, 6:630–33; Allen, "Efficiency and Distributional Consequences."

APPENDIX C
THE ECONOMICS OF URBAN FERTILIZER

1. Technically, such an isoquant violates our assumption of constant shares, but that assumption should be thought of as only an approximation.

APPENDIX D
HEDONIC WAGE REGRESSIONS

1. MacLeod and Malcomson, "Reputation and Hierarchy."

2. Rosenzweig, "Determinants of Wage Rates"; Sicsic, "City-Farm Wages Gaps." See also Chapter 4 and Appendix A, part 7.

3. Since t does not refer to time, I am in effect assuming that the wages of a servant (given his or her skills and personal characteristics) are constant over time, apart from seasonal variations and raises with tenure. Given the stickiness of nominal wages, such an assumption seems to be reasonable, particularly for the short periods covered by my data (1473–85 and 1691–1705). During these two periods average wages did not vary greatly in Normandy. It would in any case be easy to

relax the assumption of constant wages by inserting a time variable into the regressions—either a time trend, dummies for the years involved, or average wage trends for a nearby labor market. I experimented with adding the average wage trends, but the regression results were by and large unchanged. My tactic was to add average wages for unskilled labor in nearby Caen to the independent variables in table D.1. The average unskilled wage here came from the sources described in Appendix B, part 2; and like other independent variables, the average unskilled wage was measured as a difference from the value it had when the servant first went to work for the Cairon. If the constant wage assumption is inappropriate for our two periods, then the trend of average wages should explain a great deal of the wage variation we observe. Its coefficient should then be positive and significant. It never is, though; furthermore, adding it does not greatly disturb the coefficients of the other independent variables, or at least those that are estimated with some certainty. In the ln(wage) regression for 1473–85, for example, the coefficients change by less than 1 percent when average wages for Caen are added.

4. The cash wage may itself have been paid at least partially in kind, but such in-kind payments were always converted to a cash equivalent.

5. An alternative is to take first differences and see if wages increase with t; it leads to nearly identical results.

6. Wages of workers hired during the harvest itself—a shorter period of perhaps a month—were probably higher still, but the journal contains no information about harvest workers.

7. Obviously, this coefficient would be diluted somewhat if it were difficult to hire between fairs.

Sources and Bibliography

Space limitations preclude an elaborate bibliography, and in any case there are thorough references in the notes. But a brief description of the sources I consulted might prove useful, along with a list of printed works cited repeatedly in the text. In my research, I relied on a variety of manuscripts and printed sources. The printed works came from archives and libraries in France, Germany, and the United States. The manuscripts I read during visits to a number of collections in France, including the Bibliothèque Nationale in Paris and the Bibliothèque Municipale in Avignon; the Archives Municipales of Lyon and Nantes; and the Archives Départementales of the Ain, Bouches-du-Rhône, Dordogne, Drôme, Haute-Garonne, Gers, Gironde, Isère, Lot-et-Garonne, Pas-de-Calais, Puy-de-Dôme, Seine-et-Marne, Seine-Maritime, and Val-d'Oise. The bulk of the manuscripts, though, came from the Archives Nationales in Paris and the Archives Départementales of the Calvados, Cantal, Loire-Atlantique, Meurthe-et-Moselle, Moselle, Hautes-Pyrénées, Rhône, Vaucluse, and Yvelines. Some of the documents I read in the Yvelines have now been dispersed among the other departments that constitute the old Seine-et-Oise.

The sources that I relied upon most heavily fell into four categories. The first—a broad and disparate group—included the items unearthed in the initial stages of my research, when I imagined that my book would revolve about the study of eleven communities scattered about France: Brétigny-sur-Orge in the Essonne, La Grande-Paroisse in the Seine-et-Marne, Bretteville-l'Orgueilleuse in the Calvados, Jumièges in the Seine-Maritime, Vionville in the Moselle, Roville and Neuviller in the Meurthe-et-Moselle, Saint-Genis-Laval in the Rhône, Grillon in the Vaucluse, Varades in the Loire-Atlantique, and the hamlets and villages of the valley of Barèges in the Hautes-Pyrénées. Before selecting the eleven communities, I actually looked at many other villages in the same regions, and in other parts of France as well, such as the Massif Central or the southwest. The search for suitable villages exposed me to sources that ranged from local monographs and the records of both royal and local authorities to communal archives, *terriers*, *cadastres*, tax rolls, notarial registers, probate inventories, family papers, and the documents left by civil and criminal proceedings before royal and seigneurial courts. These texts shed light on commons and enclosures, on strife in villages, and on the workings of the labor market, the rental market, and the local economy. They also helped with the calculation and analysis of total factor productivity.

The second set of sources were *livres de raison*, or journals of farmers and landlords. Some—those of the Cairon family, for instance—were in manuscript. Others were printed. Whether printed or not, they proved useful for the workings of the labor market, the rental market, and the local economy. They proved essential as well for calculating and analyzing total factor productivity.

The third set of sources were handbooks for landlords and books about agriculture and its improvement. The texts here ranged from the works of Charles Estienne and Olivier de Serres to the comments of lesser known agricultural reformers in the eighteenth and nineteenth centuries. Many of the authors were French, but some hailed from abroad—Arthur Young, for instance, or examples of the German *Hausväterliteratur*. Evaluating the French authors was made easier thanks to Jean Meuvret's *Subsistances*—especially his judicious observations in volume 1, part 1 (*Texte*), pp. 55–97. To this agricultural literature, I might add contemporary analyses of the French economy by knowledgeable observers, like Lavoisier, and two works of literature that shed light on rural life, Noel du Fail's *Les propos rustiques* and Rétif de la Bretonne's *La vie de mon père*.

The final set of sources were the leases, land sales, and prices series that made possible my computations of total factor productivity. Some of the leases and sales records came from manuscript sources, as with the Notre Dame sample or in Grillon and outside Nantes. Others derived from published series. Here, one of the essential tools for the French material was Jean-Yves Grenier's *Séries économiques françaises (XVI–XVIII siècles)*, which listed published price and rental series. For comparable material from England and Germany, I was fortunate enough to have the bibliographies in the *Agrarian History of England and Wales* and Abel's *Geschichte der deutschen Landwirtschaft*.

The following bibliography is not complete. It lists only those works that are cited in more than one chapter:

Abel, Wilhelm. *Geschichte der deutschen Landwirtschaft vom frühen Mittelalter bis zum 19. Jahrhundert*. 3d revised edition. Stuttgart, 1978.

Allen, Robert C. "The Efficiency and Distributional Consequences of Eighteenth-Century Enclosures." *Economic Journal* 92 (December 1982): 937–53.

———. *Enclosure and the Yeoman*. Oxford, 1992.

Allen, Robert C., and Cormac Ó Gráda. "On the Road Again with Arthur Young: English, Irish, and French Agriculture during the Industrial Revolution." *JEH* 48 (1988): 93–116.

Arbellot, Guy. "La grande mutation des routes de France au milieu du XVIIIe siècle." *AESC* 28 (1973): 765–91.

Armstrong, W. A. "Labour I: Rural Population Growth, Systems of Employment, and Incomes." *AHEW*, 6:641–728.

Aston, T. H., and C.H.E. Philpin, eds. *The Brenner Debate: Agrarian Class Structure and Economic Development in Pre-Industrial Europe*. Cambridge, 1985.

Aubert, Abbé. "Notes extraites de trois livres de raison de 1473 à 1550. Comptes d'une famille de gentilshommes campagnards normands." France. Comité des travaux historiques et scientifiques. Section de philologie et d'histoire. *Bulletin philologique et historique* (Paris, 1898): 447–99.

Avenel, Georges d'. *Histoire économique de la propriété, des salaires, des denrées et de tous les prix en général depuis l'an 1200 jusqu'en l'an 1800*. 7 vols. Paris, 1894–1926; reprint, Lenox Hill, 1969.

Baehrel, René. *Une croissance: La Basse-Provence rurale de la fin du XVIe siècle à 1789*. Paris, 1961; new edition, Paris, 1988.

Baulant, Micheline. "Le prix des grains à Paris de 1431 à 1788." *AESC* 23 (1968): 520–40.

———. "Prix et salaires à Paris au XVIe siècle: Sources et résultats." *AESC* 31 (1976): 954–95.

———. "Le salaire des ouvriers du bâtiment à Paris de 1400 à 1726." *AESC* 26 (1971): 463–83.

Baulant, Micheline, and Jean Meuvret. *Prix des céréales extraits de la mercuriale de Paris (1520–1698)*. 2 vols. Paris, 1960–62.

Béaud, Jacques, and Georges Bouchart. "Le dépôt des pauvres de Saint-Denis (1768–1792)." *Annales de démographie historique* (1974): 127–43.

Béaur, Gérard. *Le marché foncier à la veille de la Révolution*. Paris, 1984.

———. "Prezzo della terra, congiuntura e società alla fine del XVIII secolo: L'esempio di un mercato della Beauce." *Quaderni storici* 65 (1987): 523–48.

Beckett, J. B. "Landownership and Estate Management." *AHEW*, 6:545–640.

Benedict, Philip. "Was the Eighteenth Century an Era of Urbanization in France?" *Journal of Interdisciplinary History* 21(1990): 179–215.

Bertrandy-Lacabane, M. *Brétigny-sur-Orge, Marolles-en-Hurepoix, Saint-Michel-sur-Orge*. Versailles, 1886.

Bloch, Marc. *French Rural History*, trans. Janet Sondheimer. Berkeley, 1966.

———. "La lutte pour l'individualisme agraire dans la France du XVIIIe siècle." *Annales d'histoire économique et sociale* 2 (1930): 329–83, 511–56.

Bompard, Jean-Pierre, Thierry Magnac, and Gilles Postel-Vinay. "Emploi, mobilité et chômage en France au XIXe siècle: Migrations saisonnières entre industrie et agriculture." *AESC* 45 (1990): 55–76.

———. "Migrations saisonnières de main-d'oeuvre: Le cas de la France en 1860." *Annales d'économie et de statistique* 19 (1990): 97–129.

Bossy, John. *Christianity in the West, 1400–1700*. Oxford, 1985.

Bottin, Jacques. *Seigneurs et paysans dans l'ouest du pays de Caux: 1540–1650*. Paris, 1983.

Boulay, Henri. *De la dispersion des propriétés et des moyens d'y remédier*. Nancy, 1902.

Bourde, André J. *Agronomie et agronomes en France au XVIIIe siècle*. 3 vols. Paris, 1967.

Bowden, Peter J. "Agricultural Prices, Wages, Farm Profits and Rents, 1640–1750." In *AHEW*, vol. 1: *Economic Change: Prices, Wages, Profits, and Rents, 1500–1750*, ed. Peter J. Bowden, 189–306. Cambridge, 1990.

Brenner, Robert. "Agrarian Class Structure and Economic Development in Pre-Industrial Europe." In *The Brenner Debate: Agrarian Class Structure and Economic Development in Pre-Industrial Europe*, ed. T. H. Aston and C.H.E. Philpin, 10–63. Cambridge, 1985.

———. "The Agrarian Roots of European Capitalism." In ibid., 213–327.

Campbell, Bruce M. S., and Mark Overton, eds. *Land, Labour, Livestock: Historical Studies in European Agricultural Productivity*. Manchester, 1991.

Cavaillès, Henri. *La route française, son histoire, sa fonction: Etude de géographie humaine*. Paris, 1946.

Chambers, Robert G. *Applied Production Analysis*. Cambridge, 1988.

Chevet, Jean-Michel. "Le Marquisat d'Ormesson, 1700–1840. Essai d'analyse économique." 2 vols. Doctoral thesis, Ecole des Hautes Etudes en Sciences Sociales, Paris, 1983.

Clark, Gregory. "The Economics of Exhaustion, the Postan Thesis, and the Agricultural Revolution." *JEH* 52, no. 1 (March 1992): 61–84.

Claverie, Elisabeth, and Pierre Lamaison. *L'impossible mariage: Violence et parenté en Gévaudan: XVIIe, XVIIIe, XIXe siècles*. Paris, 1982.

Clément, Pierre, ed. *Lettres, instructions et mémoires de Colbert*. 8 vols. Paris, 1861–82.

de Vries, Jan. *The Dutch Rural Economy in the Golden Age*. New Haven, 1974.

Deyon, Pierre. *Amiens, capitale provinciale: Etude sur la société urbaine au 17e siècle*. Paris, 1967.

————. *Contribution à l'étude des revenus fonciers en Picardie: Les fermages de l'Hôtel-Dieu d'Amiens et leurs variations de 1515 à 1789*. Lille, 1967.

Dion, Roger. *Histoire de la vigne et du vin en France*. Paris, 1959; reprint, Paris, 1977.

Dombasle, Christophe Joseph Alexandre Mathieu de. "Des réunions territoriales." In Dombasle, *Annales agricoles de Roville*. 2d edition, 1:264–318. Paris, 1829.

Dupâquier, Jacques. *La population rurale du Bassin Parisien à l'époque de Louis XIV*. Paris, 1979.

Dupâquier, Jacques, ed. *Histoire de la population française*. 4 vols. Paris, 1988.

Dupâquier, Jacques, M. Lachiver, and Jean Meuvret. *Mercuriales du pays de France et du Vexin français (1640–1792)*. Paris, 1968.

Durand, Georges. *Le patrimoine foncier de l'Hôtel-Dieu de Lyon (1482–1791)*. Lyon, 1974.

————. *Vin, vigne, vignerons en Lyonnais et Beaujolais*. Paris, 1979.

El Kordi, Mohamed. *Bayeux aux XVIIe et XVIIIe siècles*. Paris, 1970.

Ferejohn, John. "Rationality and Interpretation: Parliamentary Elections in Early Stuart England." In *The Economic Approach to Politics*, ed. Kristen Renwick Moore, 279–305. New York, 1991.

Forster, Robert. *The House of Saulx-Tavanes: Versailles and Burgundy, 1700–1830*. Baltimore, 1971.

Frêche, Georges. *Toulouse et la région Midi-Pyrénées au siècle des lumières (vers 1670–1789)*. Paris, 1974.

Garnier, Bernard. "La mise en herbe dans le pays d'Auge aux XVIIe et XVIIIe siècles." *Annales de Normandie* 25 (1975): 157–80.

————. "Pays herbagers, pays céréaliers et pays 'ouverts' en Normandie (XVIe–début du XIXe siècle)." *Revue d'histoire économique et sociale* 53 (1975): 493–525.

Glennie, Paul. "Continuity and Change in Hertfordshire Agriculture 1550–1700: II-Trends in Crop Yields and their Determinants." *Agricultural History Review* 36 (1988): 145–61.

————. "Measuring Crop Yields in Early Modern England." In *Land, Labour, Livestock: Historical Studies in European Agricultural Productivity*, ed. Bruce M. S. Campbell and Mark Overton, 255–83. Manchester, 1991.

Goldsmith, James Lowth. "The Agrarian History of Preindustrial France. Where Do We Go from Here?" *Journal of European Economic History* 13 (1984): 175–199.

————. *Les Salers et les d'Escorailles: Seigneurs de Haute Auvergne, 1500–1789*, trans. Jacques Buttin. Clermont-Ferrand, 1984.

Goubert, Pierre. *Beauvais et le Beauvaisis de 1600 à 1730*. 2 vols. Paris, 1960; reprint, Paris, 1982.

Goy, Joseph, and Emmanuel Le Roy Ladurie, eds. *Les fluctuations du produit de la dîme: Conjoncture décimale et domaniale de la fin du Moyen Age au XVIIIe siècle*. Paris, 1972.

———. *Prestations paysannes: Dîmes, rente foncière et mouvement de la production agricole à l'époque préindustrielle*. 2 vols. Paris, 1982.

Grantham, George W. "Agricultural Supply during the Industrial Revolution: French Evidence and European Implications." *JEH* 49 (March 1989): 43–72.

———. "The Diffusion of the New Husbandry in Northern France, 1815–1840." *JEH* 38 (June 1978): 311–37.

———. "The Growth of Labour Productivity in the *Cinq Grosses Fermes* of France, 1750–1929." In *Land, Labour, and Livestock: Historical Studies in European Agricultural Productivity*, ed. Bruce M. S. Campbell and Mark Overton, 340–63. Manchester, 1991.

———. "The Persistence of Open-Field Farming in Nineteenth-Century France." *JEH* 40 (September 1980): 515–31.

Greif, Avner. "Contract Enforceability and Economic Institutions in Early Trade: The Maghribi Traders' Coalition." *American Economic Review* 83 (1993): 525–48.

———. "Cultural Beliefs and the Organization of Society: A Historical and Theoretical Reflection on Collectivist and Individualist Societies." *Journal of Political Economy* 102 (1994): 912–50.

———. "Reputation and Coalitions in Medieval Trade: Evidence on the Maghribi Traders." *JEH* 49 (1989): 857–81.

Grenier, Jean-Yves. *Séries économiques françaises (XVIe–XVIIIe siècles)*. Paris, 1985.

Grenier, Jean-Yves, and Bernard Lepetit. "L'expérience historique: A propos de C. E. Labrousse." *AESC* 44 (1989): 1337–60.

Gruter, Edouard. *La naissance d'un grand vignoble: Les seigneuries de Pizay et Tanay en Beaujolais au XVIe et au XVIIe siècles*. Lyon, 1977.

Gutton, Jean-Pierre. *Domestiques et serviteurs dans la France de l'ancien régime*. Paris, 1981.

Guyot, Charles. "Essai sur l'aisance relative du paysan lorrain à partir du XVe siècle." *Mémoires de l'Académie de Stanislas* series 5, no. 6 (1888): 1–130.

———. *Histoire d'un domaine rural en Lorraine*. Nancy, 1887.

Hassenfratz, [Jean-Henri]. "Mémoire sur la comparaison des produits de la culture du Bourbonnais avec celle de la Picardie." *Mémoires d'agriculture, d'économie rurale et domestique* (Fall 1786): 105–22.

Hauser, Henri. *Recherches et documents sur l'histoire des prix en France de 1500 à 1800*. Paris, 1936.

Hickey, Daniel. "Innovation and Obstacles to Growth in the Agriculture of Early Modern France: The Example of Dauphiné." *French Historical Studies* 15, no. 2 (Fall 1987): 208–40.

Hoffman, Philip T. *Church and Community in the Diocese of Lyon, 1500–1789*. New Haven, 1984.

———. "Early Modern France, 1450–1700." In *Fiscal Crises, Liberty, and Representative Government, 1540–1789*, ed. Philip T. Hoffman and Kathryn Norberg, 226–52. Stanford, 1994.

Hoffman, Philip T. "The Economic Theory of Sharecropping in Early Modern France." *JEH* 44 (1984): 309–19.

———. "Institutions and Agriculture in Old Regime France." *Politics and Society* 16 (1988): 241–64.

———. "Land Rents and Agricultural Productivity: The Paris Basin, 1450–1789." *JEH* 51 (1991): 771–805.

———. "Taxes and Agrarian Life in Early Modern France: Land Sales, 1550–1730." *JEH* 46 (1986): 37–55.

Hoffman, Philip T., and Kathryn Norberg, eds. *Fiscal Crises, Liberty, and Representative Government, 1540–1789*. Stanford, 1994.

Hoffman, Philip T., Gilles Postel-Vinay, and Jean-Laurent Rosenthal. "Private Credit Markets in Paris, 1690–1840." *JEH* 52 (1992): 293–306.

Husson, Armand. *Les consommations de Paris*. 2d edition. Paris, 1875.

Jacquart, Jean. *La crise rurale en Ile-de-France, 1550–1670*. Paris, 1974.

———. "La rente foncière, indice conjoncturel?" *Revue historique* 514 (1975): 355–76.

John, A. H. "Statistical Appendix." *AHEW*, 6: 972–1155.

Jones, P. M. *The Peasantry in the French Revolution*. Cambridge, 1988.

Kaplan, Steven Lawrence. *Bread, Politics and Political Economy in the Reign of Louis XV*. 2 vols. The Hague, 1976.

———. *Provisioning Paris: Merchants and Millers in the Grain and Flour Trade during the Eighteenth Century*. Ithaca, 1984.

Laboulinière, P. *Annuaire statistique du département des Hautes-Pyrénées*. Tarbes, 1807; reprint, Marseille, 1980.

Labrousse, Ernest. *Esquisse du mouvement des prix et des revenus en France au XVIIIe siècle*. 2 vols. Paris, 1933; reprint, Paris, 1984.

Lachiver, Marcel. "L'approvisionnement de Paris en viande au XVIIIe siècle." In *La France d'ancien régime: Etudes réunies en l'honneur de Pierre Goubert*. 2 vols. 1:345–54. Paris, 1984.

Lavoisier, Antoine. *Oeuvres de Lavoisier*. 6 vols. Paris, 1864–93.

Le Brun, François. *Les hommes et la mort en Anjou aux 17e et 18e siècles*. Paris, 1971.

Le Goff, T.J.A., and D.M.G. Sutherland. "The Revolution and the Rural Economy." In *Reshaping France: Town, Country, and Region during the French Revolution*, ed. Alan Forrest and Peter Jones, 52–85. Manchester, 1991.

Le Mené, Michel. *Les campagnes angevines à la fin du Moyen Age (vers 1350–vers 1530)*. Nantes, 1982.

Léon, Pierre, and Charles Carrière. "L'appel des marchés." *HESF*, 2:161–215.

Lepetit, Bernard. *Chemins de terre et voies d'eau*. Paris, 1984.

Le Roy Ladurie, Emmanuel. "De la crise ultime à la vraie croissance, 1690–1789." *HFR*, 2:359–599.

———. *The French Peasantry, 1450–1660*, trans. Alan Sheridan. Berkeley, 1987.

———. *Les paysans de Languedoc*. 2 vols. Paris, 1966.

Le Roy Ladurie, Emmanuel, and Joseph Goy. "Première esquisse d'une conjoncture du produit décimal et domanial: Fin du Moyen Age–XVIIIe siècle." In *Les fluctuations du produit de la dîme: Conjoncture décimale et domaniale de la fin du*

Moyen Age au XVIIIe siècle, ed. Joseph Goy and Emmanuel Le Roy Ladurie, pp. 335–74.

Le Roy Ladurie, Emmanuel, and Béatrice Veyrassat-Herren. "La rente foncière autour de Paris au XVIIe siècle." *AESC* 23 (1968): 541–55.

Levi, Giovanni. *Inheriting Power: The Story of an Exorcist*, trans. Lydia G. Cochrane. Chicago, 1988.

Liger, Louis. *Nouvelle maison rustique*. 2 vols. Paris, 1721.

Macfarlane, Alan. *The Origins of English Individualism*. Cambridge, 1978.

MacLeod, W. Bentley, and James M. Malcomson. "Reputation and Hierarchy in Dynamic Models of Employment." *Journal of Political Economy* 96 (1988): 832–54.

Malestroit, Jean de, and R. P. Emile Laure. *Histoire de Vallet*. Maulévrier, 1985.

Mantellier, P. *Mémoire sur la valeur des principales denrées et marchandises qui se vendaient ou se consommaient en la ville d'Orléans, au cours des XIVe, XVe, XVIe, XVIIe et XVIIIe siècles*. Orléans, 1861.

Marx, Karl. *Capital: A Critique of Political Economy*, ed. Ernest Untermann. Revised edition. 3 vols. Chicago, 1906–9.

McCloskey, Donald. "The Economics of Enclosure: A Market Analysis." In *European Peasants and Their Markets*, ed. William N. Parker and Eric L. Jones, 132–33. Princeton, 1975.

Merle, Louis. *La métairie et l'évolution agraire de la Gâtine poitevine de la fin du Moyen Age à la Révolution*. Paris, 1958.

Meuvret, Jean. *Le problème des subsistances à l'époque Louis XIV*. 3 vols. Paris, 1977–88.

Meyer, Jean. *La noblesse bretonne au XVIIIe siècle*. 2 vols. Paris, 1966.

Michel, L. "Quelques données sur le mouvement de la rente foncière en Anjou, du milieu du XVIIe siècle à la Révolution." In *Prestation paysannes: Dîmes. rente foncière et mouvement de la production agricole à l'époque préindustrielle*, ed. Joseph Goy and Emmanuel Le Roy Ladurie, 2:607–24. Paris, 1982.

Mingay, G. E., et al. "Farming Techniques." *AHEW*, 6:275–383.

Mireaux, Emile. *Une province française au temps du grand roi: La Brie*. Paris, 1958.

Moriceau, Jean-Marc. *Les fermiers de l'Ile-de-France: XVe–XVIIIe siècle*. Paris, 1994.

———. "Au rendez-vous de la 'révolution agricole' dans la France du XVIIIe siècle: A propos des régions de grande culture." *AESC* 49 (1994): 27–63.

Moriceau, Jean-Marc, and Gilles Postel-Vinay. *Ferme, entreprise, famille: Grande exploitation et changements agricoles, XVIIe–XIXe siècles*. Paris, 1992.

Morineau, Michel. "Cambrésis et Hainaut: Des frères ennemis?" In *Prestations paysannes: Dîmes, rente foncière et mouvement de la production agricole à l'époque préindustrielle*, ed. Joseph Goy and Emmanuel Le Roy Ladurie, 2:625–643. Paris, 1982.

———. *Les faux-semblants d'un démarrage économique: Agriculture et démographie en France au XVIIIe siècle*. Cahier des Annales 30. Paris, 1971.

Mulliez, Jacques. "Du blé, 'mal nécessaire.' Réflexions sur les progrès de l'agriculture de 1750–1850." *Revue d'histoire moderne et contemporaine* 26 (1979): 3–47.

Musset, René. *L'élevage du cheval en France.* Paris, 1917.

Neveux, Hugues. *Vie et déclin d'une structure économique: Les grains du Cambrésis (fin du XIVe–début du XVIIe siècle).* Paris, 1980.

Newbery, David M. G., and Joseph E. Stiglitz. *The Theory of Commodity Price Stabilization: A Study in the Economics of Risk.* Oxford, 1981.

Nottin, Léopold. *Recherches sur les variations des prix dans le Gâtinais, du XVIe au XIX siècles.* Paris, 1935.

Parker, William N., and Eric L. Jones, eds. *European Peasants and Their Markets: Essays in Agrarian Economic History.* Princeton, 1975.

Pavard, J. M. "Productions et rendements céréaliers à Cheux au début du XVIIe siècle." *Annales de Normandie* 26 (1976): 41–65.

Peltre, Jean. *Recherches métrologiques sur les finages lorrains.* Doctoral dissertation, University of Paris IV. Lille, 1975.

Peret, Jacques. *Seigneurs et seigneuries en Gâtine poitevine: Le duché de la Meilleraye, XVIIe–XVIIIe siècles.* Poitiers, 1976.

Perren, Richard. "Markets and Marketing." *AHEW,* 6: 190–274.

Perrot, Jean-Claude. *Genèse d'une ville moderne: Caen au XVIIIe siècle.* 2 vols. Paris, 1975.

Piel, Jean. *Essai sur la réforme de l'impôt direct au XVIIe siècle: La taille proportionnelle dans les généralités de Caen et d'Alençon.* Caen, 1937.

Polanyi, Karl. *The Great Transformation.* New York, 1944.

Popkin, Samuel. *The Rational Peasant: The Political Economy of Rural Society in Vietnam.* Berkeley, 1979.

Postel-Vinay, Gilles. "A la recherche de la révolution économique dans les campagnes (1789–1815)." *Revue économique* 40 (1989): 1015–46.

Rebeyrol, Charles. *De la grande et de la petite culture chez les physiocrates.* Paris, 1912.

Rétif de la Bretonne, Nicolas-Edme. *La vie de mon père,* ed. Gilbert Rouger. Paris, 1970.

Root, Hilton L. *Peasants and King in Burgundy: Agrarian Foundations of French Absolutism.* Berkeley, 1987.

Rösener, Werner. *Bauern im Mittelalter.* Munich, 1986.

Rosenthal, Jean-Laurent. *The Fruits of Revolution: Property Rights, Litigation, and French Agriculture, 1700–1860.* Cambridge, 1992.

Rosenzweig, Mark R. "Determinants of Wage Rates and Labor Supply Behavior in the Rural Sector of a Developing Country." In *Contractual Arrangements, Employment, and Wages in Rural Labor Markets in Asia,* ed. Hans P. Binswanger and Mark R. Rosenzweig, 211–41. New Haven, 1984.

Rozier, François. *Cours complet d'agriculture.* 10 vols. Paris, 1781–1800.

Sabean, David Warren. *Power in the Blood: Popular Culture and Village Discourse in Early Modern Germany.* Cambridge, 1984.

Sahlins, Marshall. *Stone Age Economics.* Chicago, 1972.

Saint-Jacob, Pierre. *Les paysans de la Bourgogne du nord au dernier siècle de l'ancien régime.* Dijon, 1960.

Scott, James C. *The Moral Economy of the Peasant: Rebellion and Subsistence in Southeast Asia.* New Haven, 1976.

Sée, Henri. *Les classes rurales en Bretagne du XVIe siècle à la Révolution.* Paris, 1906.

Sicsic, Pierre. "City-Farm Wages Gaps in Late Nineteenth-Century France." *JEH* 52 (1992): 675–95.

Stiglitz, Joseph E. "Economic Organization, Information, and Development." In *Handbook of Development Economics*, ed. Hollis Chenery and T. N. Srinivasan, 2 vols. 1:93–160. Amsterdam, 1988.

Tessier, Alexandre-Henri, et al. *Encyclopédie méthodique ou par ordre de matières. Agriculture.* 7 vols. Paris, 1787–1821.

Thompson, E. P. *Customs in Common.* New York, 1991.

Vallez, J. M. "Le commerce des bestiaux en Normandie: L'activité de la famille Mollet (1680–1730)." *Annales de Normandie* 38 (1988): 342–43.

Vardi, Liana. *The Land and the Loom: Peasants and Profit in Northern France.* Durham, 1993.

Walter, John, and Roger Schofield. "Famine, Disease and Crisis Mortality in Early Modern Society." In *Famine, Disease and the Social Order in Early Modern Society*, ed. John Walter and Roger Schofield, 1–73. Cambridge, 1989.

Weir, David R. "Les crises économiques et les origines de la Révolution française." *AESC* 46 (1991): 917–47.

———. "Life under Pressure: France and England, 1670–1870." *JEH* 44 (1984): 27–47.

———. "Markets and Mortality in France, 1600–1789." In *Famine, Disease and the Social Order in Early Modern Society*, ed. John Walter and Roger Schofield, 201–34. Cambridge, 1989.

Wiese, H., and J. Bölts, *Rinderhandel und Rinderhaltung in nordwesteuropaischen Küstengebiet vom 15. bis zum 19. Jahrhundert.* Stuttgart, 1966.

Wunder, Heidi. *Die bäuerliche Gemeinde in Deutschland.* Göttingen, 1986.

Young, Arthur. *Voyages en France en 1787, 1788, et 1789*, ed. and trans. by Henri Sée. 3 vols. Paris, 1931.

Index

Abel, Wilhelm, 215

absentee landlords. *See* landlords

afféagements, 21

agricultural capital, rental price of in Notre Dame lease sample, 214–20, 221–22, 333–34nn. 10, 13, 15, 21, 24, 26

agricultural economy: economic history of, 4–5; enclosures and, 14, 16, 277n.19; evolution of author's hypothesis on, 5–7; historical consensus about, 12–20; overview of, 198–205, 332n.14; tenant farmers and, 13–14

agricultural productivity, 81–84, 132–42; drainage and, 169–70, 194; economic analysis of, 81–82; in England versus France, 132–33, 139–42, 156–57, 162, 183, 186–87, 190, 191, 197–98, 312n.99, 316nn. 113, 114, 317nn. 115–117, 331n.122; for France as a whole, 133–36, 313nn. 100, 101, 104; French Revolution and, 193–98, 331–32nn. 6, 9; in Germany, 183, 190; historical consensus about, 81, 132, 136, 313n.104; issues defined, 81–82; labor productivity and, 82–83, 301–2n.2; land productivity (grain output) and, 83, 302n.3; in the Netherlands, 133, 312n.98; in Normandy, 137–38, 314–15n.107–10; in the Paris Basin, 133, 136–39, 313–14nn. 105, 106, 315–16nn. 111, 112; tithing records and, 83–84. *See also* total factor productivity

agricultural productivity growth, 143–92, 198–205; absentee landlords and, 186–88, 330n.115; enclosures and, 15–16, 165–70, 203–4, 324–25nn. 54–56, 58, 59, 61, 64, 68; farm size and, 15–16, 144–45, 146–47, 151–70, 189–91, 203–4, 320nn. 25, 28, 30, 321–23nn. 34–38, 41–43, 48; historical consensus about, 143–45, 189–90; new crops and crop rotations and, 165–66, 202, 323n.51; overview of, 143–45, 184, 191–92, 201–5, 329n.103, 332n.14; in Paris Basin, 145–51, 156, 162–63, 171, 173, 174–80, 318nn. 6, 8, 9, 11, 12, 319–20nn. 13, 15–18, 19; peasants as obstacles to, 15–20, 144–45, 188–91, 201–2, 205;

taxes and, 184–85, 203; transportation costs and, 179–84, 204, 328–29nn. 86, 92, 95, 100, 101; urbanization, city markets and, 170–84, 204–5, 326nn. 70, 72–74, 327nn. 77, 79, 80, 328–29nn. 86, 92, 95, 100, 101, 331n.122; war and, 185–86, 198, 202–3

L'agriculture et la maison rustique (Estienne), 44

Albigeois, 125, 256–57, 342nn. 42, 43

Allen, Robert C., 84, 85, 141, 151, 191, 312n.99, 316n.114, 331n.122

Alps, 108, 127–28, 130–31

Amiens, 113–14, 239–40, 308–9nn. 61, 62, 338n.5

ancient versus modern economies, 77, 200–201

animals, renting draft animals, 70, 298n.118

anthropology, economics and, 8, 75–76

artificial meadows, 171, 176–78, 204

auctions, of leases, 64

Auge, 119, 247–48, 340n.21

Avenel, Georges d', 338n.58

averaging: rents in Notre Dame lease sample, 209–10; total factor productivity in Notre Dame lease sample, 230–31, 337n.50

barter, versus credit, 70, 71

Baulant, Micheline, 94, 220–21, 334–35n.28

Beaujolais, 108, 128–29, 260–61, 312n.92, 342n.53

Beauvais et le Beauvaisis (Goubert), 12

Benedict, Philip, 237

Bentham, Jeremy, 43

Bloch, Marc: on enclosures, 16, 27–28, 116, 151–52, 165, 277n.19; on French rural history, 3, 4, 5, 12, 13, 15–16, 144

Bois, Guy, 339–40n.18

Bottin, Jacques, 339–40n.18

Boudin, M., 320n.25

Brenner, Robert, 16–17, 132, 144, 190, 331n.122

Bretteville-l'Orgueilleuse: agricultural productivity in, 133, 137–38, 142; credit in, 69–71; farm size in, 151–62, 166–67; labor market in, 39, 44, 45, 47–49; sources

About the Author

PHILIP T. HOFFMAN is Professor of History and Social Science at the California Institute of Technology. He is the author of *Church and Community in the Diocese of Lyon, 1500–1789* and, with Kathryn Norberg, *Fiscal Crises, Liberty, and Representative Government, 1450–1789.*